ONE-STORY HOMES

Design 9748

448 Designs
For All Lifestyles
468 to 5,400 square feet

HOME PLANNERS

Published by Home Planners
A Divison of Hanley-Wood, Inc.
Editorial and Corporate Offices:
3275 West Ina Road, Suite 110
Tucson, Arizona 85741

Distribution Center:
29333 Lorie Lane
Wixom, Michigan 48393

Rickard D. Bailey, President and Publisher
Cindy Coatsworth Lewis, Publications Manager
Paulette Mulvin, Senior Editor
Amanda Kaufmann, Project Editor
Paul D. Fitzgerald, Book Designer

Photo Credits

Front Cover: Jon Riley

Back Cover: Design Basics, Inc.

First Printing, January 1996

10 9 8 7 6 5 4 3

Printed in the United States of America.
Library of Congress Catalog Card Number: 95-081067
ISBN: 1-881955-29-X

On the front cover: Brighten your corner of the world with this charming country-inspired plan. See page 126 for floor plans.

On the back cover: The incorporation of arches and varied exterior materials creates wonderful curb appeal in this modest one-story home. Page 7 offers floor plans and more information.

Table of Contents

Design 3630

About the Designers

The Blue Ribbon Designer Series™ is a collection of books featuring the home plans of a diverse group of outstanding home designers and architects known as the Blue Ribbon Network of Designers. This group of companies is dedicated to creating and marketing the finest possible plans for home construction on a regional and national basis. Each of the companies exhibits superior work and integrity in all phases of the stock-plan business including modern, trendsetting floor planning, a professionally executed blueprint package and a strong sense of service and commitment to the consumer.

Design Basics, Inc.

For nearly a decade, Design Basics, a nationally recognized home design service located in Omaha, has been developing plans for custom home builders. Since 1987, the firm has consistently appeared in *Builder* magazine, the official magazine of the National Association of Home Builders, as the top-selling designer. The company's plans also regularly appear in numerous other shelter magazines such as *Better Homes and Gardens, House Beautiful* and *Home Planner.*

Design Traditions

Design Traditions was established by Stephen S. Fuller with the tenets of innovation, quality, originality and uncompromising architectural techniques in traditional and European homes. Especially popular throughout the Southeast, Design Traditions' plans are known for their extensive detail and thoughtful design. They are widely published in such shelter magazines as *Southern Living* magazine and *Better Homes and Gardens.*

Alan Mascord Design Associates, Inc.

Founded in 1983 as a local supplier to the building community, Mascord Design Associates of Portland, Oregon began to successfully publish plans nationally in 1985. With plans now drawn exclusively on computer, Mascord Design Associates quickly received a reputation for homes that are easy to build yet meet the rigorous demands of the buyers' market, winning local and national awards. The company's trademark is creating floor plans that work well and exhibit excellent traffic patterns. Their motto is: "Drawn to build, designed to sell."

Larry E. Belk Designs

Through the years, Larry E. Belk has worked with individuals and builders alike to provide a quality product. After listening to over 4,000 dreams and watching them become reality all across America, Larry's design philosophy today combines traditional exteriors with upscale interiors designed for contemporary lifestyles. Flowing, open spaces and interesting angles define his interiors. Great emphasis is placed on providing views that showcase the natural environment. Dynamic exteriors reflect Larry's extensive home construction experience, painstaking research and talent as a fine artist.

Frank Betz Associates, Inc.

Frank Betz Associates, Inc., located in Smyrna, Georgia, is one of the nation's leaders in the design of stock plans. FBA, Inc. has provided builders and developers with home plans since 1977. With their vast knowledge of the speculative home builders business, they specialize in products for a wide variety of locations, price ranges, and markets. Frank Betz Associates, Inc. prides itself in its bi-annual plan magazine, *HOMEPLANS, Designed for Today's Market*, released every February and August featuring the firm's newest and most innovative plans.

Larry W. Garnett & Associates, Inc.

Starting as a designer of homes for Houston-area residents, Garnett & Associates has been marketing designs nationally for the past ten years. A well-respected design firm, the company's plans are regularly featured in *House Beautiful, Country Living, Home* and *Professional Builder.* Numerous accolades, including several from the Texas Institute of Building Design and the American Institute of Building Design, have been awarded to the company for excellence in architecture.

Home Planners

Headquartered in Tucson, Arizona, with additional offices in Detroit, Home Planners is one of the longest-running and most successful home design firms in the United States. With over 2,500 designs in its portfolio, the company provides a wide range of styles, sizes and types of homes for the residential builder. All of Home Planners' designs are created with the care and professional expertise that fifty years of experience in the home-planning business affords. Their homes are designed to be built, lived in and enjoyed for years to come.

Donald A. Gardner, Architects, Inc.

The South Carolina firm of Donald A. Gardner was established in response to a growing demand for residential designs that reflect constantly changing lifestyles. The company's specialty is providing homes with refined, custom-style details and unique features such as passive-solar designs and open floor plans. Computer-aided design and drafting technology resulting in trouble-free construction documents places the firm at the leading edge of the home plan industry.

The Sater Design Collection

The Sater Design Collection has a long established tradition of providing South Florida's most diverse and extraordinary custom designed homes. Their goal is to fulfill each client's particular need for an exciting approach to design by merging creative vision with elements that satisfy a desire for a distinctive lifestyle. This philosophy is proven, as exemplified by over 50 national design awards, numerous magazine features and, most important, satisfied clients. The result is an elegant statement of lasting beauty and value.

Home Design Services, Inc.

For the past fifteen years, Home Design Services of Longwood, Florida, has been formulating plans for the sun-country lifestyle. At the forefront of design innovation and imagination, the company has developed award-winning designs that are consistently praised for their highly detailed, free-flowing floor plans, imaginative and exciting interior architecture and elevations which have gained international appeal.

Editor's Note

There's no time like the present to build your one-story home. Today's design sensibility helps turn lightless, cramped quarters into bright, voluminous homes—all conveniently arranged on a single level. Large gathering rooms, thoughtful kitchen designs, sumptuous master suites, zoned bedroom arrangements, large gathering rooms, finish-later bonus rooms—all serve to create well-patterned living spaces. In this new collection of One-Story Homes, nearly 450 designs span the style spectrum, from traditional to contemporary and sun-country to just plain country—all your favorites are right here.

If **traditional** is your style preference, pages 6-121 hold a variety of floor plans. Design 8159 on page 12 serves as a fine example with its elegant stuccoed facade and arched entry. An exciting floor plan focuses on zoned livability with split sleeping arrangements and separate formal and informal dining areas. Family expansion is possible with a front study that may also serve as a fourth bedroom.

You don't have to build an expansive farmhouse to enjoy the **country** feeling you desire. The homes featured on pages 122-147 embody this rural charm through the use of airy porches, wood siding, dormers and gables. Design 9749 on page 133 welcomes all with its generous front porch. Inside, a great room, with a cathedral ceiling and a fireplace, opens onto a rear porch and deck for wonderful outdoor livability. Split bedrooms are highlighted by a private master bedroom suite. With such a functional floor plan, this home's 1,864 square feet lives like a much larger plan.

For another twist on the country theme, pages 148-189 exhibit a selection of **ranch** designs. Perhaps the most well-known one-story style, the ranch benefits from years of experience. Today, you'll discover raised ceilings, increased indoor/outdoor livability and floor plans that emphasize multi-purpose living patterns. Design 3332 on page 165 is a fine choice with its covered porch and rear terrace, country kitchen, airy living room and master suite with an amenity-laden bath.

Go **European** with one of the plans presented in pages 190-225. A full range of distinguished exteriors complements modern floor planning. Design 9872 on page 190 features a stucco exterior and an efficient interior. The octagonal gourmet kitchen deserves special mention with its island work counter and easy accessibility to the breakfast and dining rooms.

For some, **contemporary** is the only way to go. The selection presented here covers all bases, from luminous stucco homes to rustic Northwestern-influenced designs—even earth-sheltered styles. Design 2902 on page 259 rises to an impressive height. Inside, living areas interact seamlessly with a porch, terrace and sun space. Scan pages 226-291 for your favorite.

If Floridian is your forte, or Santa Fe your satisfaction, the section on **Sunshine Design** will provide plenty of options. Design 2875 on page 299 sets the stage with an arched garden court. A tiled roof and stucco walls further the warm welcome. Pages 292-329 offer more choices.

And because sometimes you want the best of both worlds, a selection of **one-story designs with an extra level** are found on pages 330-359. Here, such features as future second floors, walk-out basements and bonus rooms add to one-story livability. A fine bungalow design, 3315 on page 344, adds an upper-level lounge, which can function as an office or play room.

To finish the book, and your home-building experience, a collection of our best yard and garden plans can be found on pages 360-371. From two- and three-car garages to gazebos, potting sheds and playhouses, these plans will complement your new home.

Whatever your style or size considerations, *One-Story Homes* will provide you with an outstanding home. And, with the many home-design options offered by the Blue Ribbon Network of Designers, it's never been easier to realize your dream home. Our exclusive Quote One™ service allows you to estimate the costs of building select designs in this book—see page 374 for more information. Complete ordering instructions, along with a host of helpful additional products, are available at the back of the book. All are designed to make your homebuilding dreams come true!

Design 3319

Tell-Tale Traditionals:

Designs with traditional flair

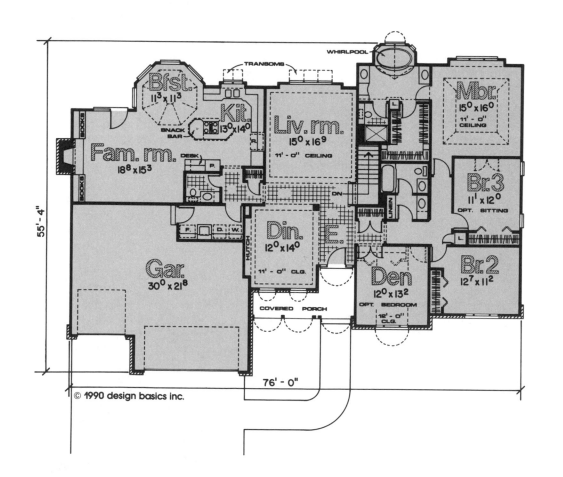

© 1990 design basics inc.

55' - 4"

76' - 0"

Bfst. 11³ x 11³

Kit. 13⁰ x 14⁰

Liv. rm. 15⁰ x 16⁹
11' - 0" CEILING

Mbr. 15⁰ x 16⁰
11' - 0" CEILING

Fam. rm. 18⁸ x 15³

Br.3 11¹ x 12⁰
OPT. SITTING

Gar. 30⁰ x 21⁸

Din. 12⁰ x 14⁰
11' - 0" CLG.

Den 12⁰ x 13²
OPT. BEDROOM
12' - 0" CLG.

Br.2 12⁷ x 11²

COVERED PORCH

WHIRLPOOL

TRANSOMS

SNACK BAR

DESK

LINEN

Design by
**Design
Basics,
Inc.**

Design 9258
Square Footage: 2,498

● Elegant arches at the covered entry of this home give way to beautiful views of the formal dining room and living room inside. Ceilings in the main living areas and the master bedroom are vaulted. The gazebo dinette is open to the family room and to the gourmet kitchen, which includes an island cooktop and a snack bar. Three bedrooms and a den are provided. One of these could become a sitting area for the master suite, if desired. A luxurious master bath provides twin vanities, a large walk-in closet and an oval whirlpool tub.

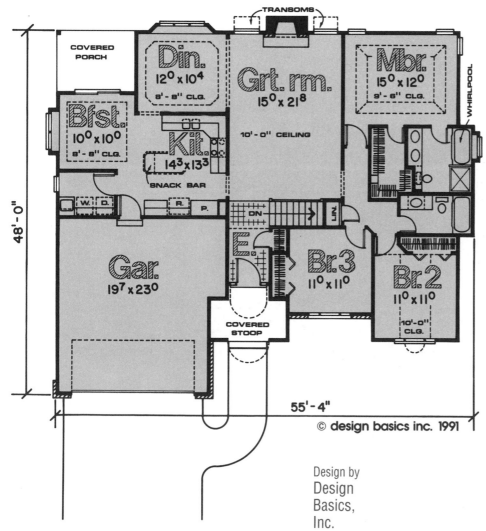

TRANSOMS

COVERED PORCH

Din.
12⁰ x 10⁴
8' - 8" CLG.

Grt. rm.
15⁰ x 21⁸
10' - 0" CEILING

Mbr.
15⁰ x 12⁰
9' - 8" CLG.

WHIRLPOOL

Bfst.
10⁰ x 10⁰
8' - 8" CLG.

Kit.
14³ x 13³

SNACK BAR

W. D.

R. P.

DN

LIN.

Gar.
19⁷ x 23⁰

Br.3
11⁰ x 11⁰

Br.2
11⁰ x 11⁰
10' - 0" CLG.

COVERED STOOP

48' - 0"

55' - 4"

© design basics inc. 1991

Design by
Design
Basics,
Inc.

Design 9361

Square Footage: 1,666

● This delightfully different plan has brick and stucco on the dramatic front elevation, showcased by sleek lines and decorative windows. An inviting entry has a view into the great room and is enhanced by an arched window and plant shelves above. The great room's fireplace is framed by sunny windows with transoms above. The bay-windowed dining room is nestled between the great room and the superb kitchen/breakfast area. Sleeping areas are positioned to buffer noise between the master bedroom and secondary bedrooms. The master suite enjoys a vaulted ceiling, roomy walk-in closet and sunlit master bath with dual lavatories and whirlpool.

Design 7230
Square Footage: 1,806

● Beautiful columns and arched transoms are the focal points of this ranch home. The ten-foot entry opens to the formal dining room and the great room, which features a brick fireplace and arched windows. The large island kitchen offers an angled range, a pantry and a sunny breakfast area with an atrium door to the back yard. Separate bedroom wings provide optimum privacy. The master wing to the right includes a whirlpool tub with a sloped ceiling, a plant shelf above dual lavatories and a large walk-in closet. The secondary bedrooms are at the opposite end of the house and share a full bath. The laundry room serves as a mud room entry from the garage.

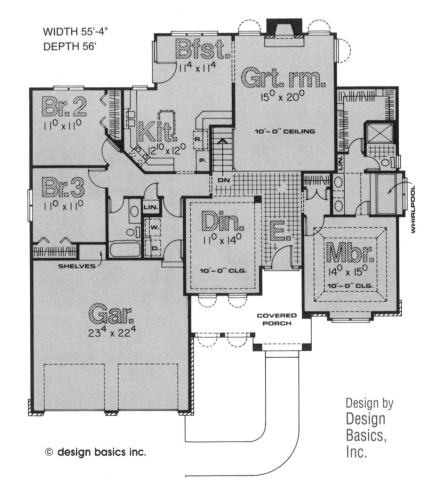

WIDTH 55'-4"
DEPTH 56'

Design by
Design Basics, Inc.

Design 9256

Square Footage: 1,347

● Though it may appear
oversized, this plan is really
quite compact and economical. From the ten-foot ceiling
in the entry to the spacious
great room with fireplace, it
has an open feeling. A snack
bar and pantry in the kitchen
complement the work area.
Bright windows light up the
entire breakfast area. To the
left side of the plan are three
bedrooms, two of which share
a full bath. The master suite
has a boxed window, built-in
bookcase and tiered ceiling.
The skylit dressing area features a double vanity and
there's a whirlpool in the bath.

Design by
Design
Basics,
Inc.

9

Design 7226
Square Footage: 1,479

● A covered porch and interesting window treatments add charisma to this ranch home. The entry opens onto a sunny great room warmed by a center fireplace framed by transom windows. Nearby, an efficient kitchen is highlighted by an island snack bar and access to the back yard. The spacious master suite features a walk-in closet and a pampering master bath with a whirlpool tub. Two secondary bedrooms—one an optional den—share a hall bath.

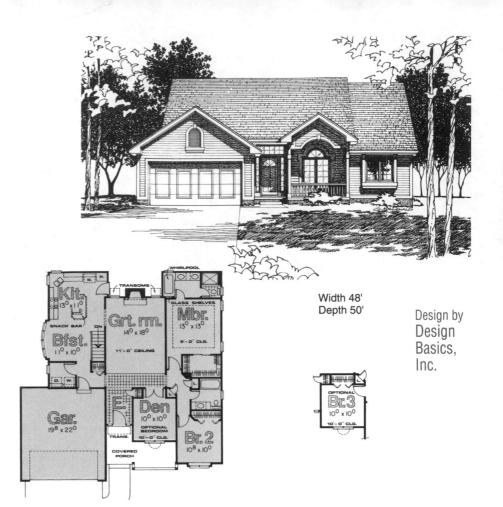

Width 48'
Depth 50'

Design by
Design Basics, Inc.

Design 7228
Square Footage: 1,651

● Front and rear covered porches extend outdoor livability on this lovely traditional home. A servery located between the volume dining room and expansive great room handily serves both areas. An adjacent, well-planned kitchen features a generous pantry and a snack bar, which separates the bright, bayed breakfast room. The spacious master suite is highlighted by a lavish master bath. A den with a wet bar enhances the master suite or can be converted to a third bedroom.

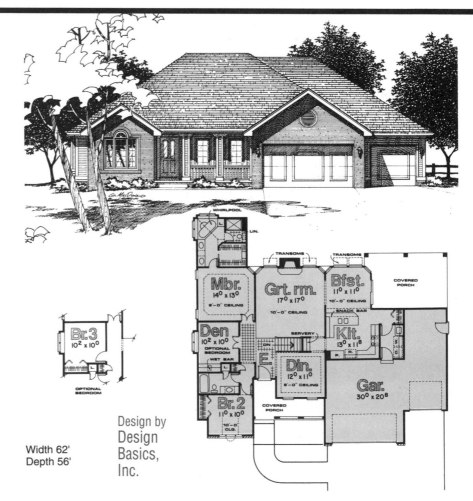

Width 62'
Depth 56'

Design by
Design Basics, Inc.

Design by
Design
Basics,
Inc.

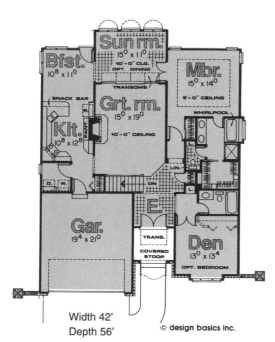

Sun rm.
15⁰ x 11⁰
10'-0" CLG.
OPT. DINING

Bfst.
10⁸ x 11⁰

TRANSOMS

Mbr.
15⁰ x 14⁰

9'-0" CEILING

SNACK BAR

Grt. rm.
15⁰ x 19⁰

10'-0" CEILING

WHIRLPOOL

Kit.
10⁸ x 12⁸

PANTRY

LIN.

D. W.

ON

Gar.
19⁴ x 21⁰

TRANS.

COVERED
STOOP

Den
13⁰ x 13⁴

OPT. BEDROOM

Width 42'
Depth 56'

© design basics inc.

Design 7214
Square Footage: 1,658

● The prominent entry of this home enhances a captivating elevation. Inside, the entry captures fantastic views from the great room to the sun room with its arched windows. A peninsula kitchen features a corner sink and a snack bar that opens to the breakfast area. The sun room offers access to the breakfast area, the great room and the master suite; or use it as a lovely dining room. The spacious master suite includes a whirlpool bath with dual lavs and a walk-in closet. The den off the entry has a bedroom option.

Design 7213
Square Footage: 1,422

● This small ranch home makes a grand statement with its prominent entry. A twelve-foot ceiling integrates the great room, the semi-formal dining room and the kitchen. Arched openings to the kitchen, with built-in bookcases, provide a dramatic backdrop for the dining area. The efficient kitchen features two Lazy Susans, a plant shelf above the upper cabinets and an airy window. The spacious covered porch opens off the dining room. The master suite features a boxed nine-foot ceiling, a whirlpool bath and a walk-in closet. A hall bath serves the secondary bedrooms. Bedroom 3 can easily convert to a den.

Design by
Design
Basics,
Inc.

LIN.

WHIRLPOOL

Mbr.
14⁰ x 12²

9'-0" CEILING

Grt. rm.
14⁰ x 20⁰

12'-0" CEILING

Din.
12³ x 10⁰

COVERED
PORCH

BOOKS

Kit.
12⁰ x 10⁰

P.

Sto.
8⁴ x 10⁴

Br. 2
10⁰ x 11⁰

Br. 3
10⁰ x 11²
10'-0" CLG.
OPT. DEN

DN

CVRD.
STOOP

WORK
BENCH

Gar.
20⁴ x 21⁸

Width 50'
Depth 58'

11

COPYRIGHT LARRY E. BELK

Design 8159
Square Footage: 2,583

● Stucco appointments give this home a European flavor. Arch-top windows flank the entry and add an air of formality to the study and dining room. The large great room is visible through a pair of arched openings and features a center-piece fireplace and twelve-foot ceilings. The plan is designed with split bedrooms. The master suite is privately located and complete with a luxury master bath. Bedrooms 2 and 3 are conveniently grouped to share Bath 2 with private dressing areas for each bedroom. Please specify crawlspace or slab foundation when ordering.

Width 67'-1"
Depth 79'-4"

Design by
Larry E. Belk
Designs

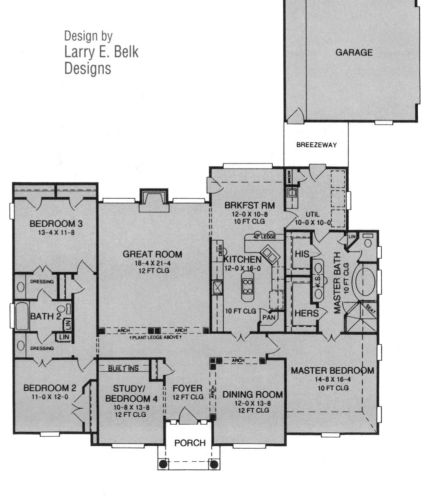

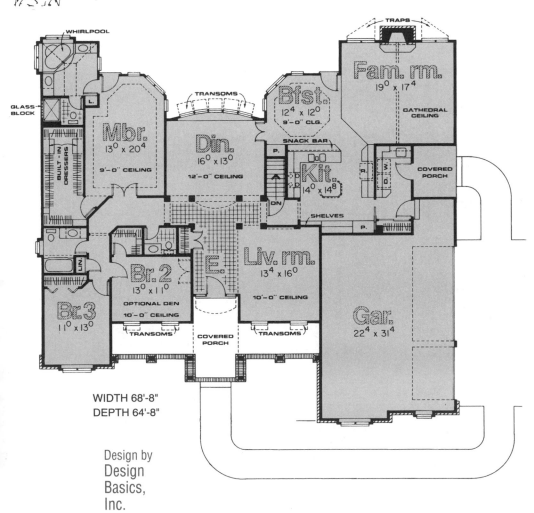

WIDTH 68'-8"
DEPTH 64'-8"

Design by
Design Basics, Inc.

Design 7233
Square Footage: 2,538

● The grand front porch gives this home a unique style and majestic curb appeal. Inside, the twelve-foot entry centers on the stately dining room with its bowed window. Both the living room and the second bedroom, which can be converted into a den, have ten-foot ceilings. The island kitchen features abundant pantries, a Lazy Susan and a snack bar. A sun-filled breakfast area opens to the large family room with its cathedral ceiling and central fireplace. The private bedroom wing offers two secondary bedrooms and a luxurious master suite featuring a spacious walk-in closet with built-in dressers and private access to the back yard. It also includes a vaulted ceiling, a corner whirlpool and His and Hers vanities in the master bath.

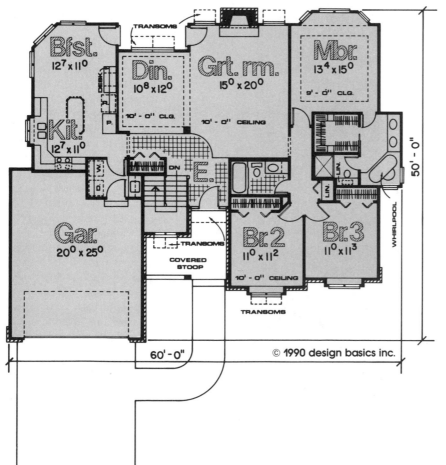

Design 9257
Square Footage: 1,735

● A covered porch at the entry to this home welcomes family and guests alike. Ten-foot ceilings at the entry foyer, great room and dining room give a feeling of open spaciousness to living areas. The formal dining room sits between the kitchen area and great room—a perfect spot for entertaining. Note service entrance with laundry just off the kitchen en route to the garage. Three bedrooms include two secondary bedrooms with shared bath and a master suite with elegant bayed window and bath with angled whirlpool, double vanity and walk-in closet. An open staircase in the entry allows for the possibility of a finished basement area in the future.

Design by
Design
Basics,
Inc.

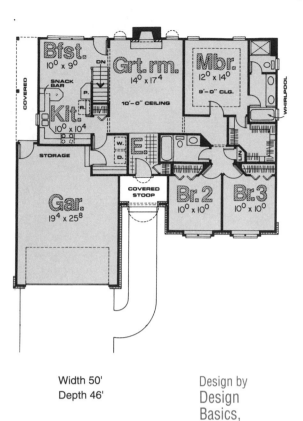

Width 50'
Depth 46'

Design by
Design
Basics,
Inc.

Design 7224
Square Footage: 1,339

● This home's arched entry complements a brick-and-siding elevation. The great room features arched windows. In the kitchen, a snack bar and convenient access to a utility room are fine attributes. Secondary bedrooms share a hall bath while the master bedroom contains its own whirlpool bath with a compartmented stool and shower.

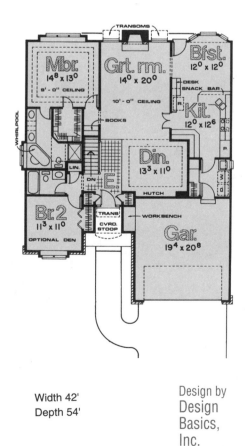

Width 42'
Depth 54'

Design by
Design
Basics,
Inc.

Design 7227
Square Footage: 1,499

● A pleasant mix of materials, shapes and textures creates an eye-catching facade. A practical use of space is demonstrated by two closets flanking the entry. An optional den/bedroom provides design flexibility. In the lofty great room, windows surround a fireplace. Double doors privatize the kitchen from the great room. The master suite features a deluxe bath with a sloped ceiling and plant shelves above an open shower.

15

Design 9375
Square Footage: 2,456

● Tapered columns at the entry help to create a majestic front elevation. Inside, an open great room features a wet bar, a fireplace, tall windows and access to a covered porch with skylights. A wide kitchen features an ideally placed island, two pantries and easy laundry access. Double doors open to the master suite where attention is drawn to French doors leading to the master bath and the covered porch. The master bath provides beauty and convenience with a whirlpool, dual lavatories, plant shelves and a large walk-in closet. Two secondary bedrooms share a compartmented bath.

QUOTE ONE®
Cost to build? See page 374
to order complete cost estimate
to build this house in your area!

Design by
**Design
Basics,
Inc.**

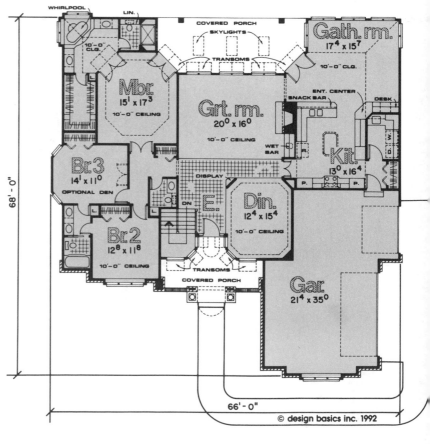

WHIRLPOOL
LIN.
COVERED PORCH
SKYLIGHTS
TRANSOMS
Gath. rm.
17⁴ x 15⁷
10'-0" CLG.

10'-0"
CLG.

Mbr.
15¹ x 17³
10'-0" CEILING

Grt. rm.
20⁰ x 16⁰
10'-0" CEILING

ENT. CENTER
SNACK BAR
DESK

WET
BAR

Kit.
13⁰ x 16⁴

Br. 3
14¹ x 11⁰
OPTIONAL DEN

DISPLAY

Din.
12⁴ x 15⁴
10'-0" CEILING

68' - 0"

Br. 2
12⁸ x 11⁸
10'-0" CEILING

TRANSOMS
COVERED PORCH

Gar.
21⁴ x 35⁰

66' - 0"

© design basics inc. 1992

Design 9362

Square Footage: 2,172

● This one-story with grand rooflines holds a most convenient floor plan. The great room with fireplace to the rear complements a front-facing living room. The formal dining room with tray ceiling sits just across the hall from the living room and is also easily accessible to the kitchen. An island, pantry, breakfast room and patio are highlights in the kitchen. A bedroom with full bath at this end of the house works fine as an office or guest bedroom since a full bath is close by. Two additional bedrooms are to the right of the plan: a master suite with grand bath and one additional secondary bedroom. The three-car garage provides extra storage space.

Quote One®

Cost to build? See page 374 to order complete cost estimate to build this house in your area!

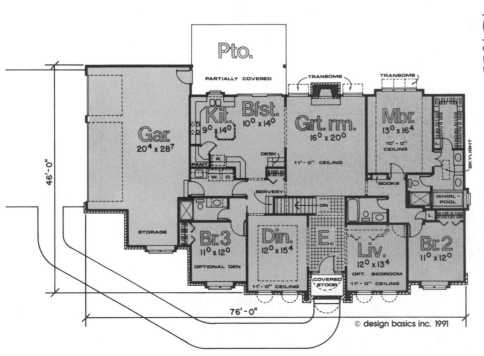

Design by
Design
Basics,
Inc.

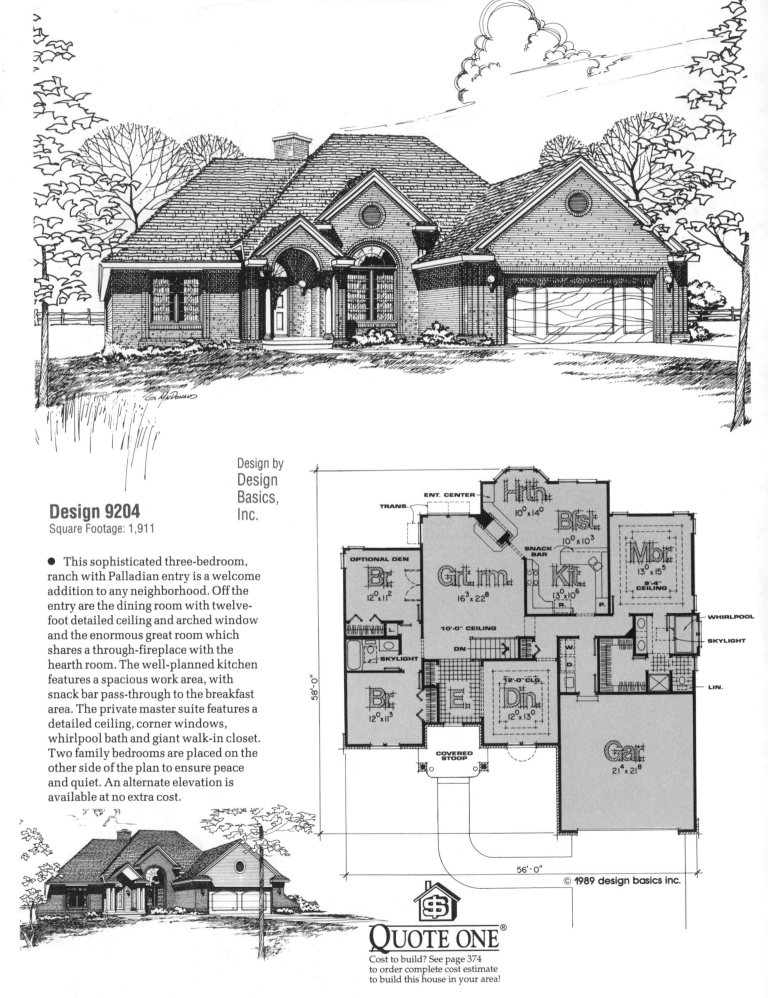

Design 9204

Square Footage: 1,911

● This sophisticated three-bedroom, ranch with Palladian entry is a welcome addition to any neighborhood. Off the entry are the dining room with twelve-foot detailed ceiling and arched window and the enormous great room which shares a through-fireplace with the hearth room. The well-planned kitchen features a spacious work area, with snack bar pass-through to the breakfast area. The private master suite features a detailed ceiling, corner windows, whirlpool bath and giant walk-in closet. Two family bedrooms are placed on the other side of the plan to ensure peace and quiet. An alternate elevation is available at no extra cost.

Design by
Design Basics, Inc.

ENT. CENTER
TRANS.
Hth
10⁰ x 14⁰
Bfst
10⁰ x 10³
SNACK BAR
Mbr
13⁰ x 15⁵
9'-4" CEILING
OPTIONAL DEN
Br
12⁰ x 11²
Grt. rm.
16³ x 22⁸
Kit
13⁰ x 10⁶
R.
P.
WHIRLPOOL
SKYLIGHT
SKYLIGHT
10'-0" CEILING
DN
LIN.
Br
12⁰ x 11³
12'-0" CLG.
Dn
12⁰ x 13⁰
W. D.
Gar
21⁴ x 21⁸
COVERED STOOP

58'-0"
56'-0"

© 1989 design basics inc.

QUOTE ONE®

Cost to build? See page 374 to order complete cost estimate to build this house in your area!

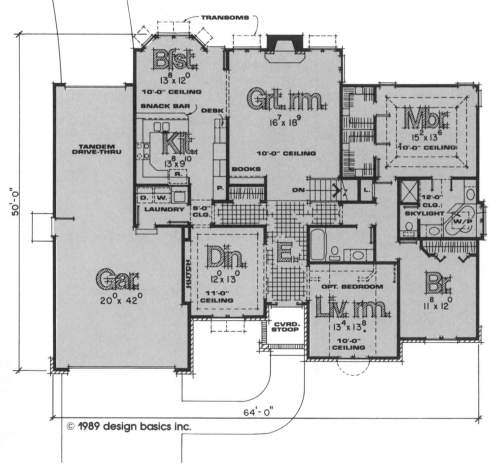

TRANSOMS

Bfst.
13⁸ x 12⁰
10'-0" CEILING

SNACK BAR   DESK

Grt. rm.
16⁷ x 18⁹

10'-0" CEILING

TANDEM
DRIVE-THRU

Kit.
13⁸ x 9¹⁰

BOOKS

Mbr
15² x 13⁶
10'-0" CEILING

R.

D. W.

LAUNDRY

P.

DN

L.

9'-0"
CLG.

12'-0"
CLG.
SKYLIGHT

W/P

HUTCH

Dn.
12 x 13

11'-0"
CEILING

E.

OPT. BEDROOM

Br.
8⁰ x 11²

Gar.
20⁰ x 42⁰

CVRD.
STOOP

Liv. rm.
13⁴ x 13⁸

10'-0"
CEILING

50'-0"

64'-0"

© 1989 design basics inc.

Design 9201

Square Footage: 1,996

● Practical, yet equipped with a variety of popular amenities, this pleasant ranch home is an excellent choice for empty nesters or small families. The front living room can become a third bedroom if you choose. The great room with dramatic fireplace serves as the main living area. The luxurious master suite features a ten-foot tray ceiling and a large bath with whirlpool, skylight, plant ledge and twin vanities. A kitchen with breakfast room serves both the dining and great rooms. Also note the tandem drive-through garage with space for a third car or extra storage.

Quote One®

Cost to build? See page 374 to order complete cost estimate to build this house in your area!

Design by
**Design
Basics,
Inc.**

19

Design 9323

Square Footage: 2,276

● Drama and harmony are expressed through the use of a variety of elegant exterior materials. An expansive entry views the private den with French doors and an open dining room (both rooms have 10-foot, 8-inch ceilings). The great room with a window-framed fireplace is conveniently located next to the kitchen/bayed breakfast area. Special amenities include a wet bar/servery, two pantries, planning desk, and snack bar. Two secluded secondary bedrooms enjoy easy access to a compartmented bath with two lavs. His and Hers closets and a built-in entertainment center grace the master bedroom. A luxurious master bath features glass blocks over the whirlpool, double lavs and an extra linen storage cabinet. An alternate elevation is provided at no extra cost.

Design by
Design
Basics,
Inc.

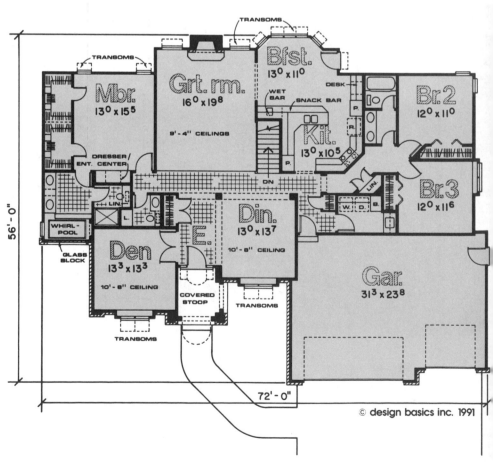

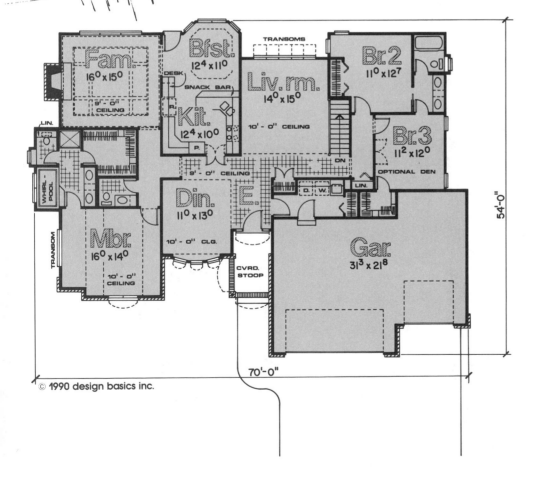

Fam.
16⁰ x 15⁰
9' - 0"
CEILING

Bfst.
12⁴ x 11⁰

TRANSOMS

Br. 2
11⁰ x 12⁷

DESK

SNACK BAR

Kit.
12⁴ x 10⁰

Liv. rm.
14⁰ x 15⁰
10' - 0" CEILING

P.

R.

Br. 3
11² x 12⁰

OPTIONAL DEN

ON

LIN.

LIN.

WHIRL-POOL

9' - 0" CEILING

Din.
11⁰ x 13⁰
10' - 0" CLG.

E.

D. W.

TRANSOM

Mbr.
16⁰ x 14⁰
10' - 0" CEILING

CVRD. STOOP

Gar.
31³ x 21⁸

54'-0"

70'-0"

© 1990 design basics inc.

Design 9347
Square Footage: 2,149

● Beautiful and accommodating, this ranch home features open entry views into formal rooms and volume ceilings in major living spaces. The family room has a spider-beamed ceiling and cozy fireplace. In the kitchen are a snack bar through to the octagonal breakfast area, a built-in desk and pantry. An open staircase leads to a basement that can be finished later as needs arise. Sleeping areas are comprised of three bedrooms including a master with walk-in closet, double vanity and whirlpool. Bedroom 3 may be used as a den with French doors to the hall. A Hollywood bath serves both secondary bedrooms.

Design by
Design
Basics,
Inc.

Design 9200
Square Footage: 1,604

● Thoughtful arrangement makes this uncomplicated three-bedroom plan comfortable. The living and working areas are grouped together for convenience—a great room with cathedral ceiling, dining room with wet bar pass-through and kitchen with breakfast room. The sleeping area features a spacious master suite with skylight bath and whirlpool and large walk-in closet. Two smaller bedrooms accommodate the rest of the family. Don't miss the deck off the breakfast room— a great spot for outdoor dining. An alternate elevation is available at no extra cost.

Design by
Design Basics, Inc.

Width 48'-8"
Depth 48'

QUOTE ONE®
Cost to build? See page 374 to order complete cost estimate to build this house in your area!

Design by
Design Basics, Inc.

Width 54'
Depth 54'

Design 9237
Square Footage: 1,697

● This volume-look home gives the impression of size and scope in just under 1,700 square feet. The large great room with fireplace is perfect for entertaining. Its proximity to the kitchen, with breakfast room, and to the formal dining room ensures easy serving and clean-ups. Besides a large walk-in closet, other features in the master bedroom include a whirlpool tub, double vanity, skylit dressing area and convenient linen storage. Two family bedrooms share a full bath with skylight and offer ample closet space.

Design 9202

Square Footage: 1,808

● Discriminating buyers will love the refined yet inviting look of this three-bedroom ranch plan. A tiled entry with ten-foot ceilings leads into the spacious great room with large bay window. An open-hearth fireplace warms both the great room and kitchen. The sleeping area features a large master suite with dramatic arched window and bath with whirlpool, His and Hers vanities and walk-in closet. Don't miss the storage space in the oversized garage.

Design by
Design Basics, Inc.

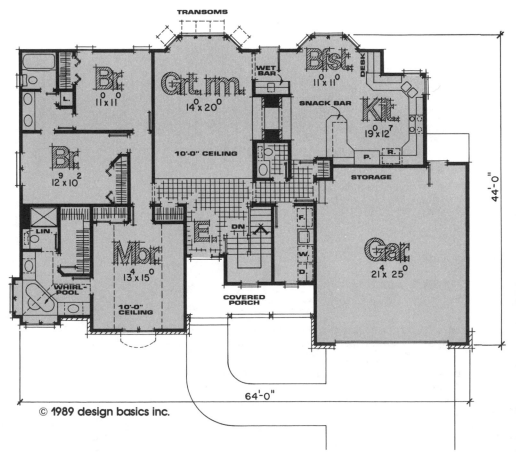

TRANSOMS

Br. 11 x 11

Grt. rm. 14⁰ x 20⁰

10'-0" CEILING

WET BAR

Bfst. 11⁰ x 11⁰

DESK

SNACK BAR

Kit. 19⁰ x 12⁷

P. R.

STORAGE

Br. 12 x 10²

LIN.

Mbr. 13⁴ x 15⁰

WHIRL-POOL

10'-0" CEILING

DN

F.

W. D.

Gar. 21⁴ x 25⁰

COVERED PORCH

44'-0"

64'-0"

© 1989 design basics inc.

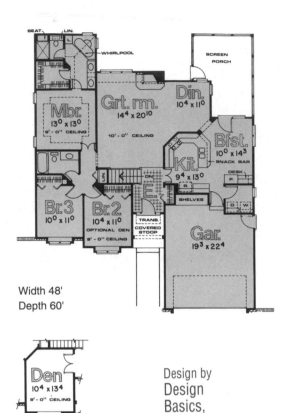

Width 48'
Depth 60'

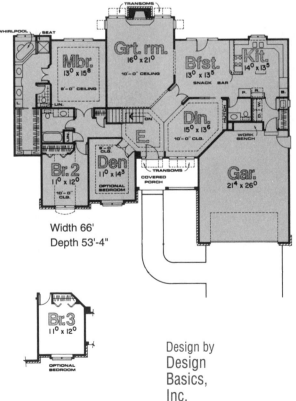

Design 7221
Square Footage: 1,580

● Brick wing walls provide a visually expansive front elevation. From the entry, traffic flows into the bright great room with an impressive two-sided fireplace. The dining room opens to the great room, offering a view of the fireplace. French doors off the entry open into the kitchen. Here, a large pantry, a planning desk and a snack bar are appreciated amenities. The breakfast nook accesses a large, comfortable screened porch. French doors access the master suite with its formal ceiling and pampering bath. Two secondary bedrooms could be one bedroom and a den.

Design by
Design
Basics,
Inc.

Width 66'
Depth 53'-4"

Design 7231
Square Footage: 2,047

● This handsome ranch home features wood railings on the lovely covered porch. Inside, the plan allows for the private den off the entry to be converted into a third bedroom, if preferred. Ten-foot ceilings in the dining room and the great room add depth and sophistication. Accessed by French doors, the master bedroom indulges with a generous walk-in closet.

Design by
Design
Basics,
Inc.

COPYRIGHT LARRY E. BELK

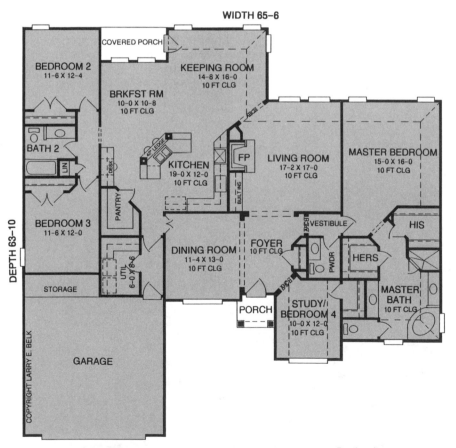

WIDTH 65-6

COVERED PORCH

BEDROOM 2
11-6 X 12-4

KEEPING ROOM
14-8 X 16-0
10 FT CLG

BRKFST RM
10-0 X 10-8
10 FT CLG

BATH 2

KITCHEN
19-0 X 12-0
10 FT CLG

FP

LIVING ROOM
17-2 X 17-0
10 FT CLG

MASTER BEDROOM
15-0 X 16-0
10 FT CLG

PANTRY

DESK

LEDGE

BUILT INS

HIS

DEPTH 63-10

BEDROOM 3
11-6 X 12-0

VESTIBULE

DINING ROOM
11-4 X 13-0
10 FT CLG

FOYER
10 FT CLG

HERS

UTIL
6-0 X 8-6

PWDR

STORAGE

PORCH

STUDY/
BEDROOM 4
10-0 X 12-0
10 FT CLG

MASTER
BATH
10 FT CLG

GARAGE

COPYRIGHT LARRY E. BELK

Design 8140

Square Footage: 2,559

● Traditional in character, this efficiently designed one-story home comes with all the amenities. Ten-foot ceilings in all major living areas give the plan a big-home feel. The kitchen, breakfast room and keeping room are adjacent and open to one another for family gatherings. The kitchen features a large walk-in pantry, a desk and a 42"-high breakfast bar. Bedrooms 2 and 3 are located away from the master suite. An owner's study is situated off the foyer and could be used for an in-home office or nursery. Please specify crawlspace or slab foundation when ordering.

Design by
Larry E. Belk
Designs

Design 8155
Square Footage: 1,973

● An angled entry is defined by arches and columns to give this traditional home an elegant flavor. Designed as a split-bedroom plan, the master suite is privately located off the entry. Bedrooms 2 and 3 are grouped off the kitchen area. The kitchen includes a large walk-in pantry and lots of counter and cabinet space. An oversized great room provides a roomy area for family gatherings and entertaining. Please specify crawlspace or slab foundation when ordering.

WIDTH 74–2

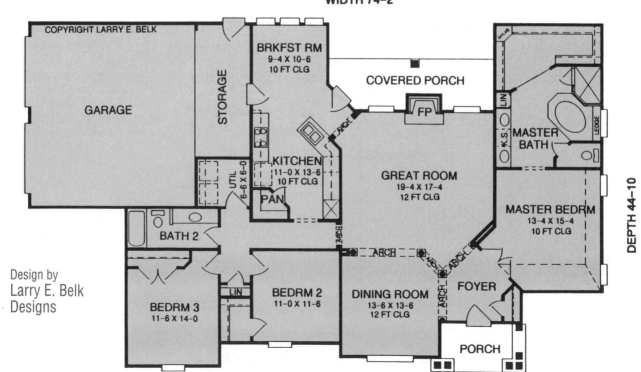

Design by
Larry E. Belk
Designs

WIDTH 61–6

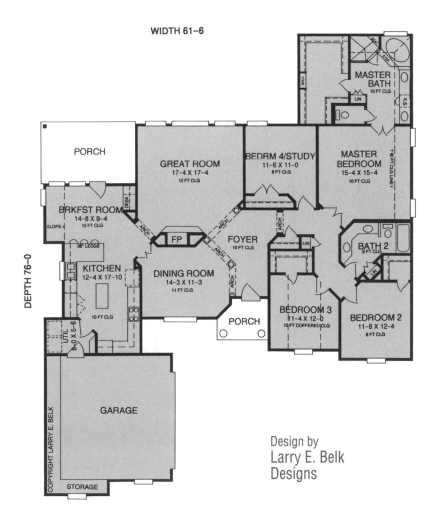

PORCH

GREAT ROOM
17-4 X 17-4
12 FT CLG

BEDRM 4/STUDY
11-6 X 11-0
8 FT CLG

MASTER
BEDROOM
15-4 X 15-4
10 FT CLG

MASTER
BATH
10 FT CLG

BRKFST ROOM
14-8 X 9-4
10 FT CLG

SLOPE

38" LEDGE

FP

FOYER
10 FT CLG

KITCHEN
12-4 X 17-10

10 FT CLG

DINING ROOM
14-3 X 11-3
11 FT CLG

BATH 2
8 FT CLG

UTIL
8-0 X 5-6

BEDROOM 3
11-4 X 12-6
10 FT COFFERED CLG

PORCH

BEDROOM 2
11-8 X 12-4
8 FT CLG

DEPTH 76–0

GARAGE

STORAGE

Design by
Larry E. Belk
Designs

Design 8137
Square Footage: 2,307

● A charming swoop roof distinguishes this efficiently designed one story. The angled foyer is created by a series of classic columns and provides views to the dining room and great room. The kitchen features a large work island and lots of cabinets and counter space. The roomy breakfast room is close by. The master suite includes a huge walk-in closet and a bath with His and Hers vanities, a corner whirlpool tub and a separate shower. Bedrooms 2 and 3 include large walk-in closets. Bedroom 4 can be used as an owner's study or an in-home office. Please specify crawlspace or slab foundation when ordering.

Copyright 1992 Stephen S. Fuller, Inc.

Width 69'
Depth 49'-6"

Design 9885
Square Footage: 2,295

● One-story living takes a lovely traditional turn in this brick one-story home. The entry foyer opens directly to the dining room and great room, with columned accents to separate the areas. A large island kitchen adjoins a combination breakfast room/keeping room with fireplace. The bedrooms are found to the left of the plan. A master suite is cloistered to the rear and has a large master bath and bayed sitting area. Two additional bedrooms share a full bath. This home is designed with a basement foundation.

DECK

SITTING AREA
12'-0" X 12'-0"

MASTER SUITE
13'-0" X 17'-6"

M.BATH

M.CLOSET

BREAKFAST
11'-4" X 10'-0"

KITCHEN
10'-0" X 18'-0"

KEEPING ROOM
11'-4" X 11'-0"

GREAT ROOM
20'-6" X 19'-0"

CLO. CLO.

BATH

LIN.

PNTRY

DN. LAUNDRY

BEDROOM NO. 3
12'-0" X 11'-8"

CØAT

FOYER
8'-0" X 14'-4"

DINING ROOM
12'-0" X 14'-4"

TWO CAR GARAGE
21'-4" X 21'-5"

BEDROOM NO. 2
13'-10" X 12'-6"

STOOP

Design by
Design Traditions

Copyright 1992 Stephen S. Fuller, Inc.

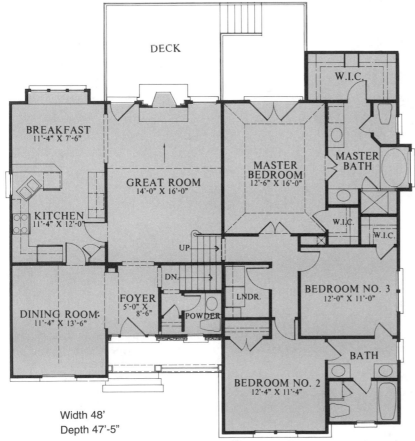

DECK

BREAKFAST
11'-4" X 7'-6"

GREAT ROOM
14'-0" X 16'-0"

KITCHEN
11'-4" X 12'-0"

MASTER
BEDROOM
12'-6" X 16'-0"

W.I.C.

MASTER
BATH

W.I.C.

W.I.C.

UP

DN

FOYER
5'-0" X
8'-6"

POWDER

LNDR.

BEDROOM NO. 3
12'-0" X 11'-0"

DINING ROOM
11'-4" X 13'-6"

BATH

BEDROOM NO. 2
12'-4" X 11'-4"

Width 48'
Depth 47'-5"

Design by
Design Traditions

Design 9949
Square Footage: 1,770

● Wood frame, weatherboard siding
and stacked stone give this home its
country cottage appeal. The concept
is reinforced by the double elliptical-
arched front porch, the Colonial
balustrade and the roof-vent dormer.
Inside, the foyer leads to the great
room and the dining room. The well-
planned kitchen easily serves the
breakfast room. A rear deck makes
outdoor living extra enjoyable. The
bi-level nature of the home puts three
bedrooms upstairs. They include a
master suite with a tray ceiling and
a luxurious bath. The two secondary
bedrooms share a compartmented
bath. A basement foundation provides
extra storage.

QUOTE ONE®
Cost to build? See page 374
to order complete cost estimate
to build this house in your area!

Design by
Design Traditions

DECK

BREAKFAST
11'-4" X 8'-6"

BEDROOM NO. 3
11'-6" X 11'-0"

GREAT ROOM
14'-0" X 17'-6"

KITCHEN
11'-4" X 10'-0"

MASTER BEDROOM
12'-4" X 15'-6"

BATH

FOYER
6'-6" X 6'-6"

DN

HIS

BEDROOM NO. 2
11'-0" X 14'-8"

DINING ROOM
11'-4" X 10'-6"

PWDR

MASTER BATH

LAUNDRY

HERS

TWO-CAR GARAGE
20'-4" X 19'-4"

Width 55'-6"
Depth 57'-6"

Design 9894
Square Footage: 1,733

● Delightfully different, this brick one-story home has everything for the active family. The entry foyer opens to a formal dining room on the right, accented with four columns, and a great room with fireplace and French doors to the rear deck. The efficient kitchen has an attached, light-filled breakfast nook. The master bath features His and Hers walk-in closets, a double vanity and huge garden tub. The other full bath is compartmented to serve both secondary bedrooms. This home is designed with a basement foundation.

DECK

BREAKFAST
11'-4" X 8'-6"

BATH

BEDROOM NO. 2
11'-0" X 12'-0"

FAMILY ROOM
17'-8" X 15'-4"

MASTER BEDROOM
13'-8" X 15'-4"

KITCHEN
10'-8" X 12'-2"

BEDROOM NO. 3
11'-0" X 12'-0"

DN

LAUNDRY

POWDER

MASTER BATH

DINING ROOM
11'-8" X 15'-0"

FOYER
6'-0" X 12'-0"

LIVING ROOM
11'-4" X 14'-0"

W.I.C.

TWO CAR GARAGE
20'-4" X 19'-10"

STOOP

Width 65'
Depth 55'-11"

Design 9874
Square Footage: 2,095

QUOTE ONE®
Cost to build? See page 374
to order complete cost estimate
to build this house in your area!

Design by
Design Traditions

● Inside this home, the foyer opens to the living room defined through the use of columns and the large dining room accented by dramatic window detail. A butler's pantry is strategically located just off the kitchen to provide ease of access when entertaining. The open family room displays a fireplace and built-in cabinetry for added storage. In the master bedroom suite, a large bath with dual vanities, jacuzzi tub and shower is complete with a spacious walk-in closet. On the opposite side of the home are two additional bedrooms. This home is designed with a basement foundation.

Design 9806

Square Footage: 2,697

● Dual chimneys (one a false chimney created to enhance the aesthetic effect) and a double stairway to the covered entry of this home create a balanced architectural statement. The sunlit foyer leads straight into the spacious great room, where French doors and large side windows provide a generous view of the covered veranda in back. The great room features a tray ceiling and a fireplace, bordered by twin bookcases. Another great view is offered from the spacious kitchen with breakfast bar and a roomy work island. The master suite provides a large balanced bath, a spacious closet, and a glassed sitting area with access to the veranda. This home is designed with a basement foundation.

WIDTH 65'-3"
DEPTH 67'-3"

QUOTE ONE®

Cost to build? See page 374 to order complete cost estimate to build this house in your area!

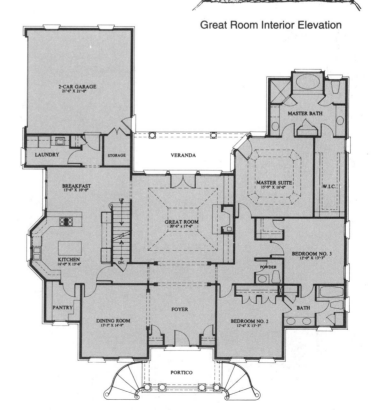

Great Room Interior Elevation

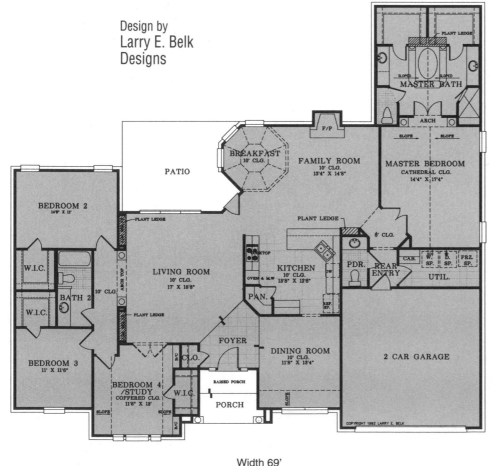

Design by
**Larry E. Belk
Designs**

PATIO

BREAKFAST
10' CLG.

FAMILY ROOM
10' CLG.
13'4" X 14'8"

MASTER BEDROOM
CATHEDRAL CLG.
14'4" X 17'4"

BEDROOM 2
14'8" X 11'

PLANT LEDGE

PLANT LEDGE

8' CLG.

W.I.C.

BATH 2

W.I.C.

LIVING ROOM
10' CLG.
17' X 18'8"

KITCHEN
10' CLG.
13'8" X 12'6"

PDR.

REAR
ENTRY

CAB.

UTIL.

OVEN & M.W.

PAN.

BEDROOM 3
11' X 11'6"

FOYER

DINING ROOM
10' CLG.
11'8" X 13'4"

2 CAR GARAGE

BEDROOM 4
/STUDY
COFFERED CLG.
11'6" X 13'

CLO.

W.I.C.

RAISED PORCH

PORCH

COPYRIGHT 1992 LARRY E. BELK

MASTER BATH

ARCH

F/P

Width 69'
Depth 63'-6"

Design 8071
Square Footage: 2,517

● A graceful stucco arch supported by columns gives this home instant curb appeal. Stucco quoins are used to further accent its traditional brick finish. Inside, the angled foyer steps down into the living room and draws the eye to a duplicate of the exterior arch with columns. Built-in display shelves on either side provide plenty of room for books or treasures. Step down again to enter the formal dining room. The kitchen features a coffered ceiling and is conveniently grouped with a sunny bayed breakfast room and the family room, the perfect place for informal gatherings. Upon entering the master suite, the master bath becomes the focal point. Columns flank the entry to this luxurious bath with a whirlpool tub as its centerpiece. His and Hers walk-in closets, a separate shower and a double-bowl vanity complete the design. This plan is available with either a crawlspace or slab foundation. Please specify when ordering.

Copyright 1992 Stephen S. Fuller, Inc.

Design 9884
Square Footage: 2,120

● Arched-top windows act as graceful accents for this wonderful design. Inside, the floor plan is compact but commodious. A central family room serves as the center of activity. It has a fireplace and connects to a lovely sun room with rear porch access. The formal dining room is to the front of the plan and is open to the entry foyer. A private den also opens off the foyer with double doors. It has its own private, cozy fireplace. The kitchen area opens to the sun room and it contains an island work counter. Bedrooms are split, with the master suite to the right side of the design and family bedrooms to the left. There are also three full baths in this plan. This home is designed with a basement foundation.

Design by
Design Traditions

QUOTE ONE®
Cost to build? See page 374 to order complete cost estimate to build this house in your area!

Width 62'
Depth 62'-6"

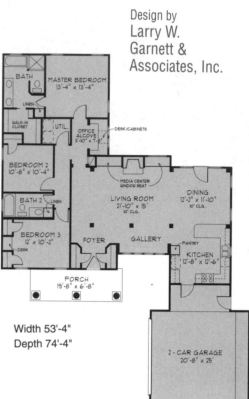

Design by
Larry W.
Garnett &
Associates, Inc.

Design 9191

Square Footage: 1,672

● This one-story traditional home features open floor planning for a comfortable, modern feel. The columned porch leads to a foyer flanked by coat closets. A columned gallery introduces a living room with a built-in media center and a warming fireplace. The dining room opens to the outdoors for enhanced livability. Three bedrooms include two secondary bedrooms separated by a full hall bath and a private master suite. Here, a walk-in closet and a contemporary bath are sure to please. Right outside the master bedroom, an office alcove accommodates home computing.

Width 53'-4"
Depth 74'-4"

Design by
Alan Mascord
Design Associates, Inc.

Design 9580

Square Footage: 2,155

● The stately appearance of this home complements a very livable interior. A columned great room gains attention from the front entry. A corner fireplace warms gatherings. The gourmet kitchen serves a nook and a dining room. The master suite is privately located behind the kitchen and features outdoor access and a luxury bath. Two bedrooms and a den finish the plan. A three-car garage provides lots of storage space.

Width 79'
Depth 60'

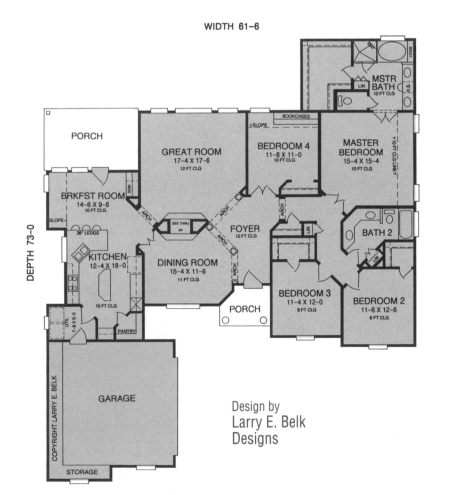

WIDTH 61-6

PORCH

GREAT ROOM
17-4 X 17-6
12 FT CLG

BEDROOM 4
11-8 X 11-0
10 FT CLG

MASTER
BEDROOM
15-4 X 15-4
10 FT CLG

BOOKCASES

SLOPE

MSTR
BATH
10 FT CLG

LIN

W.S.

BRKFST ROOM
14-6 X 9-6
10 FT CLG

SLOPE

36" LEDGE

SEE THRU
FP

FOYER
10 FT CLG

ARCH

ARCH

ARCH

BATH 2

LIN

10 FT CLG LINE

LEDGE

DEPTH 73-0

KITCHEN
12-4 X 18-0

10 FT CLG

DINING ROOM
15-4 X 11-6
11 FT CLG

ARCH

BEDROOM 3
11-4 X 12-0
8 FT CLG

BEDROOM 2
11-6 X 12-6
8 FT CLG

PORCH

7-8 X 5-5

PANTRY

GARAGE

STORAGE

Design by
Larry E. Belk
Designs

Design 8136
Square Footage: 2,247

● The combination of stucco and
brick materials gives this one-story
home a European feel. The dining
room and great room are showcased by the dramatic entry,
formed by classic columns. A see-
through fireplace serves both the
dining room and great room. All
bedrooms are conveniently
grouped on one side of the house.
Bedroom 4 is perfect for a study.
Should an additional bedroom be
needed, simply switch the location
of the doors and closet and the
study becomes a private bedroom.
A large kitchen and breakfast room
complete the efficiently designed
plan. Please specify crawlspace or
slab foundation when ordering.

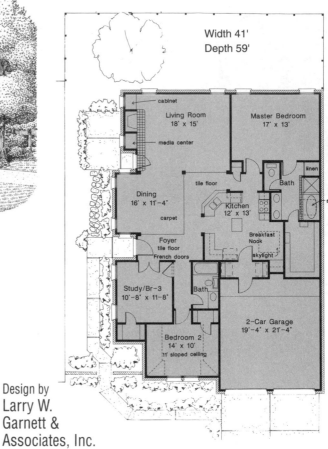

Width 41'
Depth 59'

cabinet

Living Room
18' x 15'

Master Bedroom
17' x 13'

media center

linen

tile floor

Bath

skylic

Dining
16' x 11'-4"

Kitchen
12' x 13'

carpet

Breakfast
Nook

skylight

Foyer
tile floor
French doors

Study/Br-3
10'-8" x 11-8"

Bath

2-Car Garage
19'-4" x 21'-4"

Bedroom 2
14' x 10'
11' sloped ceiling

Design 8980
Square Footage: 1,824

● Volume looks grace this one-story brick home. Combined dining and living areas are enhanced by built-ins and a fireplace. The
hub of the plan, the kitchen, serves a skylit breakfast nook. Two
bedrooms, one an optional study, share a full bath at the front of
the home. The master suite is located to the rear of the plan for
privacy and features a huge walk-in closet. The master bath contains a skylit tub, a separate shower, a double-bowl vanity and a
compartmented toilet. Linen storage completes this private
retreat.

Design by
Larry W.
Garnett &
Associates, Inc.

Design by
Larry W.
Garnett &
Associates, Inc.

Bonus Room
13'-4" x 21'
8' ceiling

4' walls

Bath

down

BONUS ROOM ABOVE GARAGE

Width 75'-2"
Depth 88'-6"

Bath

Dressing

Porch
11' x 10'

3-Car Garage
21'-4" x 32'

Utility

Porch
10' ceiling

Bedroom 3
13'-4" x 12'-8"

Master Bedroom
13'-4" x 17'-4"
11' ceiling

Family Room
16' x 21'
12' ceiling

Breakfast Room
12'-8" x 11'

Kitchen
12'-8" x 13'

Bath

Gallery
18' x 6'

Master Bath
13' x 11'

1/2 Bath

books

linen

Foyer
7' x 8'

Bedroom 2
13'-4" x 13'

13' x 6'

Study
13'-4" x 14'
11' ceiling

Dining Room
13'-4" x 15'
12' ceiling

Design 9189
Square Footage: 2,908
Bonus Room: 479 square feet

● The livability presented by this house is outstanding. From a
large family gathering area to a cozy study with a fireplace,
you're sure to find many pleasing attributes. The formal dining
room opens to the right of the foyer. Conveniently accessed by
the kitchen, meals will take on a special air when served here.
Two bedrooms make up the right side of the house. In the master
bedroom, a private bath, an expansive walk-in closet and outdoor
passage create a true retreat. A three-car garage with a bonus
room above and a pool dressing room complete the plan.

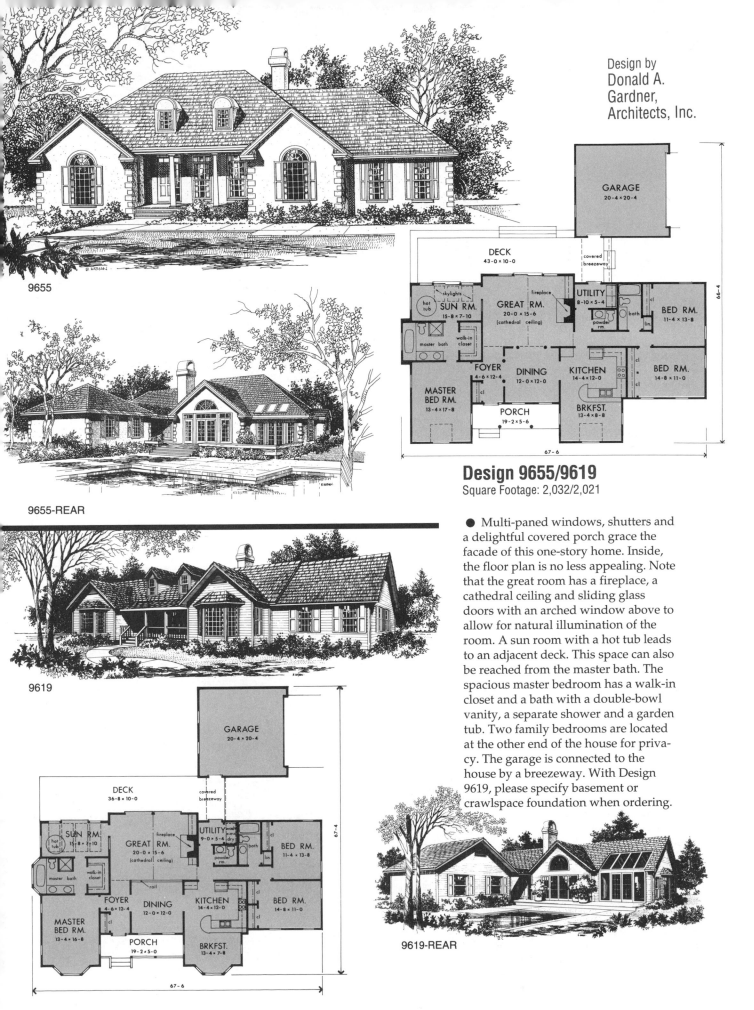

9655

9655-REAR

9619

Design by
Donald A.
Gardner,
Architects, Inc.

GARAGE
20-4 × 20-4

DECK
43-0 × 10-0

covered breezeway

skylights

hot tub

SUN RM.
15-8 × 7-10

master bath

fireplace

GREAT RM.
20-0 × 15-6
(cathedral ceiling)

walk-in closet

UTILITY
8-10 × 5-4

powder rm.

bath

lin.

cl

BED RM.
11-4 × 13-8

FOYER
4-6 × 12-4

DINING
12-0 × 12-0

KITCHEN
14-4 × 12-0

cl

cl

BED RM.
14-8 × 11-0

MASTER BED RM.
13-4 × 17-8

cl

PORCH
19-2 × 5-6

BRKFST.
13-4 × 8-8

66-4

67-6

Design 9655/9619
Square Footage: 2,032/2,021

● Multi-paned windows, shutters and
a delightful covered porch grace the
facade of this one-story home. Inside,
the floor plan is no less appealing. Note
that the great room has a fireplace, a
cathedral ceiling and sliding glass
doors with an arched window above to
allow for natural illumination of the
room. A sun room with a hot tub leads
to an adjacent deck. This space can also
be reached from the master bath. The
spacious master bedroom has a walk-in
closet and a bath with a double-bowl
vanity, a separate shower and a garden
tub. Two family bedrooms are located
at the other end of the house for privacy. The garage is connected to the
house by a breezeway. With Design
9619, please specify basement or
crawlspace foundation when ordering.

GARAGE
20-4 × 20-4

DECK
36-8 × 10-0

covered breezeway

hot tub

SUN RM.
15-8 × 7-10

GREAT RM.
20-0 × 15-6
(cathedral ceiling)

fireplace

UTILITY
9-0 × 5-4

wash
dry

powder rm.

bath

lin.

cl

BED RM.
11-4 × 13-8

master bath

walk-in closet

rail

FOYER
4-6 × 12-4

DINING
12-0 × 12-0

KITCHEN
14-4 × 12-0

cl

cl

BED RM.
14-8 × 11-0

MASTER BED RM.
13-4 × 16-8

cl

PORCH
19-2 × 5-0

BRKFST.
13-4 × 7-8

67-4

67-6

9619-REAR

Design 9023

Square Footage: 1,373

● While relatively small in terms of square footage, this home possesses the design characteristics and fine crafts-manship of another era. Influenced by Shingle Style cottages, the exterior features a sloping gable with a gentle curve over the front porch. Shingle siding is accented by expansive windows surround-ed with wide wood trim. Inside, the living area offers a fireplace and built-in media center. Decorative columns separate the living and dining areas. French doors open to a 6' x 17' rear porch from both the dining area and the master bedroom. The well-appointed master bath has ample linen storage, a private water closet and a garden tub with adja-cent glass-enclosed shower.

Design by
Larry W.
Garnett &
Associates, Inc.

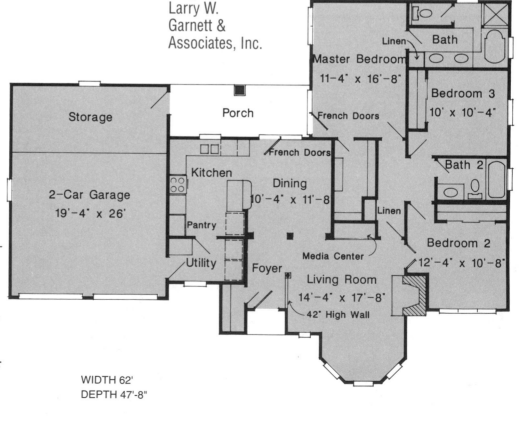

Storage

Porch

Linen   Bath

Master Bedroom
11'-4" x 16'-8"

Bedroom 3
10' x 10'-4"

French Doors

French Doors

Kitchen

Dining
10'-4" x 11'-8"

Bath 2

2-Car Garage
19'-4" x 26'

Linen

Pantry

Media Center

Bedroom 2
12'-4" x 10'-8"

Utility

Foyer

Living Room
14'-4" x 17'-8"

42" High Wall

WIDTH 62'
DEPTH 47'-8"

Design 8978
Square Footage: 468

● This delightful cottage features a columned porch and a side terrace—perfect for outdoor relaxation. Inside, the front-facing living room shares space with the efficiently patterned kitchen and has a window overlooking the terrace. A large storage closet, between the kitchen and bath, will serve nicely as a pantry or a linen closet. The bedroom, with a large, walk-in closet, enjoys peace and quiet at the rear of the plan. A step away, the full hall bath is also convenient to living areas.

Design by
Larry W.
Garnett &
Associates, Inc.

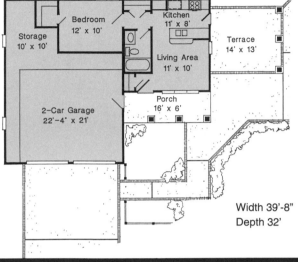

Width 39'-8"
Depth 32'

Width 62'
Depth 67'-10"

Design 8923
Square Footage: 2,361

● The combination of finely detailed brick and shingle siding recalls some of the distinctive architecture of the East Coast during the early part of this century. The foyer and gallery provide for a functional traffic pattern. The extensive living area offers a corner fireplace. A screened porch surrounding the breakfast room is an ideal entertainment area. The master suite features two spacious closets and a bath with a garden tub and an oversized shower. Bedroom 4 can serve as a study, nursery, guest room or home office.

Design by
Larry W.
Garnett &
Associates, Inc.

Cost to build? See page 374
to order complete cost estimate
to build this house in your area!

QUOTE ONE®

Cost to build? See page 374
to order complete cost estimate
to build this house in your area!

Design 9025

Square Footage: 2,481

● Multiple gables, bay windows and corner windows with transoms above provide an exterior reminiscent of English countryside homes. A marble floor in the foyer extends into the living room as an elegant fireplace hearth. The formal dining room features an eleven-foot ceiling, bay window, and French doors that open onto a private dining terrace. A spacious kitchen overlooks the breakfast area and the family room which has a corner fireplace and dramatic fourteen-foot ceiling with transom windows above triple French doors. Another corner fireplace is located in the master bedroom, which also contains a built-in desk and triple French doors. The luxurious master bath features mirrored doors at the large walk-in closet, a dressing table, and a whirlpool tub inset in a bay window.

Design by
Larry W.
Garnett &
Associates, Inc.

Kitchen

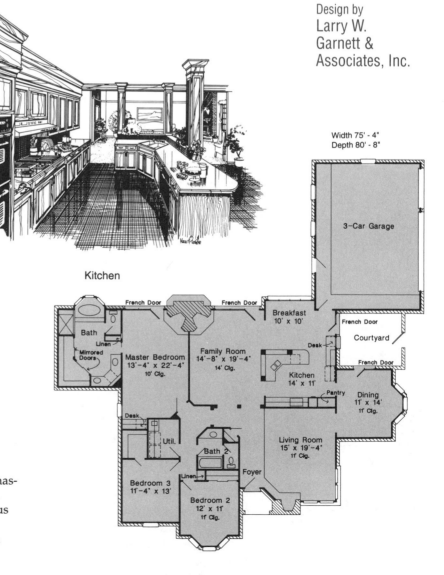

Width 75' - 4"
Depth 80' - 8"

40

Design by
Larry W.
Garnett &
Associates, Inc.

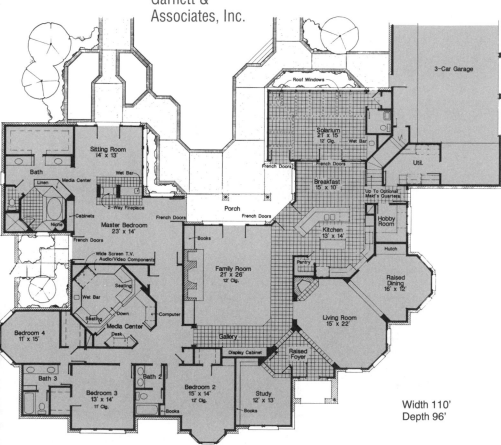

Width 110'
Depth 96'

Design 8905
Square Footage: 4,958

● The amenities in this home are almost too numerous to mention them all. Three family bedrooms, one with a bay window, are accompanied by two full baths. The master suite, to the rear of the home, includes a two-way fireplace to the bedroom and the sitting room, easy access to three separate outdoor areas, a built-in media center and a bath with dual vanities and a separate shower and tub. A modern media center is sunken and features built-in seating and a wet bar. Fireplaces warm the spacious family and living rooms. A study to the left of the foyer provides built-in bookshelves. The kitchen, with a work island and a large pantry, serves the family room, the breakfast room and the raised dining room with ease. French doors open to a commodious solarium. Maid's quarters may be built above the three-car garage.

Design 8029 Square Footage: 3,461

● This home provides a commanding entry with an octagonal shaped porch supported by large columns. This home is a sure winner for the corner or pie-shaped lot. Through the foyer is a large living room which opens to a covered porch. Flanking the foyer are the dining room and study. The gourmet kitchen includes a small bay window over the sink and an adjacent breakfast area including a small service sink. The master bedroom and bath are spacious and provide ample His and Hers closet space. A fourth bedroom and a full bath are privately located off the kitchen area. The permanent staircase is included to provide easy access to floored attic space above.

Design by
Larry E. Belk
Designs

Width 87'
Depth 77'-4"

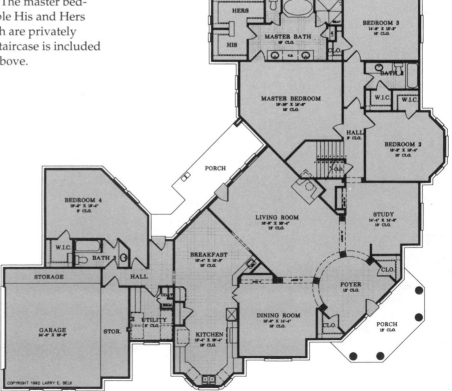

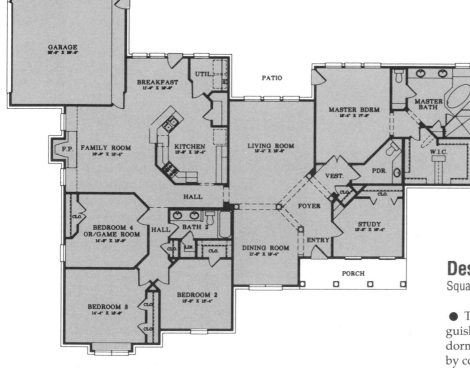

Design 8018

Square Footage: 2,846

● This Southern Colonial home is distinguished by its columned porch and double dormer. Inside, the angled foyer is defined by columns and connecting arches. The master suite is located away from the other bedrooms for privacy and includes a large master bath and a walk-in closet. Three additional bedrooms are located adjacent to the family room. The kitchen, breakfast area and family room are open and perfect for informal entertaining and family gatherings. The foyer, living room and dining room have twelve-foot ceilings. Ten-foot ceilings are used in the family room, kitchen, breakfast area and master suite to give this home an open, spacious feeling. This plan is available with either a crawlspace or slab foundation. Please specify when ordering.

Width 84'-6"
Depth 64'-2"

Design by
Larry E. Belk
Designs

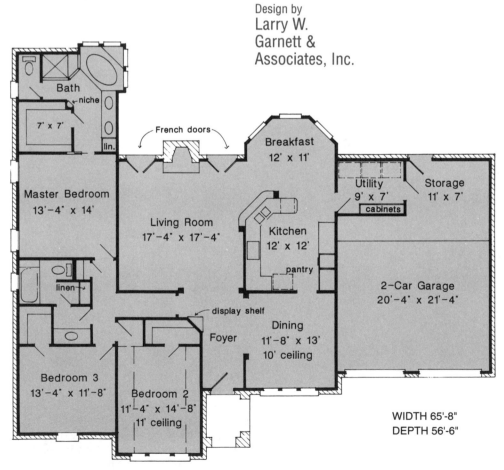

Design by
Larry W.
Garnett &
Associates, Inc.

Design 9088
Square Footage: 1,994

● This charming budget-conscious design provides an abundance of living space. Radiating around the roomy kitchen are the dining room with ten-foot ceiling and living room with French doors and fireplace. A glass-surrounded breakfast area near the kitchen provides space for casual eating. Three bedrooms, all with walk-in closets, dominate the left wing of the home. Bedroom 2 has an eleven-foot sloped ceiling. The master suite features a corner tub and a glass-enclosed shower with seat. Note the large utility room and storage space in the garage.

WIDTH 65'-8"
DEPTH 56'-6"

Cost to build? See page 374
to order complete cost estimate
to build this house in your area!

WIDTH 62'
DEPTH 57'-4"

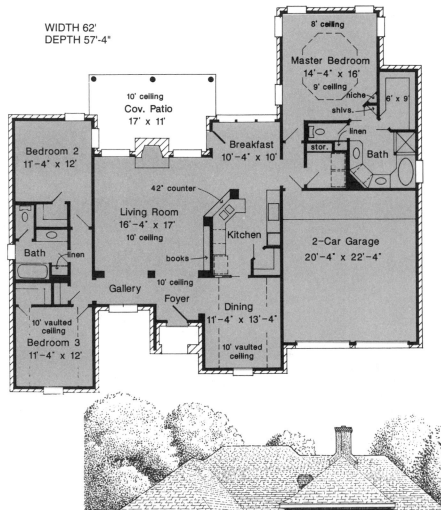

8' ceiling

Master Bedroom
14'-4" x 16'
9' ceiling
niche
6' x 9'
shlvs.
linen
Breakfast
10'-4" x 10'
stor.
Bath

10' ceiling
Cov. Patio
17' x 11'

Bedroom 2
11'-4" x 12'

42" counter

Living Room
16'-4" x 17'
10' ceiling

Kitchen

books

Bath
linen

2-Car Garage
20'-4" x 22'-4"

Gallery

10' ceiling

Foyer

Dining
11'-4" x 13'-4"

10' vaulted
ceiling

Bedroom 3
11'-4" x 12'

10' vaulted
ceiling

Design by
Larry W.
Garnett &
Associates, Inc.

Quote One®

Cost to build? See page 374
to order complete cost estimate
to build this house in your area!

Design 9161
Square Footage: 1,923

● Brick, shutters and graceful
roof lines lend a timeless
beauty in this traditional
design. Greet guests in the
ten-foot-high foyer, walk them
through the gallery and into
the impressive fireplace-
graced living room which
opens onto a covered patio.
Dining is a delight beneath a
ten-foot vaulted ceiling. The
secluded master bedroom
gives way to a glass-enclosed
shower, spa bath, double-bowl
vanity and dressing table. At
the other end of the house,
two family bedrooms—one
with a ten-foot vaulted ceiling—share a full bath.

Design by
**Alan Mascord
Design Associates, Inc.**

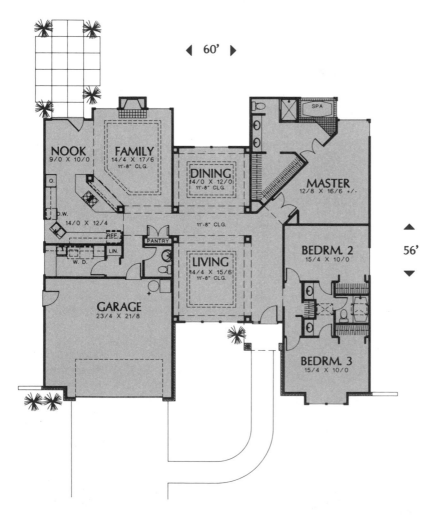

Design 9432
Square Footage: 2,276

● This elegant single-level plan puts its best foot forward with a brick facade, deeply hipped roof and multi-paned windows. The interior is something to brag about as well. All main living areas have tall ceilings with stepped tray vaults and transom windows. The large kitchen features an island with built-in cabinet on the opposite side that is perfect for the home entertainment system in the family room. Formal living and dining rooms face one another in the central hallway. Note the open feeling in both rooms. Three bedrooms include the master suite with angled wall and double doors. A convenient full bath with double vanity is shared by the two family bedrooms. The two-car garage allows space for a workshop along one side.

Design 3559
Square Footage: 2,916

L D

● Intricate details make the most of this lovely one-story. Besides the living room/dining room area to the rear, there is a large conversation area with a fireplace and plenty of windows. The kitchen is separated from the living areas by an angled snackbar counter. Three bedrooms grace the right side of the plan. The master suite features a tray ceiling and sliding glass doors to the rear terrace. The dressing area is graced by His and Hers walk-in closets, a double-bowl lavatory and a compartmented commode. The shower area is highlighted with glass block and is sunken down one step. A garden whirlpool finishes off this area.

California Engineered Plans and California Stock Plans are available for this home. Call 1-800-521-6797 for more information.

Design by
Home Planners,
Inc.

Width 77'-10"
Depth 73'-10"

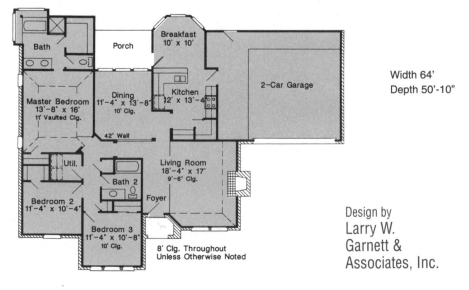

Design 9028
Square Footage: 1,707

● No slouch on amenities, this plan is a popular choice with those looking for a smaller-sized home. The openness of the floor plan makes it seem much larger than it really is. Note, for example, the high ceilings in the living room and master bedroom, and the short front wall defining the dining area. A bay-windowed breakfast room opens the kitchen area (don't miss the attached porch for outdoor dining). Three bedrooms include a large master suite. The laundry area is conveniently located near the bedrooms and a shared bath.

Width 64'
Depth 50'-10"

Design by
Larry W.
Garnett &
Associates, Inc.

Design 3612

Square Footage: 2,946

L

● This home's varying hipped-roof planes make a strong statement. Exquisite classical detailing includes delightfully proportioned columns below a modified pedimented gable and masses of brick punctuated by corner quoins. The central foyer, with its high ceiling, leads to interesting traffic patterns. This extremely functional floor plan fosters flexible living patterns. There are formal and informal living areas which are well defined by the living and family rooms. The family room is sunken and wonderfully spacious with its high, sloping ceiling. It has a complete media-center wall and a fireplace flanked by doors to the entertainment patio. Occupying the isolated end of the floor plan is the master suite and its adjacent office/den with private porch.

Design by
Home Planners,
Inc.

Width 94'-1"
Depth 67'-4"

QUOTE ONE™
Cost to build? See page 374
to order complete cost estimate
to build this house in your area!

Design by
Donald A.
Gardner,
Architects, Inc.

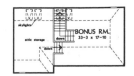

Design 9709

Square Footage: 2,663
Bonus Room: 653 square feet

● This home displays large arched windows, round columns, a covered porch and brick veneer siding. The arched window in the clerestory above the entrance provides natural light to the interior. The great room boasts a cathedral ceiling, a fireplace, built-in cabinets and bookshelves. Sliding glass doors lead to the sun room. The L-shaped kitchen services the dining room, the breakfast area and the great room. The master bedroom suite, with a fireplace, uses private passage to the deck and its spa. Three additional bedrooms—one could serve as a study—are at the other end of the house for privacy. This plan is available with a crawlspace foundation.

Width 72'-7"
Depth 78"

Design 9695

Square Footage: 2,526

● The spacious master suite with a fireplace occupies the right side of this home, while three bedrooms (or two with a study) are to the far left. Another fireplace and built-in cabinets are found in the great room. The sun room and breakfast area let plenty of sunlight in to brighten each day. Please specify crawlspace or basement foundation when ordering.

Design by
Donald A.
Gardner,
Architects, Inc.

Width 76'-11"
Depth 71'-7"

ALTERNATE PLAN
FOR BASEMENT

Design 9634
Square Footage: 2,099

● This enchanting design incorporates the best in floor planning–all on one level. The central great room is the hub of the plan from which all other rooms radiate. It is highlighted with a fireplace and cathedral ceiling. Nearby is a skylit sun room with sliding glass doors to the rear deck and a built-in wet bar. The galley-style kitchen adjoins an attached breakfast room that also connects to the sun room. The master suite is split from the family bedrooms and contains access to the rear deck. Its bathroom contains such special amenities as a large walk-in closet and double vanity. Family bedrooms share a full bath also with double vanity. Extra storage space is contained in the garage. Please specify basement or crawlspace foundation.

**Design by
Donald A.
Gardner,
Architects, Inc.**

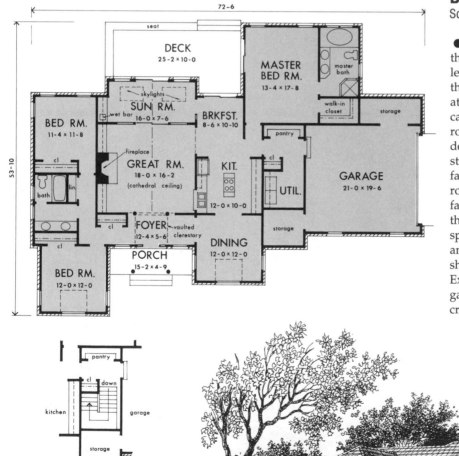

Floor plan labels

72-6

53-10

seat

DECK
25-2 × 10-0

MASTER
BED RM.
13-4 × 17-8

master
bath

walk-in
closet

storage

skylights

SUN RM.
16-0 × 7-6

wet bar

BRKFST.
8-6 × 10-10

BED RM.
11-4 × 11-8

pantry

cl

fireplace

GREAT RM.
18-0 × 16-2
(cathedral ceiling)

KIT.
12-0 × 10-0

cl

bath

lin

GARAGE
21-0 × 19-6

UTIL.

cl

FOYER
12-4 × 5-6

vaulted
clerestory

storage

BED RM.
12-0 × 12-0

PORCH
15-2 × 4-9

DINING
12-0 × 12-0

Alternate plan for basement

pantry

cl   down

kitchen

garage

storage

**ALTERNATE PLAN
FOR BASEMENT**

Design by
Donald A. Gardner, Architects, Inc.

Design 9734
Square Footage: 1,977
Bonus Room: 430 square feet
Optional Basement: 2,025 square feet

● A two-story foyer with a Palladian window sets the tone for this sunlit home. Columns mark the passage from the foyer to the great room, where a centered fireplace and built-in cabinets are found. A screened porch with skylights and a wet bar provides a pleasant place to start the day or to wind down after work. The kitchen is flanked by the formal dining room and the breakfast room, which has sliding doors to the rear deck and spa. Hidden quietly to the rear of the plan, the master suite includes a bath with dual vanities and skylights. Two family bedrooms (one an optional study) share a bath with twin sinks. Please specify basement or crawl-space foundation when ordering.

Cost to build? See page 374 to order complete cost estimate to build this house in your area!

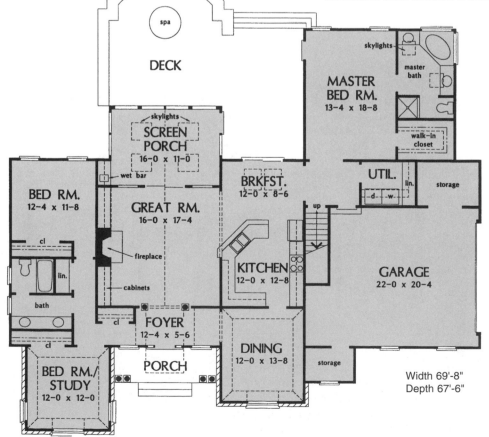

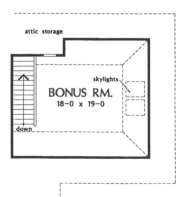

51

Design 9660

Square Footage: 2,108

● Multi-paned windows, dormers, copper-covered bay windows, a covered porch with round columns and brick veneer siding help to emphasize the sophisticated appearance of this three-bedroom home. An added special feature to this plan is the sun room with hot tub adjacent to and accessible to both the master bath and great room. The great room has a fireplace, cathedral ceiling and sliding glass door with arched window above to allow plenty of natural light. The spacious master bedroom contains a walk-in closet and a bath with double-bowl vanity, shower and garden tub. Two family bedrooms are located at the opposite end of the house for privacy. The plan includes a crawl-space foundation.

Design by
Donald A. Gardner, Architects, Inc.

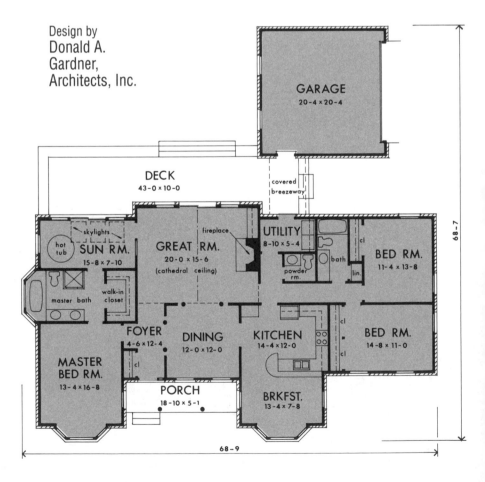

Design 9728
Square Footage: 1,576

● This stately, three-bedroom, one-story home exhibits sheer elegance with its large, arched windows, round columns, covered porch and brick veneer. In the foyer, a multitude of natural light enters through arched windows in clerestory dormers. In the great room, a dramatic cathedral ceiling and a fireplace set the mood. Through gracious, round columns, the kitchen and breakfast room open up. For sleeping, turn to the master bedroom. Here, a large, walk-in closet and a well-planned master bath with a double-bowl vanity, a garden tub and a shower will pamper. Two additional bedrooms are located at the opposite end of the house for privacy.

Design by
Donald A.
Gardner,
Architects, Inc.

53

Design 9765

Square Footage: 1,537

● The intricate window treatment
and stately columns give this home
magnificent curb appeal. Inside,
the columns continue from the
foyer into the spacious great room
with its cathedral ceiling and
raised-hearth fireplace. The fireplace is flanked by windows with a
view to the rear deck and the spa.
The great room opens to the large
island kitchen and the formal dining room with its dramatic tray
ceiling. Another tray ceiling can be
found in the master bedroom. It
includes a large bath with dual
vanities, a whirlpool tub, a separate
shower and a walk-in closet. The
remaining bedrooms, a shared full
bath and a conveniently placed
utility room are located in the right
wing of the house.

Design by
Donald A.
Gardner,
Architects, Inc.

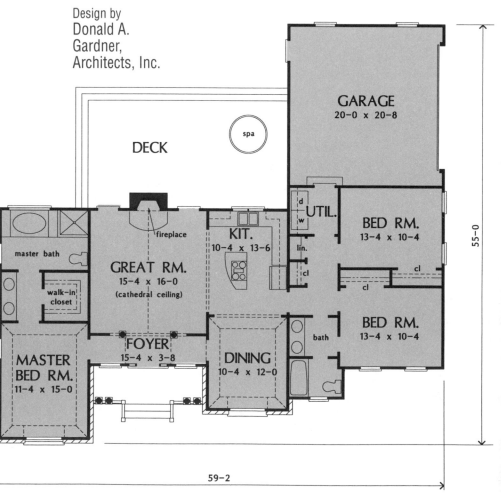

**Design by
Donald A.
Gardner,
Architects, Inc.**

Design 9760

Square Footage: 1,475

● Timeless appeal is exhibited in this design. The front porch leads to the columned foyer. A cathedral ceiling in the great room lends height and a feeling of openness. A fireplace here is framed by doors leading to a rear deck with a spa. The kitchen easily serves an elegant dining room. In the quiet master bedroom, a tiered ceiling, a private bath and a walk-in closet are appreciated features. Two secondary bedrooms reside on the left side of the plan and share a full hall bath.

Width 59'-6"
Depth 54'-7"

Design 9739

Square Footage: 2,211
Bonus Room: 408 square feet

● This home is built for entertaining. The large great room is perfect for parties and the kitchen, with sunny skylights and an adjoining dining room, creates a cozy breakfast buffet. Access from both rooms to the expansive deck completes the picture perfectly. The location of the kingly master bedroom and the other bedrooms allows for quiet comfort. Notice the bonus room which can be made into a game room or a study.

Design by
Donald A.
Gardner,
Architects, Inc.

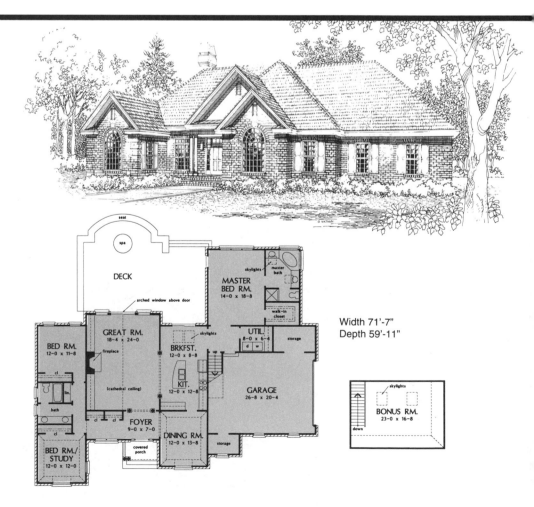

Width 71'-7"
Depth 59'-11"

Copyright 1992 Stephen S. Fuller, Inc.

Design 9854
Square Footage: 2,770

● This English cottage with its cedar shake exterior displays the best qualities of a traditional design. With the bay window and recessed entry, visitors will feel welcomed. The foyer opens to both the dining room and the great room with its fireplace and built-in cabinetry. Surrounded by windows, the breakfast room opens to a gourmet kitchen and a laundry room conveniently located near the garage entrance. To the right of the foyer is a hall powder room. Two bedrooms with large closets are joined by a full bath with individual vanities and a window seat. Through double doors at the end of a short hall, the master suite awaits with a tray ceiling and an adjoining sunlit sitting room. The master bath has His and Hers walk-in closets, separate vanities, an individual shower and a garden tub with a bay window. This home is designed with a basement foundation.

Design by
Design Traditions

Width 73'-6"
Depth 78'

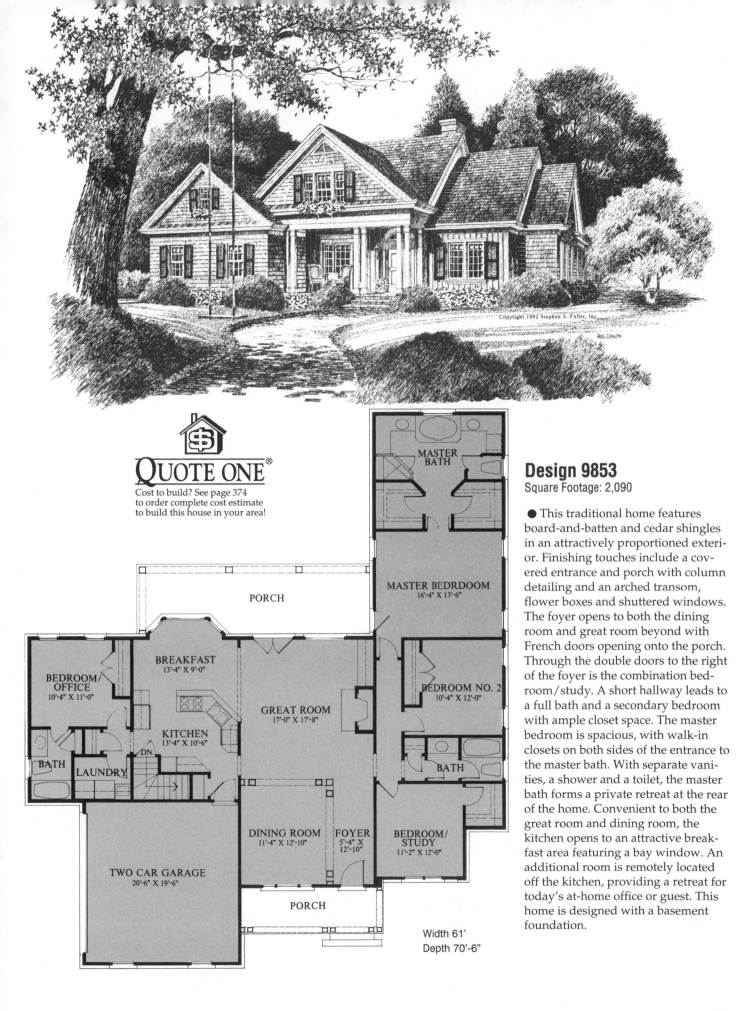

Copyright 1992 Stephen S. Fuller, Inc.

QUOTE ONE®

Cost to build? See page 374
to order complete cost estimate
to build this house in your area!

PORCH

MASTER BATH

MASTER BEDRDOOM
16'-4" X 13'-6"

BEDROOM/
OFFICE
10'-4" X 11'-0"

BREAKFAST
13'-4" X 9'-0"

KITCHEN
13'-4" X 10'-6"

GREAT ROOM
17'-0" X 17'-8"

BEDROOM NO. 2
10'-4" X 12'-0"

BATH

LAUNDRY

DN.

BATH

TWO CAR GARAGE
20'-6" X 19'-6"

DINING ROOM
11'-4" X 12'-10"

FOYER
5'-4" X
12'-10"

BEDROOM/
STUDY
11'-2" X 12'-0"

PORCH

Width 61'
Depth 70'-6"

Design 9853

Square Footage: 2,090

● This traditional home features
board-and-batten and cedar shingles
in an attractively proportioned exteri-
or. Finishing touches include a covered entrance and porch with column
detailing and an arched transom,
flower boxes and shuttered windows.
The foyer opens to both the dining
room and great room beyond with
French doors opening onto the porch.
Through the double doors to the right
of the foyer is the combination bed-
room/study. A short hallway leads to
a full bath and a secondary bedroom
with ample closet space. The master
bedroom is spacious, with walk-in
closets on both sides of the entrance to
the master bath. With separate vanities, a shower and a toilet, the master
bath forms a private retreat at the rear
of the home. Convenient to both the
great room and dining room, the
kitchen opens to an attractive breakfast area featuring a bay window. An
additional room is remotely located
off the kitchen, providing a retreat for
today's at-home office or guest. This
home is designed with a basement
foundation.

Design 9187
Square Footage: 1,462

● Start small with this charming
cottage and grow-as-you-go! The
basic design offers amenities often
found in homes twice the size.
Special features include French
doors flanking the warming fireplace in the living room, a window
seat bordered by twin closets in
Bedroom 2, a laundry room conveniently located to the bedrooms
and bath, and an efficient kitchen
nestled between the formal dining
room and breakfast nook. When
you're ready, enlarging the plan is
simple, and designed to finish in
stages. A sumptuous master suite
with a large walk-in closet and
pampering bath may be added as
the need for additional space arises. A two-car garage with a large
shop area, utility room and half
bath may be completed in the next
phase. Completing the expansion
of this terrific plan is the guest
quarters located above the garage.

Design by
Larry W.
Garnett &
Associates, Inc.

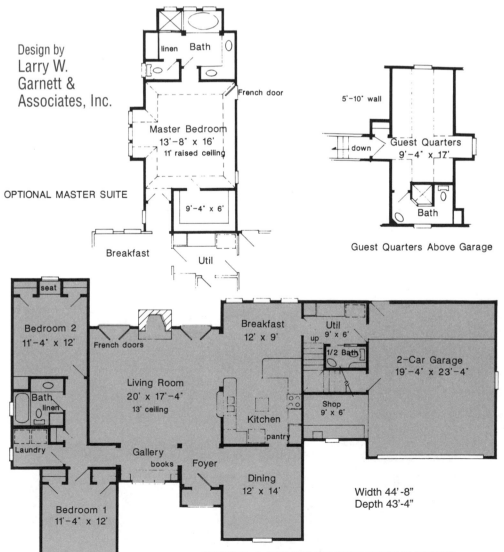

OPTIONAL MASTER SUITE

linen   Bath

French door

Master Bedroom
13'-8" x 16'
11' raised ceiling

9'-4" x 6'

Breakfast   Util

5'-10" wall

down   Guest Quarters
9'-4" x 17'

Bath

Guest Quarters Above Garage

seat

Bedroom 2
11'-4" x 12'

French doors

Bath
linen

Laundry

Living Room
20' x 17'-4"
13' ceiling

Gallery
books

Foyer

Breakfast
12' x 9'

up

Kitchen

pantry

Util
9' x 6'

1/2 Bath

Shop
9' x 6'

2-Car Garage
19'-4" x 23'-4"

Dining
12' x 14'

Bedroom 1
11'-4" x 12'

Width 44'-8"
Depth 43'-4"

OPTIONAL 2-CAR GARAGE WITH GUEST QUARTERS

Width 58'
Depth 52'-6"

Design by
**Home Planners,
Inc.**

Design 3340

Square Footage: 1,611

L

● You may not decide to build this design simply because of its delightful covered porch. But it certainly will provide its share of enjoyment if this plan is your choice. Notice also how effectively the bedrooms are arranged out of the traffic flow of the house. One bedroom could double nicely as a TV room or study. The living room/dining area is highlighted by a fireplace, sliding glass doors to the porch and an open staircase with built-in planter.

Design by
Design Traditions

Design 9862

Square Footage: 2,170

● This classic cottage features a stone-and-wooden exterior with an arch-detailed porch and box-bay window. From the foyer, double doors open to the den with a fireplace. The family room is centrally located, just beyond the foyer. The master bedroom opens onto the rear porch. A short hallway from the sun room leads to two bedrooms with large closets and a shared full bath featuring double vanities. This home is designed with a basement foundation.

Width 62'-4"
Depth 62'-2"

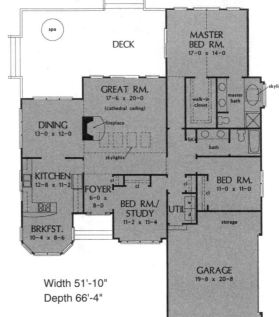

**Design by
Donald A.
Gardner,
Architects, Inc.**

Design 9772

Square Footage: 1,829

● Ample windows allow lots of sunshine to penetrate the interior of this cozy one-story home. The foyer leads to a study on the right. This room may convert to a bedroom, if desired. In the great room, skylights, a fireplace and a cathedral ceiling are pleasing enhancements. Sliding glass doors open to a rear deck. Bedrooms include a private master suite with a sloping ceiling and luxury bath. Here, double lavatories and a garden tub with a skylight create an elegant atmosphere. A large walk-in closet accommodates even expansive wardrobes.

Width 51'-10"
Depth 66'-4"

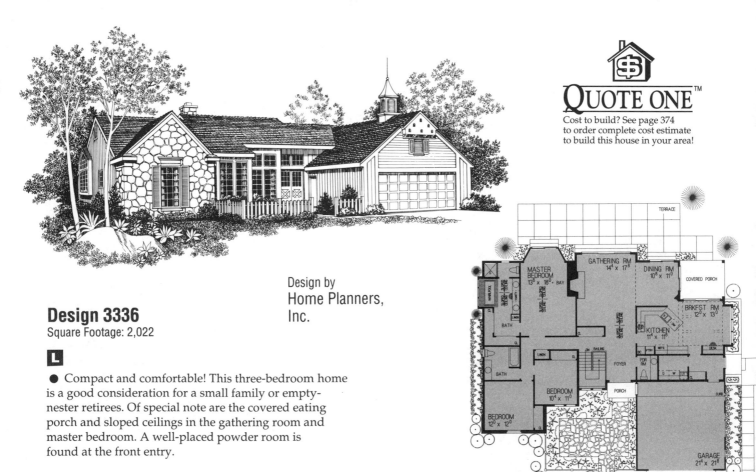

QUOTE ONE™
Cost to build? See page 374
to order complete cost estimate
to build this house in your area!

**Design by
Home Planners,
Inc.**

Design 3336

Square Footage: 2,022

L

● Compact and comfortable! This three-bedroom home is a good consideration for a small family or empty-nester retirees. Of special note are the covered eating porch and sloped ceilings in the gathering room and master bedroom. A well-placed powder room is found at the front entry.

Width 64'
Depth 55'4"

Design 2805

Quote One®

Cost to build? See page 342
to order complete cost estimate
to build this house in your area!

Design by
Home Planners

Design 2806

OPTIONAL NON-BASEMENT

Width 60'-4"
Depth 51'-5"

Design 2807

Design 2805/2806/2807

Square Footage: 1,547/1,584/1,576

L **D**

● Three different exterior facades share one compact, practical and economical floor plan. The major design variations are roof pitch, window placement and garage openings. Each design will hold its own, whether you select the romantic stone-and-shingle cottage design (2805), the brick and half-timbered stucco Tudor version (2806) or the sleek contemporary-style home (2807). Inside, the living-dining room expands across the rear of the plan, with a fireplace at one end and direct access to the skylit covered porch. The breakfast room also provides a view of the porch. A desk, snack bar and mud room housing the laundry facilities are near the U-shaped kitchen in a convenient clustering of work areas. Notice the attractive built-in planter adjacent to the open basement staircase. The master bedroom has a private bath with a shower, while two family bedrooms (one of which could be a TV room or study) share a full bath with a tub.

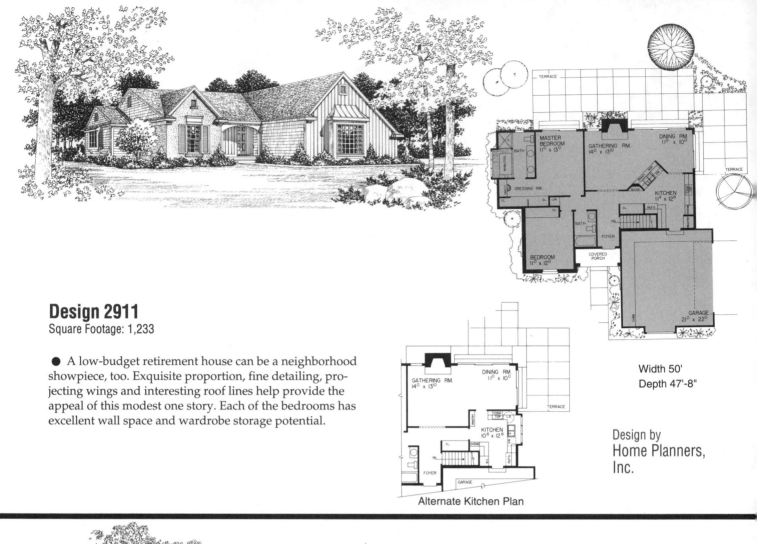

Design 2911
Square Footage: 1,233

● A low-budget retirement house can be a neighborhood showpiece, too. Exquisite proportion, fine detailing, projecting wings and interesting roof lines help provide the appeal of this modest one story. Each of the bedrooms has excellent wall space and wardrobe storage potential.

Alternate Kitchen Plan

Width 50'
Depth 47'-8"

Design by
Home Planners,
Inc.

Design 2878
Square Footage: 1,521

● Postcard-perfect, this is an economical one story that still has all the basics covered—and then some. It's got a gathering room with a fireplace and a sloped ceiling, a formal dining room adjacent to a rear terrace, a roomy kitchen and a breakfast room and a study off the foyer that could be a third bedroom. The master suite shows off a dressing room, a walk-in closet and access to its own private terrace.

California Engineered Plans and California Stock Plans are available for this home. Call 1-800-521-6797 for more information.

QUOTE ONE™
Cost to build? See page 374 to order complete cost estimate to build this house in your area!

Design by
Home Planners,
Inc.

Width 51'-4"
Depth 52'-4"

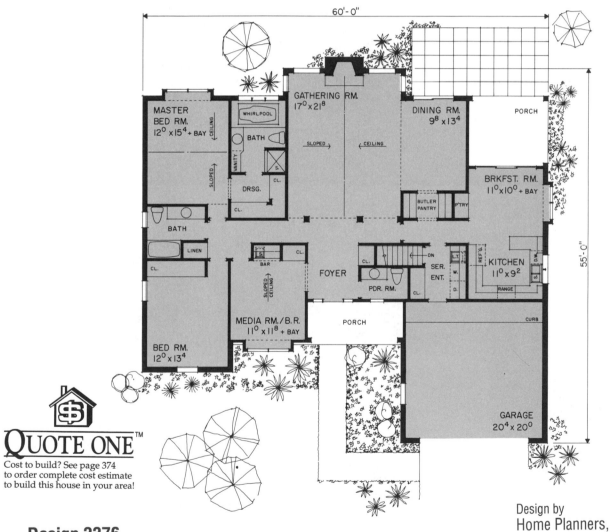

60'-0"

MASTER
BED RM.
12⁰ x 15⁴ + BAY

GATHERING RM.
17⁰ x 21⁸

DINING RM.
9⁸ x 13⁴

PORCH

WHIRLPOOL

BATH

SLOPED   CEILING

BRKFST. RM.
11⁰ x 10⁰ + BAY

VANITY

DRSG.

BUTLER
PANTRY

P'TRY

CL.

BATH

REF'G.

KITCHEN
11⁰ x 9²

LINEN

BAR

CL.

CL.

FOYER

PDR. RM.

SER.
ENT.

W.

D.

DW.

RANGE

CL.

55'-0"

SLOPED
CEILING

MEDIA RM./B.R.
11⁰ x 11⁸ + BAY

PORCH

DN

CURB

BED RM.
12⁰ x 13⁴

GARAGE
20⁴ x 20⁰

Design by
Home Planners,
Inc.

Design 3376

Square Footage: 1,999

L **D**

● Small families or empty nesters will appreciate the layout of this traditional ranch. The foyer opens to the gathering room with fireplace and sloped ceiling. The dining room is open to the gathering room for entertaining ease and contains sliding doors to a rear terrace. The breakfast room also provides access to a covered porch for dining outdoors. The media room to the left of the home offers a bay window and a wet bar, or it can double as a third bedroom.

Design 3314

Square Footage: 1,951

L

● Formal living areas in this plan are joined by a three-bedroom sleeping wing. One bedroom, with foyer access, could function as a study. Two verandas and a screened porch enlarge the plan and enhance indoor/outdoor livability. The sloped ceiling in the gathering room gives this area an open, airy quality.

California Engineered Plans and California Stock Plans are available for this home. Call 1-800-521-6797 for more information.

Cost to build? See page 374
to order complete cost estimate
to build this house in your area!

Width 56'
Depth 48'-8"

Design by
Home Planners, Inc.

Design 3319

Square Footage: 2,274

L **D**

● This attractive bungalow design separates the master suite from family bedrooms and puts casual living to the back in a family room. The gathering room and dining area are centrally located and have access to a rear terrace, as does the master suite. The kitchen sits between formal and informal living areas. The two family bedrooms are found to the front of the plan. A home office or study opens off the front foyer and the master suite.

Cost to build? See page 374
to order complete cost estimate
to build this house in your area!

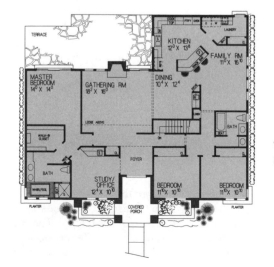

Design by
Home Planners, Inc.

Width 58'
Depth 54'

64

Design 1323
Square Footage: 1,344

L **D**

● Incorporated in the set of blueprints for this design are details for building each of the three charming, traditional exteriors. Each of the three alternate exteriors has a distinction all its own. A study of the floor plan reveals fine livability. There are two full baths, a fine family room, an efficient work center, a formal dining area, bulk storage facilities and sliding glass doors to the quiet and living terraces. The laundry is strategically located near the kitchen.

QUOTE ONE™

Cost to build? See page 374 to order complete cost estimate to build this house in your area!

Floor plan labels:

68'-0"
48'-0"
20'-0"
28'-0"

QUIET TERRACE — SCREEN — LIVING TERRACE

MASTER BED RM. 13⁰ x 13⁶ — BATH — FAMILY RM 10⁶ x 13⁶ — S — D.W. O. W. D. — STORAGE 16⁰ x 8⁰

CL. — KIT. 10⁶ x 8⁰ — RANGE — LAUNDRY

BATH — REF'G — CL. — CARPORT-GARAGE 20⁰ x 20⁰

CL. — AIR COND. — CHINA — DINING

LIN. CL. — CL.

BED RM. 10⁰ x 13⁶ — BED RM. 10⁸ x 10⁰ — CL. — ENTRY — LIVING RM. 18⁰ x 19⁶

R

FENCE

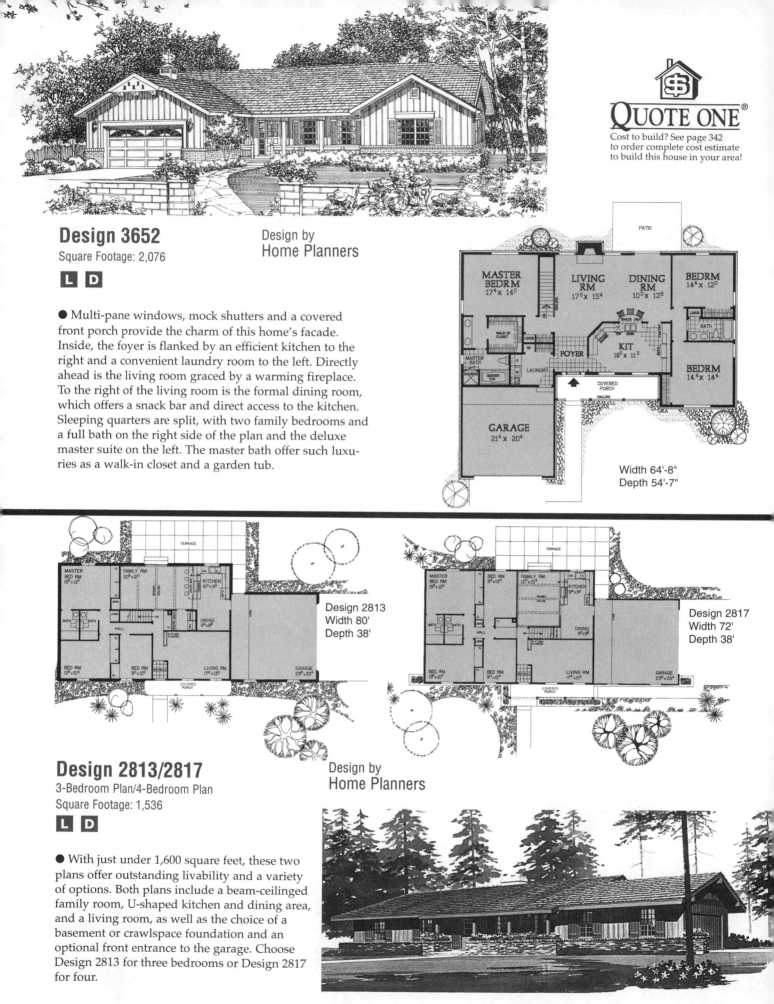

QUOTE ONE®
Cost to build? See page 342
to order complete cost estimate
to build this house in your area!

Design 3652

Square Footage: 2,076

L D

Design by
Home Planners

● Multi-pane windows, mock shutters and a covered front porch provide the charm of this home's facade. Inside, the foyer is flanked by an efficient kitchen to the right and a convenient laundry room to the left. Directly ahead is the living room graced by a warming fireplace. To the right of the living room is the formal dining room, which offers a snack bar and direct access to the kitchen. Sleeping quarters are split, with two family bedrooms and a full bath on the right side of the plan and the deluxe master suite on the left. The master bath offer such luxuries as a walk-in closet and a garden tub.

Width 64'-8"
Depth 54'-7"

Design 2813
Width 80'
Depth 38'

Design 2817
Width 72'
Depth 38'

Design 2813/2817

3-Bedroom Plan/4-Bedroom Plan
Square Footage: 1,536

L D

Design by
Home Planners

● With just under 1,600 square feet, these two plans offer outstanding livability and a variety of options. Both plans include a beam-ceilinged family room, U-shaped kitchen and dining area, and a living room, as well as the choice of a basement or crawlspace foundation and an optional front entrance to the garage. Choose Design 2813 for three bedrooms or Design 2817 for four.

Design 2693
Square Footage: 3,462

● This elegant Georgian manor is reminiscent of historic Rose Hill, built 1818 in Lexington, Kentucky. It is typical of the classic manors with Greek Revival features built in Kentucky as the 19th Century dawned. Note the classical portico of four Ionic columns plus the fine proportions. Also noteworthy is the updated interior, highlighted by a large country kitchen with fireplace and an efficient work center that includes an island cooktop. The country kitchen leads directly into a front formal dining room, just off the foyer. On the other side of the foyer is a front living room. A large library is located in the back of the house. It features built-in bookcases plus a fireplace, one of four fireplaces.

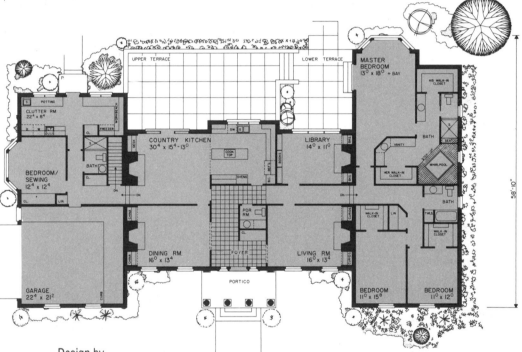

Design by
Home Planners, Inc.

Design 9439

Square Footage: 1,338

● This classic single-story home invites a second look—particularly for those who are planning to build for affordability. Special features make it attractive while budget-worthy: the living room, nook and master suite all contain vaulted ceilings; the covered patio provides outdoor enjoyment even in inclement weather. Notice that the living and dining areas remain open to each other—this creates a friendly atmosphere for entertaining. Of course, the fireplace in the living room adds additional warmth to the setting. Each of the family bedrooms enjoys ample closet space as well as lots of privacy. The master bedroom, opening through double doors, spotlights its own bath.

◄ 48' ►

48'

COVERED PATIO

VAULTED
NOOK
7/0 X 10/0

VAULTED
MASTER
14/8 X 14/0 +/-

8/0 X 14/0

DINING
12/0 X 10/0

P. REF.

LINEN

BR. 2
12/0 X 10/0

VAULTED
LIVING
12/0 X 13/0

BR. 3
9/6 X 12/8

GARAGE
19/4 X 21/8

Design by
Alan Mascord
Design Associates, Inc.

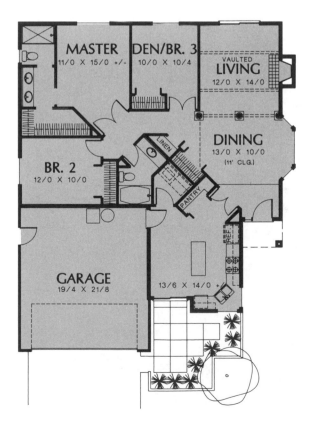

Design 9429
Square Footage: 1,367

● Featuring a combination of cedar shingles and vertical cedar siding, this ranch home has a compact, convenient floor plan. Both kitchen and nook face the front where a courtyard wall provides privacy for outdoor relaxation. The entry and dining room both have eleven-foot ceilings, allowing for attractive transom windows. This area is also enhanced by a series of columns separating the vaulted living room from the dining room. Opening off the hallway with a pair of French doors is a den which could be used as a third bedroom.

Design by
Alan Mascord
Design Associates, Inc.

Design 9431
Square Footage: 1,316

● An exceptional use of cedar shingles, horizontal cedar siding and brick highlights the exterior of this one-story home. And the floor plan is bursting with amenities found normally on much larger homes. Note, for example, the dramatically vaulted great room with the plant shelf floating across the entry. The master bedroom is also vaulted. The covered patio lends itself to great outdoor living even in inclement weather. Opening off the entry with a pair of French doors is a den which could be used as a third bedroom.

◄ 46' ►

50'

COVERED PATIO

DINING
10/0 X 10/4

VAULTED
GREAT RM.
15/0 X 15/0

VAULTED
MASTER
12/0 X 15/0

PLANT SHELF

9/6 X 11/8

LIN.

P.

VAULTED
DEN/ BR. 3
11/0 X 11/0 +/-

BR. 2
12/8 X 10/0

GARAGE
19/4 X 21/8

Design by
Alan Mascord
Design Associates, Inc.

9529

Design 9529/9530/9531
Square Footage: 1,420

● This efficient floor plan carries three different exterior elevations for just the right look. Inside, a living room or den opens to the right of the entry. It offers an optional built-in or closet. In the kitchen, an abundance of counter space and an accommodating layout make meal preparations simple. A great room and dining room connect to this area and will conform to everyday living. Two bedrooms include a master suite with a private bath and ample closet space. The master bedroom also accesses the outdoors for an added treat.

Design by
Alan Mascord
Design Associates, Inc.

9530

9531

◀ 40' ▶

58'

MASTER
13/8 X 12/4 +/-

DINING
10/0 X 11/0

GREAT RM.
14/4 X 15/0 +/-

BR. 2
11/0 X 11/0

13/0 X 13/0

LINEN

PAN. REF.

GARAGE
19/4 X 21/8

LR./DEN
13/0 X 11/8 +/-

OPTIONAL
BUILT-IN
OR CLOSET

PORCH

Design 9528

Square Footage: 1,843

● The vaulted living room of this design makes a grand first impression. A niche in the entry hall further accentuates this area. On the right, a dining room accommodates formal meals well. In the kitchen, an island cooktop will please cooks of any caliber. A sunny nook opens to the vaulted family room with its warming fireplace. Nearby, two secondary bedrooms—or a bedroom and a den—offer ample closet space. A full hall bath features interesting angles. In the master bedroom suite, a bathroom with a spa tub, a large walk-in closet and outdoor access all command attention.

SPA

MASTER
12/0 X 17/6 +/-

VAULTED
FAMILY
13/0 X 16/0

NOOK
8/6 X 11/0

54'

BEDRM. 2
12/0 X 10/0

LINEN

14/6 X 11/4 +/-

O. REF.

DEN/BR. 3
12/0 X 10/0

PANTRY

W. D.

GARAGE
21/2 X 21/4

OPT. DR.

NICHE

DINING
10/0 X 12/0

VAULTED
LIVING
14/0 X 13/0

56'

Design by
Alan Mascord
Design Associates, Inc.

Width 44'-4"
Depth 47'-4"

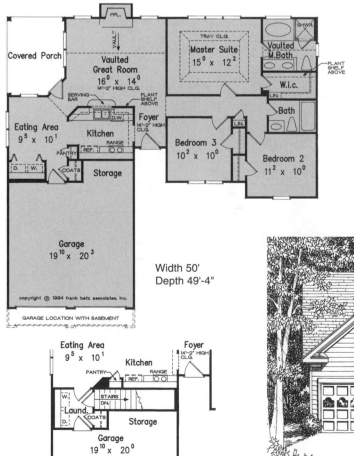

Design by
Home Planners

QUOTE ONE®

Cost to build? See page 342
to order complete cost estimate
to build this house in your area!

Design 3659

Square Footage: 1,118

L

● Compact and perfect for starters or empty-
nesters, this is one wonderful single-level
home. Just to the left of the entry is a roomy
kitchen with bright windows and convenient
storage. The octagonal dining room shares a
three-sided fireplace with the living room. A
covered patio to the rear enhances outdoor
living. A fine master suite with a grand bath
is complemented by a secondary bedroom
and bath.

Design by
Frank Betz
Associates, Inc.

Design P239

Square Footage: 1,185

● The living areas of this attractive plan curve around a
covered porch, with the well-designed kitchen conveniently close to all. The vaulted great room features a fireplace and a serving bar from the kitchen. The master suite
is sure to please, with a tray ceiling and a private bath that
includes a large walk-in closet, separate tub and shower,
double-bowl vanity and decorative plant shelf.

Design by
Alan Mascord
Design Associates, Inc.

Design 9428
Square Footage: 1,546

● Highlighting the exterior
of this home are brick accents
and a variety of interesting
lines and angles. It exudes a
sense of space that far exceeds
its actual square footage.
Inside, the floor plan offers a
number of amenities. Featured
in the living room is an
immense bay window that
encloses the entire end of the
room in glass. A pair of doors
opens to the large master suite
with a compartmented shower
and large closet with space-
expanding mirrored doors.
Two family bedrooms and
another full bath round out
this unique plan.

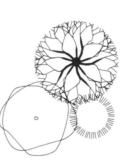

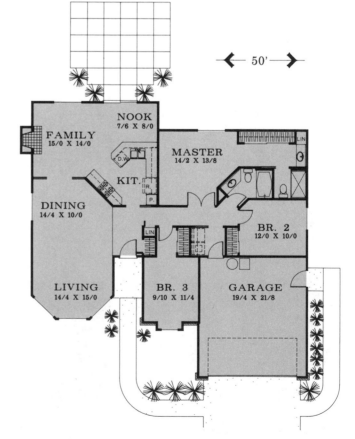

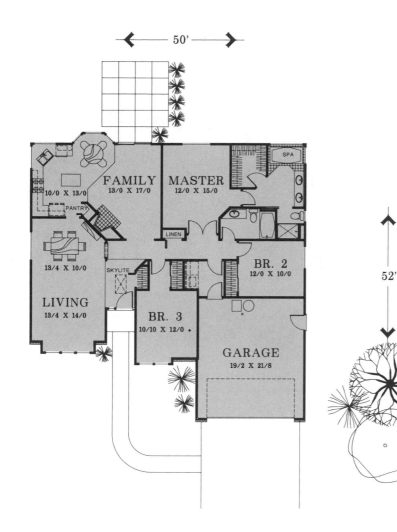

FAMILY
13/0 X 17/0

MASTER
12/0 X 15/0

SPA

10/0 X 13/0

PANTRY

LINEN

13/4 X 10/0

SKYLITE

BR. 2
12/0 X 10/0

LIVING
13/4 X 14/0

BR. 3
10/10 X 12/0 +

GARAGE
19/2 X 21/8

50'

52'

Design 9427
Square Footage: 1,687

● Intriguing roof lines create a dynamic exterior for this home. It is even further enhanced by a tasteful accenting of brick. The interior floor plan is equally attractive. Towards the rear a wide archway forms the entrance to the spacious family living area with its centrally placed fireplace and bay-windowed nook area. An island and a walk-in pantry complete the efficient kitchen (note the corner window treatment overlooking the yard). This home also boasts a terrific master suite complete with walk-in wardrobe, spa tub with corner windows and a compartmentalized shower and toilet area.

Design by
**Alan Mascord
Design Associates, Inc.**

NOOK
8/8 X 9/8

VAULTED
MASTER
12/0 X 14/0

VAULTED
FAMILY
12/0 X 14/0

11/2 X 12/0

SPA

BR. 2
12/0 X 10/0

DINING

DEN/BR. 3
10/6 X 10/8

VAULTED
LIVING
13/0 X 20/8

GARAGE
19/4 X 21/8

Width 50'
Depth 52'-10"

Design 9403

Square Footage: 1,565

● If you're looking for a traditional-styled ranch, this one with front-facing gables and a combination of cedar siding may be just right for you. The vaulted living room faces the street and is set off with a gorgeous Palladian window. The family room (note angled fireplace here) and master bedroom also have vaulted ceilings. Look for a spa tub, large shower and walk-in closet in the master bedroom. Through French doors in the entry is a den that could be used as a third bedroom.

Design by
Alan Mascord
Design Associates, Inc.

QUOTE ONE™

Cost to build? See page 374
to order complete cost estimate
to build this house in your area!

Design 3355

Square Footage: 1,387

L **D**

● Though it's only just under 1,400 total
square feet, this plan offers three bedrooms (or
two with study) and a sizable gathering room
with fireplace and sloped ceiling. The galley
kitchen provides a pass-through snack bar and
has a planning desk and attached breakfast
room. Besides two smaller bedrooms with a
full bath, there's an extravagant master suite
with large dressing area, double vanity and
raised whirlpool tub. The full-length terrace to
the rear of the house extends the living potential to the outdoors.

Design by
Home Planners

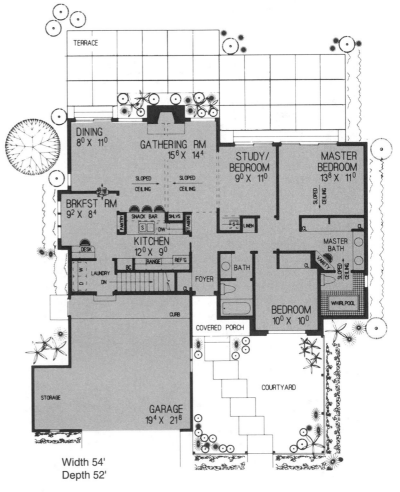

Width 54'
Depth 52'

Design by
**Home Planners,
Inc.**

Width 36'
Depth 26'

Design 2165
Square Footage: 880

● Whether called upon to function as a two- or a three-bedroom home, this attractive design will serve its occupants ideally for many years. The efficient kitchen accommodates informal eating space.

Design 1107
Square Footage: 1,416

● A smart looking traditional adaptation which, because of its perfectly rectangular shape, will be most economical to build. The low-pitched roof has a wide overhang which accentuates its low-slung qualities. The attached two-car garage is oversized to permit the location of extra bulk storage space. Further, its access to the house is through the handy separate laundry area. This house will function as either a four bedroom home, or as one that has three bedrooms, plus a quiet study. Features include a fireplace in the living room, built-in china cabinet in the breakfast room, sizable vanity in the main baths and more.

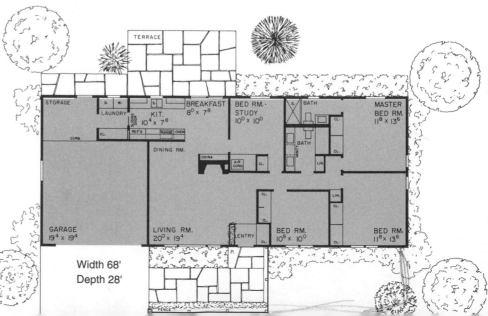

Width 68'
Depth 28'

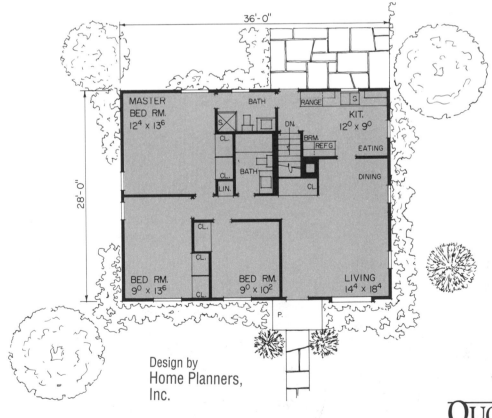

Design 1113
Square Footage: 1,008

L **D**

● A cozy plan, but just right
for a small family or empty
nesters. A covered front porch
shelters visitors from inclement
weather. An ample living
room/dining room area leads
the way to a rear kitchen overlooking a terrace. Two full baths
serve three bedrooms—one a
master suite. The kitchen
includes informal eating space.
Stairs lead to a full basement
that may be developed as
desired. Multi-lite windows
with quaint shutters add a touch
of charm to the design.

Design by
Home Planners,
Inc.

QUOTE ONE™

Cost to build? See page 374
to order complete cost estimate
to build this house in your area!

Design 1191

Square Footage: 1,232

L **D**

● A careful study of the floor plan for this cozy, appealing traditional home reveals a fine combination of features which add tremendously to convenient living. For instance, observe the wardrobe and storage facilities of the bedroom area. Built-in chests are located in one bedroom and the family room. Notice the economical plumbing of the two full back-to-back baths. Positively a great money-saving feature. Don't overlook the location of the washer and dryer which have cupboards above. An optional two-car garage is available if necessary.

Design by
Home Planners,
Inc.

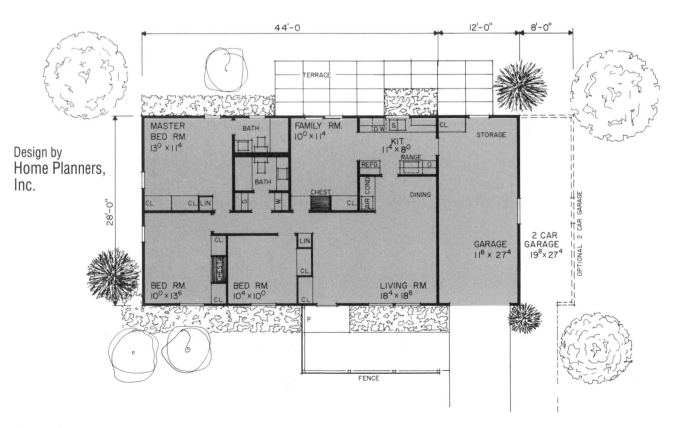

OPTIONAL BASEMENT PLAN

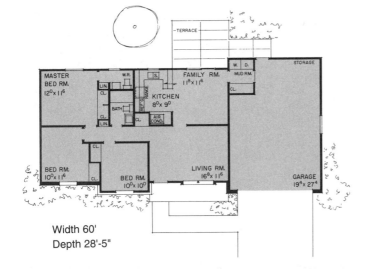

Width 60'
Depth 28'-5"

Design 1311
Square Footage: 1,050

L

Design by
Home Planners, Inc.

● Delightful design and effective, flexible planning come in little packages, too. This fine traditional exterior with its covered front entrance features an alternate basement plan. Note how the non-basement layout provides a family room and mud room, while the basement option shows kitchen eating and dining room. Sensible planning.

Design 1373
Square Footage: 1,200

● Here's a traditional L-shaped home with an attractive recessed front entrance, which leads to an ideal traffic pattern. The U-shaped kitchen has an abundance of cupboard and counter space, plus a pass-through to the snack bar in the family room. Three bedrooms are away from living areas; the master suite features its own bath.

Design by
Home Planners, Inc.

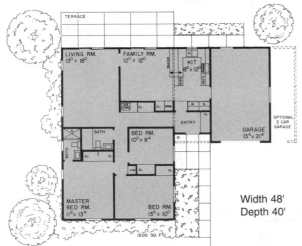

Width 48'
Depth 40'

Enhanced Plan

MERCED
Design 3705
Square Footage: 1,200

● This three-bedroom ranch home contains many spacious features. It includes a full-size bath in the master bedroom, plus a full-size bath adjoining the other bedrooms. The dining room and living room flow together giving the appearance of one large gathering room. Every foot of space makes its vital contribution to total livability. A two-car garage, standard deck, decorative louvers and a centrally located fireplace are optional.

Blueprints and a complete lumber and materials package are also available for this home at your local 84 Lumber dealer.

Design by
Home Planners,
Inc.

56'-0"

36'-0"

RAILING

DECK
14⁴ X 12⁰

MASTER BEDROOM
12⁴ X 13⁰

DINING RM
8⁸ X 13⁰

LIVING RM
14⁰ X 13⁰

CURB

BATH

LINEN

W
D

5 SHLS

LINEN

OPT. FIREPLACE

KITCHEN
14⁸ X 10⁰

S
DW

COOK TOP

REF'G

ENTRY

FURN

WH

OPTIONAL 1 CAR GARAGE

2 CAR GARAGE
19⁸ X 21⁴

BATH

BEDROOM
10¹⁰ X 9⁴

BEDROOM
10¹⁰ X 9⁴

Basic Plan

Enhanced Plan

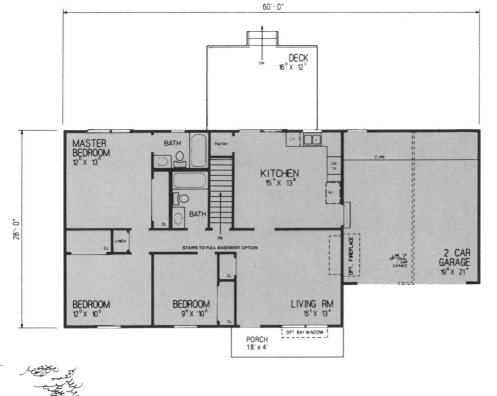

60'-0"

DECK
16'0" X 12'0"

MASTER
BEDROOM
12'0" X 13'0"

BATH

PANTRY

KITCHEN
15'0" X 13'0"

BATH

28'-0"

CL LINEN

STAIRS TO FULL BASEMENT OPTION

DN

2 CAR
GARAGE
19'0" X 21'4"

OPT. FIREPLACE

BEDROOM
12'0" X 10'0"

BEDROOM
9'0" X '10'0"

CL

CL

LIVING RM
15'0" X 13'0"

OPT BAY WINDOW

PORCH
18' x 4'

ST. ALBANS
Design 3701
Square Footage: 1,130

● Traditional charm is an apt description of this economical ranch home. Every foot of space makes its vital contribution to total livability. Within three bedrooms it offers a full bath in the master bedroom, plus ample closet space. A full-size bath adjoins the other two bedrooms. The large kitchen is designed to serve as an eat-in kitchen for this efficient home. The exterior is dressed with vertical siding and window and door shutters. Options include a one- or two-car garage, front porch, rear deck with railing, box bay window and fireplace.

Blueprints and a complete lumber and materials package are also available for this home at your local 84 Lumber dealer.

Basic Plan

DINING ROOM 14⁴ x 12⁰

GATHERING ROOM 20² x 15¹⁰

STUDY 11⁸ x 19²

MASTER BEDRM 13⁴ x 18⁸

WALK-IN CLOSET

BRKFST ROOM 13¹⁰ x 11⁰

SNACK BAR

MASTER BATH

WHIRL POOL

KIT 12¹¹ x 10⁶

PANTRY

FOYER

WALK-IN CLOSET

LAUNDRY

BEDRM 10¹¹ x 12⁰

BATH

BEDRM 10¹¹ x 12⁰

COVERED PORCH

STEP-UP

TUB

GARAGE 28⁸ x 31⁸

Design 3359

Square Footage: 2,473

L **D**

Width 82'-6"
Depth 81'-10"

Cost to build? See page 342
to order complete cost estimate
to build this house in your area!

Quote One®

● Multiple rooflines and vertical windows give this design plenty of curb appeal. Inside, the two-story foyer leads to a sunken gathering room, which shares a through-fireplace with the study. The large island kitchen and a sunny breakfast room are also on the lower level. The master suite is designed for pampering, with a double-door entry, access to a private terrace, a large walk-in closet and a lavish bath with a whirlpool tub.

Design by
Home Planners

TERRACE

Width 72'
Depth 36'

BED RM. 10⁰ x 13⁶

BED RM. 10⁰ x 10⁰

FAMILY RM. 14⁰ x 13⁶

SNACKS

KIT. 12⁸ x 10⁰

STORAGE 9⁴ x 8⁰

RANGE

PANTRY

MUD RM.

BATH

STOR.

GRILLE

4'HI CHINA

LIVING RM. 19⁰ x 13⁶

DINING RM. 11⁰ x 13⁶

ENTRY

MASTER BED RM. 13⁴ x 12⁰

GARAGE 21⁴ x 21⁴

Design by
Home Planners

Design 1864

Square Footage: 1,598

D

● Multi-pane windows and a double-door entry welcome you to this attractive design. The floor plan provides ample living space in a front living/dining room and a family room with sliding glass doors to a terrace. The roomy kitchen offers plenty of counter space, a pantry and a snack bar. Notice the convenient mud room and washroom next to the side entry.

Design by
Home Planners,
Inc.

Design 2505

Square Footage: 1,366

L D

● This design offers you a choice of
three distinctively different exteriors.
Which is your favorite? Blueprints
show details for all three optional
elevations. A study of the floor plan
reveals a fine measure of livability. In
less than 1,400 square feet there are
features galore. An excellent return on
your construction dollar. In addition to
the two eating areas and the open
planning of the gathering room, the
indoor-outdoor relationships are of
great interest. The basement may be
developed for recreational activities.
Be sure to note the storage potential,
particularly the linen closet, the pantry,
the china cabinet and the broom closet.

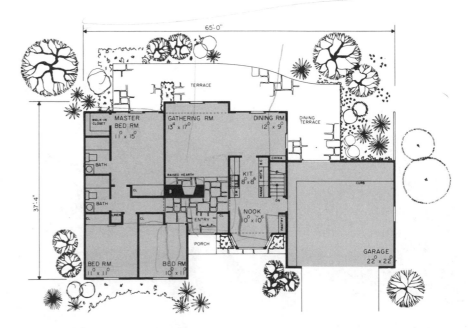

Design by
Home Planners

Design 3688

Square Footage: 1,646

L

Cost to build? See page 342
to order complete cost estimate
to build this house in your area!

● From a wraparound covered porch the foyer opens directly into the attractive living room, which is enhanced by a warming fireplace, a vaulted ceiling and a bayed dining area. A U-shaped kitchen offers a snack bar to the sunny family room. Across the back of the house, two secondary bedrooms share a full bath, and a master suite waits to pamper the lucky home-owner with a walk-in closet, access to the porch and a luxurious bath.

Width 64'
Depth 44'-8"

Design 3689

Square Footage: 1,295

L **D**

Cost to build? See page 342
to order complete cost estimate
to build this house in your area!

● This one- or two-bedroom cottage has a post-and-rail covered porch hugging one wing, with convenient access through double doors or pass-through windows in the dining room and kitchen. The columned foyer leads past a family bedroom or media room into a great room with a fireplace and a low wall along the staircase to the attic. Filling the right wing, the master suite features a plant shelf in the bedroom and garden tub in the master bath, plus a large walk-in closet and laundry facilities.

Width 48'
Depth 59'

Design by
Home Planners

Width 64'-5"
Depth 32'-5"

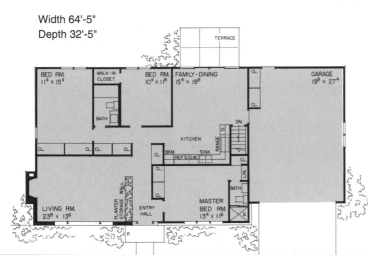

Design 1025
Square Footage: 1,426

● A real charmer. At the front of the house, parents have a private master suite with a full bath and generous closet space. Opposite the master bedroom is a secluded living room, without any through-traffic, and a center fireplace that provides a focus of interest for arranging furniture. Recreational facilities may be developed in the full basement. This area also lends itself to developing additional storage.

Design by
Home Planners,
Inc.

Design 1075
Square Footage: 1,232

L D

Design by
Home Planners,
Inc.

● This picturesque traditional one-story home has much to offer the young family. Because of its rectangular shape and its predominantly frame exterior, construction costs will be economical. Passing through the front entrance, visitors will be surprised to find so much livability in only 1,232 square feet. The attached garage is extra long to accommodate the storage of garden equipment, lawn furniture, bicycles, etc.

Width 56'
Depth 38'-3"

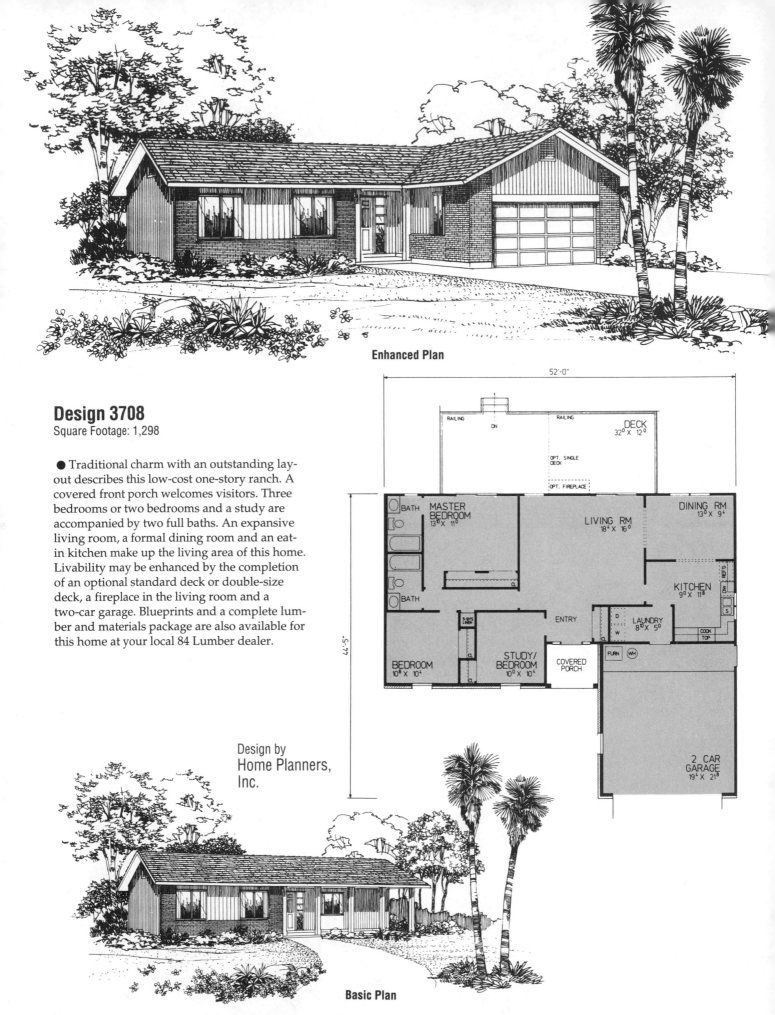

Enhanced Plan

Design 3708
Square Footage: 1,298

● Traditional charm with an outstanding lay-out describes this low-cost one-story ranch. A covered front porch welcomes visitors. Three bedrooms or two bedrooms and a study are accompanied by two full baths. An expansive living room, a formal dining room and an eat-in kitchen make up the living area of this home. Livability may be enhanced by the completion of an optional standard deck or double-size deck, a fireplace in the living room and a two-car garage. Blueprints and a complete lumber and materials package are also available for this home at your local 84 Lumber dealer.

Design by
Home Planners,
Inc.

Basic Plan

Enhanced Plan

HICKORY
Design 3704
Square Footage: 1,492

● The comfort and charm of this lovely ranch home are surprisingly affordable. Featuring an old-fashioned front porch, this three-bedroom home includes two full baths. A large dining area and a pantry adjoin a large work area to form a country kitchen. Livability can be enhanced with the optional one- or two-car garage, rear deck with railing, two angle-bay windows and fireplace.
Blueprints and a complete lumber and materials package are also available for this home at your local 84 Lumber dealer.

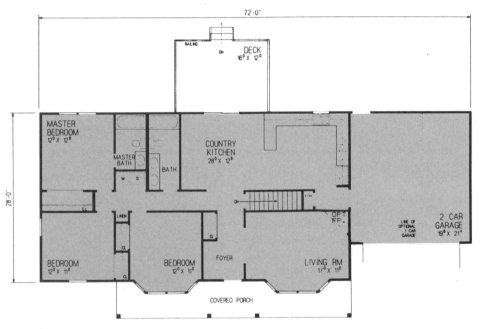

Design by
Home Planners, Inc.

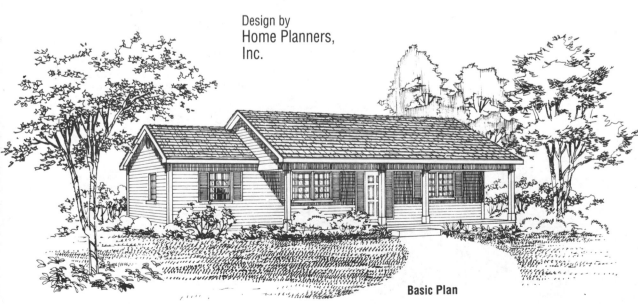

Basic Plan

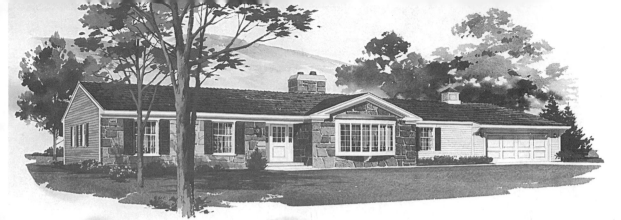

Design by
Home Planners

Design 2204

Square Footage: 2,016

● This is a delightful design that you will enjoy for years to come. Family and friends alike will enjoy the beam-ceilinged family room and the living room with its bowed window and fireplace. The U-shaped kitchen easily serves a nearby breakfast nook and the formal dining room. The sleeping zone includes a master bedroom with a private bath. Sliding glass doors provide access to the rear terrace from the master bedroom, family room and breakfast nook.

Width 94'
Depth 30'-5"

Design 8177

Square Footage: 1,834

● Reminiscent of America's farmhouses, this home comes complete with two covered porches perfect for summer evenings. The foyer opens to the great room, with French doors flanking the fireplace, and to the dining room, where square columns add a formal flair. An angled bar in the kitchen opens the area to the great room. A deluxe master suite and two family bedrooms complete the plan. Please specify crawlspace or slab foundation when ordering.

Width 78'
Depth 48'-7"

Design by
Larry E. Belk Designs

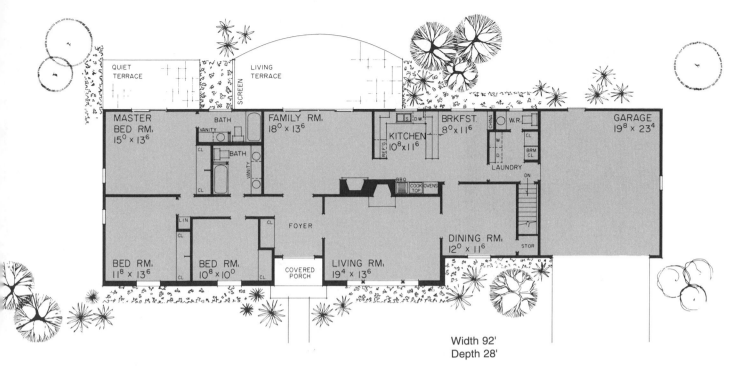

QUIET TERRACE

LIVING TERRACE

SCREEN

MASTER BED RM. $15^0 \times 13^6$

BATH
VANITY
CL
BATH
VANITY
CL
CL

FAMILY RM. $18^0 \times 13^6$

REF'G
KITCHEN $10^8 \times 11^6$
S DW

BBQ
COOK TOP OVENS

BRKFST. $8^0 \times 11^6$

CHINA
W.R.
CL
W
D
LAUNDRY
BRM CL

GARAGE $19^8 \times 23^4$

DN

LIN
CL
CL

FOYER

DINING RM. $12^0 \times 11^6$

STOR

BED RM. $11^8 \times 13^6$

BED RM. $10^8 \times 10^0$

CL

COVERED PORCH

LIVING RM. $19^4 \times 13^6$

Width 92'
Depth 28'

Design 1325

Square Footage: 1,942

L **D**

● Double doors introduce the large front entry hall, which permits direct access to the formal living room, the sleeping area and the informal family room. Both of the living areas have fireplaces. When formal dining is the occasion of the evening, the separate dining room is but a step from the living room. The U-shaped kitchen is strategically flanked by the family room and the breakfast area. The master bedroom has a private bath and a quiet terrace.

Design by
Home Planners, Inc.

Design 2778

Square Footage: 2,761

D

● No matter what the occasion, family and friends alike will enjoy the sizable gathering room which is featured in this plan. A spacious 20' x 23', this room has a thru-fireplace to the study and two sets of sliding glass doors to the large rear terrace. Indoor-outdoor living can also be enjoyed from the dining room, study and master bedroom; all located to face the rear yard. There is a covered dining porch, too, accessible through sliding glass doors in the dining and breakfast rooms. A total of three bedrooms are planned for this design. Each has plenty of closet space. Notice the high lights of the master suite: large walk-in closet, tub plus stall shower and exercise area.

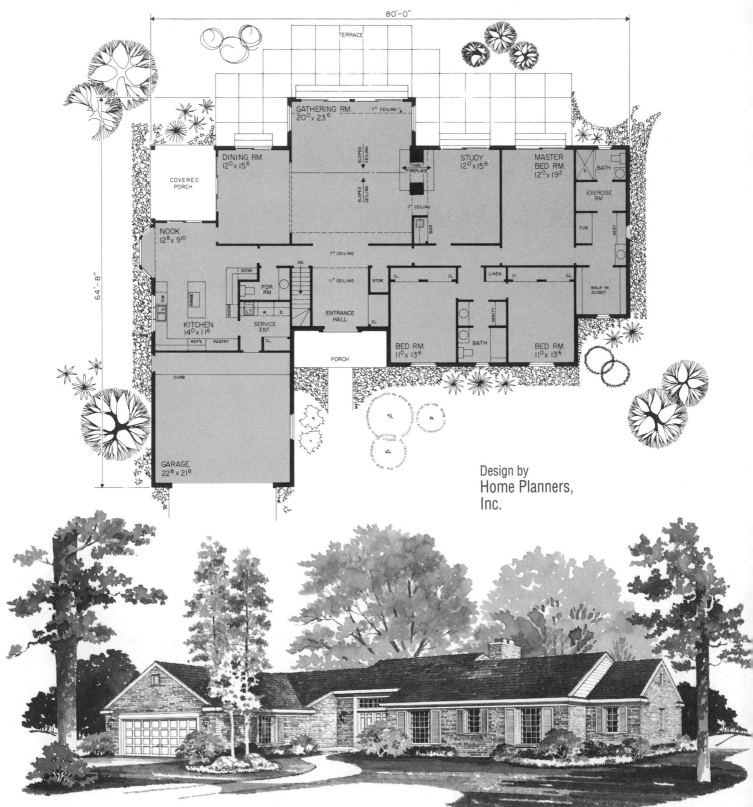

Design by
Home Planners,
Inc.

Design 2777
Square Footage: 2,006

L **D**

● Many years of delightful living will surely be enjoyed in this one-story traditional. The covered front porch adds a charm to the exterior as do the paned windows and winding drive. Inside there is livability galore. An efficient kitchen with island range and adjacent laundry make this work area very pleasing. There is also a breakfast nook with bay window and built-in desk to serve the family when informal dining is called upon plus a formal dining room with sliding glass doors to the rear terrace. The large gathering room with raised hearth fireplace can serve the family on any occasion gracefully. The sleeping wing consists of two bedrooms and a study [or make it three bedrooms]. The master bedroom includes all the fine features one would expect: a huge walk-in closet, a vanity, a bath and sliding glass doors to a private terrace.

Design by
Home Planners, Inc.

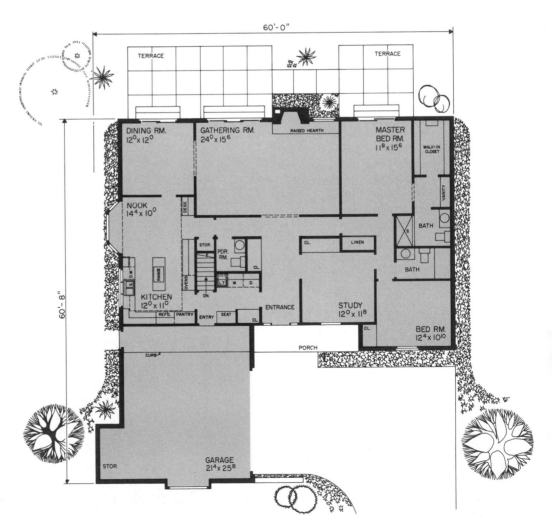

Design 1761
Square Footage: 2,548

L D

● Low, strong roof lines and solid, enduring qualities of brick give this house a permanent, here-to-stay appearance. The bedroom wing is isolated, and the baths and closets deaden the noise from the rest of the house. Center fireplaces in the family and living rooms make furniture arrangement easy. There are a number of extras including a workshop garage and an indoor barbecue.

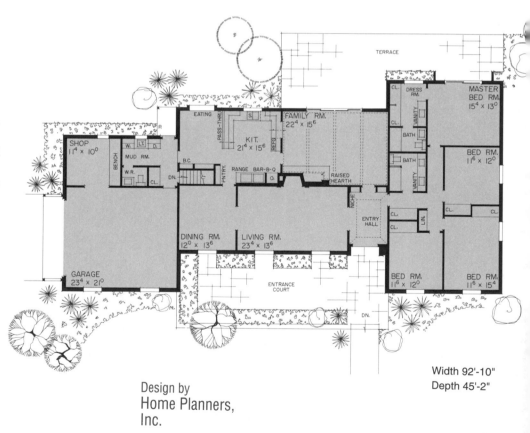

Design by
Home Planners, Inc.

Width 92'-10"
Depth 45'-2"

Design 1939

Square Footage: 1,387

L **D**

● This finely proportioned house has more than its full share of charm. The brick veneer exterior contrasts pleasingly with the narrow horizontal siding of the oversized attached two-car garage. Perhaps the focal point of the exterior is the recessed front entrance with its double Colonial-styled doors. The secondary service entrance through the garage to the kitchen area is a handy feature. The plan features three bedrooms, one a master suite, and two full baths. A living room with fireplace, front kitchen with an eating area and formal dining room make up the living area of the home. There is plenty of storage space, plus a basement for additional storage or development as a recreational area.

Design by
Home Planners, Inc.

Width 74'-9"
Depth 30'-5"

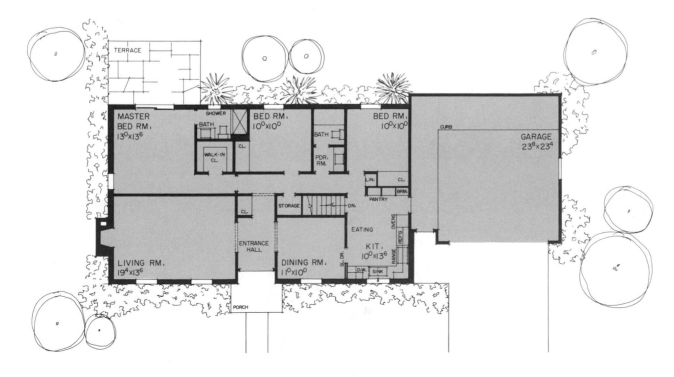

Design by
Home Planners,
Inc.

Design 2941
Square Footage: 1,842

D

● Here is a basic floor plan which goes with each of the differently styled exteriors. The Early American version above is charming, indeed. Horizontal siding, stone, window boxes, a dovecote, a picket fence and a garden court enhance its appeal. Note the covered entrance.

Design 2942
Square Footage: 1,834

D

● The Tudor exterior above will be the favorite of many. Stucco, simulated timber work and diamond-lite windows set its unique character. Each of the delightful exteriors features eye-catching roof lines. Inside, there is an outstanding plan to cater to the living patterns of the small family, empty nesters, or retirees.

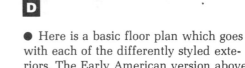

Design 2943
Square Footage: 1,834

D

Width 58'-2"
Depth 59'-9"

● The Contemporary optional exterior above features vertical siding and a wide-overhanging roof with exposed rafter ends. The foyer is spacious with sloped ceiling and a dramatic open staircase to the basement recreation area. Other ceilings in the house are also sloped. The breakfast, dining and media rooms are highlights, along with the laundry, the efficient kitchen, the snack bar and the master bath.

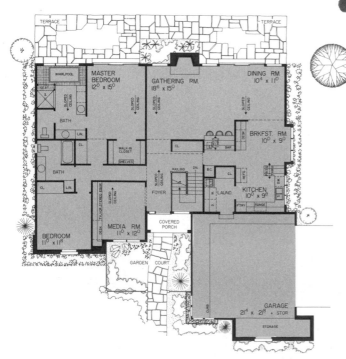

QUOTE ONE™

Cost to build? See page 374
to order complete cost estimate
to build this house in your area!

Design 2802
Square Footage: 1,729

● The three exteriors shown at the left house the same efficiently planned one-story floor plan shown below. Be sure to notice the design variations in the window placement and roof pitch. This Tudor version has an authenic bay window at the front. The Quote One™ custom price quote system is available for this design.

Design 2803
Square Footage: 1,679

● Housed in varying facades, this floor plan is very efficient. The front foyer leads to each of the living areas. The sleeping area of two, or optional three, bedrooms is ready to serve the family. Then there is the gathering room. This room is highlighted by its size, 16 x 20 feet. A contemporary mix of fieldstone and vertical wood siding characterizes this exterior. The absence of columns or posts gives a modern look to the covered porch.

Design 2804
Square Footage: 1,674

● Stuccoed arches, multi-paned windows and a gracefully sloped roof accent the exterior of this Spanish-inspired design. Like the other two designs, the interior kitchen will efficiently serve the dining room, covered dining porch and breakfast room with great ease. Blueprints for all three designs include details for an optional non-basement plan.

Design by
Home Planners,
Inc.

OPTIONAL NON-BASEMENT

Width 68'-2"
Depth 48'-10"

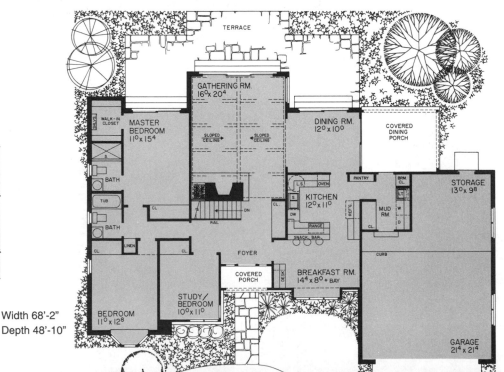

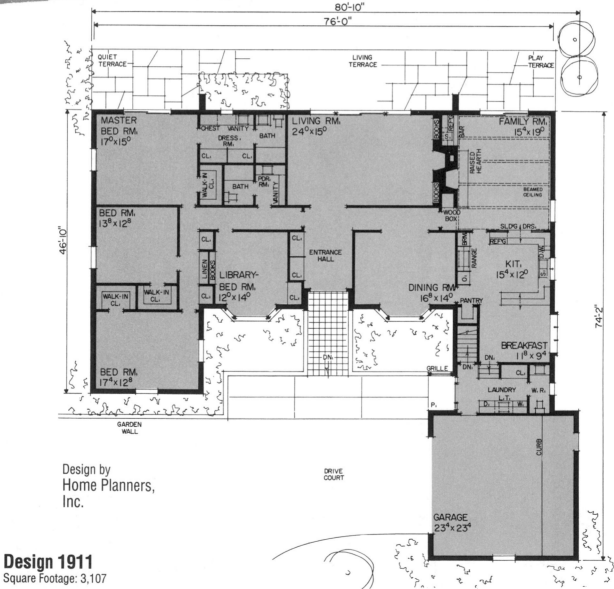

Design by
Home Planners,
Inc.

Design 1911
Square Footage: 3,107

● For luxurious, country-estate living it would be difficult to beat the livability offered by these two impressive traditional designs. To begin with, their exterior appeal is, indeed, gracious. Their floor plans highlight plenty of space, excellent room arrangements, fine traffic circulation, and an abundance of convenient living features. It is interesting to note that each design features similar livability facilities. Both may function as four bedroom homes . . .

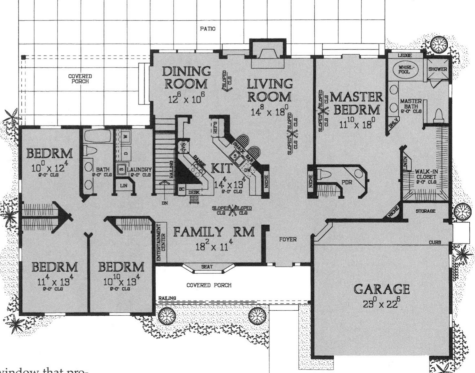

Quote One®

Cost to build? See page 374
to order complete cost estimate
to build this house in your area!

Design by
Home Planners

Design 3685

Square Footage: 2,415

● A covered porch, shutters and a
centered dormer with an arched
window dress up this country home
with blue-ribbon style. To the left of
the foyer, the family room features a
built-in entertainment center and a bay window that provides a window seat overlooking the front yard. Nearby,
the kitchen—angled for interest—contains a large pantry
and a snack bar that opens onto the adjacent living room.
The dining room provides access to the rear covered porch,
supplying a spacious area for outdoor dining. Split planning places the restful master suite to the rear for privacy.
Amenities include a large walk-in closet and a soothing
master bath with a whirlpool, separate shower and double-
bowl vanity. Three secondary bedrooms share a full bath
and easy access to the laundry room.

Width 74'
Depth 54'

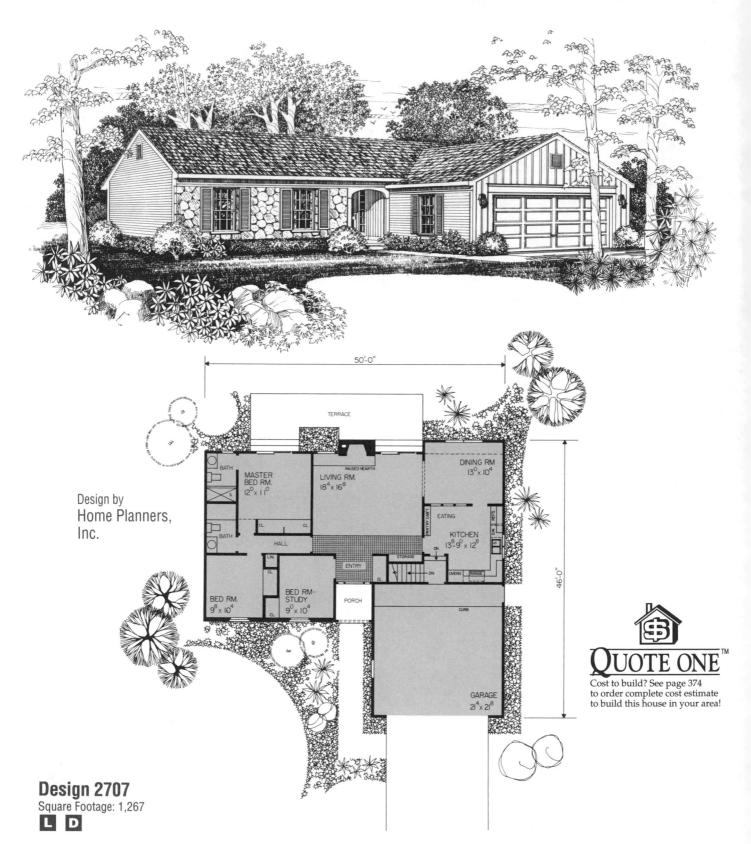

Design by
Home Planners,
Inc.

QUOTE ONE™
Cost to build? See page 374
to order complete cost estimate
to build this house in your area!

Design 2707

Square Footage: 1,267

L **D**

● Here is a charming Early American
adaptation that will serve as a picturesque and practical retirement home.
Also, it will serve admirably those with
a small family in search of an efficient,
economically built home. The living
area, highlighted by the raised hearth

fireplace, is spacious. The kitchen features eating space and easy access to
the garage and basement. The dining
room is adjacent to the kitchen and
views the rear yard. Then, there is the
basement for recreation and hobby
pursuits. The bedroom wing offers

three bedrooms and two full baths.
Don't miss the sliding doors to the terrace from the living room and the master bedroom. Storage units are plentiful
including a pantry cabinet in the eating area of the kitchen. This plan will
be efficient and livable.

Design 2316

Square Footage: 2,000

● If you are looking for a cozy four-bedroom design, look no further. This Colonial adaptation will accommodate even expanded families. Four bedrooms comprise a wing of their own with the quiet master bedroom at the forefront. Gather informally in the family room with its fireplace or entertain in the front living and dining rooms. Don't miss the work space in the utility room and garage, the abundance of storage space and the many built-ins.

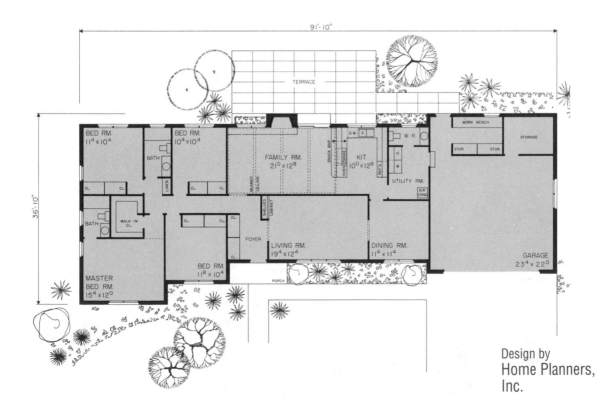

Design by
Home Planners,
Inc.

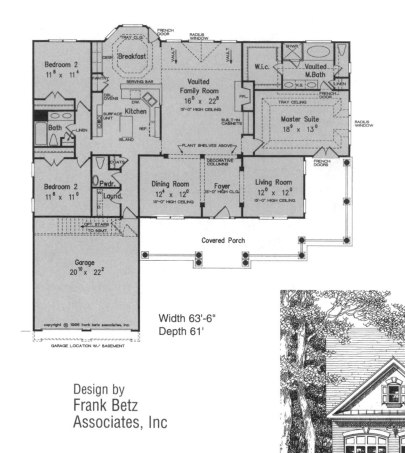

Design P242

Square Footage: 2,170

● An exterior highlighted by multiple arches and gables welcomes you to a home well designed for family living and for entertaining. Formal dining and living rooms flank the foyer, defined by decorative columns. The spacious family room opens to the bayed breakfast room, which provides a French door to the outside. An efficient island kitchen is centrally located to serve all of the living areas of the home. The luxurious master suite is separated from two family bedrooms for privacy.

Width 63'-6"
Depth 61'

Design by
**Frank Betz
Associates, Inc**

Design P107

Square Footage: 1,373

● Columns add style as well as support to the covered porch that dresses up this petite home. The foyer opens onto a family room that combines with the dining room to create a space sized to accommodate every occasion. The adjacent kitchen is designed for efficiency, uniting with the breakfast room for casual meals. Sleeping quarters include two family bedrooms and a spacious master suite. Please specify basement or crawlspace foundation when ordering.

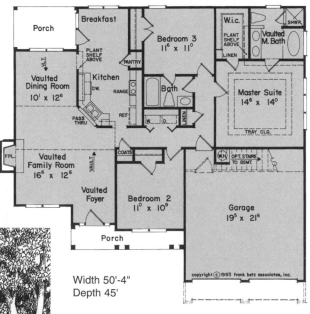

Width 50'-4"
Depth 45'

Design by
**Frank Betz
Associates, Inc.**

Quote One®

Cost to build? See page 374 to order complete cost estimate to build this house in your area!

Design by
Home Planners

Design 3662

Square Footage: 1,937
Bonus Room: 414 square feet

L

● The traditions of country are alive and well within this transitional home. A covered porch introduces a warm welcome through the angled entry into the spacious great room. A crackling fire in the hearth further extends an invitation to stretch out and relax. The adjacent dining room is sized for formal occasions while the morning nook that adjoins the island kitchen accommodates casual meals. Planned for privacy, the master bedroom has been split from two secondary bedrooms that share a full bath. A bumped-out sitting room located to the rear of the master suite overlooks the back yard while double doors offer access to the patio deck retreat. A walk-in closet and a luxurious master bath with a garden tub complete this area. A bonus room over the garage offers flexible space for a future guest suite, home office or hobby room.

Width 76'-4"
Depth 73'-4"

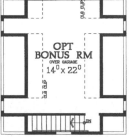

Design 2888
Square Footage: 3,018

L

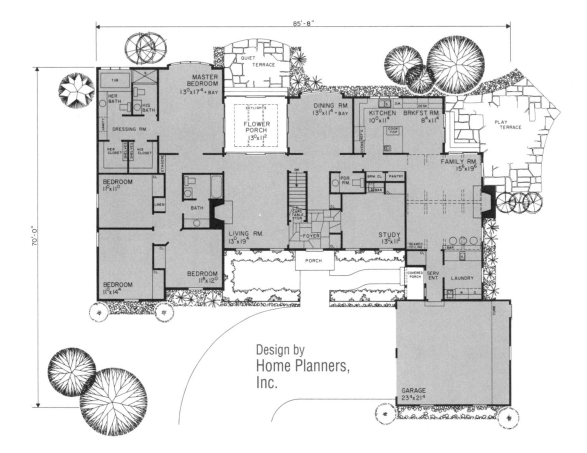

Design by
Home Planners,
Inc.

● This is an outstanding Early American design for the 20th-Century. The exterior detailing with narrow clapboards, multi-paned windows and cupola are the features of yesteryear. Interior planning, though, is for today's active family. Formal living room, informal family room plus a study are present. Every activity will have its place in this home. Picture yourself working in the kitchen. There's enough counter space for two or three helpers. Four bedrooms are in the private area. Stop and imagine your daily routine if you occupied the master bedroom. Both you and your spouse would have plenty of space and privacy. The flower porch, accessible from the master bedroom, living and dining rooms, is a very delightful "plus" feature. Study this design's every detail.

Design 3655/3656

Square Footage: 1,418/1,414

L

● If you need a guest or mother-in-law suite, you'll love this compact design. The suite—which could be used as a home office—enjoys its own courtyard, a cozy fireplace and a private bath. The efficient floor plan features a spacious living area, which offers patio access and a three-sided fireplace that shares its warmth with a formal dining area with built-in shelves. A thoughtfully planned kitchen is highlighted by a corner sink with a view and lots of counter space. The large master suite has access to the covered patio and includes a luxury bath. Design 3655 offers two additional family bedrooms; Design 3656 comes with one family bedroom and a larger master suite.

Design 3655
Width 44'-8"
Depth 52'-4"

Design by
Home Planners

QUOTE ONE®

Cost to build? See page 374
to order complete cost estimate
to build this house in your area!

Design 3656
Width 44'-8"
Depth 54'-4"

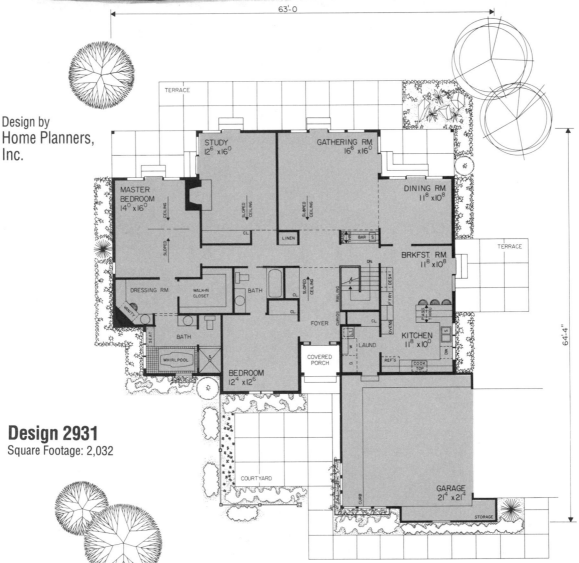

63'-0

64'-4"

TERRACE

STUDY
12⁶ x16⁰

GATHERING RM
16⁶ x16⁰

Design by
Home Planners,
Inc.

MASTER
BEDROOM
14⁰ x16⁰

DINING RM
11⁸ x10⁸

CL

LINEN

BAR

DRESSING RM

WALK-IN
CLOSET

BATH

BRKFST. RM
11⁸ x10⁸

TERRACE

CL

CL

DN

BATH

FOYER

CL

KITCHEN
11⁸ x10⁰

WHIRLPOOL

REF'G

COOK
TOP

Design 2931
Square Footage: 2,032

BEDROOM
12⁴ x12⁶

COVERED
PORCH

LAUND

COURTYARD

CURB

GARAGE
21⁴ x21⁴

STORAGE

● Little details make the difference. Consider these that make this such a charming showplace: Picket-fenced courtyard, carriage lamp, window boxes, shutters, muntined windows, multi-gabled roof, cornice returns, vertical and horizontal siding with corner boards, front door with glass side lites, etc. Inside this appealing exterior there is a truly outstanding floor plan for the small family or empty-nesters. The master bedroom suite is long on luxury, with a separate dressing room, private vanities, and whirlpool bath. An adjacent study is just the right retreat. There's room to move and — what a warm touch! — it has its own fireplace. Other attractions: roomy kitchen and breakfast area, spacious gathering room, rear and side terraces, and an attached two-car garage with storage.

Design 2810

Square Footage: 1,536

L **D**

Design by Home Planners

● A sheltering covered porch furnishes a delightful introduction to this traditional home. The vestibule opens to a spacious living room graced by a built-in planter. Straight ahead is a beam-ceilinged family room with sliding glass doors to the terrace. An adjacent kitchen supplies a snack bar for quick meals and an eating nook for casual dining. Two family bedrooms share a hall bath, while the master bedroom features its own private bath. Plans for an alternate garage are included for those who prefer a front-loading garage.

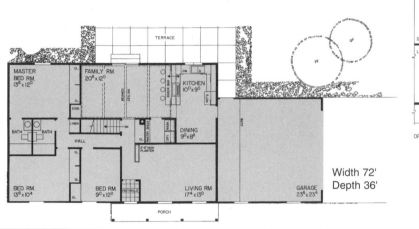

Width 72'
Depth 36'

OPTIONAL FRONT ENTRANCE GARAGE

OPTIONAL CRAWL SPACE PLAN

QUOTE ONE®

Cost to build? See page 374 to order complete cost estimate to build this house in your area!

Design P241

Square Footage: 1,374

● Two covered porches encourage outdoor relaxing while an open floor plan provides for easy entertaining indoors. The vaulted family room/dining room area is served by a handy pass-through from the kitchen, which includes a pantry and a sunny breakfast nook. Two family bedrooms share a full hall bath; each has a large closet. The master suite includes a large walk-in closet, decorative plant shelf and pampering bath.

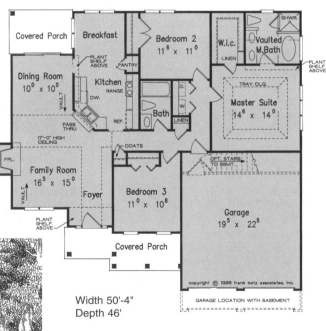

Width 50'-4"
Depth 46'

Design by Frank Betz Associates, Inc.

Design 2261
Square Footage: 1,825

● This distinctive L-shaped home virtually exudes traditional warmth and charm. Little wonder, for the architectural detailing is exquisite. Notice the fine window detailing, the appealing cornice work, the attractiveness of the garage door and the massive chimney. The dovecote and the weather vane add to the design impact. The covered front porch shelters the entry, which is strategically located to provide excellent traffic patterns. A service entry from the garage is conveniently located near the laundry, washroom, kitchen and stairs to the basement. The beamed-ceilinged family room will naturally be everyone's favorite spot for family living. The master bedroom features a private bath.

Design by
Home Planners,
Inc.

Design 3651

Square Footage: 2,213

L D

Design by
Home Planners

● This home's two projecting wings with low-pitched, wide, overhanging roofs provide a distinctive note. The compact, efficient floor plan assures convenient living patterns. In the kitchen, a planning desk, an island cooktop counter with storage below, double ovens, a pantry, fine counter space and a handy snack bar capture attention. The open planning of the living and dining rooms provides a big, spacious area for functional family living. The master bedroom has French doors to provide outdoor living potential.

Quote One®

Cost to build? See page 374
to order complete cost estimate
to build this house in your area!

Width 60'
Depth 68'

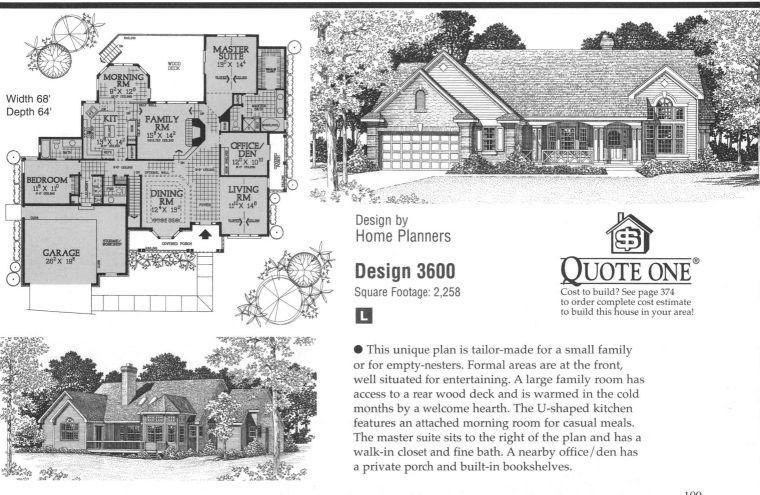

Width 68'
Depth 64'

Design by
Home Planners

Design 3600

Square Footage: 2,258

L

Quote One®

Cost to build? See page 374
to order complete cost estimate
to build this house in your area!

● This unique plan is tailor-made for a small family or for empty-nesters. Formal areas are at the front, well situated for entertaining. A large family room has access to a rear wood deck and is warmed in the cold months by a welcome hearth. The U-shaped kitchen features an attached morning room for casual meals. The master suite sits to the right of the plan and has a walk-in closet and fine bath. A nearby office/den has a private porch and built-in bookshelves.

Design by
Home Planners,
Inc.

Design 1890

Square Footage: 1,628

● The pediment gable and columns set the charm of this modestly sized home. The pleasant symmetry of the windows and the double front doors complete the picture. Inside, each square foot is wisely planned to assure years of convenient living. There are three bedrooms and two full baths.

Width 78'-10"
Depth 28'-10"

Design 2550

Square Footage: 1,892

D

● Stone and vertical siding provide a pleasing contrast on this charming one-story traditional ranch. Diamond lite windows, the fence with its lamp post and the dovecote above the carriage lamp add interest to the exterior. Inside, there are four bedrooms and two full baths in the sleeping wing. The L-shaped living area is spacious and features a sloping ceiling for the gathering and dining rooms.

Design by
Home Planners,
Inc.

Width 56'
Depth 60'-8"

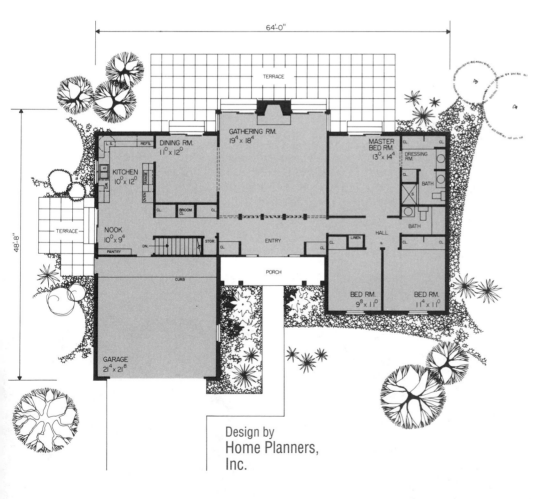

TERRACE

DINING RM.
11⁰ x 12⁰

KITCHEN
10⁰ x 12⁰

GATHERING RM.
19⁴ x 18⁴

MASTER BED RM.
13⁰ x 14⁴

DRESSING RM.

BATH

BATH

NOOK
10⁰ x 9⁴

TERRACE

PANTRY

DN.

STOR.

ENTRY

PORCH

CURB

LINEN

HALL

CL.

GARAGE
21⁴ x 21⁸

BED RM.
9⁸ x 11⁰

BED RM.
11⁴ x 11⁰

64'-0"

48'-8"

Design by
Home Planners,
Inc.

Design 2704

Square Footage: 1,746

L **D**

● This Colonial design offers a covered front porch with columns and double doors. The gathering room is impressive in size and design with its fireplace flanked by sliding glass doors leading to the terrace. A formal dining room is nearby and leads to an L-shaped kitchen. A breakfast nook with a pantry features sliding glass doors to a second terrace. Three bed-rooms include a master suite with private dressing area and bath. The rear terrace may also be accessed from this room. The back-to-back plumbing is economical. Addition-al space can be developed in the basement.

Design by
Frank Betz
Associates, Inc.

Design P100

Square Footage: 1,945

● Corner quoins and keystones above graceful windows decorate the exterior of this lovely home. The foyer is beautifully framed by columns marking the entrances to the dining room and vaulted great room. To the right of the combined kitchen and breakfast room you will find the private master suite. A relaxing bath and a large walk-in closet complete this splendid retreat. Please specify basement or crawlspace foundation when ordering.

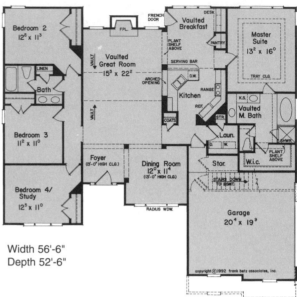

Width 56'-6"
Depth 52'-6"

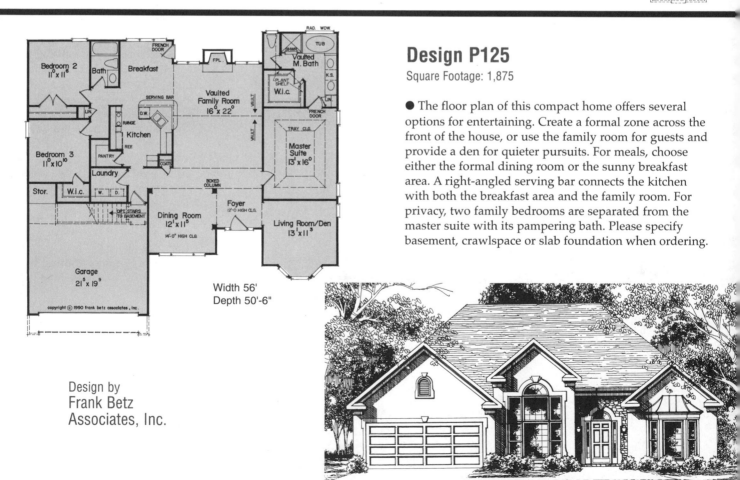

Width 56'
Depth 50'-6"

Design by
Frank Betz
Associates, Inc.

Design P125

Square Footage: 1,875

● The floor plan of this compact home offers several options for entertaining. Create a formal zone across the front of the house, or use the family room for guests and provide a den for quieter pursuits. For meals, choose either the formal dining room or the sunny breakfast area. A right-angled serving bar connects the kitchen with both the breakfast area and the family room. For privacy, two family bedrooms are separated from the master suite with its pampering bath. Please specify basement, crawlspace or slab foundation when ordering.

Design 1337
Square Footage: 1,606

● This traditional facade captures a full measure of warmth. Exterior appeal results from a symphony of such features as: attractive window detailing, a raised planter, a carriage light and a cupola located on the garage. The floor plan is designed for the family whose requirements include formal and informal living areas. An exceptional amount of livability is found in this modest-sized design.

Width 64'-10"
Depth 40'-10"

Design 1367
Square Footage: 1,432

● Brick veneer, a projecting two-car garage with a gabled end, wood shutters, attractive window treatment, paneled front door and a wood fence with lamp post are among the features that make the exterior of this traditional house so charming. The formal living room with all that blank wall space for effective furniture placement, is just the right size for quiet conversation. The family room will be the hub of the informal activities with a snack bar and pass-thru to the kitchen. Adjacent to the kitchen is a room which may function as a study, sewing room, TV room or formal dining room. Note the two full baths and stall shower.

Width 66'-10"
Depth 36'-10"

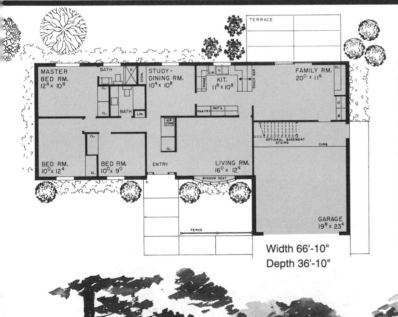

Design 2153

Square Footage: 960

D

● One floor plan carries three distinct exteriors from which to choose. Livability excels with multipurpose living and dining areas. A walk-in closet graces the living room and will be appreciated for storing guests' coats. Three bedrooms share a hall bath; one also has access to a wash room off the kitchen. A basement offers space for storage or future expansion, making this a perfect home for young families or empty-nesters. With shutters and flower boxes, this home will be a pleasure to come home to.

Design by
Home Planners

Width 52'
Depth 24'

BED RM.
12⁰×11⁶

W.R.

KIT.
10⁴×8⁰

RANGE

DINING
8⁸×11⁶

GARAGE
11⁸×23⁴

CL.

BATH

CL.

S.   REF'G

WALK-IN CL.

DN.

LIN.

BED RM.
10⁰×11⁶

CL.

CL.

BED RM.
10⁰×8⁰

LIVING RM.
16⁴×11⁶

Design by
**Home Planners,
Inc.**

QUOTE ONE™

Cost to build? See page 374
to order complete cost estimate
to build this house in your area!

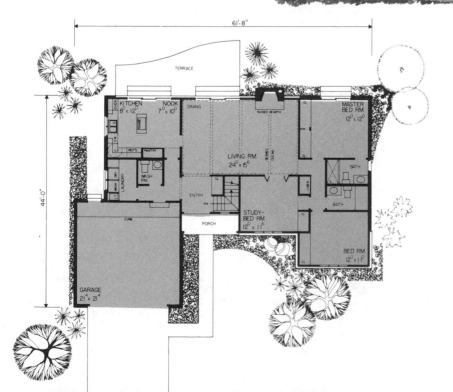

Design 2565

Square Footage: 1,540

L **D**

● This modest sized floor plan has
much to offer in the way of livability.
It may function as either a two or
three bedroom home. The living
room is huge and features a fine,
raised hearth fireplace. The open
stairway to the basement is handy
and will lead to what may be developed as the recreation area. In addition to the two full baths, there is an
extra wash room. Adjacent is the
laundry room and the service entrance from the garage. The blueprints
you order for this design will show
details for each of the three delightful
elevations above. Which is your favorite? The Tudor, the Colonial or the
Contemporary?

Design 8174

Square Footage: 1,136

● Corner quoins, multi-pane windows and a brick exterior give this home plenty of curb appeal. An efficient floor plan makes it attractive inside as well. The large family room is perfect for both formal and informal gatherings, while the bay-windowed breakfast room brightens early morning meals. The feeling of spaciousness is enhanced by vaulted ceilings in the family room, breakfast room, kitchen and master bedroom. The master bath pampers with a dual-bowl vanity and built-in linen closet. Two family bedrooms share a second linen closet and a full hall bath. A two-car garage easily handles the family fleet. Please specify crawlspace or slab foundation when ordering.

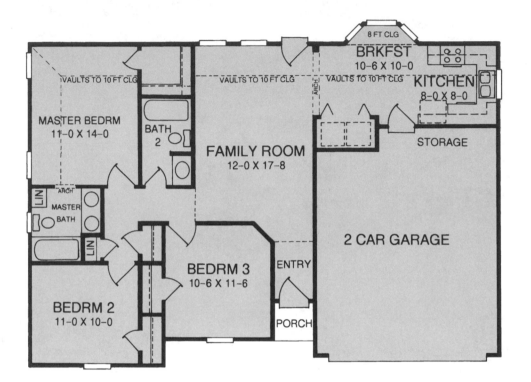

Width 48'-10"
Depth 35'-6"

Design 2671
Square Footage: 1,589

L **D**

● The rustic exterior of this one-story home features vertical wood siding. The entry foyer is floored with flagstone and leads to the three areas of the plan: sleeping, living and work center. The sleeping area has three bedrooms. The master bedroom has sliding glass doors to the rear terrace. The living area, consisting of gathering and dining rooms, also has access to the terrace. The work center is efficiently planned. It houses the kitchen with snack bar, breakfast room with built-in china cabinet and stairs to the basement. This is a very livable plan. Special amenities include a raised-hearth fireplace and a walk-in closet in the master bedroom.

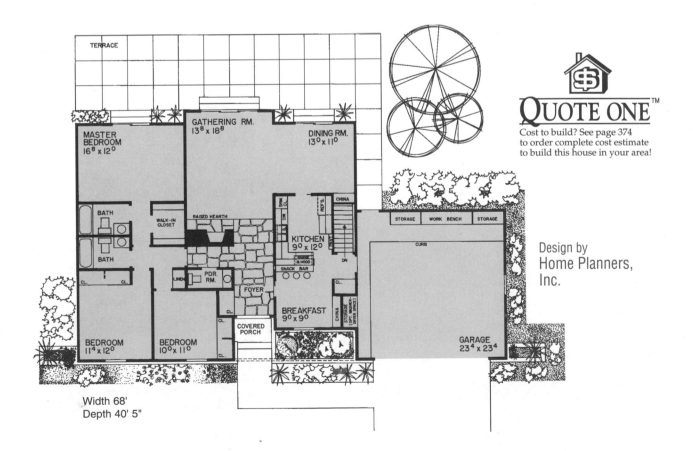

QUOTE ONE™

Cost to build? See page 374 to order complete cost estimate to build this house in your area!

Design by
Home Planners, Inc.

TERRACE

GATHERING RM.
13⁸ x 18⁸

DINING RM.
13⁰ x 11⁰

MASTER BEDROOM
16⁸ x 12⁰

BATH

BATH

WALK-IN CLOSET

RAISED HEARTH

KITCHEN
9⁰ x 12⁰

CHINA

STORAGE   WORK BENCH   STORAGE

CURB

SNACK BAR

LIN.

PDR. RM.

FOYER

BREAKFAST
9⁰ x 9⁰

CHINA

BEDROOM
11⁴ x 12⁰

BEDROOM
10⁰ x 11⁰

COVERED PORCH

GARAGE
23⁴ x 23⁴

Width 68'
Depth 40' 5"

Design 8633

Square Footage: 1,865

● This innovative plan takes advantage of an angled entry to the home, maximizing visual impact and making it possible to include four bedrooms. The joining of the great room and dining space makes creative interior decorating possible. The master suite also takes advantage of angles in creating long vistas into the space. The master bath is designed with all the amenities usually found in much larger homes. The kitchen and breakfast nook overlook the outdoor living space where you can even have an outdoor kitchen area—great for entertaining. The traditional feel of the exterior and the up-to-date interior make this house the perfect design for the nineties.

WIDTH 45'
DEPTH 66'

Design by
**Home Design
Services, Inc.**

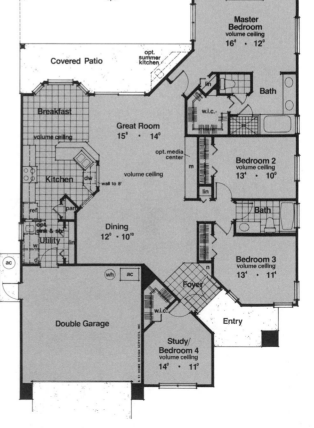

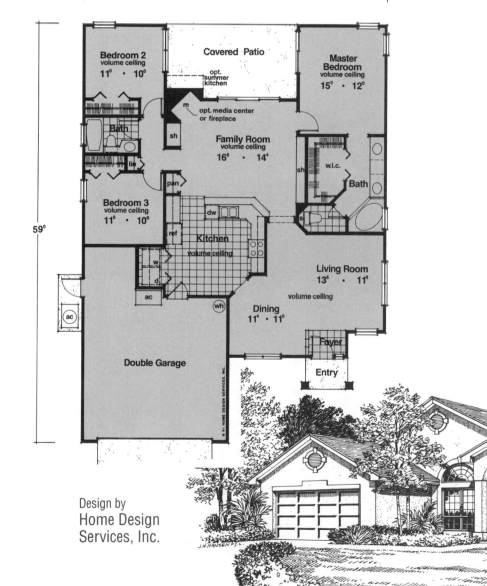

Design 8630
Square Footage: 1,550

● This plan has it all! A formal living and dining area as you enter is just the beginning. The eat-in country kitchen overlooking the family room and outdoor living space makes this plan the ultimate family house. The home is designed for adults, however, because it pampers with a master suite featuring a vaulted ceiling and oversized master bath with sitting area. The private toilet room adds a special touch. Even though the look of this home is traditional, special details such as the media space in the family room make it very current. Plans for this home include a choice of two exterior elevations.

Design by
Home Design
Services, Inc.

119

Design 8666

Square Footage: 2,931

● The bricked, French-door entrance, the stone corner quoins and the keyed windows are icing on this lovely home. Inside, rich tile flows throughout. The foyer opens to a large living room with a vaulted ceiling. The wonderfully equipped kitchen with a walk-in pantry opens up to the windowed breakfast area and the immense family room with built-in shelves and a fireplace. The large covered patio with a summer kitchen is perfect for cookouts and entertaining and is accessible through the breakfast area, the living room and the master bedroom. His and Hers walk-in closets, individual sinks, a separate shower, a compartmented toilet and a windowed tub make the master bedroom and bathroom a study in elegance.

Design by
Home Design
Services, Inc.

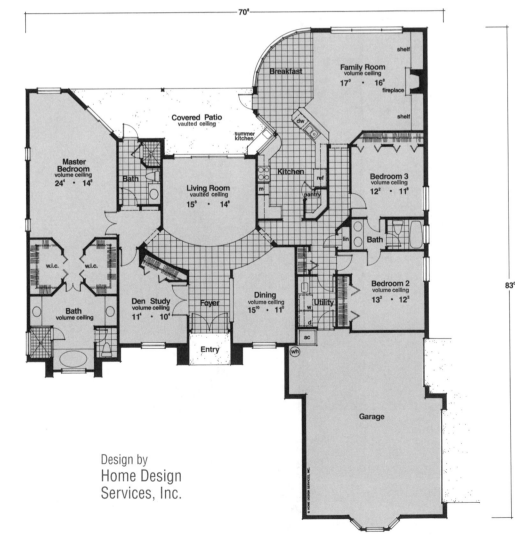

Design 3631

Square Footage: 2,831

L

● Symmetry reigns supreme on the exterior of this Spanish-style design. A portico with three arches frames the entryway, while turrets on either side feature multi-pane windows with circle-head tops. The floor plan allows for the open lifestyle so enjoyed in the Southwest. Flanking the foyer are the formal living and dining rooms, each large enough for carefree entertaining. The rear of the home is wonderfully open—with a family room and U-shaped kitchen and easy access to a covered patio for indoor and outdoor casual living. To further pamper homeowners, the master suite offers a walk-in closet, a private office with covered porch, an exercise area and access to a deck with spa tub. Three family bedrooms—one with a private porch—share a full bath.

Design by
Home Planners

Quote One®

Cost to build? See page 374
to order complete cost estimate
to build this house in your area!

Width 84'
Depth 77'

121

A Little Bit Country:

Homes with rural charm

Design 9788
Square Footage: 1,302

● Well designed for maximum efficiency and practical to build, this streamlined plan is big on popular innovations as well as curb appeal. A spacious cathedral ceiling expands the open great room, the dining room and the kitchen. A deck located next to the kitchen amplifies the living and entertaining space. The versatile bedroom/study features a cathedral ceiling and shares a full skylit bath with another bedroom. The master bedroom is highlighted by a cathedral ceiling for extra volume and light. The private bath opens up with a skylight and includes a double-bowl vanity, a garden tub and a separately located toilet. A walk-in closet adjacent to the bedroom completes the suite.

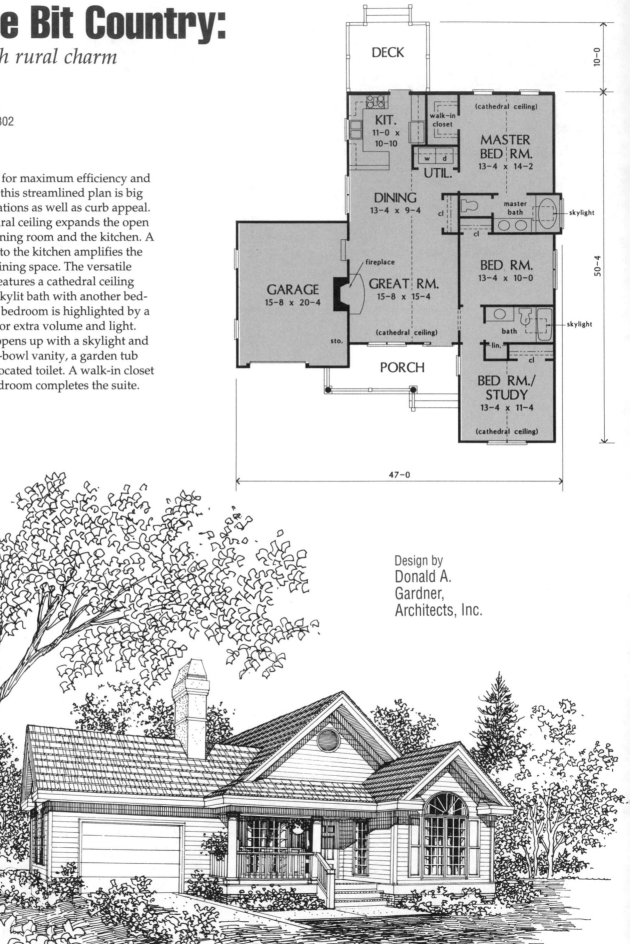

Design by
Donald A.
Gardner,
Architects, Inc.

Design 9781
Square Footage: 1,246

● This one-story home offers tremendous curb appeal and many extras found only in much larger homes. A continuous cathedral ceiling in the great room, dining room and kitchen gives a spacious feel to an efficient plan. The kitchen, brightened by a skylight, features a pantry and a peninsula counter for easy preparation and service to the dining room and screened porch. The deck joins the screened porch for extra entertaining space. The master suite opens up with a cathedral ceiling, a walk-in and linen closets and a private bath including a garden tub and a double-bowl vanity. A cathedral ceiling highlights the front bedroom/study that is separated from the other bedroom by a skylit bath.

Design by
Donald A. Gardner, Architects, Inc.

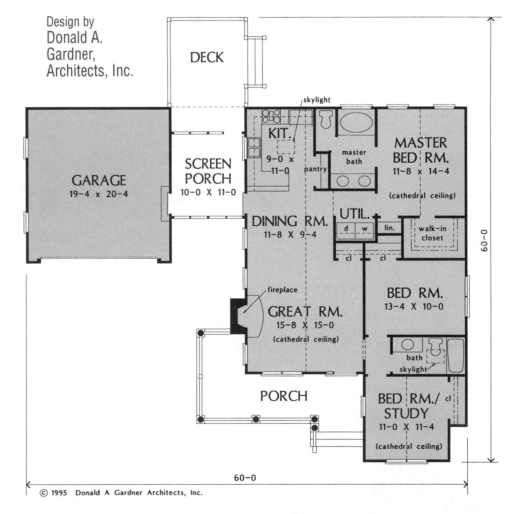

DECK

SCREEN PORCH
10-0 X 11-0

GARAGE
19-4 x 20-4

skylight

KIT.
9-0 x
11-0

pantry

master bath

MASTER BED RM.
11-8 x 14-4
(cathedral ceiling)

UTIL.
d w lin.

walk-in closet

DINING RM.
11-8 X 9-4

cl cl

fireplace

GREAT RM.
15-8 X 15-0
(cathedral ceiling)

BED RM.
13-4 x 10-0

bath
skylight

PORCH

BED RM./ STUDY
11-0 X 11-4
(cathedral ceiling)

cl

60-0

60-0

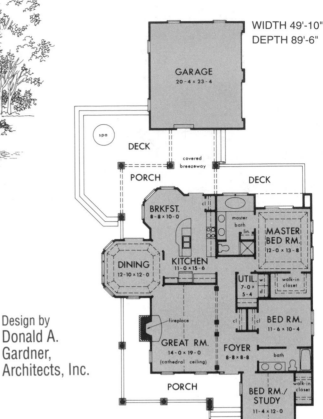

WIDTH 49'-10"
DEPTH 89'-6"

Design 9693

Square Footage: 1,677

● This narrow, three-bedroom plan with arched windows and a wraparound porch displays a sense of elegance uncommon to a plan this size. The colonnade between the great room and the foyer/hallway opens this area to the great room. Cathedral ceilings grace both the great room and the bedroom/study, while tray ceilings appear in the dining room and master bedroom. The open kitchen design allows for a serving island which is convenient to the breakfast area, dining room and deck. The master suite has direct access to the deck and also features a large walk-in closet and a master bath with a double-bowl vanity, a shower and a whirlpool tub. A covered breezeway connects the garage to the house. The plan is available with a crawl-space foundation.

Design by
Donald A. Gardner, Architects, Inc.

Design 9664

Square Footage: 1,287
Optional Basement: 1,319 square feet

● This economical plan offers an impressive visual statement with its well-proportioned exterior. Inside, the great room, dining area and kitchen are open to one another; a cathedral ceiling adds to the feeling of spaciousness. This area is further enhanced by a fireplace, built-in bookshelves and access to the back deck. The master suite boasts a cathedral ceiling, walk-in closet and private bath with double-bowl vanity, whirlpool tub and shower. Two family bedrooms complete the plan. Please specify basement or crawlspace foundation when ordering.

Design by
Donald A. Gardner, Architects, Inc.

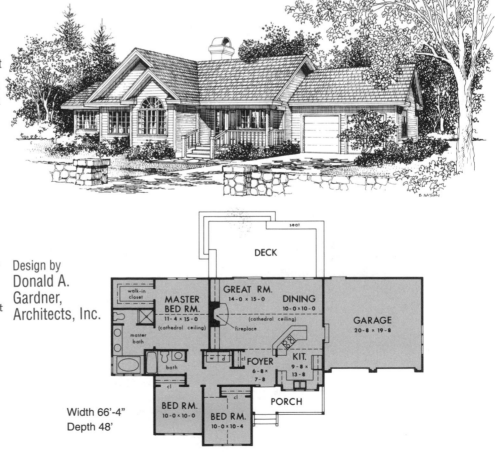

Width 66'-4"
Depth 48'

124

Design 9639

Square Footage: 1,541

● This traditional three-bedroom home projects the appearance of a much larger home. The great room features a cathedral ceiling, a fireplace and an arched window above the sliding glass door to the expansive rear deck. The master suite contains a pampering master bath and a walk-in closet. Two other bedrooms share a full bath with a double-bowl vanity. Please specify basement or crawlspace foundation when ordering.

Design by
Donald A.
Gardner,
Architects, Inc.

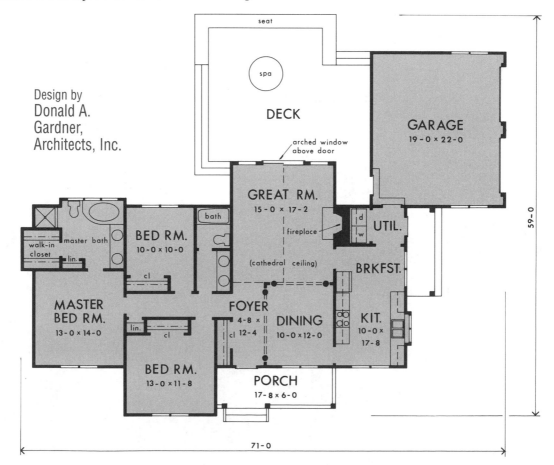

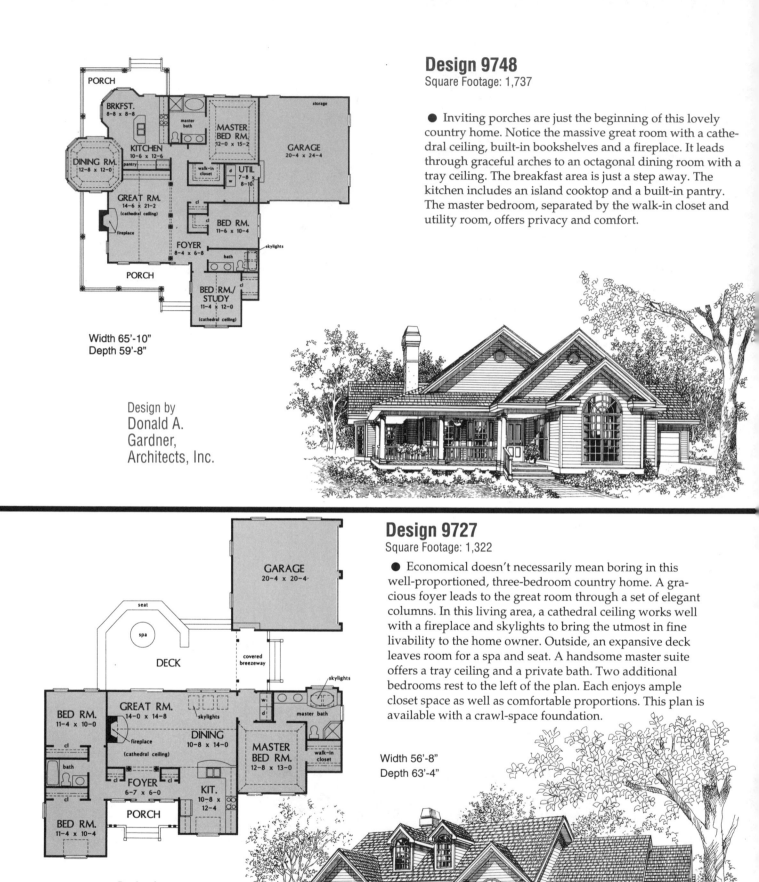

Design 9748
Square Footage: 1,737

● Inviting porches are just the beginning of this lovely country home. Notice the massive great room with a cathedral ceiling, built-in bookshelves and a fireplace. It leads through graceful arches to an octagonal dining room with a tray ceiling. The breakfast area is just a step away. The kitchen includes an island cooktop and a built-in pantry. The master bedroom, separated by the walk-in closet and utility room, offers privacy and comfort.

PORCH

BRKFST.
8-8 x 8-8

master bath

MASTER BED RM.
12-0 x 15-2

storage

GARAGE
20-4 x 24-4

KITCHEN
10-6 x 12-6

DINING RM.
12-8 x 12-0

pantry

walk-in closet

UTIL
7-8 x 8-10

d w

GREAT RM.
14-6 x 21-2
(cathedral ceiling)

fireplace

cl

BED RM.
11-6 x 10-4

FOYER
8-4 x 6-8

skylights

PORCH

bath

cl

BED RM./ STUDY
11-4 x 12-0
(cathedral ceiling)

Width 65'-10"
Depth 59'-8"

Design by
Donald A. Gardner, Architects, Inc.

Design 9727
Square Footage: 1,322

● Economical doesn't necessarily mean boring in this well-proportioned, three-bedroom country home. A gracious foyer leads to the great room through a set of elegant columns. In this living area, a cathedral ceiling works well with a fireplace and skylights to bring the utmost in fine livability to the home owner. Outside, an expansive deck leaves room for a spa and seat. A handsome master suite offers a tray ceiling and a private bath. Two additional bedrooms rest to the left of the plan. Each enjoys ample closet space as well as comfortable proportions. This plan is available with a crawl-space foundation.

GARAGE
20-4 x 20-4

seat

spa

DECK

covered breezeway

skylights

BED RM.
11-4 x 10-0

GREAT RM.
14-0 x 14-8

skylights

w d

master bath

cl

bath

DINING
10-8 x 14-0

MASTER BED RM.
12-8 x 13-0

walk-in closet

fireplace
(cathedral ceiling)

cl

cl

FOYER
6-7 x 6-0

cl

KIT.
10-8 x 12-4

BED RM.
11-4 x 10-4

PORCH

Width 56'-8"
Depth 63'-4"

Design by
Donald A. Gardner, Architects, Inc.

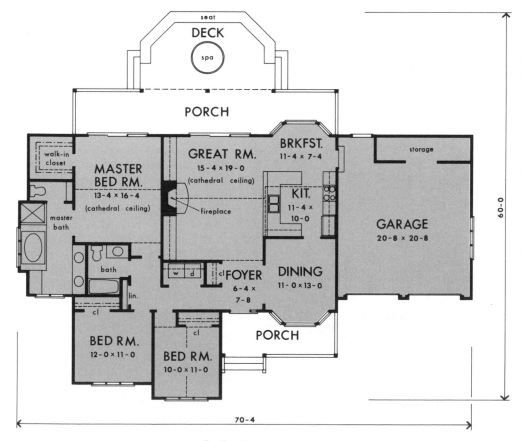

Design 9696

Square Footage: 1,625

● This family-pleasing design is thoughtful, indeed. Living areas include a kitchen with an efficient work triangle, an adjoining breakfast room, a dining room with a bay window and, of course, the great room with a fireplace and access to a rear porch. The master bedroom also has porch access, along with a walk-in closet and a lavish bath. Two family bedrooms include one featuring a half-round transom window, adding appeal to the exterior and interior. The laundry room is convenient to all three bedrooms.

Design by
Donald A.
Gardner,
Architects, Inc.

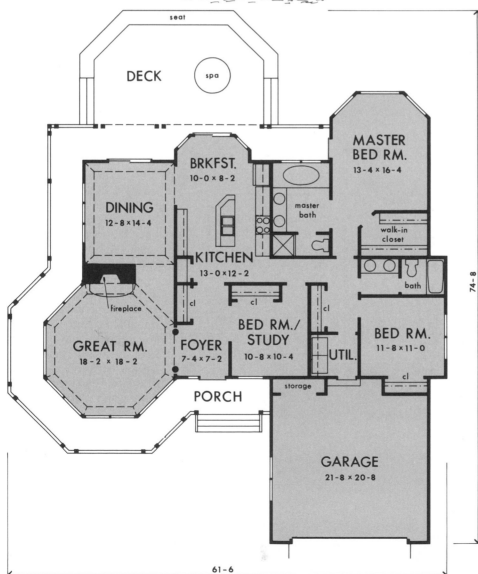

DECK   spa

seat

MASTER
BED RM.
13-4 × 16-4

BRKFST.
10-0 × 8-2

DINING
12-8 × 14-4

master
bath

walk-in
closet

KITCHEN
13-0 × 12-2

bath

fireplace

GREAT RM.
18-2 × 18-2

FOYER
7-4 × 7-2

BED RM./
STUDY
10-8 × 10-4

UTIL.

BED RM.
11-8 × 11-0

PORCH

storage

GARAGE
21-8 × 20-8

74-8

61-6

Design 9638
Square Footage: 1,865

● This distinctive Victorian exterior conceals an open, contemporary floor plan. The entrance foyer with round columns offers visual excitement. The octagonal great room has an 11' 6"-high tray ceiling and a fireplace. A generous kitchen with an elaborate island counter is centrally located, providing efficient service to the dining room, breakfast room and deck. Note the luxurious master bedroom suite with a large walk-in closet and master bath with double-bowl vanity, shower and garden tub.

Design by
Donald A.
Gardner,
Architects, Inc.

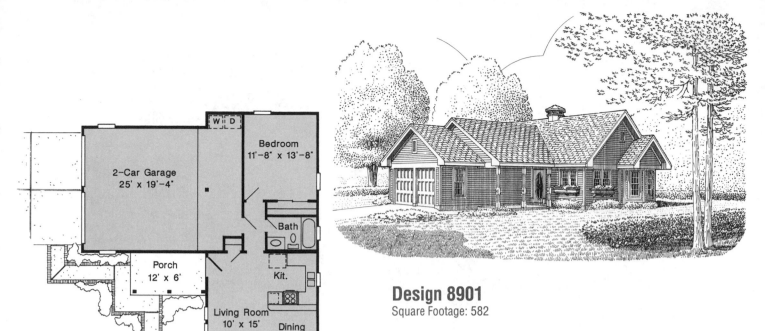

Design by
**Larry W.
Garnett &
Associates, Inc.**

Width 37'-8"
Depth 41'-2"

Design 8901
Square Footage: 582

● Perfect for narrow lots, lake-side or otherwise, this darling little Victorian-style cottage will serve as a wonderful retreat. The covered front porch leads to a bright living room and dining room area. The U-shaped kitchen includes a windowed sink area. It directly accesses the bay-windowed dining area. A full bath with natural light is conveniently located. The bedroom, with lots of closet space and views out two sides, sits quietly at the rear of the plan. In the two-car garage, space exists for the placement of a washer and a dryer.

Design by
**Larry E. Belk
Designs**

Width 45'-8"
Depth 50'-2"

Design 8165
Square Footage: 1,772

● A Victorian flair gives this home its curb appeal. Inside, a large living room boasts a centerpiece fireplace and coffered ceiling. The kitchen has a 42"-high breakfast bar and a pantry. The master suite includes a ten-foot coffered ceiling and a luxury bath complete with a corner whirlpool tub, a separate shower, His and Hers vanities and a roomy walk-in closet. Two additional bedrooms and a bath are nearby. A two-car garage plan is included with this design and can be connected to the home with a breezeway. Please specify crawlspace or slab foundation when ordering.

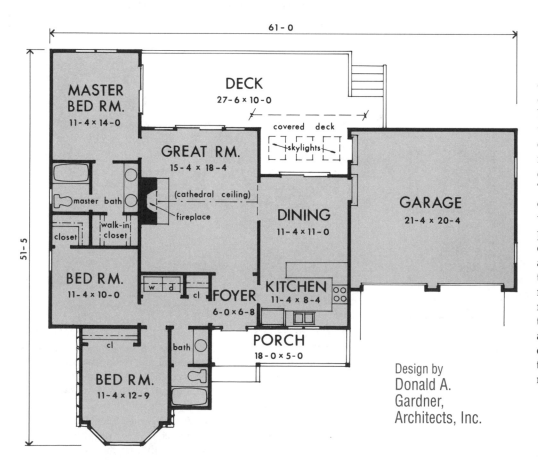

MASTER BED RM.
11-4 x 14-0

DECK
27-6 x 10-0

covered deck

skylights

GREAT RM.
15-4 x 18-4

(cathedral ceiling)

fireplace

master bath

walk-in closet

closet

GARAGE
21-4 x 20-4

DINING
11-4 x 11-0

BED RM.
11-4 x 10-0

w d cl FOYER
6-0 x 6-8

KITCHEN
11-4 x 8-4

cl

bath

PORCH
18-0 x 5-0

BED RM.
11-4 x 12-9

61-0

51-5

Design 9620
Square Footage: 1,310

● A multi-paned bay window, dormers, a cupola, a covered porch and a variety of building materials dress up this one-story cottage. The entrance foyer leads to an impressive great room with cathedral ceiling and fireplace. The U-shaped kitchen, adjacent to the dining room, provides an ideal layout for food preparation. An expansive deck offers shelter while admitting cheery sunlight through skylights. A luxurious master bedroom located to the rear of the house takes advantage of the deck area and is assured privacy from two other bedrooms at the front of the house. These family bedrooms share a full bath.

Design by
Donald A.
Gardner,
Architects, Inc.

spa

DECK

MASTER BED RM.
13-4 x 13-8

master bath

skylights

BRKFST.
11-4 x 7-4

GREAT RM.
15-4 x 16-10
(cathedral ceiling)

fireplace

walk-in closet

storage

w
d

BED RM.
11-4 x 11-4

cl

bath

cl

KITCHEN
11-4 x 10-0

GARAGE
20-0 x 19-8

FOYER
8-2 x 6-6

cl

cl

BED RM./ STUDY
11-4 x 10-4

PORCH

DINING RM.
11-4 x 11-4

50-8

59-8

Design by
**Donald A.
Gardner,
Architects, Inc.**

Design 9726

Square Footage: 1,498
Optional Basement: 1,531 square feet

● This charming home utilizes multi-pane windows, columns, dormers and a covered porch to offer a welcoming front exterior. Inside, the great room commands attention with a dramatic cathedral ceiling and fireplace. A set of columns leads to an L-shaped island kitchen and the sunny breakfast nook. The tiered-ceilinged dining room presents a delightfully formal atmosphere for dinner parties and family gatherings. A tray ceiling in the master bedroom will please, as will a large walk-in closet and a gracious master bath with dual lavatories, a garden tub and a separate shower. Two family bedrooms are located at the opposite end of the house for privacy. Please specify basement or crawlspace foundation when ordering.

131

Design 9753

Square Footage: 1,346

● A great room that stretches into the dining room makes this design perfect for entertaining. A fireplace and built-ins, as well as a cathedral ceiling, further the atmosphere. A rear deck extends livability. The ample kitchen features lots of counter and cabinet space as well as an angled cooktop. Three bedrooms include the master suite with its sloped ceiling, private bath and deck access.

Design by
Donald A.
Gardner,
Architects, Inc.

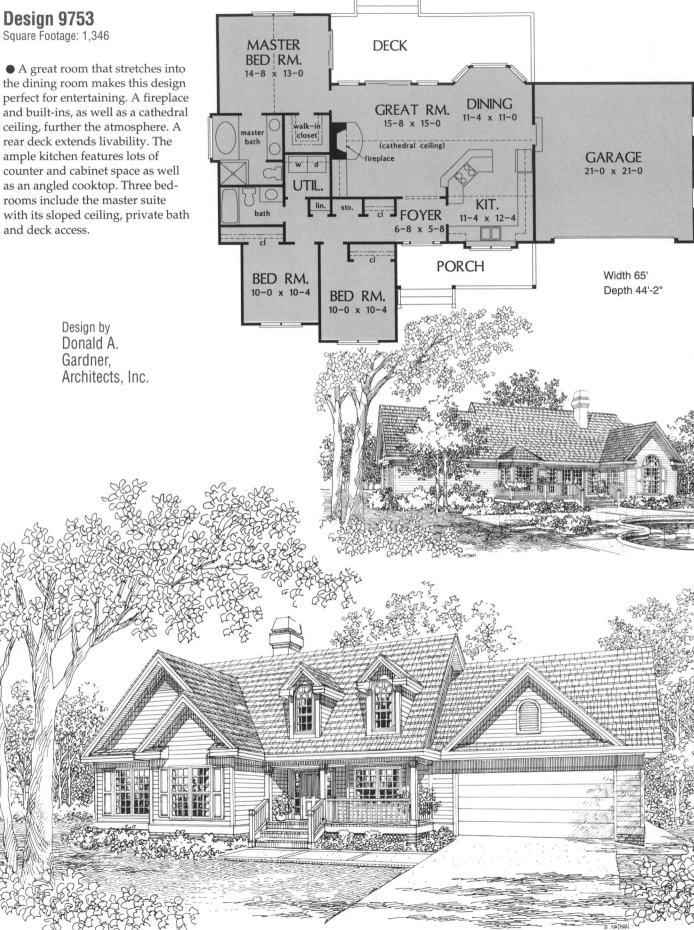

MASTER BED RM.
14-8 x 13-0

DECK

master bath

walk-in closet

w   d

UTIL.

bath

lin.   sto.

cl

BED RM.
10-0 x 10-4

cl

BED RM.
10-0 x 10-4

GREAT RM.
15-8 x 15-0

DINING
11-4 x 11-0

(cathedral ceiling)
fireplace

KIT.
11-4 x 12-4

FOYER
6-8 x 5-8

GARAGE
21-0 x 21-0

PORCH

Width 65'
Depth 44'-2"

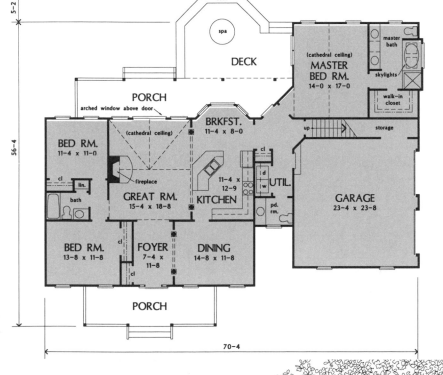

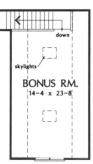

Floor plan labels:

- seat
- spa
- DECK
- PORCH
- arched window above door
- (cathedral ceiling)
- BED RM. 11-4 x 11-0
- cl
- lin.
- bath
- fireplace
- GREAT RM. 15-4 x 18-8
- BRKFST. 11-4 x 8-0
- KITCHEN
- 11-4 x 12-9
- UTIL.
- d / w
- pd. rm.
- MASTER BED RM. 14-0 x 17-0
- master bath
- skylights
- walk-in closet
- up
- storage
- GARAGE 23-4 x 23-8
- BED RM. 13-8 x 11-8
- FOYER 7-4 x 11-8
- DINING 14-8 x 11-8
- PORCH
- 5-2
- 56-4
- 70-4

Bonus room plan:

- down
- skylights
- BONUS RM. 14-4 x 23-8

Design by
Donald A.
Gardner,
Architects, Inc.

Design 9749

Square Footage: 1,864
Bonus Room: 420 square feet

● Quaint and cozy on the outside
with porches front and back, this
three-bedroom country home surpris-
es with an open floor plan featuring a
large great room with a cathedral ceiling. Nine-foot ceilings add volume
throughout the home. A central
kitchen with an angled counter opens
to the breakfast and great rooms for
easy entertaining. The privately located master bedroom has a cathedral
ceiling and adjacent access to the deck.
Operable skylights over the tub accent
the luxurious master bath. Two secondary bedrooms share a full hall
bath. A bonus room makes expanding
easy. Please specify basement or
crawlspace foundation when ordering.

Design 9778

Square Footage: 1,655
Optional Basement: 1,704 square feet

● A covered front porch, dormers and arched windows welcome you to this country home. Interior columns dramatically open the foyer and the kitchen to the spacious great room. The drama is heightened by the great room's cathedral ceiling and fireplace. The kitchen, with its food preparation island, easily serves the breakfast area and the formal dining room. The master suite boasts a tray ceiling and access to the rear deck. Added luxuries include a walk-in closet and a skylit master bath with a double vanity, a garden tub and a shower. Two generous bedrooms share the second bath. Please specify basement or crawlspace foundation when ordering.

Design by
Donald A.
Gardner,
Architects, Inc.

DECK

spa

MASTER BED RM.
13-4 x 14-8

skylights

master bath

fireplace

BRKFST.
11-4 x 8-0

walk-in closet

lin.

storage

BED RM.
11-4 x 12-4

GREAT RM.
15-4 x 19-8
(cathedral ceiling)

KIT.
11-4 x 10-4

GARAGE
20-0 x 19-8

cl

lin.

bath

FOYER
8-2 x 6-2

cl

DINING RM.
11-4 x 12-4

BED RM./
STUDY
11-4 x 11-4

PORCH

(optional door location)

53-8

61-0

© 1994 Donald A Gardner Architects, Inc.

Design 9679

Square Footage: 1,512

● A multi-pane bay window, dormers, a cupola, a covered porch and a variety of building materials all combine to dress up this intriguing country cottage. The generous entry foyer leads to a formal dining room and an impressive great room with a cathedral ceiling and a fireplace. The kitchen includes a breakfast area with a bay window overlooking the deck. The great room and master bedroom also access the deck. The master bath has a double-bowl vanity, a shower and a garden tub. Two additional bedrooms are located at the front of the house for privacy and share a full bath.

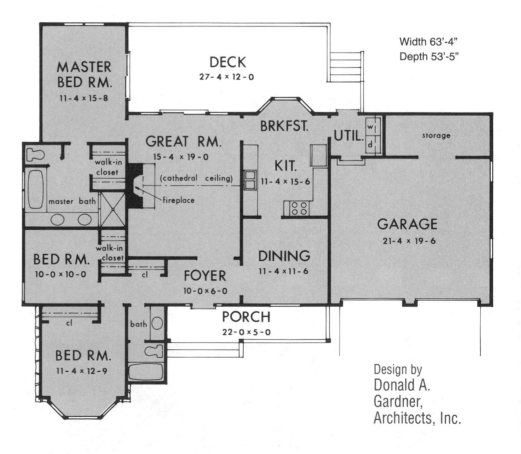

Width 63'-4"
Depth 53'-5"

MASTER BED RM.
11-4 × 15-8

DECK
27-4 × 12-0

BRKFST.

UTIL.

storage

GREAT RM.
15-4 × 19-0

walk-in closet

(cathedral ceiling)

fireplace

KIT.
11-4 × 15-6

master bath

BED RM.
10-0 × 10-0

walk-in closet

cl

GARAGE
21-4 × 19-6

cl

FOYER
10-0×6-0

DINING
11-4 × 11-6

bath

BED RM.
11-4 × 12-9

PORCH
22-0 × 5-0

Design by
Donald A. Gardner, Architects, Inc.

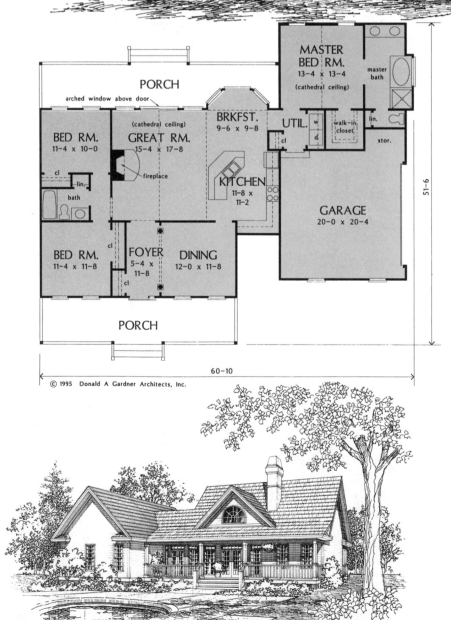

Design 9780

Square Footage: 1,561

● This country farmhouse embraces a big heart in a cozy package. Special touches such as interior columns, a bay window and dormers add their own special brand of charm. The centrally located great room features a cathedral ceiling, a fireplace and a clerestory window that fills the room with natural light. The adjoining kitchen, designed to save steps, easily services the bay-windowed breakfast room and the dining room nearby. Split for privacy, the master suite boasts amenities found in much larger homes. Efficient use of space in the master bath allows room for a whirlpool tub, a separate shower and a walk-in closet. Two additional bedrooms share a full bath.

Design by
Donald A.
Gardner,
Architects, Inc.

Width 74'-10"
Depth 55'-8"

MASTER BED RM.
14-0 x 17-4

master bath

walk-in closet

sto.

up

skylight

lin.

attic storage

down

BONUS RM.
14-4 x 21-8

skylights

GARAGE
23-0 x 25-8

storage

UTIL.

d w

KIT.
11-8 x 12-8

cl

pd. rm.

BRKFST.
11-8 x 9-0

(cathedral ceiling)

PORCH

GREAT RM.
16-4 x 18-8

fireplace

opening above

DINING
14-8 x 11-8

FOYER
6-4 x 11-8

vaulted ceiling

BED RM./ STUDY
14-8 x 11-8

PORCH

BED RM.
12-0 x 11-0

cl

BED RM.
10-10 x 11-0

cl

lin.

bath

walk-in closet

Design by
Donald A. Gardner, Architects, Inc.

Design 9782
Square Footage: 2,192

● Exciting volumes and nine-foot ceilings add elegance to a comfortable, open plan while secluded bedrooms are pleasant retreats in this home, designed for today's family. Sunlight fills the airy foyer from a vaulted dormer and streams into the great room. A formal dining room, delineated from the foyer by columns, features a tray ceiling. Hosts whose guests always end up in the kitchen will enjoy entertaining here with only columns to separate them from the great room. Children's bedrooms share a full bath complete with a linen closet. The front bedroom doubles as a study for extra flexibility and is accented by a tray ceiling. The master suite is highlighted by a tray ceiling.

Design 9783

Square Footage: 1,832

● This plan rises with a cathedral ceiling and a circle-top clerestory. The kitchen features an island for easy entertaining and is differentiated from the great room by columns. A formal colonnaded dining room is accessible from the kitchen and the foyer. The master suite pampers with a lovely garden bath.

Design by
Donald A.
Gardner,
Architects, Inc.

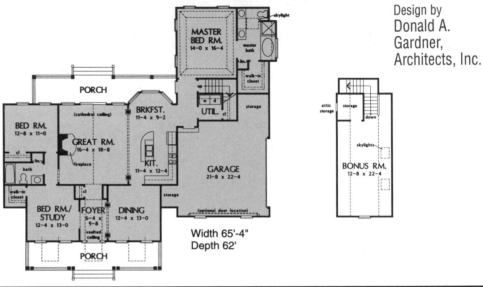

Width 65'-4"
Depth 62'

Design 9756

Square Footage: 2,207
Bonus Room: 435 square feet

● This quaint four-bedroom home with front and rear porches reinforces its beauty with arched windows and dormers. The pillared dining room opens on your right while a study that could double as a guest room is available on your left. Straight ahead lies the massive great room with its cathedral ceiling, enchanting fireplace and access to the private rear porch and the deck with a spa and seat. Within steps of the dining room is the efficient kitchen and the sunny breakfast nook. The master suite enjoys a cathedral ceiling, rear deck access and a master bath with a skylit whirlpool tub, a walk-in closet and a double vanity. Two additional bedrooms are located at the opposite end of the house.

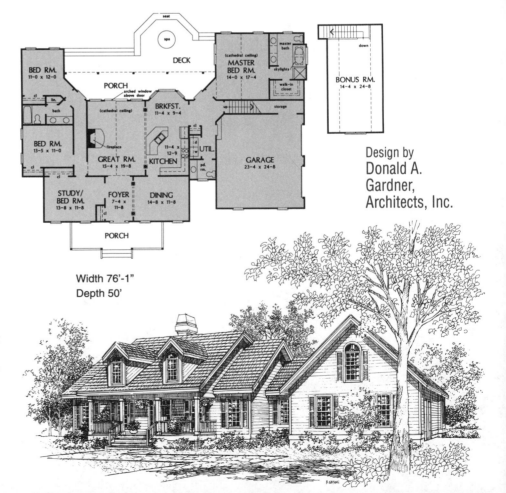

Width 76'-1"
Depth 50'

Design by
Donald A.
Gardner,
Architects, Inc.

Design by
Donald A.
Gardner,
Architects, Inc.

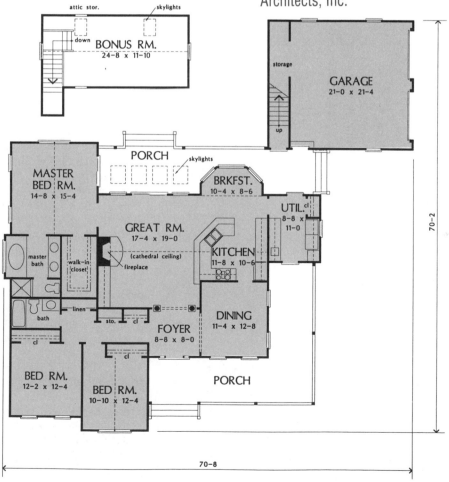

attic stor.   skylights

down   BONUS RM.
24-8 x 11-10

storage

GARAGE
21-0 x 21-4

PORCH   skylights

up

MASTER
BED RM.
14-8 x 15-4

BRKFST.
10-4 x 8-6

UTIL. cl.
8-8 x
11-0

master bath

walk-in closet

GREAT RM.
17-4 x 19-0

(cathedral ceiling)
fireplace

KITCHEN
11-8 x 10-6

linen

bath

cl

sto.   cl

FOYER
8-8 x 8-0

DINING
11-4 x 12-8

70-2

BED RM.
12-2 x 12-4

cl

BED RM.
10-10 x 12-4

PORCH

70-8

Design 9764
Square Footage: 1,815

● Dormers, arched windows
and covered porches lend this
home its country appeal. Inside,
the foyer opens to the dining
room on the right and leads
through a columned entrance to
the great room warmed by a
fireplace. Access is provided to
the covered, skylit rear porch
for outdoor livability. The open
kitchen easily serves the great
room, the bayed breakfast area
and the dining room. A cathedral ceiling graces the master
bedroom with its walk-in closet
and private bath with a dual
vanity and a whirlpool tub. Two
additional bedrooms share a full
bath. A detached garage with a
skylit bonus room is connected
to the rear covered porch.

QUOTE ONE®
Cost to build? See page 374
to order complete cost estimate
to build this house in your area!

Design by
Donald A.
Gardner,
Architects, Inc.

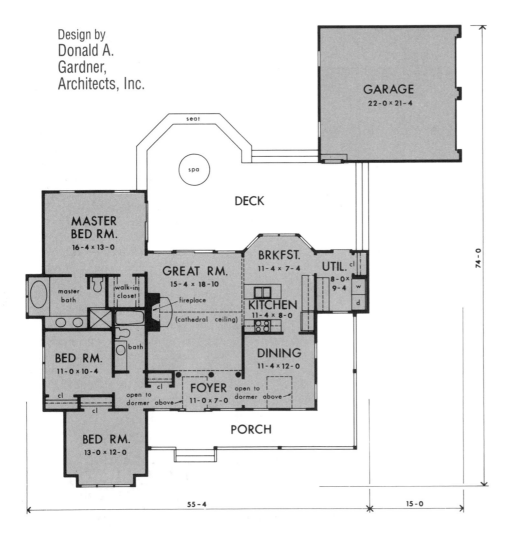

GARAGE
22-0 × 21-4

seat

spa

DECK

MASTER
BED RM.
16-4 × 13-0

master bath

walk-in closet

GREAT RM.
15-4 × 18-10

fireplace

(cathedral ceiling)

BRKFST.
11-4 × 7-4

UTIL.
8-0 × 9-4

cl

w

d

KITCHEN
11-4 × 8-0

bath

BED RM.
11-0 × 10-4

cl

cl

open to dormer above

cl

FOYER
11-0 × 7-0

open to dormer above

DINING
11-4 × 12-0

BED RM.
13-0 × 12-0

PORCH

55-4

15-0

74-0

Design 9713
Square Footage: 1,590

● The open floor plan of this country farmhouse packs in all of today's amenities in only 1,590 square feet. Columns separate the foyer from the great room with its cathedral ceiling and fireplace. Serving meals has never been easier—the kitchen makes use of direct access to the dining room as well as a breakfast nook overlooking the deck and spa. A handy utility room even has room for a counter and cabinets. Three bedrooms make this an especially desirable design. The master bedroom, off of the great room, provides private access to the deck. This design is flexible enough to be accommodated by a narrow lot if the garage is relocated. This plan includes a crawl-space foundation.

Design 9704
Square Footage: 1,687

WIDTH 77'-4"
DEPTH 62'-10"

● This traditional country three-bedroom house with front and side porches, arched windows and dormers projects a comfortable character. Elegant columns define the dining room while providing pleasing visuals in this open, modern plan. The great room has a cathedral ceiling, fireplace and arched window above sliding glass doors. Both great room and breakfast room have direct access to the deck. The master suite has a well-proportioned bedroom and master bath consisting of a whirlpool tub, shower, double-vanity and walk-in closet. Two other bedrooms share a full bath with double-bowl vanity. The plan is available with crawl-space foundation.

Design by
Donald A.
Gardner,
Architects, Inc.

Design 9685
Square Footage: 1,445

● Accommodate a narrow lot with this home by relocating the garage to the rear of the house. The entrance foyer leads to an open great room with cathedral ceiling and fireplace. A conveniently shaped rear deck enhances outdoor living. The master bedroom is located to the rear of the house in order to take advantage of the lovely deck area. Two additional bedrooms are found at the front of the house.

Width 76'-4"
Depth 56'-6"

Design by
Donald A.
Gardner,
Architects, Inc.

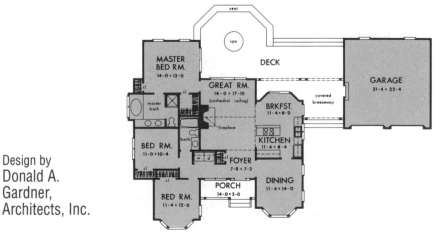

Design 9779

Square Footage: 1,632

● This country home has a big heart in a cozy package. Special touches–interior columns, a bay window and dormers–add elegance. The central great room features a cathedral ceiling and a fireplace. A clerestory window splashes the room with natural light. The open kitchen easily services the breakfast area and the nearby dining room. The private master suite, with a tray ceiling and a walk-in closet, boasts amenities found in much larger homes. The bath features skylights over the whirlpool tub. Two additional bedrooms share a bath. The front bedroom features a walk-in closet and also doubles as a study.

Width 62'-4"
Depth 55'-2"

Design by
Donald A. Gardner, Architects, Inc.

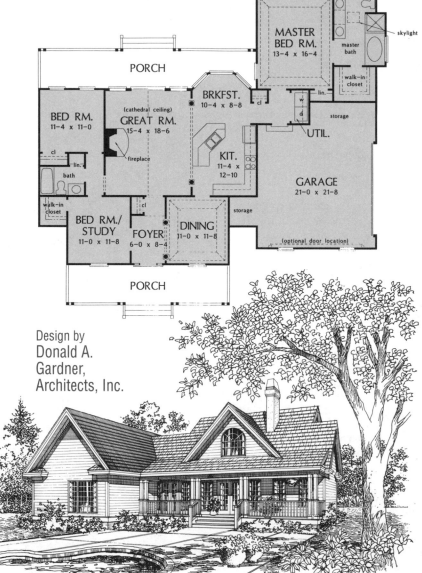

Design 9771

Square Footage: 1,927

● Sunlight takes center stage in this delightful country home. Each room has at least two windows to add warmth and radiance, and a clerestory window brightens the foyer. Two bedrooms and a full bath are to the left of the foyer. To the right is the dining room, which leads into the L-shaped kitchen with its penninsular cooktop and connecting bay-windowed breakfast area. The central great room offers a cathedral ceiling, a fireplace and access to the rear porch. The master suite is separated for privacy and features two walls of windows, a large walk-in closet and a luxurious whirlpool bath with skylights.

Design by
Donald A.
Gardner,
Architects, Inc.

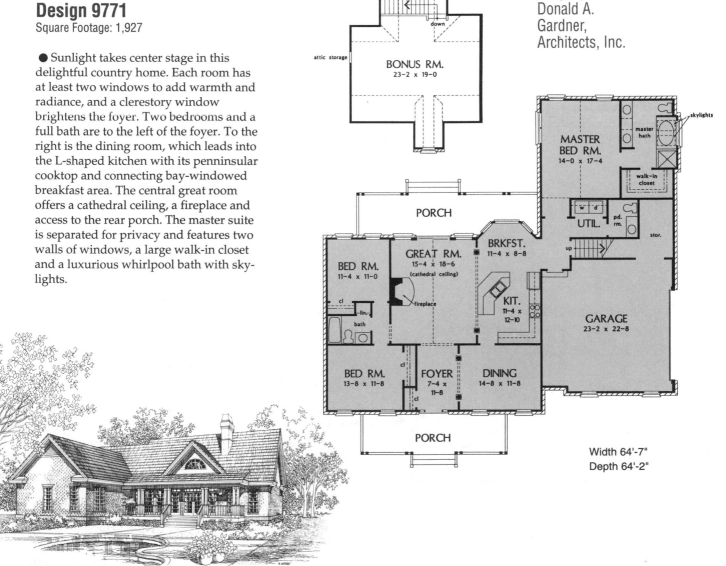

BONUS RM.
23-2 x 19-0

attic storage

PORCH

MASTER BED RM.
14-0 x 17-4

master bath

skylights

walk-in closet

UTIL.

pd. rm.

stor.

BED RM.
11-4 x 11-0

GREAT RM.
15-4 x 18-6
(cathedral ceiling)

fireplace

BRKFST.
11-4 x 8-8

KIT.
11-4 x 12-10

GARAGE
23-2 x 22-8

BED RM.
13-8 x 11-8

FOYER
7-4 x 11-8

DINING
14-8 x 11-8

PORCH

Width 64'-7"
Depth 64'-2"

Design 9742

Square Footage: 1,954
Bonus Room: 436 square feet

● This beautiful brick country home has all the amenities needed for today's active family. Covered front and back porches along with a rear deck provide plenty of room for outdoor enjoyment. Inside, the focus is on the large great room with its cathedral ceiling and welcoming fireplace. To the right, columns separate the kitchen and breakfast area while keeping this area open. Chefs of all ages will appreciate the convenience of the kitchen with its center island and additional eating space. The master bedroom provides a splendid private retreat, featuring a cathedral ceiling and a large walk-in closet. The luxurious master bath shares a double-bowl vanity, a separate shower and a relaxing skylit whirlpool tub. At the opposite end of the plan, two additional bedrooms share a full bath. A skylit bonus room above the garage allows for additional living space.

Design by
Donald A.
Gardner,
Architects, Inc.

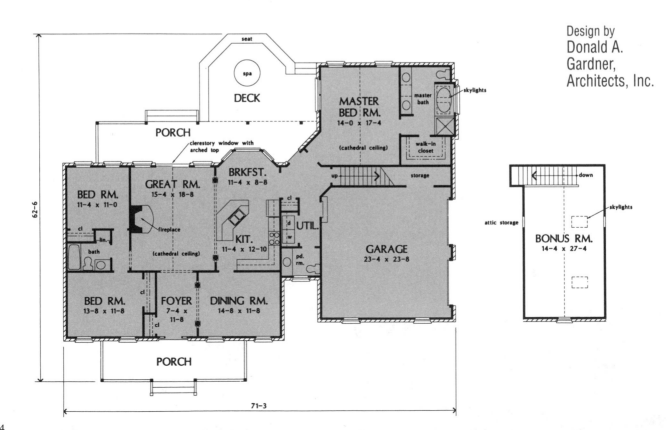

144

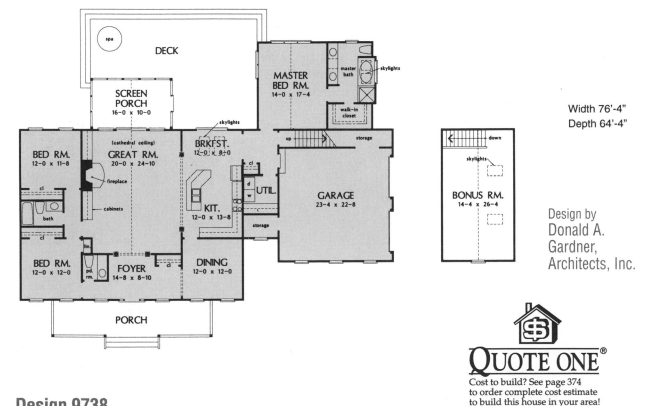

Width 76'-4"
Depth 64'-4"

Design by
Donald A.
Gardner,
Architects, Inc.

Design 9738
Square Footage: 2,136
Bonus Room: 405 square feet

● This exciting three-bedroom country home overflows with amenities. Traditional details such as columns, cathedral ceilings and open living areas combine to create the ideal floor plan for today's active family lifestyle. The spacious great room features built-in cabinets and a fireplace and a cathedral ceiling which continues into the adjoining screened porch. An efficient kitchen with a food prepara-tion island is conveniently grouped with the great room, the dining room and the skylit breakfast area for the cook who enjoys visiting while preparing meals. A private master bedroom features a cathedral ceiling, a large walk-in closet and a relaxing master bath with a skylit whirlpool tub and a separate shower. Two secondary bedrooms share a full bath at the opposite end of the home.

Enhanced Plan

LEXINGTON
Design 3718
Square Footage: 1,433

● This eye-catching three-bedroom ranch home is designed specifically for narrow lots. All the many features you've been looking for in a family home can be found. The master bedroom suite includes a full-size bath and walk-in closet. A second bath is located between the two family bedrooms. The huge great room offers plenty of space for all your family gatherings. Decorative louvers, two bay windows, a rear deck, a fireplace and a two-car garage are optional. A four-bedroom version of this plan appears on the opposite page.

Blueprints and a complete lumber and materials package are also available for this home at your local 84 Lumber dealer.

Design by
Home Planners,
Inc.

Basic Plan

Enhanced Plan

WINCHESTER
Design 3721
Square Footage: 1,648

● If you have a narrow lot to build your dream home on, then this elegant ranch design is for you! The master bedroom suite includes a full-size bath and walk-in closet, while a second full-size bath serves the remaining three bedrooms. A galley kitchen with an eat-in nook opens up to a huge great room that easily accommodates friends and family. This home is the correct choice for those who desire an affordable family plan. The house may be built with or without the two-car garage, rear deck, bay windows and fireplace.

Blueprints and a complete lumber and materials package are also available for this home at your local 84 Lumber dealer.

Floor Plan

35'-0"

76'-0"

BEDROOM 10⁴ x 10⁴
BEDROOM 10⁴ x 10⁴
RAILING
DECK 13² x 9⁸
GREAT RM 13² x 33⁴
OPT. FIREPLACE
LINEN
BEDROOM 11⁴ x 10⁴
BATH
KITCHEN 9² x 17¹⁰
OPT. BAY WINDOW
BATH
OPT. BAY WINDOW
WALK-IN CLOSET
LINEN
DW
MASTER BEDROOM 11⁴ x 16⁰
DN
FOYER
RAILING
COVERED PORCH
GARAGE 20¹⁰ x 21⁸

Design by
Home Planners, Inc.

Basic Plan

Back At The Ranch:
A collection of favorite ranch homes

This home, as shown in the photograph, may differ from the actual blueprints. For more detailed information, please check the floor plans carefully.

Photo by Andrew D. Lautman

Design 2947
Square Footage: 1,830

L **D**

● This charming, one-story traditional home greets visitors with a covered porch. A galley-style kitchen shares a snack bar with the spacious gathering room where a fireplace is the focal point. An ample master suite includes a luxury bath with a whirlpool tub and a separate dressing room. Two additional bedrooms, with one that could double as a study, are located at the front of the home.

California Engineered Plans and California Stock Plans are available for this home. Call 1-800-521-6797 for more information.

Design by
Home Planners, Inc.

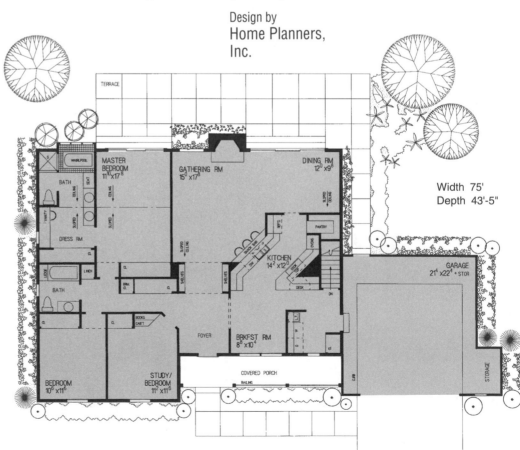

Width 75'
Depth 43'-5"

TERRACE

MASTER BEDROOM 11⁰ x17⁸

BATH

SEAT

VANITY

DRESS RM

LINEN

BATH

BOOKS CAB'T

BEDROOM 10⁶ x11⁶

STUDY/ BEDROOM 11² x11⁶

GATHERING RM 15⁰ x17⁸

DINING RM 12² x9⁶

PANTRY

KITCHEN 14² x12⁰

DESK

FOYER

BRKFST RM 8⁸ x10⁴

COVERED PORCH
RAILING

GARAGE 21⁴ x22⁴ + STOR

STORAGE

QUOTE ONE™
Cost to build? See page 374 to order complete cost estimate to build this house in your area!

148

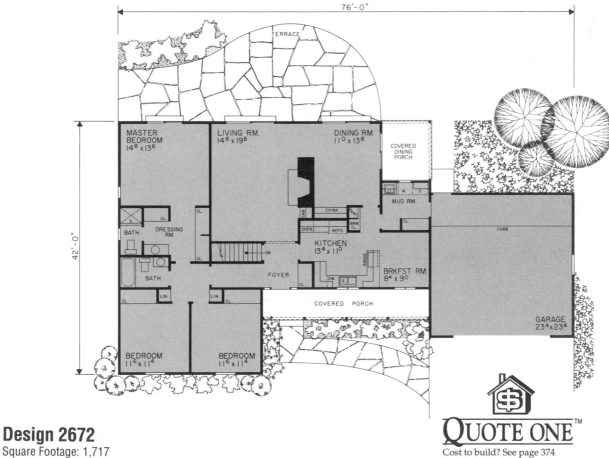

Design 2672
Square Footage: 1,717

L D

● The traditional appearance of this one-story is emphasized by its covered porch, multi-paned windows, narrow clapboard and vertical wood siding. Not only is the exterior eye-appealing but the interior has an efficient plan and is very livable. The front U-shaped kitchen will work with the breakfast room and mud room, which houses the laundry facilities. An access to the garage is here. Outdoor dining can be enjoyed on the covered porch adjacent to the dining room. Both of these areas, the porch and dining room, are convenient to the kitchen. Sleeping facilities consist of three bedrooms and two full baths. Note the three sets of sliding glass doors leading to the terrace.

Quote One™
Cost to build? See page 374 to order complete cost estimate to build this house in your area!

Design by
Donald A.
Gardner,
Architects, Inc.

Design 9622
Square Footage: 1,842

● What visual excitement is created in this country ranch with the use of a combination of exterior building materials and shapes! The angular nature of the plan allows for flexibility in design—lengthen the great room or family room, or both, to suit individual space needs. An amenity-filled master bedroom features a cathedral ceiling, private deck and master bath with whirlpool tub. Two other bedrooms share a full bath. Please specify basement or crawlspace foundation when ordering.

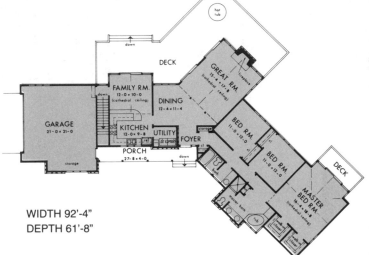

WIDTH 92'-4"
DEPTH 61'-8"

Design by
Donald A.
Gardner,
Architects, Inc.

Design 9601
Square Footage: 1,988

● This country-style ranch is the essence of interesting shapes. Because it's angled, it allows for flexibility in design—the great room and/or the family room can be lengthened. The master bedroom has a cathedral ceiling, a walk-in closet, a private deck and a spacious master bath with a whirlpool tub. Expansive deck area with space for a hot tub wraps around interior family gathering areas. Both the family room and great room have cathedral ceilings; the great room has a fireplace. This plan is available with either a crawlspace or partial basement foundation. Please specify when ordering.

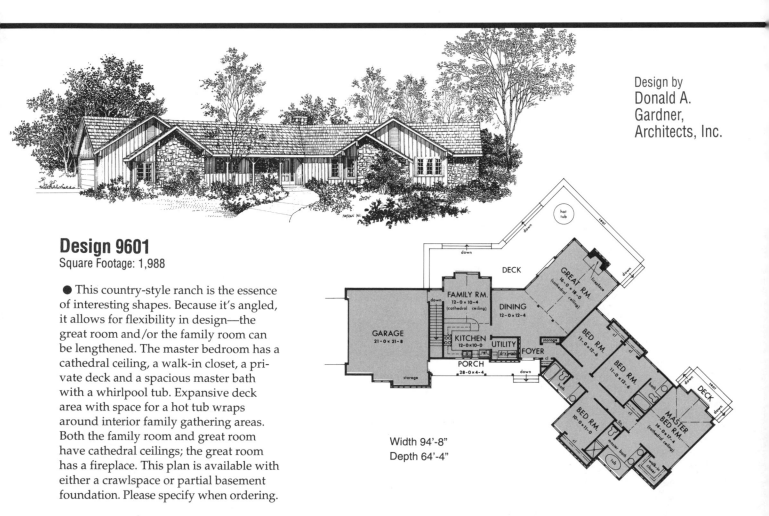

Width 94'-8"
Depth 64'-4"

Design 9674
Square Footage: 2,308

● Multi-pane windows, shutters, dormers, bay windows with metal roofs and round wood columns add intrigue to this lively country cottage. This three-bedroom plan has all the spaces necessary for the growing family, including a living room and family room. A lavish master bedroom and master bath with double-bowl vanity, shower and whirlpool tub is located at the other end of the house for privacy. The family room contains a fireplace and the sun room displays an arched window over a sliding glass door. Both rooms boast cathedral ceilings.

Design by
Donald A.
Gardner,
Architects, Inc.

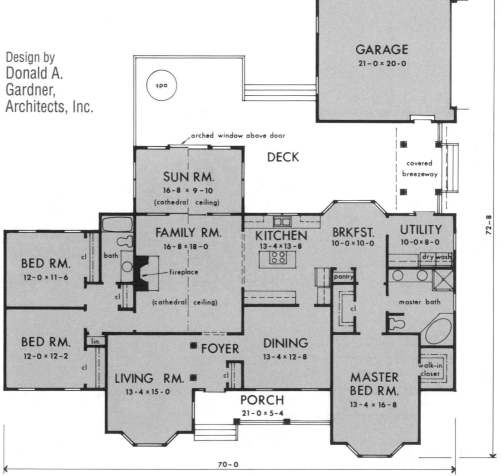

BASEMENT OPTION

Design by
Home Planners,
Inc.

Design 1343
Square Footage: 1,620

L

● This traditional, L-shaped exterior with its flower court and covered front porch is picturesque, indeed. The formal front entry routes traffic directly to the three distinctly zoned areas: the sleeping area, the living and dining area and the family kitchen area. Four bedrooms and two full baths will serve the family well.

Width 62'
Depth 50'

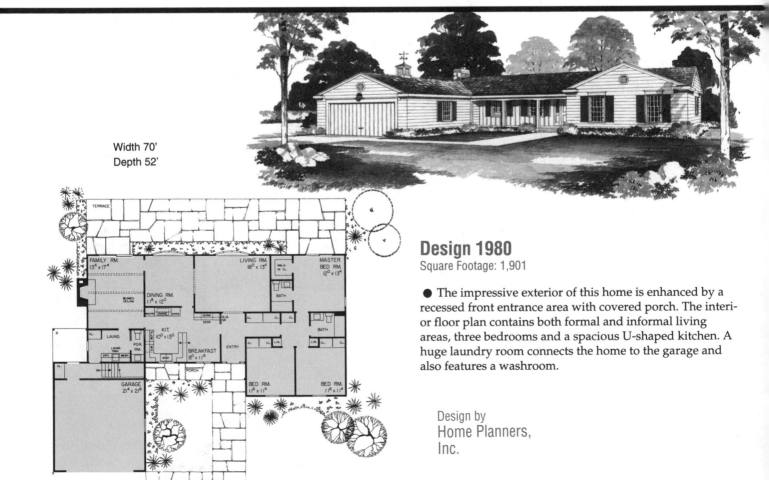

Width 70'
Depth 52'

Design 1980
Square Footage: 1,901

● The impressive exterior of this home is enhanced by a recessed front entrance area with covered porch. The interior floor plan contains both formal and informal living areas, three bedrooms and a spacious U-shaped kitchen. A huge laundry room connects the home to the garage and also features a washroom.

Design by
Home Planners,
Inc.

Design 1829

Square Footage: 1,800

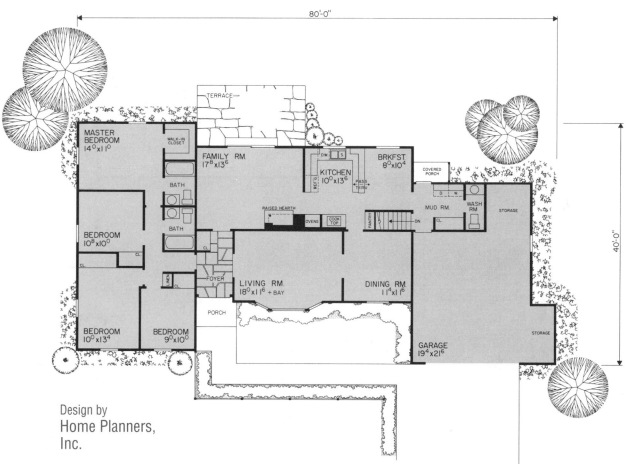

Design by
Home Planners,
Inc.

● All the charm of a traditional heritage is wrapped up in this U-shaped home with its narrow, horizontal siding, delightful window treatment and high-pitched roof. The massive center chimney, the bay window and the double front doors are plus features. Inside, the living potential is outstanding. The sleeping wing is self-contained and has four bedrooms and two baths. The large family and living rooms cater to the divergent age groups. Pay attention to the carefully thought-out room arrangement with living room and dining room to the fore, family room and kitchen to the rear. A service area with laundry and half bath is conveniently located. A rear terrace will surely be a favorite outdoor space.

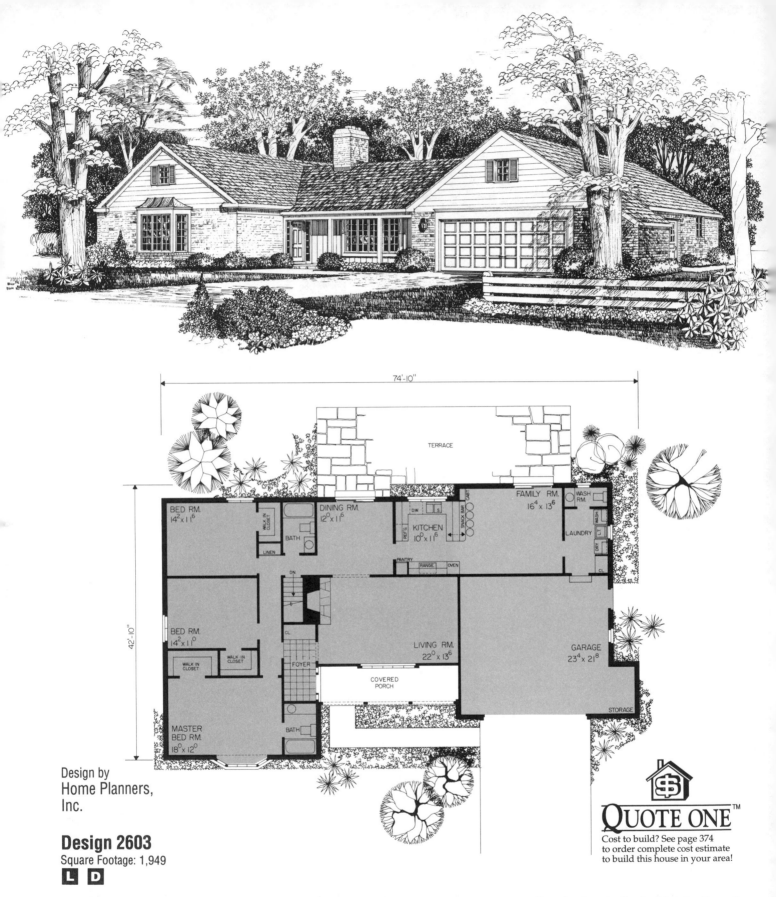

Design by
Home Planners,
Inc.

Design 2603

Square Footage: 1,949

L **D**

● Surely it would be difficult to beat the appeal of this traditional one-story home. Its slightly modified U-shape with the two front facing gables, the bay window, the covered front porch, and the interesting use of exterior materials all add to the exterior charm. Besides, there are three large bedrooms serviced by two full baths and three walk-in closets. The excellent kitchen is flanked by the formal dining room and the informal family room. Don't miss the pantry, the built-in oven, and the pass-thru to the snack bar.

QUOTE ONE™
Cost to build? See page 374
to order complete cost estimate
to build this house in your area!

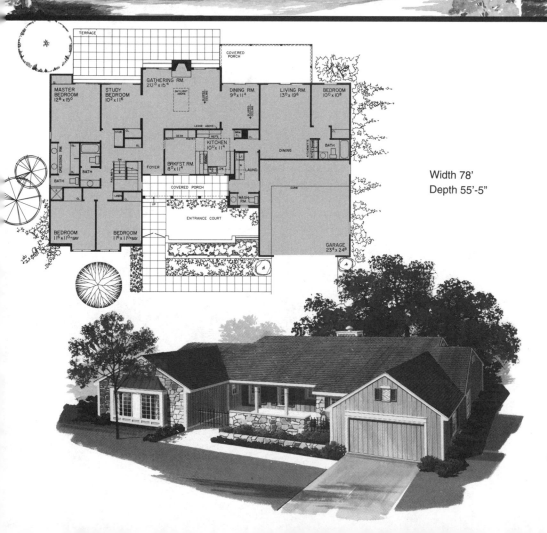

Design 1786

Square Footage: 2,370

● This is an extremely appealing design, high-lighted by its brick masses, its window detailing, its interesting shape and its inviting covered front entrance. The foyer is centrally located and but a step or two from all areas. The bedroom wing is distinctly defined. The quiet, sunken living room is off by itself. There is even a separate formal dining room. The family room has a fireplace and is adjacent to the U-shaped kitchen. Just off the garage is the mud room with washroom for quick clean-ups.

WIDTH 78'-10"
DEPTH 50'-10"

Design by
Home Planners,
Inc.

Design 2867

Square Footage: 2,388

L

● This design features a self-contained suite (473 sq. ft.) consisting of a bedroom, a bath, a living room and a kitchenette with a dining area. The rest of this traditional, one-story house, faced with fieldstone and vertical wood siding, is also very livable. One wing houses the four family bedrooms and bath facilities. The center of the plan has a front, U-shaped kitchen and breakfast room. The formal dining room and large gathering room enjoy access to, and views of, the rear grounds.

Width 78'
Depth 55'-5"

Design by
Home Planners,
Inc.

Enhanced Plan

BLUFF CITY
Design 3700
Square Footage: 1,317

● All the charm of a traditional country home is wrapped up in this efficient, economical ranch. The time-honored, three-bedroom plan can also serve as two bedrooms plus study or playroom. The formal living room provides a warm welcome to guests, while the open kitchen and family room combination offers plenty of space for active family gatherings. This functional interior is packaged in an exterior that is neat as a pin—with vertical siding, window and door shutters and a crisp brick ledge veneer. A one- or two-car garage may be attached. Other options include a front porch with railing, a rear deck with railing, a box bay window and a fireplace.

Blueprints and a complete lumber and materials package are also available for this home at your local 84 Lumber dealer.

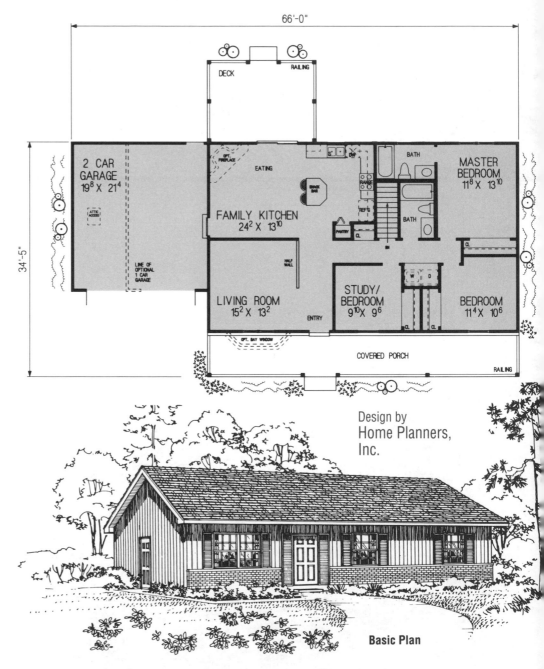

Design by
Home Planners, Inc.

Basic Plan

Design by
**Home Planners,
Inc.**

TERRACE

COVERED PORCH

MASTER
BEDROOM
13⁰ x 21⁴ + BAY

FAMILY RM
19⁸ x 13⁴

BRKFST
8⁰ x 11⁰

KITCHEN
10⁰ x 13²

MUD RM

LAUNDRY
9⁰ x 10⁰

HER
WALK-IN
CLOSET

HIS
WALK-IN
CLOSET

RAISED HEARTH

OVEN

COOK
TOP

PANTRY

SEAT

BATH

VANITY

WHIRLPOOL

BATH

LINEN

BEDROOM
11² x 10⁰

FOYER

LIVING RM
20⁰ x 13⁴

DINING
11⁸ x 12⁶

CURB

BEDROOM
11² x 13⁴

STUDY/
BEDROOM
11⁶ x 12⁰

COVERED PORCH

STORAGE

GARAGE
21⁴ x 20⁶

Quote One™
Cost to build? See page 374
to order complete cost estimate
to build this house in your area!

Width 88'-8"
Depth 53'-6"

Design 3348
Square Footage: 2,549

L

● Covered porches front and rear
will be the envy of the neighborhood
when this house is buit. The interior
plan meets family needs perfectly in
well-zoned areas: a sleeping wing

with four bedrooms and two baths,
a living zone with formal and informal gathering space and a work
zone with U-shaped kitchen and
laundry with washroom.

**California Engineered Plans and
California Stock Plans are available
for this home. Call 1-800-521-6797
for more information.**

Design by Home Planners

Design 1364
Square Footage: 1,142

D

● The family working within the confines of a restricted building budget will find this eye-catching traditional ranch home the solution to its housing needs. The living room is free of cross-room traffic and lends itself to effective and flexible furniture placement. The family-dining room is easily served by an efficient kitchen, and offers access to a terrace for outdoor living. The master bedroom has its own private bath.

Width 60'-10"
Depth 28'-10"

Design 9795
Square Footage: 1,298

● This design has plenty of curb appeal. From its gable roof and covered front porch to its large rear deck, this home will brighten any neighborhood. Inside, open planning is the theme in the dining room/great room area, with a cathedral ceiling combining the two areas into a comfortable unit. The kitchen contributes to the openness with its snack bar/work island. Three bedrooms—or two and a study—complete this attractive second home.

Width 59'
Depth 36'

Design by
Donald A. Gardner, Architects, Inc.

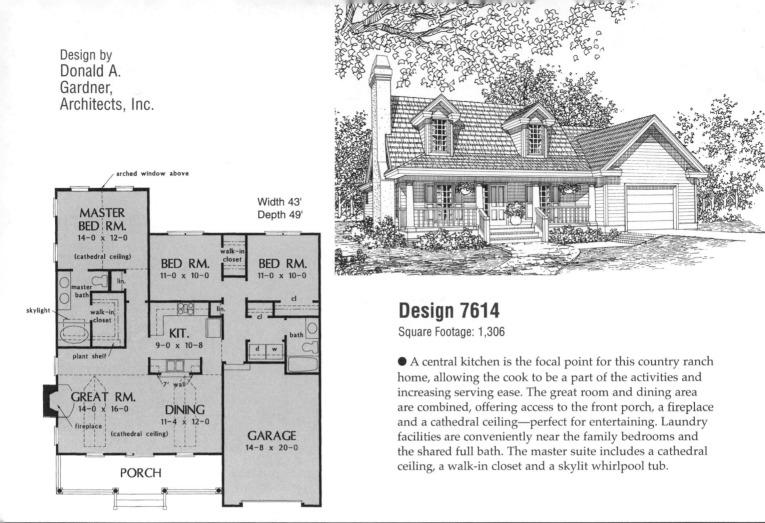

Design by
Donald A.
Gardner,
Architects, Inc.

arched window above

Width 43'
Depth 49'

MASTER
BED RM.
14-0 x 12-0
(cathedral ceiling)

master
bath

skylight

walk-in
closet

plant shelf

BED RM.
11-0 x 10-0

walk-in
closet

lin.

BED RM.
11-0 x 10-0

cl

cl

bath

KIT.
9-0 x 10-8

lin.

d   w

GREAT RM.
14-0 x 16-0

fireplace

7' wall

DINING
11-4 x 12-0
(cathedral ceiling)

GARAGE
14-8 x 20-0

PORCH

Design 7614

Square Footage: 1,306

● A central kitchen is the focal point for this country ranch home, allowing the cook to be a part of the activities and increasing serving ease. The great room and dining area are combined, offering access to the front porch, a fireplace and a cathedral ceiling—perfect for entertaining. Laundry facilities are conveniently near the family bedrooms and the shared full bath. The master suite includes a cathedral ceiling, a walk-in closet and a skylit whirlpool tub.

Design by
Donald A.
Gardner,
Architects, Inc.

Width 41'-8"
Depth 51'-4"

DECK

MASTER
BED RM.
13-8 x 12-0

walk-in
closet

BED RM.
11-0 x 10-0

walk-in
closet

lin.

bath

cl

master
bath

d
w

UTIL.

BED RM.
11-0 x 10-0

KITCHEN
12-0 x 10-0

cl

cl

storage

DINING
10-0 x 11-4

GREAT RM.
15-0 x 18-4
(cathedral ceiling)

fireplace

GARAGE
13-4 x 20-0

PORCH

Design 7615

Square Footage: 1,362

● A covered front porch and a rear deck call for cool summer evenings spent outdoors. Family members and guests will enjoy gathering inside, where the central great room, with its cathedral ceiling and warming fireplace, opens to the dining area and the U-shaped kitchen. Three bedrooms include two with a shared bath and a master suite with a walk-in closet and a large master bath. The utility area is located within the sleeping zone.

Design 3601

Square Footage: 2,424

L

● Here is a home that is tailor-made for a small family or for empty-nesters. The formal dining room features a coffered ceiling and a bay window, while the formal living room is enhanced by a sloped ceiling. A large family room to the rear provides access to a wood deck and is warmed in the cold months by a welcome hearth. The U-shaped kitchen opens into a sunny bayed morning room for casual meals. The laundry and a powder room are nearby. On the right of the plan, the master suite offers a view of the back yard, a spacious walk-in closet and a pampering bath. A nearby office or den has a private porch. Two family bedrooms on the other side of the plan share a bath.

Design by
Home Planners

Cost to build? See page 374 to order complete cost estimate to build this house in your area!

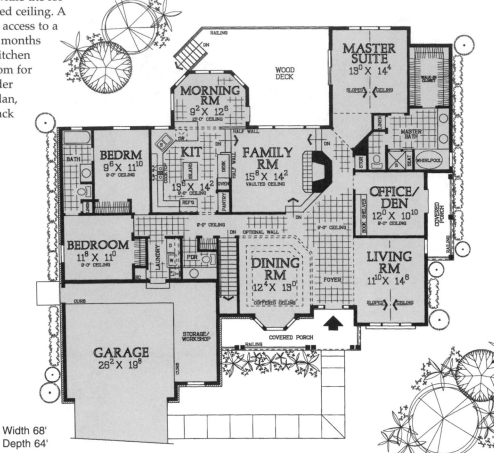

Width 68'
Depth 64'

Design by
Home Planners,
Inc.

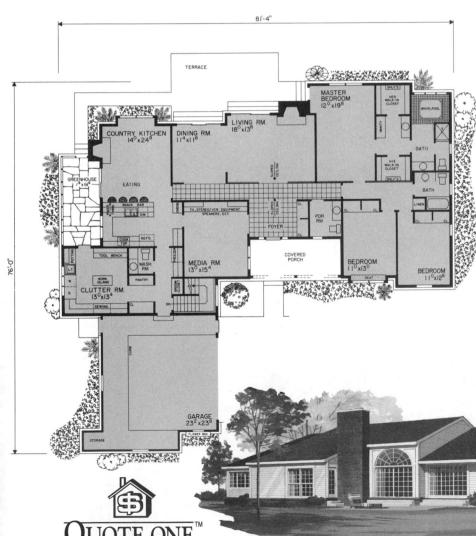

Design 2880

Living Area: 2,758 square feet
Greenhouse: 149 square feet
Total: 2,907 square feet

L **D**

● This comfortable traditional home offers plenty of modern livability. A clutter room off the two-car garage is the perfect space for workbench, sewing, and hobbies. It includes a work island and bench space. Across the hall one finds a modern media room, the perfect place for stereo speakers, videos, and more. A spacious country kitchen off the greenhouse is a cozy gathering place for family and friends, as well as convenient work area. The 149-foot greenhouse itself easily could be the focal point of this home filled with modern amenities. The house also features a formal dining room, living room with fireplace, covered porch, and three bedrooms including a master bedroom suite.

Quote One™

Cost to build? See page 374
to order complete cost estimate
to build this house in your area!

161

Design 1920
Square Footage: 1,600

L

● This home offers a charming exterior with a truly great floor plan. The covered front porch at the entrance heralds outstanding features inside. The sleeping zone has three bedrooms and two full baths. Each of the bedrooms has its own walk-in closet. Note the efficient U-shaped kitchen with the family room and dining room to each side. There is also a laundry with wash room just off the garage. Blueprints for this design include details for both basement and non-basement construction.

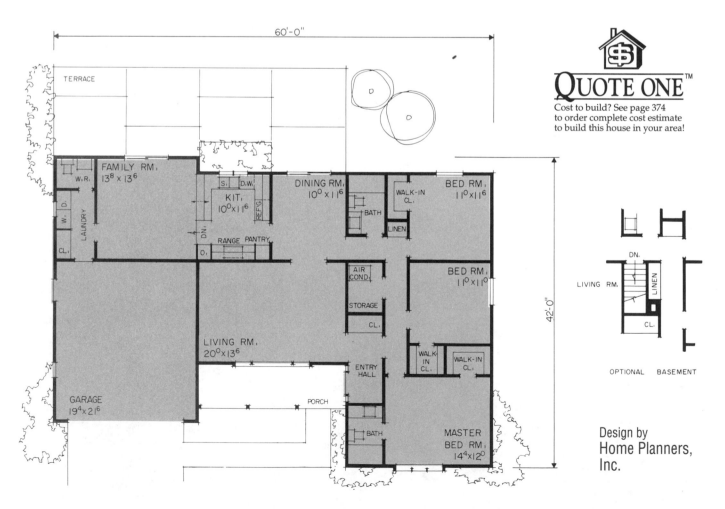

QUOTE ONE™

Cost to build? See page 374 to order complete cost estimate to build this house in your area!

Design by
Home Planners,
Inc.

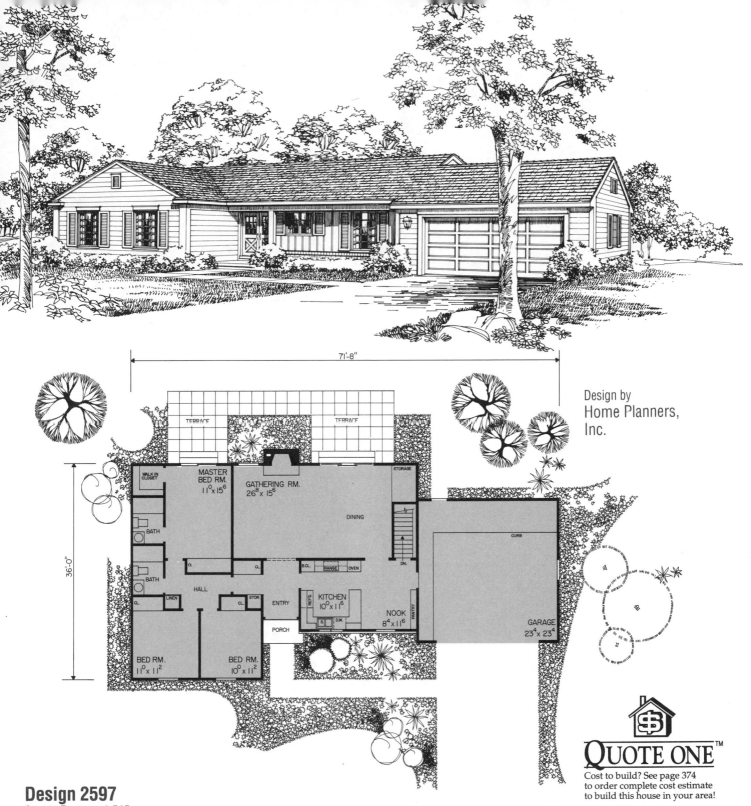

71'-8"

36'-0"

TERRACE   TERRACE

Design by
Home Planners,
Inc.

WALK-IN CLOSET
MASTER BED RM.
11⁰ x 15⁶

GATHERING RM.
26⁸ x 15⁶

STORAGE

BATH

DINING

BATH

CL.   CL.

B.CL.   RANGE   OVEN

DN.

HALL   LINEN   STOR   ENTRY   KITCHEN
10⁰ x 11⁶

CURB

CL.   CL.

REF'S   NOOK
8⁴ x 11⁶   PANTRY

BED RM.
11⁰ x 11²

PORCH   S   D.W.

BED RM.
10⁰ x 11²

GARAGE
23⁴ x 23⁴

QUOTE ONE™

Cost to build? See page 374
to order complete cost estimate
to build this house in your area!

Design 2597
Square Footage: 1,515

L **D**

● Whether it be a starter house you are after, or one in which to spend your retirement years, this pleasing frame home will provide a full measure of pride in ownership. The contrast of vertical and horizontal lines, the double front doors and the coach lamp post at the garage create an inviting exterior. The floor plan functions in an orderly and efficient manner. The 26 foot gathering room has a delightful view of the rear yard and will take care of those formal dining occasions. There are two full baths serving the three bedrooms. There are plenty of storage facilities, two sets of glass doors to the terraces, a fireplace in the gathering room, a basement and an attached two-car garage to act as a buffer against the wind. A delightful home, indeed.

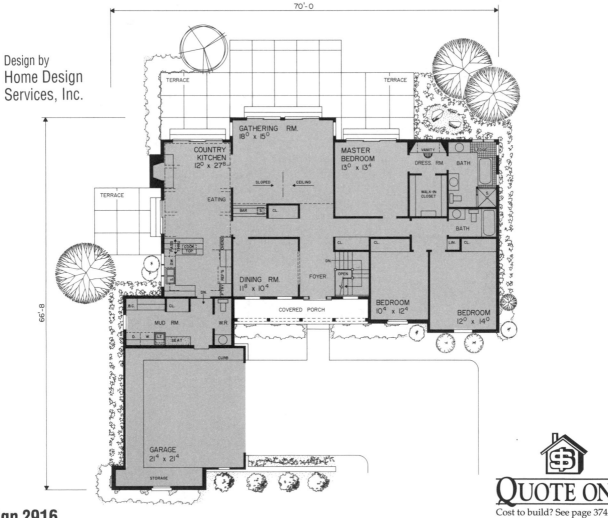

TERRACE

TERRACE

GATHERING RM.
18⁰ x 15⁰

MASTER
BEDROOM
13⁰ x 13⁴

VANITY

DRESS. RM.   BATH

COUNTRY
KITCHEN
12⁰ x 27⁸

WALK-IN
CLOSET

SLOPED   CEILING

EATING

BATH

TERRACE

BAR   S.   CL.

COOK
TOP

CL.   CL.

LIN.   CL.

DINING RM.
11⁸ x 10⁴

FOYER

OPEN
DN.

BEDROOM
10⁴ x 12⁴

BEDROOM
12⁰ x 14⁰

B.C.   CL.

COVERED PORCH

MUD RM.   W.R.

D.   W.   LT.   SEAT

CURB

GARAGE
21⁴ x 21⁴

STORAGE

70'-0

66'-8

Design by
Home Design
Services, Inc.

Design 2916
Square Footage: 2,129

L

● Pride of ownership will be forever yours as the occupant of this Early American styled one-story house. The covered front porch provides a shelter for the inviting panelled front door with its flanking side lites. Designed for fine family living, this three-

bedroom, 2½-bath home offers wonderful formal and informal living patterns. The 27-foot country kitchen has a beamed ceiling and a fireplace. The U-shaped work center is efficient. It is but a step from the mud room area with its laundry equipment, clos-

ets, cupboards, counter space and washroom. There are two dining areas — an informal eating space and a formal separate dining room. The more formal gathering room is spacious with a sloping ceiling and two sets of sliding glass doors to the rear terrace.

Design 3332 Square Footage: 2,168

L

● Nothing completes a traditional-style home quite as well as a country kitchen with a fireplace. Notice the living room with its sloped ceiling and the well-appointed master suite. A handy washroom is near the laundry, just off the garage.

California Engineered Plans and California Stock Plans are available for this home. Call 1-800-521-6797 for more information.

QUOTE ONE™

Cost to build? See page 374 to order complete cost estimate to build this house in your area!

Design by Home Planners, Inc.

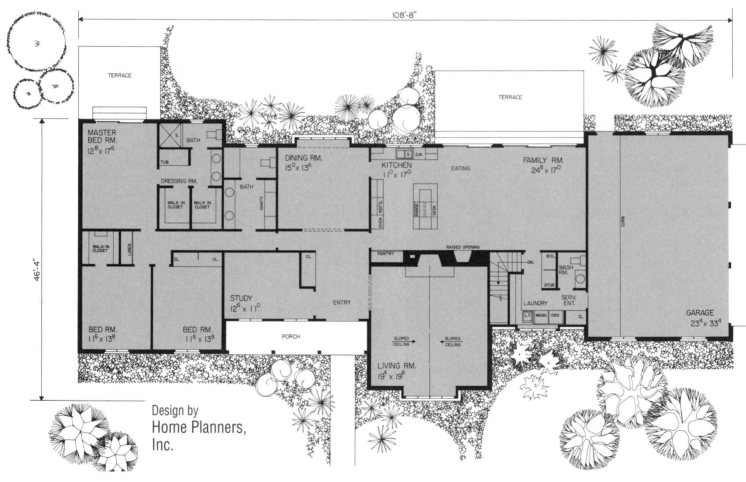

Design by
Home Planners,
Inc.

Design 2767
Square Footage: 3,000

D

● What a sound investment this impressive home will be. And while its value withstands the inflationary pressures of ensuing years, it will serve your family well. It has all the amenities to assure truly pleasurable living. The charming exterior will lend itself to treatment other than the appealing fieldstone, brick and frame shown. Inside, the plan will impress you with large, spacious living areas, formal and informal dining areas, three large bedrooms, two full baths with twin lavatories, walk-in closets and a fine study. The kitchen features an island work center with range and desk. The two fireplaces will warm their surroundings in both areas. Two separate terraces for a variety of uses. Note laundry, wash room and three-car garage with extra curb area.

Design 2181
Square Footage: 2,612

L **D**

● This home is the complete picture of charm.
The interior features are outstanding. It is possible to substitute brick or even siding when
building this home.

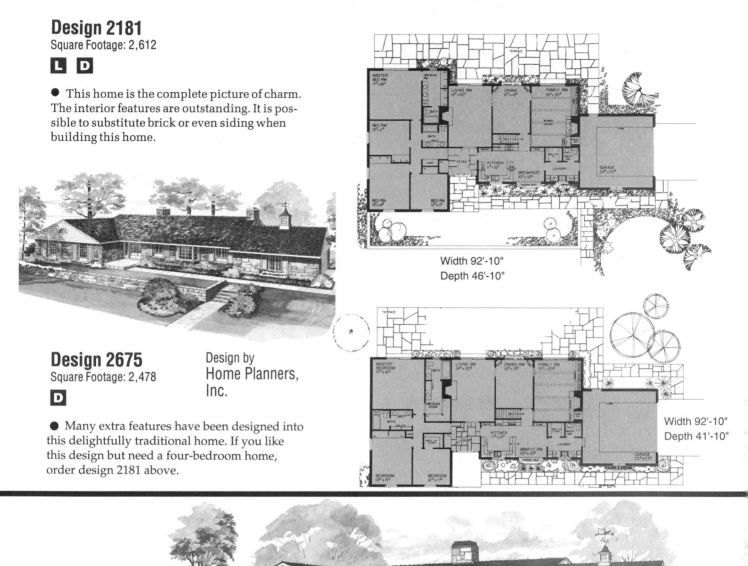

Width 92'-10"
Depth 46'-10"

Width 92'-10"
Depth 41'-10"

Design 2675
Square Footage: 2,478

D

Design by
**Home Planners,
Inc.**

● Many extra features have been designed into
this delightfully traditional home. If you like
this design but need a four-bedroom home,
order design 2181 above.

Design by
**Home Planners,
Inc.**

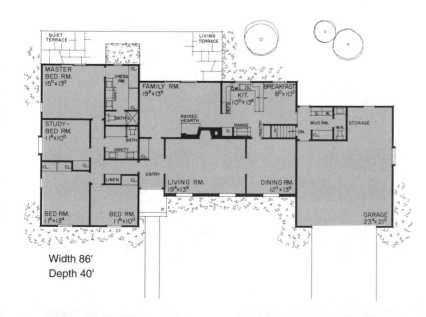

Design 1835
Square Footage: 2,144

L **D**

● Cedar shakes and quarried natural stone are the
exterior materials that adorn this traditional ranch
home. Adding to the appeal of the exterior are the
shutters and the pediment gable. Inside, formal and
informal living spaces are separated from the sleeping zone. The master bedroom includes a private
bath with a dressing room.

Width 86'
Depth 40'

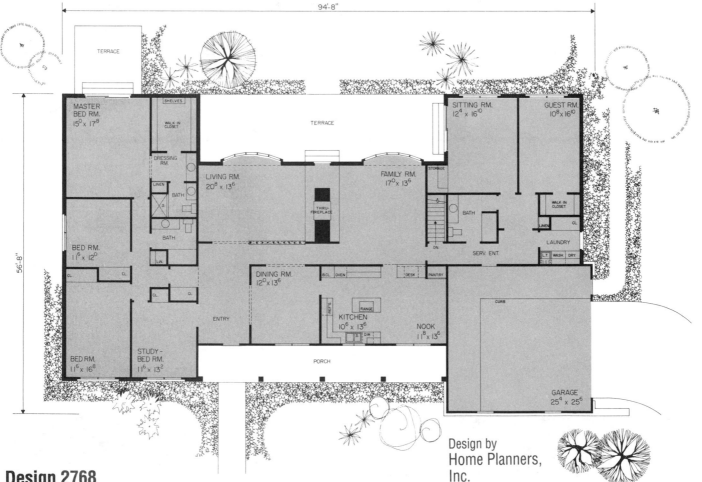

Design 2768

Square Footage: 3,436

● Besides its elegant traditionally styled exterior with its delightfully long covered front porch, this home has an exceptionally livable interior. There is the outstanding four bedroom and two-bath sleeping wing. Then, the efficient front kitchen with island range flanked by the formal dining room and the informal breakfast nook. Separated by the two-way, through-fireplace are the living and family rooms which look out on the rear yard. Worthy of particular note is the development of a potential live-in-relative facility. These two rooms would also serve the large family well as a hobby room and library or additional bedrooms. A full bath is adjacent as well as the laundry. Note curb area in the garage for the storage of outdoor equipment.

Design by
Home Planners

QUOTE ONE®

Cost to build? See page 374
to order complete cost estimate
to build this house in your area!

Design 3693

Square Footage: 3,638

● This diamond in the desert gives new meaning to old style. A courtyard gives way to a covered porch with nooks for sitting and open-air dining. The gracious living room is highlighted by a corner fireplace, while the formal dining room comes with an adjacent butler's pantry and access to the porch dining area. Two sleeping areas are luxurious with whirlpool spas and separate showers. The master suite also boasts an exercise room and a nearby private office. A guest suite has a private entrance and includes another corner fireplace.

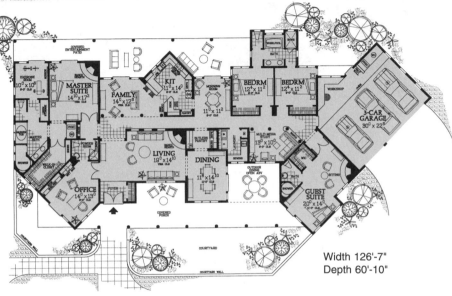

Width 126'-7"
Depth 60'-10"

Width 116'-7"
Depth 77'-5"

Design 3646

Square Footage: 2,966

L

Design by
Home Planners

● Here's a rambling ranch with a unique configuration. Massive double doors at the front entrance are sheltered by a covered porch. The angular living room has a commanding corner fireplace with a raised hearth, access to a huge rear covered patio, and a pass-through to the kitchen. The family room also has access to the patio and is handy to three family bedrooms. At the far end of the plan, the master suite offers a large bedroom and a deluxe private bath as well as a door to the patio.

QUOTE ONE®

Cost to build? See page 374
to order complete cost estimate
to build this house in your area!

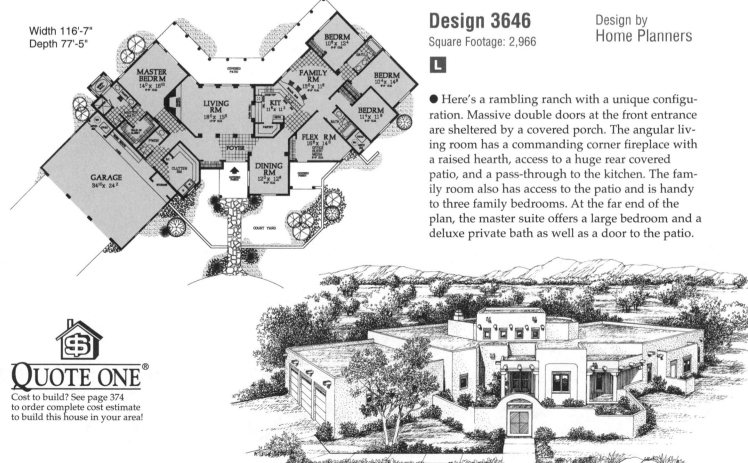

169

Design 1305

Design by
Home Planners

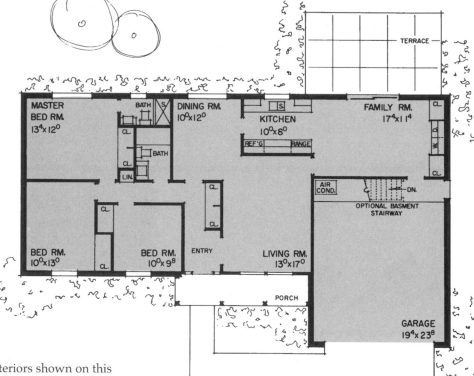

TERRACE

MASTER BED RM.
13⁴x12⁰

BATH

DINING RM.
10⁰x12⁰

KITCHEN
10⁰x8⁰

REF'G   RANGE

FAMILY RM.
17⁴x11⁴

CL.

W.

CL.

BATH

CL.

LIN.

CL.

AIR COND.

DN.

OPTIONAL BASMENT STAIRWAY

BED RM.
10⁰x13⁰

CL.

BED RM.
10⁰x9⁸

ENTRY

CL.

CL.

LIVING RM.
13⁰x17⁰

Design 1305/1382

Square Footage: 1,382

D

● Order blueprints of either of the exteriors shown on this page and you will receive details for building this outstanding floor plan. In less than 1,400 square feet you'll find three bedrooms, two full baths, a separate dining room, a formal living room, a kitchen overlooking the rear yard and an informal family room. In addition, there is the attached two-car garage. Note the location of the stairs when this plan is built with a basement. Each of the exteriors is predominantly brick—the front of Design 1305 features both stone and vertical boards and battens, with brick on the other three sides. Notice the double front doors on the French design, 1382. Multi-pane windows and shutters add to the charm of both designs.

PORCH

GARAGE
19⁴x23⁸

Width 62'-10"
Depth 36'-10"

Design 1382

170

Design 3660

Square Footage: 2,086

L

● This home exhibits wonderful dual-use space in the sunken sitting room and media area. Anchoring the ends of this spacious living zone are the raised-hearth fireplace and the entertainment center. The outstanding kitchen has an informal breakfast bay and looks over the snack bar to the family area. To the rear of the plan, a few steps from the kitchen and functioning with the upper patio, is the formal dining room. Through the archway are two children's bedrooms and a bath with twin vanities. At the far end of the plan is the master suite. It has a sitting area with fine, natural light. A few steps away, French doors open to the covered master patio.

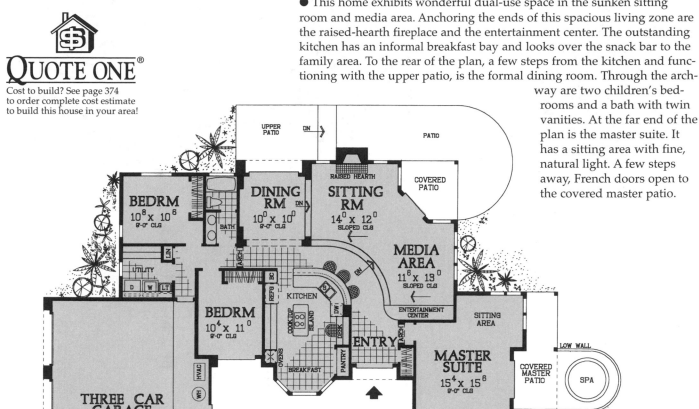

Width 82'
Depth 58'-4"

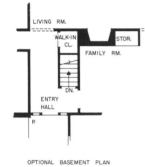

OPTIONAL BASEMENT PLAN

LIVING RM.

WALK-IN CL.   STOR.

FAMILY RM.

DN.

ENTRY HALL

Design 3144
Square Footage: 1,760

● If you are short of space and searching for a home that is long on both good looks and livability, search no more! This impressive L-shaped home measures merely 56'-5" in width. Therefore, it qualifies for placement on a relatively narrow building site. Of course, with land costs so high, the purchase of a smaller and less expensive building site can significantly reduce the building budget. Outstanding livability is apparent with three bedrooms, two baths, a formal living room, an excellent kitchen, a laundry room and a huge storage area in the garage.

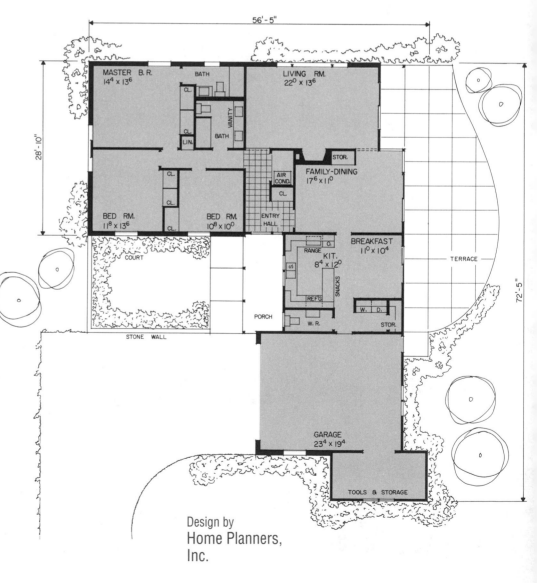

56'-5"

28'-10"

72'-5"

MASTER B.R. 14⁴ x 13⁶

BATH

LIVING RM. 22⁰ x 13⁶

CL.

CL.

VANITY

BATH

LIN.

STOR.

FAMILY-DINING 17⁶ x 11⁰

AIR COND.

CL.

CL.

CL.

BED RM. 11⁸ x 13⁶

CL.

BED RM. 10⁸ x 10⁰

ENTRY HALL

BREAKFAST 11⁰ x 10⁴

TERRACE

COURT

RANGE

O.

KIT. 8⁴ x 12⁰

SNACKS

REF'G

W. D.

PORCH

W.R.

STOR.

STONE WALL

GARAGE 23⁴ x 19⁴

TOOLS & STORAGE

Design by
Home Planners, Inc.

172

Design by Home Planners

Design 1186

Square Footage: 1,872

● This appealing home has an interesting and practical floor plan. It is cleverly zoned to cater to the living patterns of both the children and the parents. The children's wing projects to the rear and functions with the informal family room. The master bedroom and its private bath are located at the other end of the home, with the formal living and dining rooms and kitchen in between.

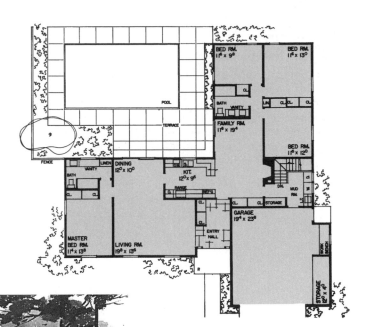

Width 64'
Depth 64'

Width 97'-2"
Depth 57'-4"

QUOTE ONE®

Cost to build? See page 374 to order complete cost estimate to build this house in your area!

Design by Home Planners

Design 3657

Square Footage: 2,344

● A magnificent arched entry opens to a spacious tiled foyer that invites guests toward a gathering room with fireplace and views to the rear property. Decorative half-walls define the formal dining area, which offers rear patio access. The U-shaped kitchen is equipped to serve formal and informal occasions, and includes a snack counter for mini-meals. An office with a nearby powder room could serve as a guest suite. Sleeping quarters include an outstanding master suite, with His and Hers walk-in closets, step-down shower, knee-space vanity and whirlpool tub.

Design 1952

Square Footage: 2,705

● This delightful home has been designed for country-estate living. L-shaped, this traditional will be a worthy addition to any building site. Its pleasing proportions are almost breathtaking. They seem to foretell the tremendous amount of livability its inhabitants are to enjoy. The interior zoning hardly could be improved upon. The children's bedrooms function together in a wing with their own bath. There is a large master bedroom suite. It features Mr. and Mrs. dressing rooms, each with a vanity, with a full bath in the middle. The dining room is nestled between the living and family rooms. Both of these living areas have a beamed ceiling and a fireplace. All of the work area, kitchen, breakfast room, laundry and washroom, is in the front of the plan.

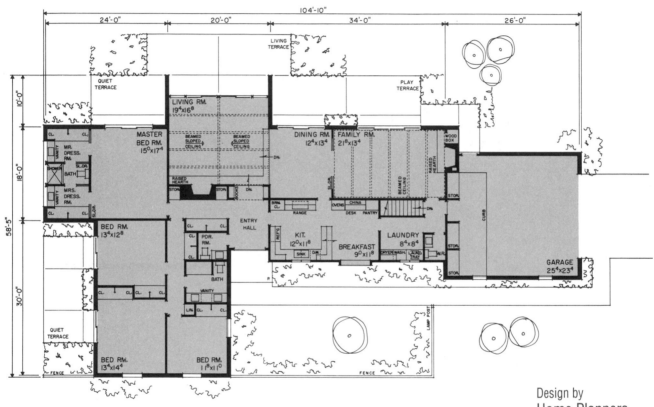

Design by
Home Planners,
Inc.

Quote One ®

Cost to build? See page 374
to order complete cost estimate
to build this house in your area!

Design by
Home Planners

Design 3613

Square Footage: 2,407

L

● A projecting portico provides shelter as well as an
appealing front entrance. At the center of the plan is the
family room, with its sloped ceiling, raised-hearth fireplace, entertainment center and access to the covered
patio. This plan offers the increasingly popular feature of
the split sleeping facilities. Two family bedrooms share a
bath at the front of the house, with the master suite
placed at the opposite corner. Here the focal point is the
raised-hearth fireplace, which can be enjoyed on three
sides—even from the whirlpool!

Width 65'-4"
Depth 55'

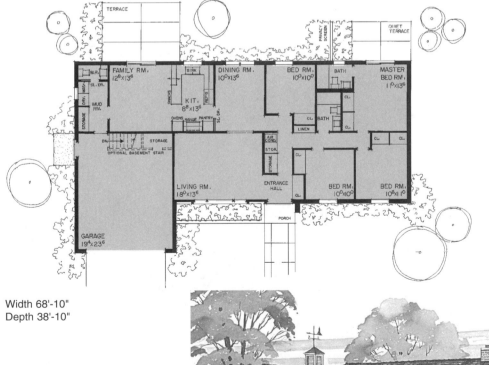

Design 1896

Square Footage: 1,690

● Complete family livability is provided in this exceptional floor plan.
The entrance hall leads to the sleeping zone on the right and to the formal living and dining rooms on the
left. The layout culminates in a casual
living area with a U-shaped kitchen
and a family room that accesses a rear
terrace. Three bedrooms will sleep
children and guests, while the master
bedroom has a private bath and
access to a its own terrace.

Width 68'-10"
Depth 38'-10"

Design by
Home Planners

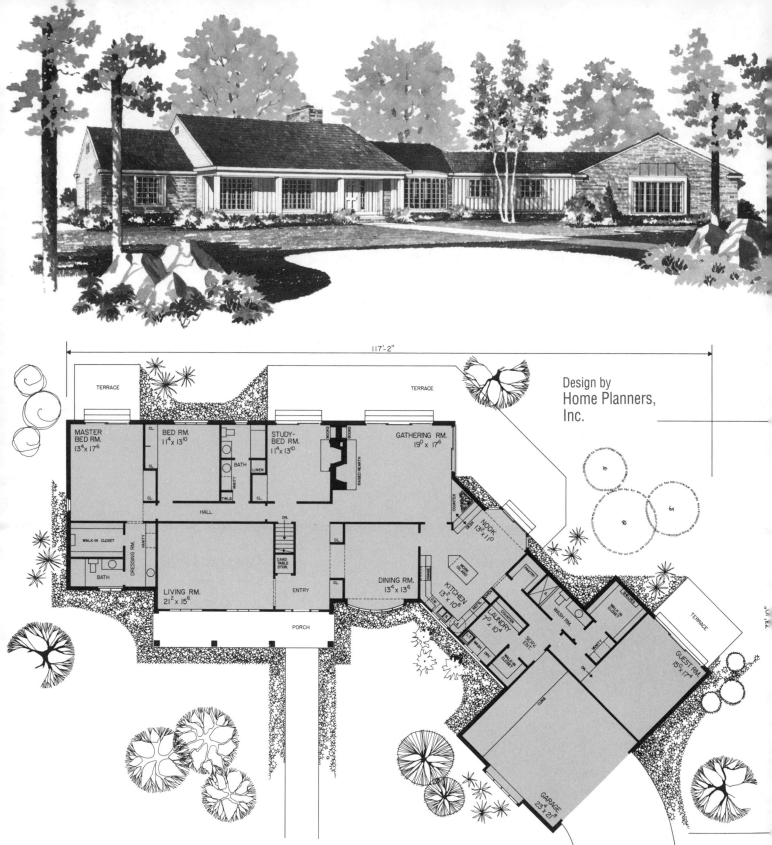

Design 2739
Square Footage: 3,313

● If you and your family are looking for new living patterns, try to envision your days spent in this traditionally styled home. Its Early American flavor is captured by effective window and door treatment, cornice work and porch pillars. Its zoning is interesting.

The spacious interior leaves nothing to be desired. There are three bedrooms and two full baths in the sleeping area. A quiet, formal living room is separated from the other living areas. The gathering and dining rooms are adjacent to each other and function with

the excellent kitchen and its breakfast eating area. Note work island, pantry and pass-thru. Then, there is an extra guest room sunken one step. A live-in relative would enjoy the privacy of this room. Full bath is nearby. This is definitely a home for all to enjoy.

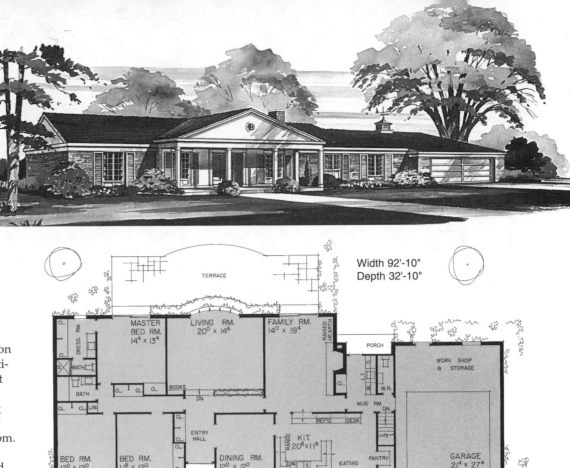

Design by
Home Planners

Design 1788
Square Footage: 2,218

L **D**

● "Charm" is one of the many words which may be used to describe this fine design. In addition to its exterior appeal, it has a practical and functional floor plan. Front entrance details are enhanced by columns supporting the projecting pediment gable. The focal point of the interior is the formal living room. It is, indeed, dramatic with its bay window overlooking the back yard.

Width 92'-10"
Depth 32'-10"

TERRACE

MASTER BED RM. 14⁴ x 13⁴

LIVING RM. 20⁰ x 14⁶

FAMILY RM. 14⁰ x 19⁴

RAISED HEARTH

PORCH

WORK SHOP & STORAGE

DRESS. RM.

BATH

BATH

CL. CL. CL.

BOOKS

DN.

CL.

MUD RM.

DN.

CL. CL. LIN

BED RM. 12⁰ x 12⁰

BED RM. 11⁹ x 12⁰

CL. CL. CL.

ENTRY HALL

DINING RM. 12⁰ x 12⁰

REF'G DESK

RANGE KIT. 20⁸ x 11⁸

EATING

PANTRY

GARAGE 21⁴ x 27⁴

PORCH

PORCH

Design 3525
Square Footage: 2,158

● Stately columns and a covered porch welcome you to this Greek Revival-style home. Impressive in any setting, it conceals an interior with great livability. The tiled foyer leads to a hallway separating the living areas from the sleeping zone and a media room. The kitchen is centrally located to serve the formal areas at the front of the house, the family room in the rear and the nearby bayed breakfast nook. The master suite includes a walk-in closet, garden tub and sit-down vanity.

COVERED PORCH

FAMILY ROOM 20⁰ x 12⁰

MASTER BEDRM 12⁰ x 16⁰

MASTER BATH

LAUNDRY

LINEN

KITCHEN 18⁴ x 12⁰

NOOK 7⁰ x 8⁰

W.I.C.

VANITY

BATH

DINING ROOM 13² x 11⁴

BEDRM 12⁰ x 11⁰

MEDIA ROOM 11¹⁰ x 11⁰

DN.

LIVING ROOM 19⁰ x 13⁰

FOYER

Width 54' 8"
Depth 56' 4'''

COVERED PORCH

Design by
Home Planners

Master
Bedroom
14⁰x18⁰

Deck

Keeping
Room
14³x12⁹

Brkfst
10³x9⁰

Great Room
18⁰x15⁰

Dining
Room
11⁹x12⁹

Bedroom
No. 2
13³x12⁹

Kitchen
14³x14⁰

Bedroom
No. 3
12³x13³

Two Car
Garage
22⁰x24⁰

Width 68'-3"
Depth 78'-3"

Design 7806

Square Footage: 2,598

● The overall design of this home is reminiscent of an English country cottage. From the double-door entry, columns add an elegance to the foyer and the great room with its warming fireplace. The formal dining room leads to the L-shaped kitchen. A bayed breakfast nook opens to a wonderful keeping room with outdoor access and a fireplace. The bayed master suite features a luxurious bath with a walk-in closet. This home is designed with a basement foundation.

Design 7820

Square Footage: 2,127

● Stone and stucco, arched windows and shutters create an attractive facade. Inside, graceful columns define an elegant formal dining room and lead to the great room, which is enhanced by windows and access to the rear porch. The kitchen/breakfast nook area is highlighted by a sunny bay window. An office or guest bedroom is located for privacy. The sleeping zone includes two family bedrooms and a luxurious master suite. A deluxe bath, two walk-in closets and private access to the rear porch make this a delightful retreat for the homeowner. This home is designed with a basement foundation.

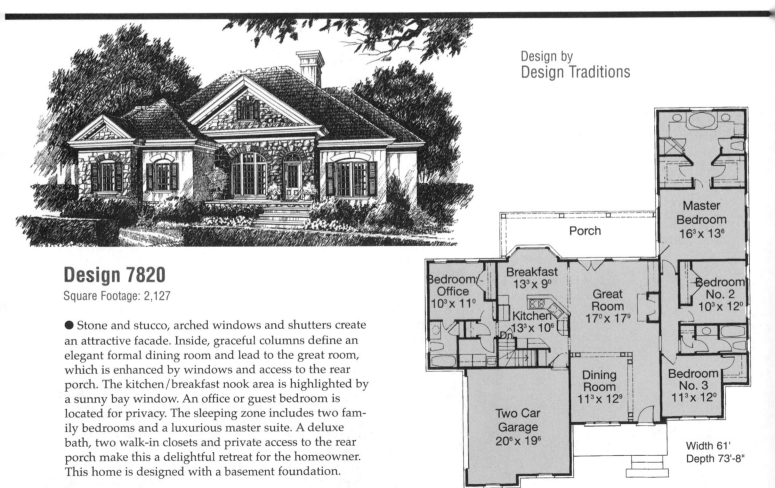

Porch

Master
Bedroom
16³ x 13⁶

Breakfast
13³ x 9⁰

Great
Room
17⁰ x 17⁹

Bedroom
No. 2
10³ x 12⁰

Bedroom/
Office
10³ x 11⁰

Kitchen
13³ x 10⁶

Dining
Room
11³ x 12⁹

Bedroom
No. 3
11³ x 12⁰

Two Car
Garage
20⁶ x 19⁶

Width 61'
Depth 73'-8"

Design 3327

Square Footage: 2,881

L **D**

QUOTE ONE®

Cost to build? See page 374
to order complete cost estimate
to build this house in your area!

Design by
Home Planners

● The massive hipped roof of this home creates an imposing facade, while varying roof planes and projecting gables enhance its appeal. A central, high-ceilinged foyer routes traffic efficiently to the formal, informal and sleeping zones of the house. Note the sliding glass doors that provide access to the back yard. A built-in china cabinet and planter unit in the dining room are fine decor features. The gourmet island kitchen opens into a bumped-out conversation room, which will be a favorite gathering place for family and friends. The spacious master bedroom boasts a tray ceiling, access to the rear yard and an abundance of wall space for effective and flexible furniture arrangement.

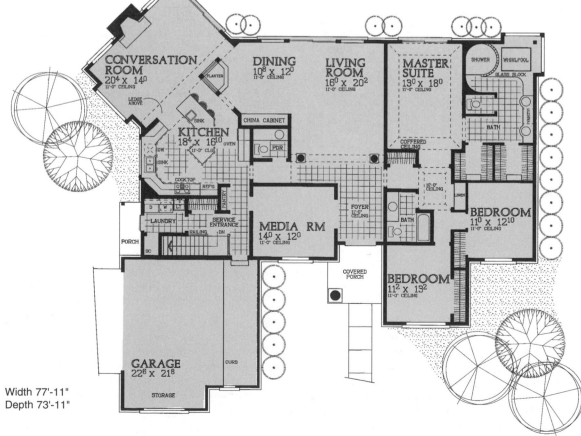

Width 77'-11"
Depth 73'-11"

179

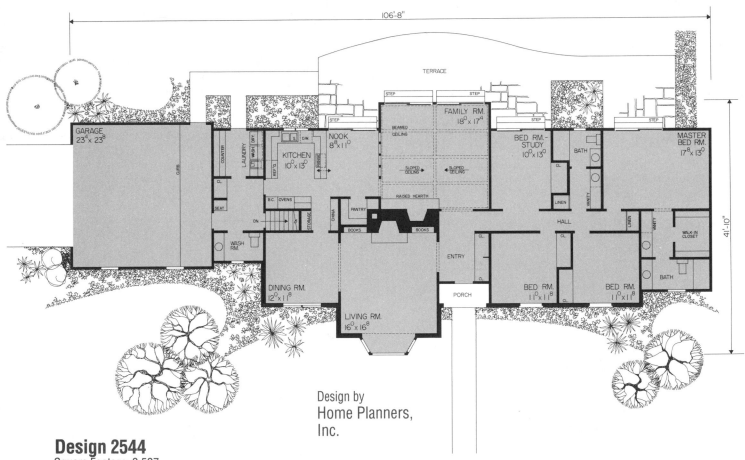

TERRACE

106'-8"

41'-10"

GARAGE
23⁴ x 23⁸

LAUNDRY

KITCHEN
10⁰ x 13⁰

NOOK
8⁸ x 11⁰

FAMILY RM.
18⁰ x 17⁴

BEAMED CEILING

SLOPED CEILING

RAISED HEARTH

BED RM.- STUDY
10⁰ x 13⁰

BATH

MASTER BED RM.
17⁸ x 13⁰

LINEN

VANITY

B.C. OVENS

STORAGE

CHINA

PANTRY

BOOKS

BOOKS

HALL

LINEN

VANITY

WALK-IN CLOSET

DN

WASH RM.

DINING RM.
12⁰ x 11⁸

ENTRY

PORCH

BED RM.
11⁰ x 11⁸

BED RM.
11⁰ x 11⁸

BATH

LIVING RM.
16⁰ x 16⁸

Design by
Home Planners, Inc.

Design 2544
Square Footage: 2,527

D

● A blend of exterior materials enhance the beauty of this fine home. Here, the masonry material used is fieldstone to contrast effectively with the horizontal siding. You may substitute brick or quarried stone if you wish. Adding appeal are the various projections and their roof planes, the window treatment and the recessed front entrance. Two large living areas highlight the interior. Each has a fireplace. The homemaking effort will be easily and enjoyably dispatched with such features as the efficient kitchen, the walk-in pantry, the handy storage areas, the first floor laundry and extra bedrooms, two baths with vanities and good closet accommodations. There's a basement for additional storage and recreation activities.

Design by
Home Planners

Design 1346
Square Footage: 1,644

● Whether you enter through the service door of the attached garage or through the centered front entry, your appreciation of this plan will grow. The mud room area is certainly an outstanding feature. Traffic flows from this area to the informal family room with its fireplace and access to the rear terrace.

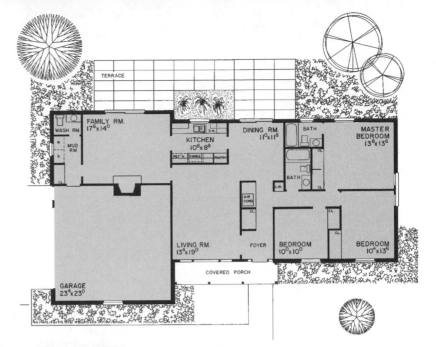

Width 68'-10"
Depth 38'-10"

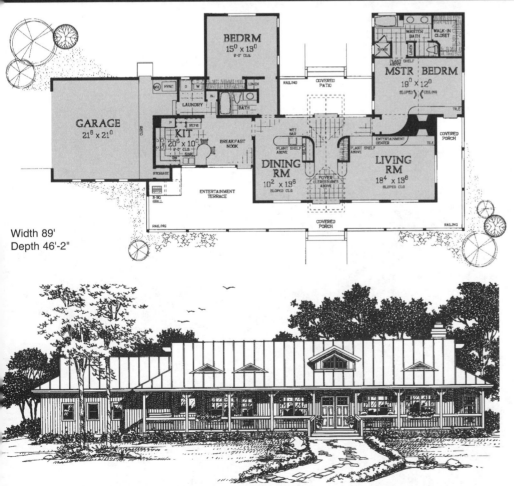

Width 89'
Depth 46'-2"

Quote One®
Cost to build? See page 374 to order complete cost estimate to build this house in your area!

Design by
Home Planners

Design 3466
Square Footage: 1,800

L **D**

● Small but inviting, this one-story ranch-style farmhouse is the perfect choice for a small family or empty-nesters. Inside, the hearth-warmed living room and formal dining room each have plant shelves and built-ins to enhance livability. A well-appointed bath with a dual vanity and a walk-in closet highlight the master suite. The additional bedroom has its own bath with linen storage. A clever bar area separates the nearby kitchen from the breakfast nook.

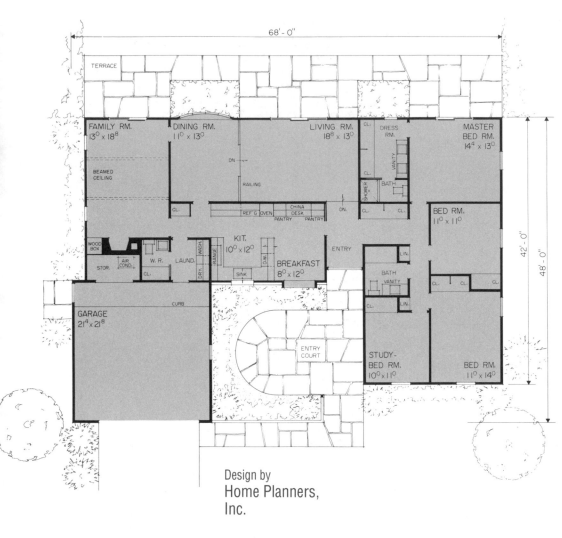

Design 1950
Square Footage: 2,076

● If you were to count the various reasons that will cause excitement over the prospect of moving into this home, you would certainly be able to compile a long list. You might head your list with the grace and charm of the front exterior. You'd certainly have to comment on the delightful entry court, the picket fence and lamp post and the recessed front entrance. Comments about the interior obviously would begin with the listing of such features as: spaciousness galore; sunken living room; separate dining room; family room with beamed ceiling; excellent kitchen with pass-thru to breakfast room; two full baths, plus washroom, etc.

Design by
Home Planners,
Inc.

Design 2317
Square Footage: 3,161

● Here's a rambling English manor with its full measure of individuality. Its fine proportions and irregular shape offer even the most casual of passers-by delightful views of fine architecture. The exterior boasts an interesting use of varying materials. In addition to the brick work, there is vertical siding, wavy-edged horizontal siding and stucco. Three massive chimneys provide each of the three major wings with a fireplace. The overhanging roof provides the cover for the long front porch. Note the access to both the foyer as well as the service hall. The formal living room, with its sloping beamed ceiling, and fireplace flanked by bookshelves and cabinets, will be cozy, indeed. Study the rest of the plan. It's outstanding. Don't miss the three fireplaces and three full baths.

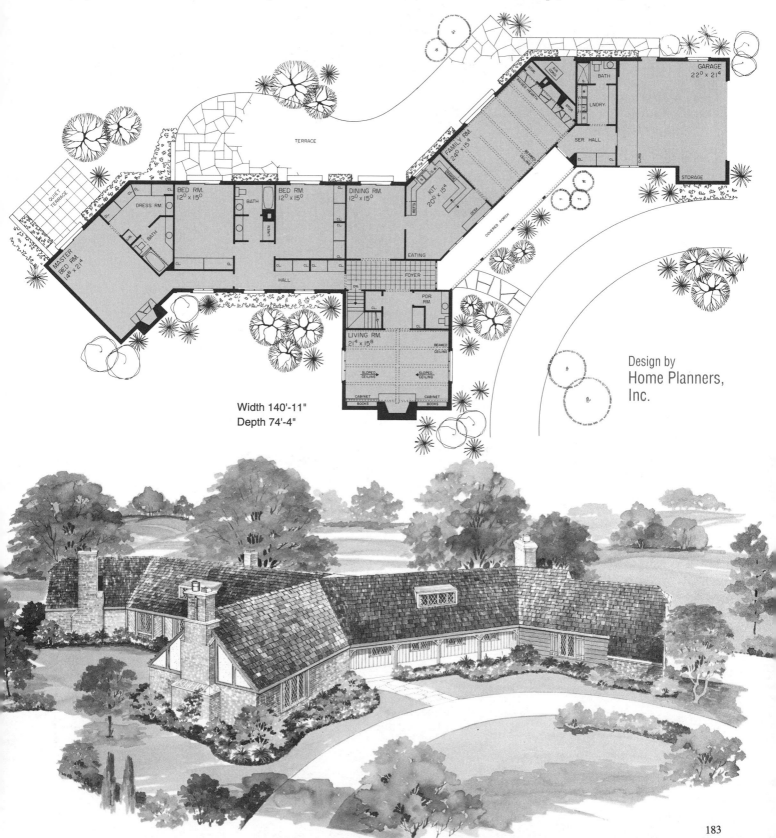

Width 140'-11"
Depth 74'-4"

Design by
Home Planners,
Inc.

Design 2604
Square Footage: 1,956

L

● A feature that will be most appreciated is this home's 26-foot-wide country kitchen. It is enhanced by an island counter. Beamed ceilings, a fireplace and sliding glass doors add to the cozy atmosphere of this area. The laundry, dining room and entry hall are but a step away. The big keeping room also has a fireplace and can function with the terrace. It is sure to provide well for relaxing as well as entertaining.

Design by
Home Planners, Inc.

74'-10"

TERRACE

COUNTRY KITCHEN
12⁰ x 10⁴ & 14⁴ x 12⁴

KEEPING RM.
20⁴ x 17⁰

COUNTER

BEAMED CEILING

PANTRY

STOR.
B.C.

LAUNDRY
DRY. WASH.

CL.

ENTRY HALL

CL. CL. LINEN

WASH RM.

DINING RM.
12⁰ x 10⁸

AIR COND.
BATH

BED RM.
11⁰ x 10⁰

VANITY

GARAGE
23⁴ x 23⁴

PORCH

BATH

52'-10"

CL. CL.

CL. CL.

BED RM.
11⁰ x 12⁸

BED RM.
12⁰ x 12⁸

KEEPING RM.

ENTRY

CL. CL. LINEN BAR

BED RM.

DN.

BATH

B.

OPTIONAL BASEMENT

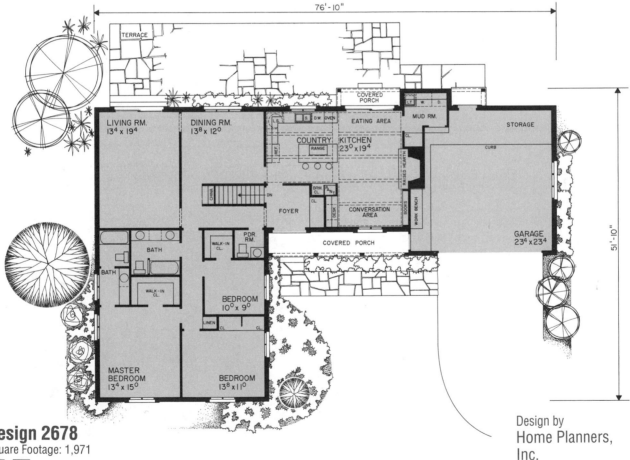

Design 2678

Square Footage: 1,971

L **D**

● If you've ever desired to have a large country kitchen in your home then this is the design for you. The features of this room are many, indeed. Begin your long list with the island range with snack bar, pantry and broom closets, eating area with sliding glass doors leading to a covered porch, adjacent mud room with laundry facilities and access to the garage, raised hearth fireplace and conversation area with built-in desk on one side and shelves on the other. Now that is some multi-purpose room! There are formal living and dining rooms, too. Two and a half baths, all grouped around the living and sleeping areas. Review the rest of this plan which is surrounded by a delightful Tudor facade. It will surely prove to be a remarkable home to live in for the entire family.

Design by
Home Planners, Inc.

Design by
Home Planners

Width 120'
Depth 76'

Design 3329

Square Footage: 3,169

L

● Projecting wood beams, called vigas,
add a decorative touch to this Santa Fe
exterior. To the left of the foyer, the living
room features a corner fireplace and a
music alcove. The beam-ceilinged family
room offers a second fireplace and outdoor access. The kitchen includes yet
another fireplace, along with a snack bar
and a sunny morning room. The master
suite pampers with a huge bedroom and a
luxury bath. At the opposite end of the
home are three family bedrooms, two full
baths and a study with a built-in bookcase.

Design 3669

Square Footage: 3,959

Design by
Home Planners

● This Santa Fe-style home is perfect in the Southwest and
eye-catching anywhere. Covered porches abound—at the
entry and the back as well as off the family room and the
master suite. Corner fireplaces add warmth to the elegant
sunken living room, the master bedroom and the spacious
family room. A wonderful kitchen serves the dining room
and a breakfast nook, while a bookcase-lined study is set
apart as a peaceful retreat. The master suite includes an
exercise room, a separate dressing area, skylights and a
deluxe bath.

Width 107'-2"
Depth 81'-3"

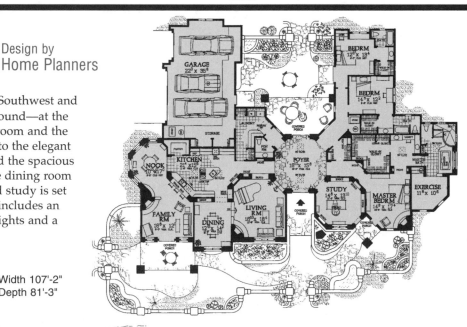

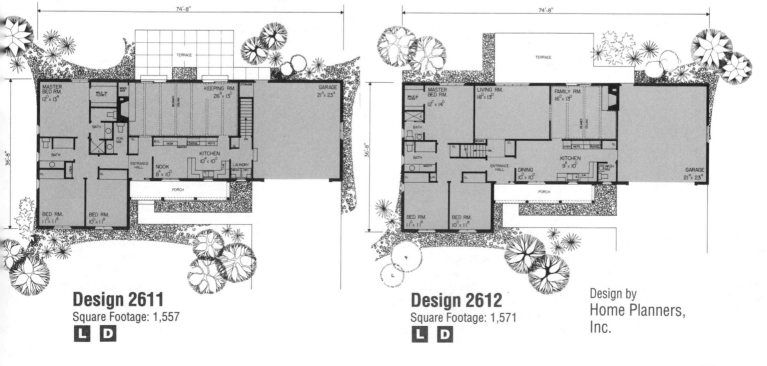

● Here is a unique series of designs with three charming exterior adaptations: Southern Colonial, Western Ranch and French Provincial. A distinctive floor plan accompanys each. Each is less than 1,600 square feet.

● If your preference is the floor plan with the 26-foot keeping room, you should order blueprints for Design 2611. Of course, the details for each of the three delightful exteriors will be included. If the plan with the living, dining and family rooms is your favorite, order blueprints for Design 2612 and get details for all three exteriors.

● There are many points of similarity in the two designs. Each has a fireplace, 2 ½ baths, sliding glass doors to a rear terrace, a master bedroom with a walk-in closet and a private bath with a stall shower and a basement.

Design 2611
Square Footage: 1,557
L D

Design 2612
Square Footage: 1,571
L D

Design by
Home Planners, Inc.

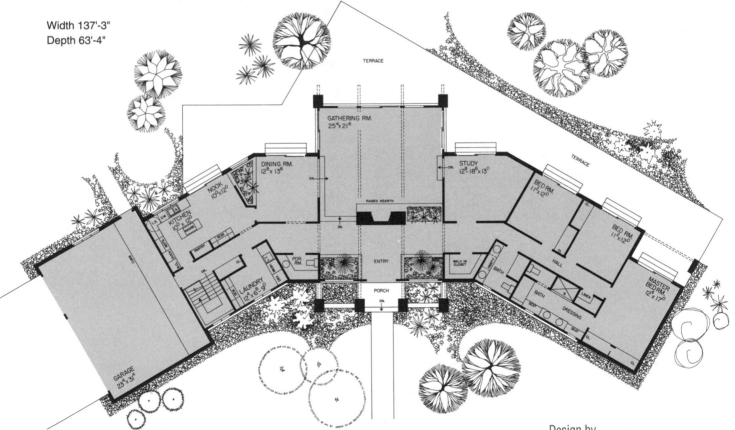

Width 137'-3"
Depth 63'-4"

TERRACE

GATHERING RM.
25⁴ x 21⁶

DINING RM.
12⁸ x 13⁶

STUDY
12⁸-18⁶ x 13⁰

TERRACE

NOOK
10⁴ x 12⁰

BED RM.
11³ x 12⁰

KITCHEN
10³ x 12⁰

RAISED HEARTH

BED RM.
11³ x 12⁰

PANTRY

PDR. RM.

ENTRY

WALK IN CLOSET

HALL

LAUNDRY
12⁴ x 6⁹

BATH

BATH

LINEN

MASTER BED RM.
12⁴ x 17⁰

PORCH

DRESSING

GARAGE
23⁴ x 3¹¹

Design by
Home Planners,
Inc.

Design 2720
Square Footage: 3,130

● A raised hearth fireplace lights up the sunken gathering room which is exceptionally large and located at the very center of this home! For more living space, a well-located study and formal dining room each having a direct entrance to the gathering room. Plus a kitchen with all the right fea-

tures . . . an island range, pantry, built-in desk and separate breakfast nook. There's an extended terrace, too . . . accessible from every room! And a master suite with double closets, dressing room and private bath. Plus two family bedrooms, a first-floor laundry and lots of storage

space. A basement too, for additional space. This is a liveable home! You can entertain easily or you can hide-out with a good book. Study this plan with your family and pick out your favorite features. Don't miss the dra-matic front entry planting areas, or the extra curb area in the garage.

Design 2534
Square Footage: 3,262

● The angular wings of this ranch home surely contribute to the unique character of the exterior. These wings effectively balance what is truly a dramatic and inviting front entrance. Massive masonry walls support the wide overhanging roof with its exposed wood beams. The patterned double front doors are surrounded by delight- ful expanses of glass. The raised plant- ers and the masses of quarried stone (make it brick if you prefer) enhance the exterior appeal. Inside, a distinc- tive and practical floor plan stands ready to shape and serve the living patterns of the active family. The spa- cious entrance hall highlights sloped ceiling and an attractive open stairway to the lower level recreation area. An impressive fireplace and an abundance of glass are features of the big gather- ing room. Interestingly shaped dining room and study flank this main living area. The large kitchen offers many of the charming aspects of the family- kitchen of yesteryear. The bedroom wing has a sunken master suite.

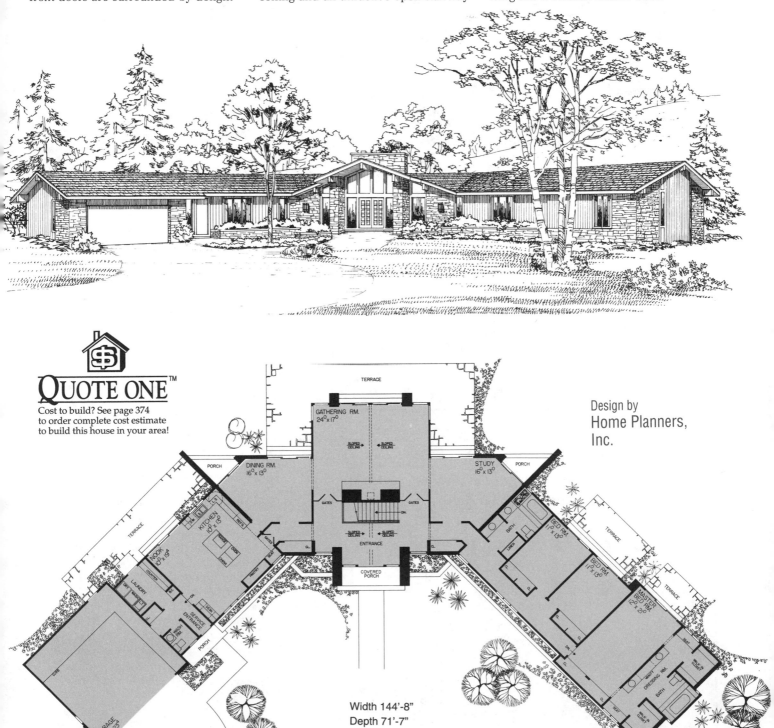

QUOTE ONE™
Cost to build? See page 374 to order complete cost estimate to build this house in your area!

Design by
Home Planners, Inc.

Width 144'-8"
Depth 71'-7"

European Essence:
European- & English-inspired designs

Copyright 1992 Stephen S. Fuller, Inc.

PORCH

BREAKFAST
10'-0" X 10'-0"

GREAT ROOM
16'-0" X 18'-0"

MASTER BEDROOM
15'-0" X 14'-0"

W.I.C.

MASTER BATH

POWDER

KITCHEN
14'-0" X 11'-4"

BEDROOM NO. 2
11'-2" X 11'-0"

FOYER
5'-0" X 9'-0"

DINING ROOM
10'-6" X 13'-0"

BEDROOM
NO. 3
10'-6" X 10'-0"

BATH

LAUND
5'-2" X
10'-6"

DN.

TWO CAR GARAGE
20'-4" X 19'-4"

WIDTH 60'
DEPTH 58'-6"

Design by
Design Traditions

QUOTE ONE®
Cost to build? See page 374
to order complete cost estimate
to build this house in your area!

Design 9872
Square Footage: 1,815

● The approach to this European home has an inviting quality about it. The stucco exterior with arched detail on the windows furthers the feel of style and grace while the front door adds a majestic touch to an already stately presence. Inside, the foyer opens into the great room with a vaulted ceiling and a dining room defined by an asymmetrical column arrangement. Kitchen tasks are made easy with this home's step-saving kitchen and breakfast bar. Nestled away at the opposite end of the home, the master suite combines perfect solitude with elegant luxury. Features include a double-door entry, a tray ceiling, niche detail and a private rear deck. Additional bedrooms and a bath are provided for children and guests. This home is designed with a basement foundation.

Design 9904

Square Footage: 2,090

● People will surely stop to admire this exquisite house. Its European styling will work well in a variety of environments. As for livability, this plan has it all. Begin with the front door which opens into the dining and great rooms—the latter complete with a fireplace and doors that open onto the back porch. The kitchen combines with the breakfast nook to create ample space for meals and quiet socializing—whatever your fancy. This plan incorporates four bedrooms; you may want to use one bedroom as an office and another as a study. The master bedroom houses a fabulous bath; be sure to check out the walk-in closets and spa tub. This home is designed with a basement foundation.

Width 61'
Depth 72'

Quote One®
Cost to build? See page 374 to order complete cost estimate to build this house in your area!

MASTER BATH

MASTER BEDRDOOM
16'-4" X 13'-6"

PORCH

BEDROOM NO. 2
10'-4" X 12'-0"

BREAKFAST
13'-4" X 9'-0"

BEDROOM/
OFFICE
10'-4" X 11'-0"

GREAT ROOM
17'-0" X 17'-8"

KITCHEN
13'-4" X 10'-6"

BATH

BATH

LAUNDRY

DN.

DINING ROOM

BEDROOM/
STUDY

TWO CAR GARAGE
20'-6" X 19'-6"

Design by
Design Traditions

![Quote One logo]

Quote One®

Cost to build? See page 374 to order complete cost estimate to build this house in your area!

Design by
Design Traditions

Design 9808
Square Footage: 2,902

● To highlight the exterior of this brick home, window jack arches have been artfully combined with arched transoms, gables and a sweeping roofline. The foyer opens into the formal dining room, which is highlighted by the vaulted ceiling treatment and the stunning triple window. Also open to the foyer is the great room with its dramatic tray ceiling. The accommodating kitchen, with a generous work island/breakfast bar, adjoins the breakfast area with its bright bay window and the keeping room with a fireplace, a vaulted ceiling and abundant windows. Two bedrooms and a connecting bath offering private vanities complete the rooms set along the front. The master suite, with its garden bath and glass sitting room, provides a quiet and peaceful retreat from the noise and pace of the day. This home is designed with a basement foundation.

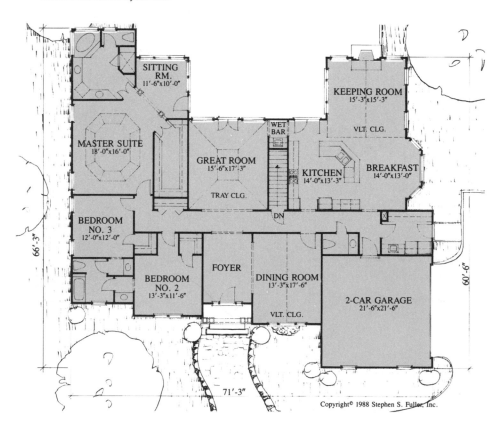

Copyright© 1988 Stephen S. Fuller, Inc.

Design by
Design Traditions

Design 9950
Square Footage: 2,095

● This special cottage design carries a fully modern floor plan. The entry leads to open living areas with a dining room and a living room flanking the foyer. The family room—with a fireplace and built-in bookcases—is nearby the bright breakfast room with deck access. The efficiently patterned kitchen provides a helpful lead-in to the dining room. Two secondary bedrooms make up the left side of the plan. A full, compartmented bath connects them. In the master bedroom suite, a tiered ceiling and a bath with dual lavatories, a whirlpool tub, a separate shower, a compartmented toilet and a walk-in closet are sure to please. The two-car, side-load garage opens to the laundry room. This home is designed with a basement foundation.

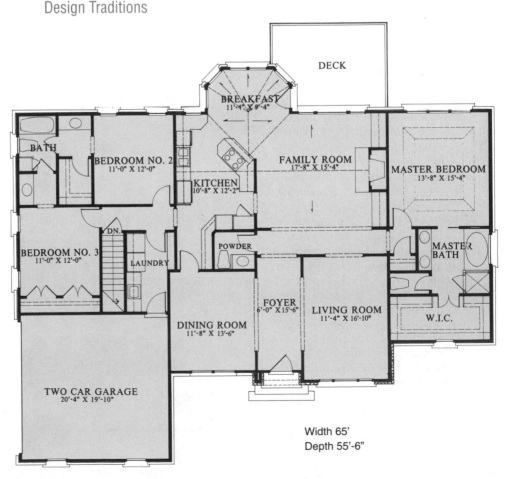

Width 65'
Depth 55'-6"

Design 9810
Square Footage: 2,770

● The European-inspired excitement of this stucco home can be seen in its use of large, abundant windows. Inside, the spacious foyer leads directly to a large great room with a massive fireplace and French doors that lead outdoors. The banquet-sized dining room, just off the foyer, receives the brilliant light of the triple window, and features a dramatic, vaulted ceiling. The kitchen and breakfast room add another plus by providing openness. The spacious kitchen also offers all the amenities of a walk-in pantry, desk, breakfast bar and a large convenient laundry room. The master suite features a separate sitting area with a cathedral ceiling and access to the patio for a private owners' retreat. The two additional bedrooms each have their own vanity within a shared bath. This home is designed with a basement foundation.

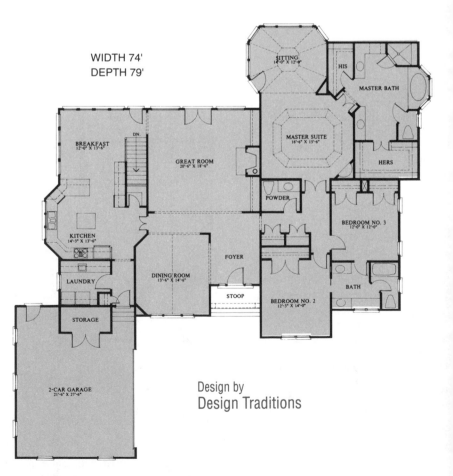

WIDTH 74'
DEPTH 79'

Design by
Design Traditions

194

Quote One®

Cost to build? See page 374
to order complete cost estimate
to build this house in your area!

WIDTH 72'
DEPTH 73'

2-CAR GARAGE
21'-3" x 26'-0"

LAUN.

BREAKFAST
11'-6" x 12'-0"

KITCHEN
14'-0" x 16'-6"

PAN.

DN

GREAT ROOM
16'-0" x 20'-6"

DINING ROOM
13'-0" x 13'-6"

FOYER

STUDY/
BEDROOM No.2
13'-0" x 13'-6"

GUEST ROOM/
CHILDRENS
DEN
13'-6" x 16'-9"

M. BATH

SITTING

MASTER SUITE
15'-6" x 23'-3"

MASTER
CLOSET

BEDROOM No.3
12'-0" x 13'-6"

Design 9807

Square Footage: 2,785

● The balance and symmetry of this European home has an inviting quality about it. An entry foyer allowing a grand view out of the back of the house leads directly to the great room. Just off the great room are a convenient and functional gourmet kitchen and an adjoining bay-windowed breakfast room. The master suite enjoys privacy in its position at the rear of the home. Three other bedrooms, one which might serve as a guest room or children's den and one that might work well as a study, round out the sleeping accommodations. This home is designed with a basement foundation.

Design by
Design Traditions

Design 8000
Square Footage: 2,540

● A gabled stucco entry with over-sized columns emphasizes the arched glass entry of this winsome one-story brick home. Arched windows on either side of the front door add symmetry and style to this pleasing exterior. An arched passage flanked by twin bookcases and plant ledges—perfect for plants and collectibles—provides interest to the living room. Pass through the arch and find three of the bedrooms in this split-bedroom plan. Bedroom 4 may also be a study and can be entered from double French doors off the living room. A large, efficient kitchen shares space with an octagonal-shaped breakfast area and a family room with a fireplace. The master bedroom is entered through angled double doors and features a cathedral ceiling. Attention centers immediately on the columned and arched entry to the relaxing master bath with its central whirlpool tub. This plan is available with either a crawlspace or slab foundation. Please specify when ordering.

Design by
Larry E. Belk
Designs

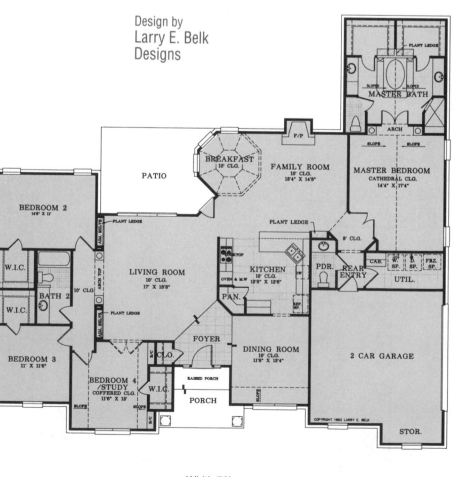

Width 70'
Depth 65'

Copyright 1992 Stephen S. Fuller, Inc.

Design by
Design Traditions

Design 9914
Square Footage: 1,770

● Perfect for a sloping lot, this
European one-story includes living
areas on one level and bedrooms
on another. The great room contains a fireplace and access to the
rear deck. Close by are the U-
shaped kitchen and breakfast room
with a boxed window. Bedrooms
are a few steps up from the living
areas and include a master suite
with two walk-in closets and a
sumptuous bath with a compartmented toilet. Secondary bedrooms
share a full bath with double-bowl
vanity. On the lower level is garage
space and bonus space that may be
used later for additional bedrooms
or casual gathering areas. This
home is designed with a basement
foundation.

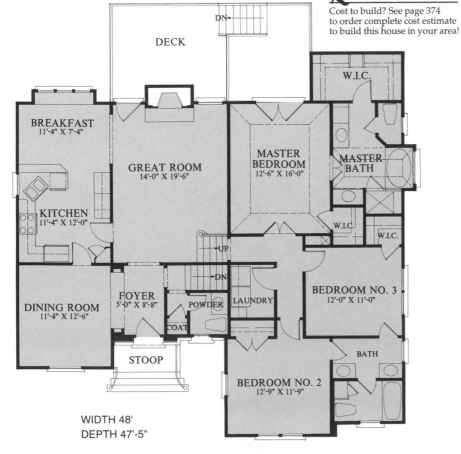

DECK

DN

BREAKFAST
11'-4" X 7'-4"

GREAT ROOM
14'-0" X 19'-6"

MASTER
BEDROOM
12'-6" X 16'-0"

W.I.C.

MASTER
BATH

KITCHEN
11'-4" X 12'-0"

W.I.C.

W.I.C.

UP

DN

DINING ROOM
11'-4" X 12'-6"

FOYER
5'-0" X 8'-8"

POWDER

COAT

LAUNDRY

BEDROOM NO. 3
12'-0" X 11'-0"

STOOP

BATH

BEDROOM NO. 2
12'-9" X 11'-9"

WIDTH 48'
DEPTH 47'-5"

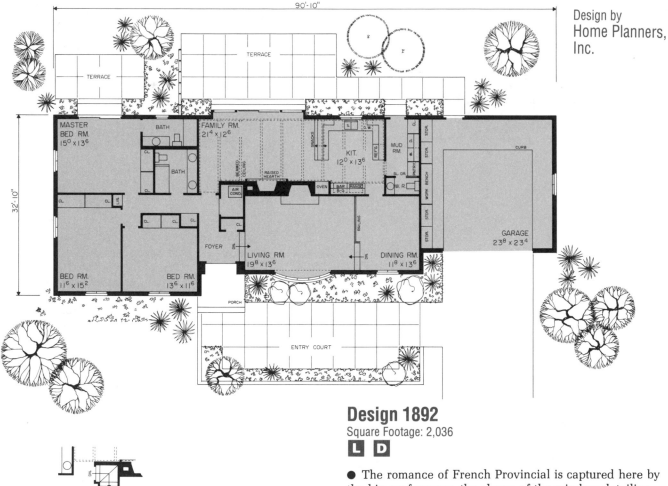

Design 1892
Square Footage: 2,036

L **D**

● The romance of French Provincial is captured here by the hip-roof masses, the charm of the window detailing, the brick quoins at the corners, the delicate dentil work at the cornices, the massive centered chimney, and the recessed double front doors. The slightly raised entry court completes the picture. The basic floor plan is a favorite of many. And little wonder, for all areas work well together, while still maintaining a fine degree of separation of functions. The highlight of the interior, perhaps, will be the sunken living room. The family room, with its beamed ceiling, will not be far behind in its popularity. The separate dining room, mud room, efficient kitchen, complete the livability.

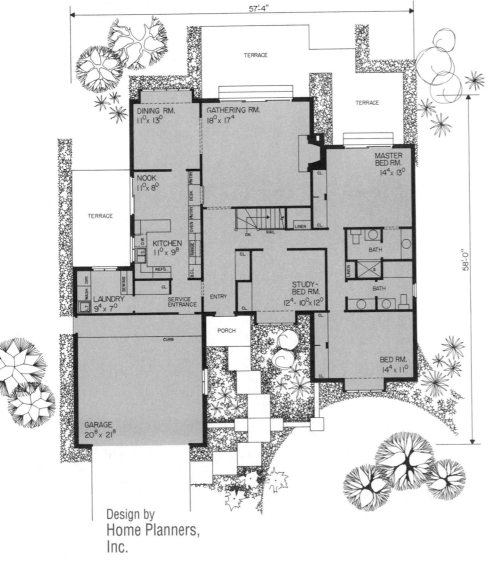

DINING RM.
11⁰ x 13⁰

GATHERING RM.
18⁰ x 17⁴

TERRACE

TERRACE

MASTER
BED RM.
14⁴ x 13⁰

NOOK
11⁰ x 8⁰

PANTRY
DESK
OVEN PANTRY

CL.

TERRACE

KITCHEN
11⁰ x 9⁸

RANGE

DN. RAIL

LINEN

CL.

BATH

REFS.

B.CL.

CL.

LINEN

DRY
WASH
SEWING

BATH

LAUNDRY
9⁴ x 7⁰

CL.

SERVICE
ENTRANCE

ENTRY

STUDY-
BED RM.
12⁴ - 10⁰ x 12⁰

CL.

GARAGE
20⁸ x 21⁸

CURB

PORCH

CL.

BED RM.
14⁴ x 11⁰

57'-4"

58'-0"

Design by
**Home Planners,
Inc.**

Design 2738
Square Footage: 1,898

● Impressive architectural
work is indeed apparent in
this three bedroom home.
The three foot high entrance
court wall, the high pitched
roof and the paned glass
windows all add to this
home's exterior appeal. It is
also apparent that the floor
plan is very efficient with
the side, U-shaped kitchen
and nook with two pantry
closets. Overlooking the
backyard, the dining and
gathering rooms will serve
your every family occasion.
Three (or make it two with a
study) bedrooms and two
baths are in the sleeping
wing. Indoor-outdoor living
also will be enjoyed in this
home with a dining terrace
off the nook and a living terrace off the gathering room
and master bedroom. Note
the fireplace in the gathering
room and bay window in
dining room. This design
will be very livable.

Design 1228

First Floor: 2,583 square feet
Second Floor: 697 square feet
Total: 3,280 square feet

L **D**

Width 93'-10"
Depth 67'-10"

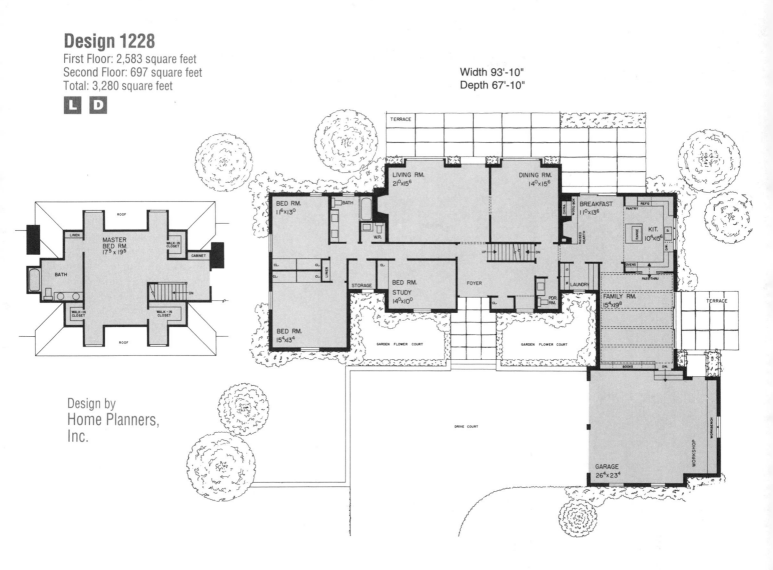

Design by
**Home Planners,
Inc.**

● This beautiful house has a wealth of detail taken from the rich traditions of French Regency design. The roof itself is a study in pleasant dormers and the hips and valleys of a big flowing area. A close examination of the plan shows the careful arrangement of space for privacy as well as good circulation of traffic. The spacious formal entrance hall sets the stage for good zoning. The informal living area is highlighted by the updated version of the old country kitchen. Observe the fireplace, built-in wood box, and china cabinet. While there is a half-story devoted to the master bedroom suite, this home funcions more as a one-story country estate design than as a 1½ story.

Design 2779

Square Footage: 3,225

L **D**

● This French design is surely impressive. The exterior appearance will brighten any area with its French roof, paned-glass windows, masonry brick privacy wall and double front doors. The inside is just as appealing. Note the unique placement of rooms and features. The entry hall is large and leads to each of the areas in this plan. The formal dining room is outstanding and guests can enter through the entry hall. While serving one can enter by way of the butler's pantry (notice its size and that it has a sink). To the right of the entry is a sizable parlor. Then there is the gathering room with fireplace, sliding glass doors and adjacent study. The work center is also outstanding. There is the U-shaped kitchen, island range, snack bar, breakfast nook, pantry, plus washroom and large laundry near the service entrance. Basement stairs are also nearby.

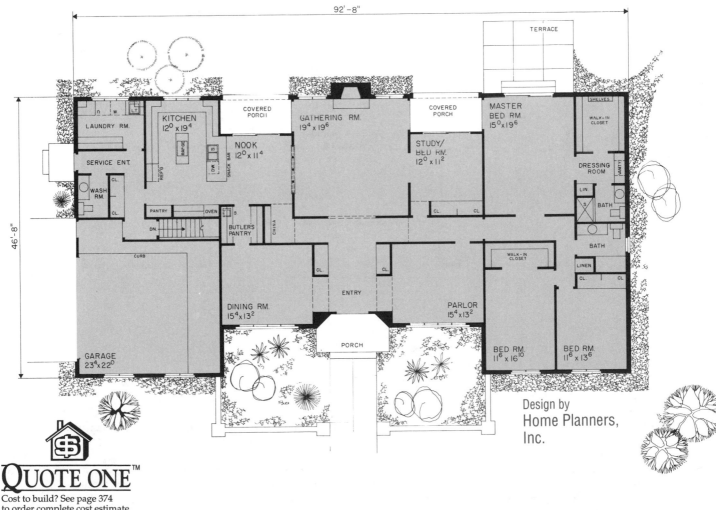

Design by
Home Planners, Inc.

QUOTE ONE™

Cost to build? See page 374
to order complete cost estimate
to build this house in your area!

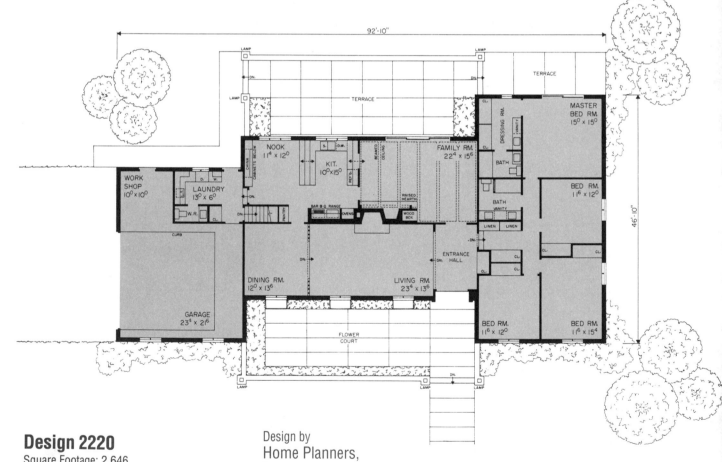

Design 2220

Square Footage: 2,646

L **D**

● The gracious formality of this home is reminiscent of a popularly accepted French styling. The hip-roof, the brick quoins, the cornice details, the arched window heads, the distinctive shutters, the recessed double front doors, the massive center chimney, and the de-

Design by
**Home Planners,
Inc.**

lightful flower court are all features which set the dramatic appeal of this home. This floor plan is a favorite of many. The four bedroom, two bath sleeping wing is a zone by itself. Further, the formal living and dining rooms are ideally located. For enter-

taining they function well together and look out upon the pleasant flower court. Overlooking the raised living terrace at the rear are the family and breakfast rooms and work center. Don't miss the laundry, extra wash room and work shop in garage.

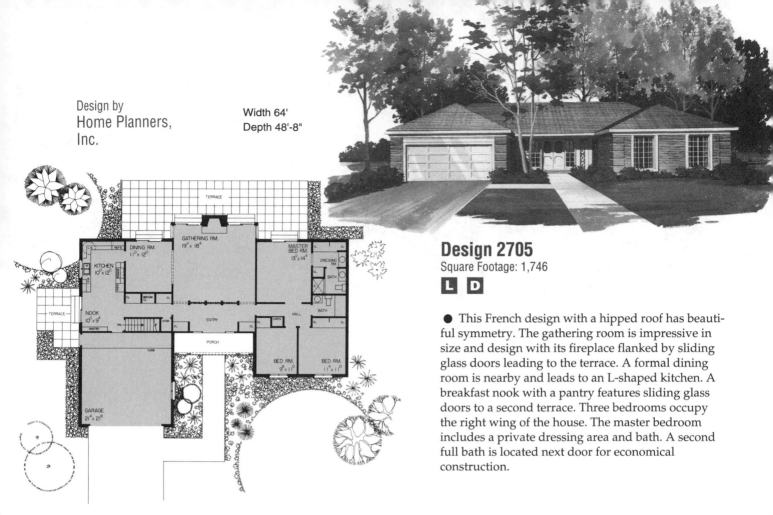

Design by
Home Planners,
Inc.

Width 64'
Depth 48'-8"

Design 2705

Square Footage: 1,746

L **D**

● This French design with a hipped roof has beautiful symmetry. The gathering room is impressive in size and design with its fireplace flanked by sliding glass doors leading to the terrace. A formal dining room is nearby and leads to an L-shaped kitchen. A breakfast nook with a pantry features sliding glass doors to a second terrace. Three bedrooms occupy the right wing of the house. The master bedroom includes a private dressing area and bath. A second full bath is located next door for economical construction.

Design 2851

Square Footage: 2,739

L

● This spacious one-story has a classic Country French hip roof. The front entrance creates a charming entry. Beyond the covered porch is an octagonal foyer. All of the living areas overlook the rear yard. Features include a fireplace in the living room, skylight in the dining room and a second set of sliding glass doors in the family room leading to a covered porch. An island range and other built-ins are featured in the spacious front kitchen. Adjacent is the breakfast room. The four bedrooms and bath facilities are all clustered in one wing.

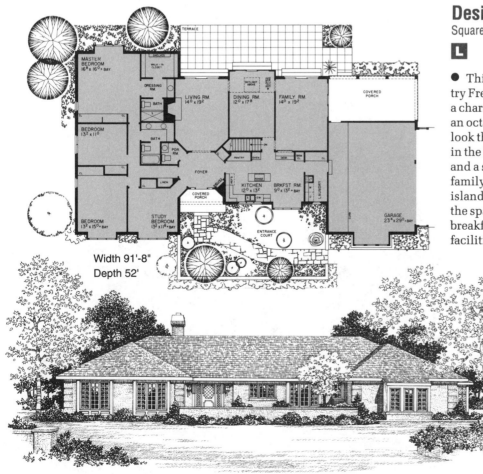

Width 91'-8"
Depth 52'

Design by
Home Planners,
Inc.

Cost to build? See page 374
to order complete cost estimate
to build this house in your area!

Design 6600

Square Footage: 1,795

● This engaging split-bedroom plan promotes casual living both inside and out. An elegant foyer opens to a spacious living area, which includes a formal dining room and an expansive great room with a fireplace and built-in entertainment center. Double French doors allow access to the veranda through the great room. The large kitchen includes a walk-in pantry and shares an eating bar with the bay-windowed breakfast nook. A secluded master suite enjoys private access to the screened veranda through lovely French doors, and offers His and Hers walk-in closets and a private bath with glass enclosed shower. Two family bedrooms share a full bath. The laundry room is nearby for convenience.

Design by
The Sater
Design Collection

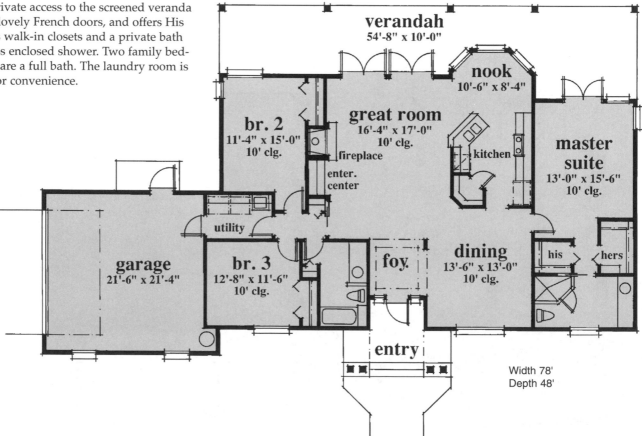

Width 78'
Depth 48'

Quote One®

Cost to build? See page 374 to order complete cost estimate to build this house in your area!

Width 84'-4"
Depth 75'-4"

● Grand style is reflected in the pediment gables, columns and keystones of this distinguished home. Inside, a formal living room, angled for interest, warmly greets friends and provides a perfect complement to the formal dining room located nearby. The island kitchen overlooks the covered entertainment terrace and easily serves both formal and informal areas. Family gatherings will be enjoyed in the light and airy family room that shares space with the breakfast nook. A secluded master suite features a spacious master bedroom with room to stretch and a walk-in closet sized for frequent shoppers. The master bath enjoys a corner whirlpool tub overlooking the garden area. Two additional bedrooms, a den/study, a full bath and a powder room complete the plan.

Design by
Home Planners

Design 3634

Square Footage: 3,264

L

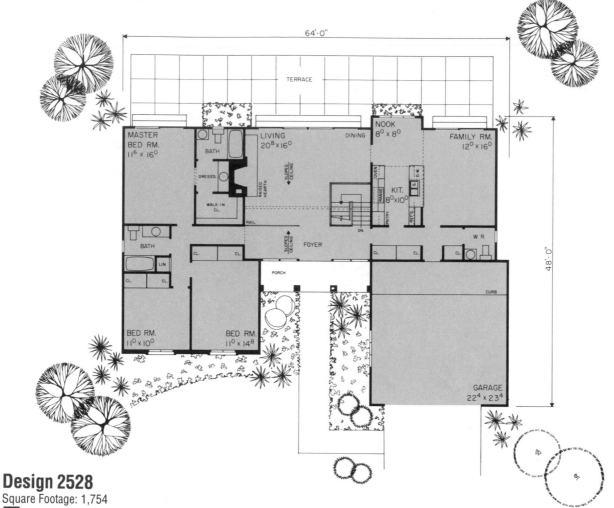

64'-0"

TERRACE

MASTER BED RM. 11⁶ × 16⁰

BATH

DRESS'G.

WALK-IN CL.

LIVING 20⁸ × 16⁰

SLOPED CEILING

RAISED HEARTH

DINING

NOOK 8⁰ × 8⁰

OVEN

RANGE

S. D.W.

KIT. 8⁰ × 10⁰

PANTRY

REF'G.

FAMILY RM. 12⁰ × 16⁰

48'-0"

BATH

LIN.

CL.

CL.

CL.

RAIL

DN.

SLOPED CEILING

FOYER

CL.

CL.

CL.

W. R.

BED RM. 11⁰ × 10⁰

BED RM. 11⁰ × 14⁸

PORCH

CURB

GARAGE 22⁴ × 23⁴

Design 2528

Square Footage: 1,754

D

● This inviting, U-shaped western ranch adaptation offers outstanding living potential behind its double front doors. In only 1,754 square feet there are three bedrooms and 2½ baths. The formal living room is open to the dining area and offers a raised-hearth fireplace and a sloped ceiling. The functional kitchen features an adjacent breakfast nook and has easy access to the informal family room. A rear terrace stretches the width of the home and is accessible from the master bedroom, living room and family room. Stairs lead to a basement which may be developed at a later time.

Design 3377

Square Footage: 2,217

L **D**

● This Tudor design provides a handsome exterior complemented by a spacious and modern floor plan. The sleeping area is positioned to the left side of the home. The master bedroom features an elegant bath with whirlpool, shower, dual lavs and a separate vanity area. Two family bedrooms share a full bath. A media room exhibits the TV, VCR and stereo. The enormous gathering room is set off by columns and contains a fireplace and sliding doors to the rear terrace. The dining room and breakfast room each feature a bay window.

Cost to build? See page 374 to order complete cost estimate to build this house in your area!

Design by
Home Planners,
Inc.

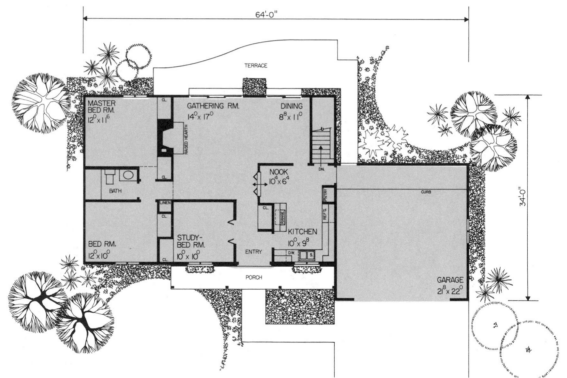

Design 2570
Square Footage: 1,176

L D

● This attractive Tudor is an economically built design which will cater admirably to the living patterns of the retired couple. In addition to the two bedrooms this plan offers a study which could double ideally as a guest room, sewing room or even serve as the TV room. The living area is a spacious L-shaped zone for formal living and dining. The efficient kitchen is handy to the front door and overlooks the front yard. It features a convenient breakfast nook for those informal meals. Handy to the entry from the garage and the yard are the stairs to the basement. Don't overlook the attractive front porch and the window flower boxes.

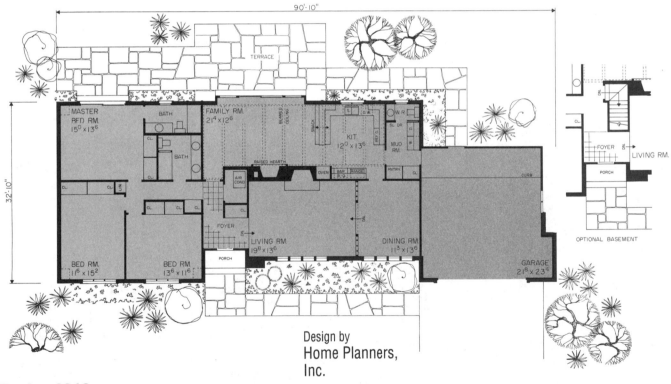

Design by
Home Planners,
Inc.

Design 2318

Square Footage: 2,029

● Warmth and charm are characteristics of Tudor adaptations. This modest sized home with its twin front-facing gabled roofs represents a great investment. While it will be an exciting and refreshing addition to any neighborhood, its appeal will never grow old.

The covered, front entrance opens to the center foyer. Traffic patterns flow in an orderly and efficient manner to the three main zones — the formal dining zone, the sleeping zone and the informal living zone. The sunken living room with its fireplace is separated

from the dining room by an attractive trellis divider. A second fireplace, along with beamed ceiling and sliding glass doors, highlights the family room. Note snack bar, mud room, cooking facilities, two full baths and optional basement.

Design 2573

Square Footage: 2,747

● A dapper Tudor ranch, this plan combines wood, brick and stucco to create an elegantly appealing exterior. Inside is a thoroughly contemporary floor plan. The open living room and dining area, with more than 410 square feet, features a fireplace, a wall of built-in shelves and a clear view to the outside through diagonally shaped windows. Other highlights include a family room with a raised-hearth fire-place, a U-shaped kitchen and adjacent breakfast nook, an optional bedroom, a study or office and a four-bedroom sleeping wing including a master suite with access to a private terrace.

California Engineered Plans and California Stock Plans are available for this home. Call 1-800-521-6797 for more information.

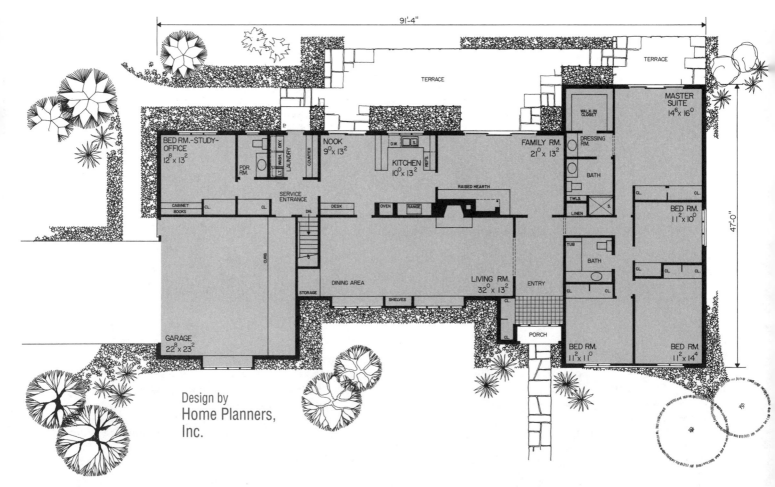

Design by
Home Planners,
Inc.

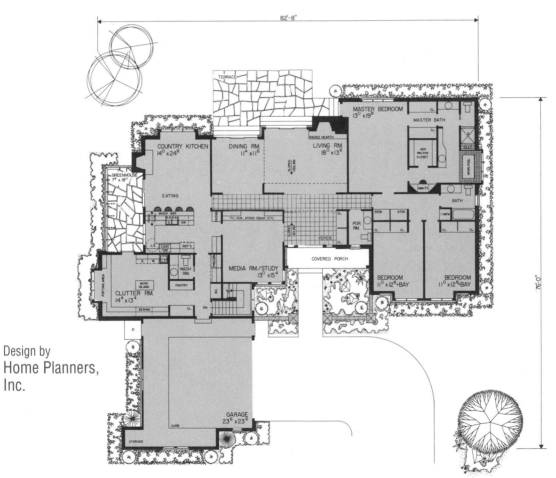

Design by
Home Planners,
Inc.

Design 2961
Square Footage: 2,919

● This is an interesting and charming L-shaped exterior one-story home. It features a Tudor exterior with varying roof plans, cornice detailing and a brick exterior with accents of stucco and beam work. A brick wall forms the front courtyard. Inside, the spacious foyer with slate floor routes traffic most effectively. Highlights include a media room, clutter room, country kitchen and 29-foot formal living/dining room area. The large master bedroom has a luxurious master bath. A walled glass greenhouse has 130 feet not included in the total above.

Design by
**Home Planners,
Inc.**

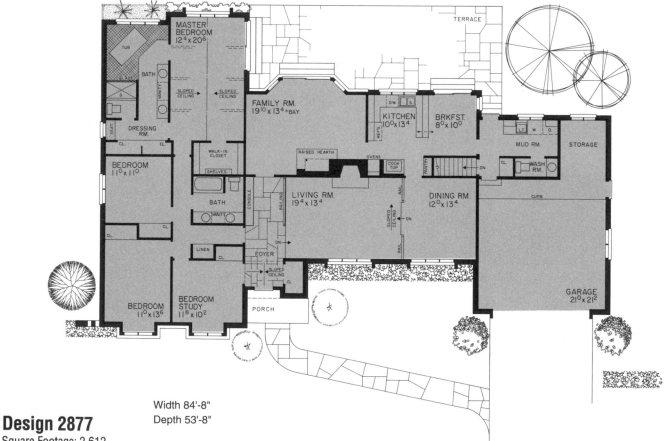

Width 84'-8"
Depth 53'-8"

Design 2877
Square Footage: 2,612

L D

● Here's a dramatic, Post-Modern exterior with a popular plan featuring an outstanding master bedroom suite. The bedroom itself is spacious, has a sloped ceiling, a large walk-in closet and sliding glass doors to the terrace. Now examine the bath and dressing area. Two large closets, twin vanities, built-in seat and a dramatically presented corner tub are present. The tub will be a great place to spend the evening hours after a long, hard day. Along with this bedroom, there are three more served by a full bath. The living area of this plan has the formal areas in the front and the informal areas in the rear. Both have a fireplace. The spacious work center is efficiently planned.

Design 2607
Square Footage: 1,208

L

● This English Tudor cottage will delight young and old with its warm, open interior. The front porch gives way to the main living area of the house. With a fireplace and windows that overlook both front and rear yards, this space becomes a most pleasant one to inhabit. The dining room features a built-in china cabinet—built-in bookshelves are just around the corner. The U-shaped kitchen is wonderfully efficient with its double sink, dishwasher, pantry and adjacent eating bay. A laundry area and half bath also occupy this end of the house. At the other end, two bedrooms share a full bath.

Design by
**Home Planners,
Inc.**

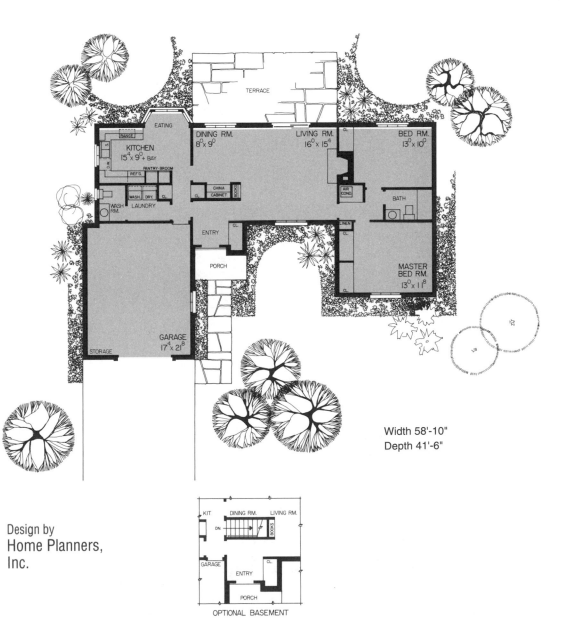

Width 58'-10"
Depth 41'-6"

OPTIONAL BASEMENT

Design by
Frank Betz
Associates, Inc.

Design P127

Square Footage: 2,322

● Gables, arches and a stone-and-stucco exterior give this home plenty of curb appeal. Inside, you'll find a floor plan designed for easy entertaining. The dining room is close to the living room for formal occasions and opens into the spacious family room for informal gatherings. High ceilings and decorative columns are added attractions. The gourmet island kitchen offers a pantry, double ovens and a snack bar that serves both the family room and the sunny breakfast nook. The master suite is a homeowner's delight with a bayed sitting area, access to the back yard, a tray ceiling, huge walk-in closet and luxurious bath. Two family bedrooms and a full bath complete the plan. Please specify basement, crawlspace or slab foundation when ordering.

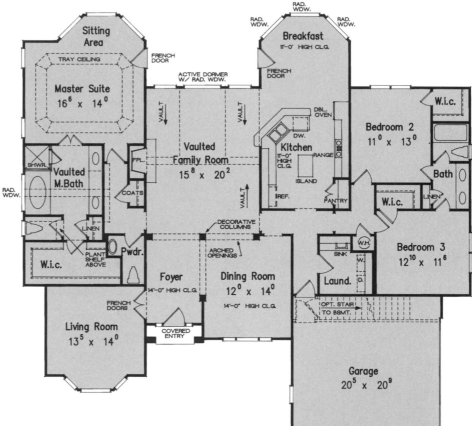

GARAGE LOCATION WITH BASEMENT

Width 62'
Depth 61'

Design by
Home Planners

Design 3664

Square Footage: 2,471

L

● Corner quoins and keystones above
the windows provide a touch of Old-
World appeal to this splendid one-story
home. From the soaring entry, views of
the rear grounds can be enjoyed through
the great room. To the left of the foyer is
an office/guest suite with a nearby bath,
supplying the flexibility to suit your
needs. The island kitchen is found to the
right, serving the breakfast nook and formal dining room with equal ease. Split
for privacy, two family bedrooms—one
with a covered patio—share a full bath.
The room-to-stretch master suite com-
prises the left wing of the house. Here,
amenities include a large walk-in closet,
a large master bath with a whirlpool tub,
a double-bowl vanity and a separate
shower, and a retreat area that opens
onto a private covered patio.

Width 86'-4"
Depth 80'-2"

Cost to build? See page 374
to order complete cost estimate
to build this house in your area!

215

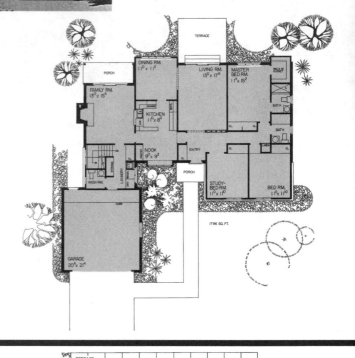

Width 62'
Depth 57'-4"

Design by
Home Planners

Design 2737
Square Footage: 1,796

L

● Tudor accents add distinction to this wonderful home. Inside, livability takes priority. The step-saving U-shaped kitchen handily services the formal dining room, the family room and the nook. Sliding glass doors in the family room provide easy access to the covered porch and back yard; the living room opens onto a rear terrace. Three bedrooms and two baths highlight the sleeping zone. Or if you prefer, one bedroom may be used as a study.

Design 2929
Square Footage: 1,608

● This efficient floor plan caters to the needs of the small family. The angled kitchen is located in a space convenient to the garage, dining room, dining terrace and front door. The spacious living area has a dramatic fireplace and rear-terrace access. A favorite spot will be the media room with built-in cabinets for the TV, VCR and stereo. Storage space abounds in the master bedroom, and its adjacent bath has twin lavatories, a tub and a separate shower. There's an extra bedroom for guests or for use as a nursery.

Width 55'-4"
Depth 46'-4"

Design by
Home Planners

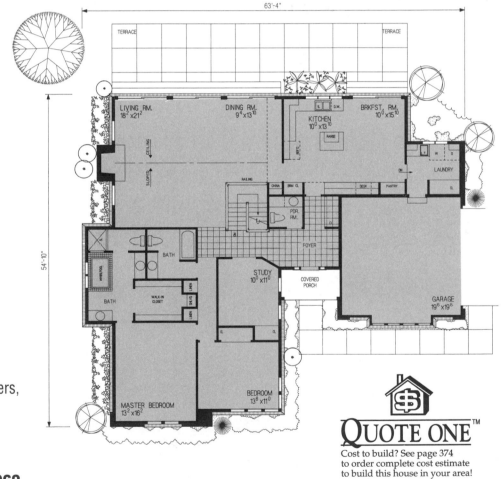

Design by
**Home Planners,
Inc.**

Quote One™
Cost to build? See page 374
to order complete cost estimate
to build this house in your area!

Design 2962
Square Footage: 2,112

● A Tudor exterior with an efficient floor plan favored by many. Each of the three main living zones — the sleeping zone, living zone, and the working zone — are but a couple steps from the foyer. This spells easy, efficient traffic patterns. Open planning, sloping ceiling and plenty of glass create a nice environment for the living-dining area. Its appeal is further enhanced by the open staircase to the lower level recreation/hobby area. The L-shaped kitchen with its island range and work surface is delightfully opened to the large breakfast room. Again, plenty of glass area adds to the feeling of spaciousness. Nearby is the step-saving first floor laundry. The sleeping zone has the flexibility of functioning as a two or three bedroom area. Notice the economical back-to-back plumbing.

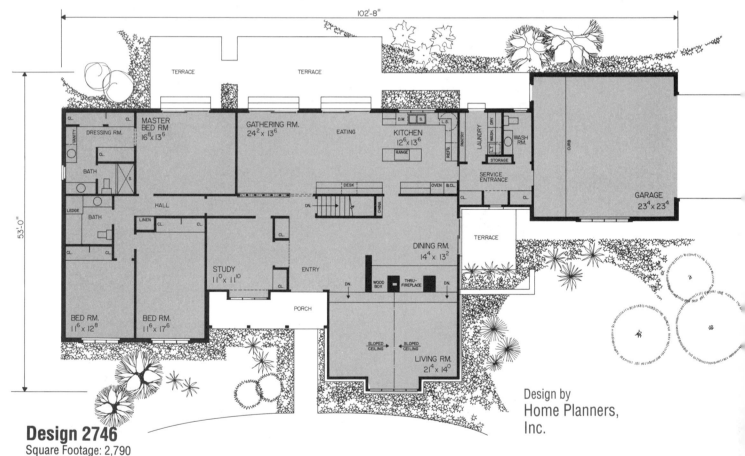

Design 2746
Square Footage: 2,790

D

● This impressive one-story will be the talk-of-the-town. And not surprisingly, either. It embodies all of the elements to assure a sound investment and years of happy family livability. The projecting living room with its stucco, simulated wood beams and

effective window treatment adds a dramatic note. Sunken by two steps, this room will enjoy privacy. The massive double front doors are sheltered by the covered porch and lead to the spacious entry hall. The interior is particularly well-zoned. The large, rear

gathering room will cater to the family's gregarious instincts. Outdoor enjoyment can be obtained on the three terraces. Also, a study is available for those extra quiet moments. Be sure to observe the plan closely for all of the other fine features.

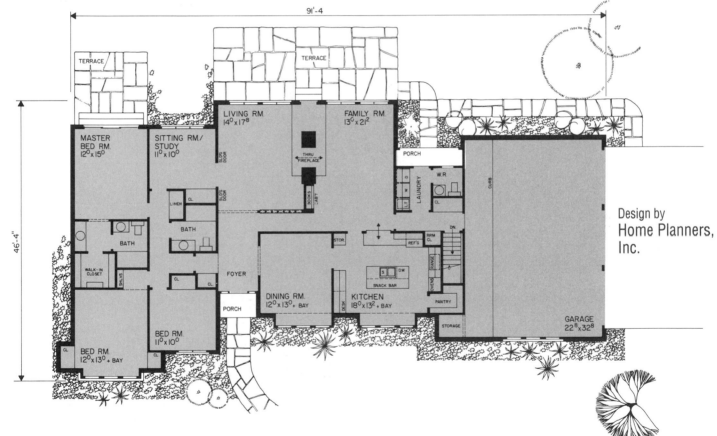

Design 2785
Square Footage: 2,375

L **D**

● Exceptional Tudor design! Passers-by will take a second glance at this fine home wherever it may be located. And the interior is just as pleasing. As one enters the foyer and looks around, the plan will speak for itself in the areas of convenience and efficiency.

Cross room traffic will be avoided. There is a hall leading to each of the three bedrooms and study of the sleeping wing and another leading to the living room, family room, kitchen and laundry with washroom. The formal dining room can be entered from both

the foyer and the kitchen. Efficiency will be the by-word when describing the kitchen. Note the fine features: a built-in desk, pantry, island snack bar with sink and pass-thru to the family room. The fireplace will be enjoyed in the living and family rooms.

Design 3346

Square Footage: 2,032

L

● This home boasts a delightful Tudor exterior with a terrific interior floor plan. Though compact, there's plenty of living space: large study with fireplace, gathering room, dining room, and breakfast room. The master bedroom has an attached bath with whirlpool tub. Note the double walk-in closets.

Design by
Home Planners,
Inc.

QUOTE ONE™

Cost to build? See page 374
to order complete cost estimate
to build this house in your area!

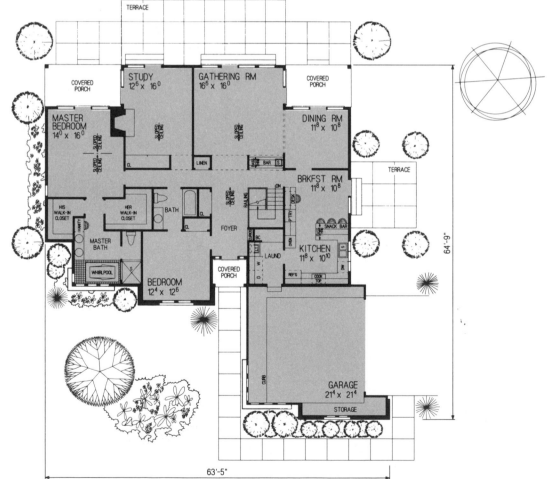

220

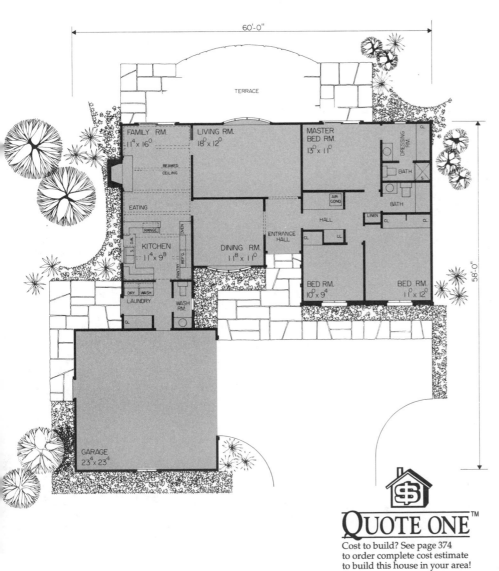

Design by
Home Planners,
Inc.

Design 2606

Square Footage: 1,499

L

OPTIONAL BASEMENT

● This modest sized house with its 1,499 square feet could hardly offer more in the way of exterior charm and interior livability. Measuring only 60 feet in width means it will not require a huge, expensive piece of property. The orientation of the garage and the front drive court are features which promote an economical use of property. In addition to the formal, separate living and dining rooms, there is the informal kitchen/family room area. Note the beamed ceiling, the fireplace, the sliding glass doors and the eating area of the family room.

QUOTE ONE™

Cost to build? See page 374
to order complete cost estimate
to build this house in your area!

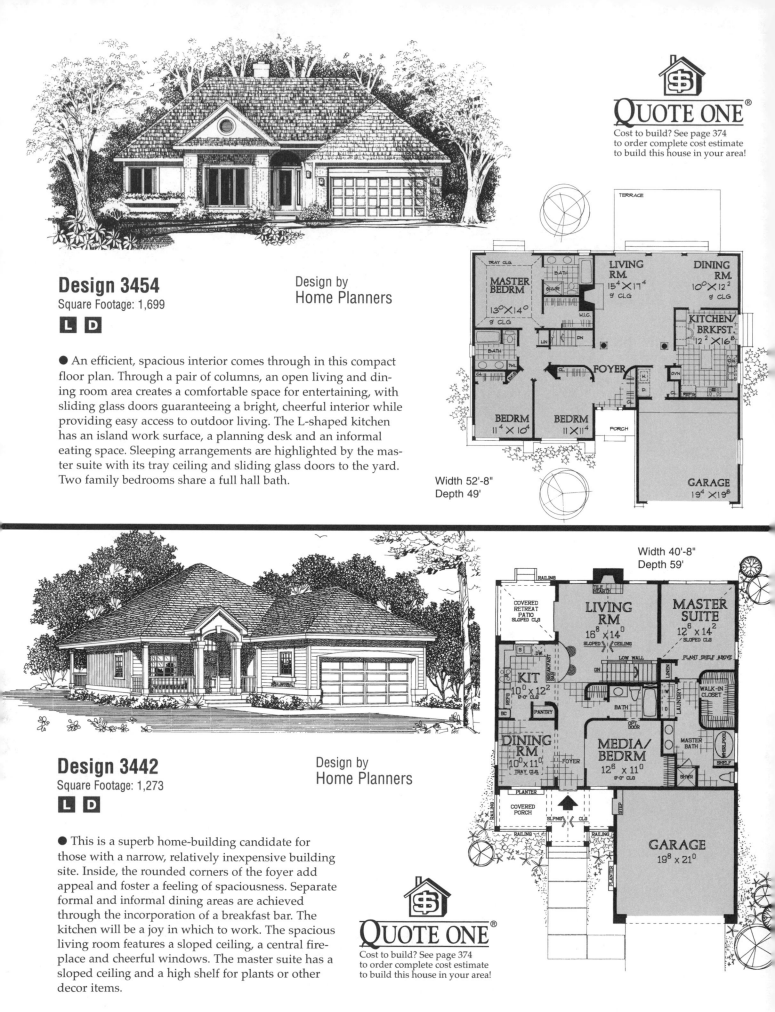

Cost to build? See page 374
to order complete cost estimate
to build this house in your area!

Design 3454
Square Footage: 1,699

L **D**

Design by
Home Planners

● An efficient, spacious interior comes through in this compact floor plan. Through a pair of columns, an open living and dining room area creates a comfortable space for entertaining, with sliding glass doors guaranteeing a bright, cheerful interior while providing easy access to outdoor living. The L-shaped kitchen has an island work surface, a planning desk and an informal eating space. Sleeping arrangements are highlighted by the master suite with its tray ceiling and sliding glass doors to the yard. Two family bedrooms share a full hall bath.

Width 52'-8"
Depth 49'

Width 40'-8"
Depth 59'

Design 3442
Square Footage: 1,273

L **D**

Design by
Home Planners

● This is a superb home-building candidate for those with a narrow, relatively inexpensive building site. Inside, the rounded corners of the foyer add appeal and foster a feeling of spaciousness. Separate formal and informal dining areas are achieved through the incorporation of a breakfast bar. The kitchen will be a joy in which to work. The spacious living room features a sloped ceiling, a central fireplace and cheerful windows. The master suite has a sloped ceiling and a high shelf for plants or other decor items.

QUOTE ONE®
Cost to build? See page 374
to order complete cost estimate
to build this house in your area!

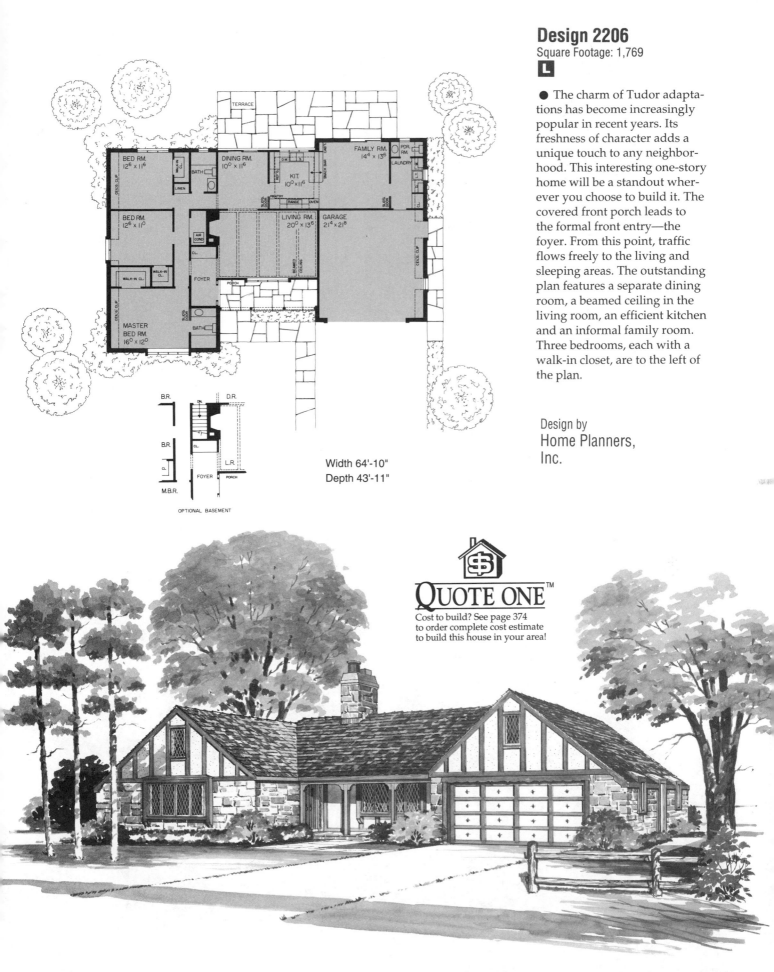

Design 2206
Square Footage: 1,769

L

● The charm of Tudor adaptations has become increasingly popular in recent years. Its freshness of character adds a unique touch to any neighborhood. This interesting one-story home will be a standout wherever you choose to build it. The covered front porch leads to the formal front entry—the foyer. From this point, traffic flows freely to the living and sleeping areas. The outstanding plan features a separate dining room, a beamed ceiling in the living room, an efficient kitchen and an informal family room. Three bedrooms, each with a walk-in closet, are to the left of the plan.

Design by
Home Planners, Inc.

Width 64'-10"
Depth 43'-11"

QUOTE ONE™

Cost to build? See page 374 to order complete cost estimate to build this house in your area!

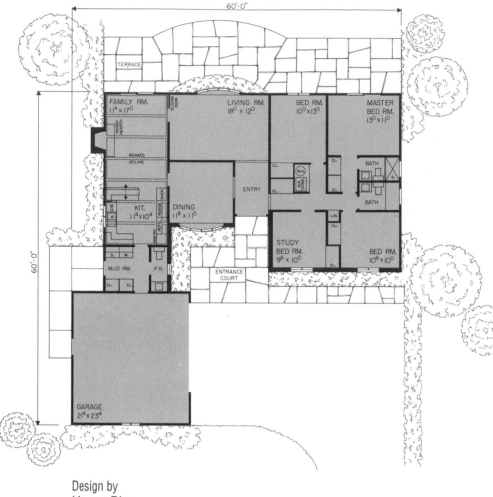

60'-0"

TERRACE

FAMILY RM.
11⁴ x 17⁰

RAISED HEARTH

BEAMED CEILING

KIT.
11⁴x10⁴

DINING
11⁸ x 11⁰

MUD RM.

P.R.

CL.   CL.

GARAGE
21⁴ x 23⁴

60'-0"

SLIDING DOOR

LIVING RM.
18⁰ x 12⁰

ENTRY

ENTRANCE COURT

BED RM.
10⁰ x 13⁰

MASTER BED RM.
13⁰ x 11⁰

W.H.

AIR COND.

BATH

BATH

S.

LIN.

CL.

STUDY BED RM.
9⁶ x 10⁰

BED RM.
10⁸ x 10⁰

Design by
**Home Planners,
Inc.**

Design 2170
Square Footage: 1,646

L

● An L-shaped home with an enchanting Olde English styling. The wavy-edged siding, the similated beams, the diamond lite windows, the unusual brick pattern and the interesting roof lines all are elements which set the character of authenticity. The center entry routes traffic directly to the formal living and sleeping zones of the house. Between the kitchen-family room area and the attached two-car garage is the mud room. Here is the washer and dryer with the extra powder room nearby. The family room is highlighted by the beamed ceilings, the raised hearth fireplace and sliding glass doors to the rear terrace. The work center with its abundance of cupboard space will be fun in which to function. Four bedrooms, two full baths and good closet space are features of the sleeping area.

Design 2728
Square Footage: 1,825

L **D**

● This lovely L-shaped English adaptation presents a wonderful face with impressive exterior features. Its floor plan adds livability for modern families. Note the fireplace — a focal point in the living/dining room area. The kitchen is strategically placed to serve the dining room and family room. In addition to the two full baths in the sleeping zone, there is a handy washroom at the entrance from the garage. Note the fine master bath.

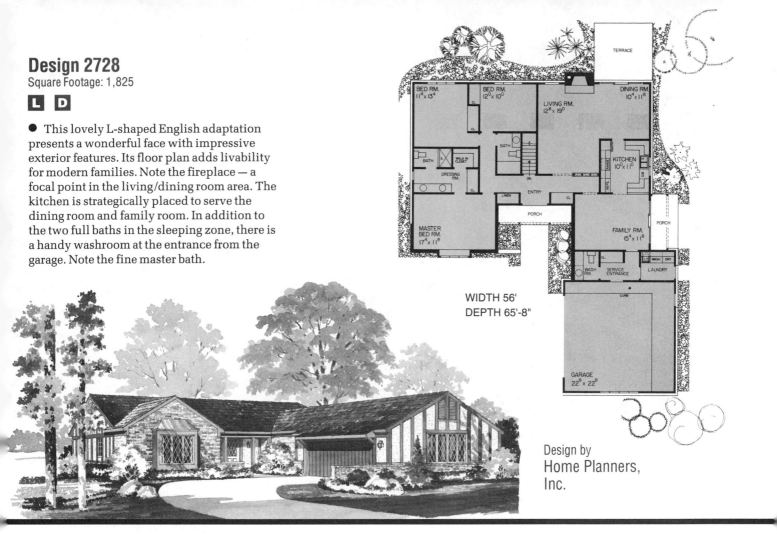

WIDTH 56'
DEPTH 65'-8"

Design by
Home Planners,
Inc.

Design 1989
Square Footage: 2,282

L **D**

● High style abounds in this picturesque, ground-hugging design. The plan calls for a sunken living room and separate dining room. Overlooking the rear yard is an informal family room with beamed ceiling. Note the proximity of the kitchen and breakfast room. A master bedroom suite is one of four bedrooms found to the left of the entry foyer.

Width 86'-10"
Depth 40'-10"

Design by
Home Planners,
Inc.

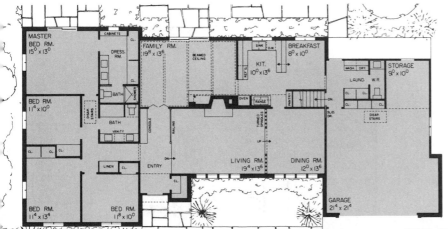

225

On The Cutting Edge:

Contemporary-style homes

Design 8672
Square Footage: 2,397

● Low-slung, hipped rooflines
and an abundance of glass enhance
the unique exterior of this fine
one-story home. Inside, the use of
soffits and tray ceilings heighten
the distinctive style of the floor
plan. To the left, double doors lead
to the private master suite which
is bathed in natural light—compliments of an abundant use of
glass—and enjoys a garden setting
from the corner tub. Convenient
planning of the gourmet kitchen
places everything at minimum
distances and serves the outdoor
kitchen, breakfast nook and family
room with equal ease. Completing
the plan are two family bedrooms
that share a full bath.

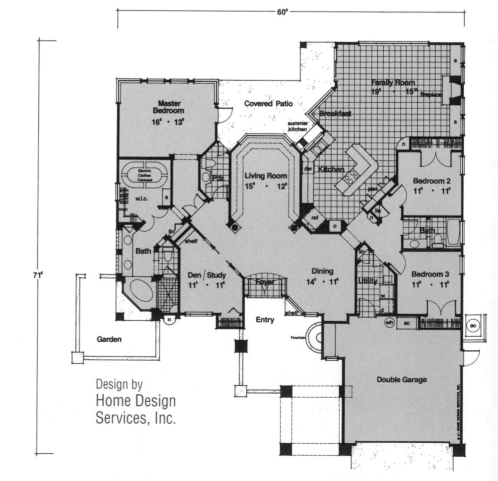

Design by
Home Design
Services, Inc.

Width 70'
Depth 67'-4"

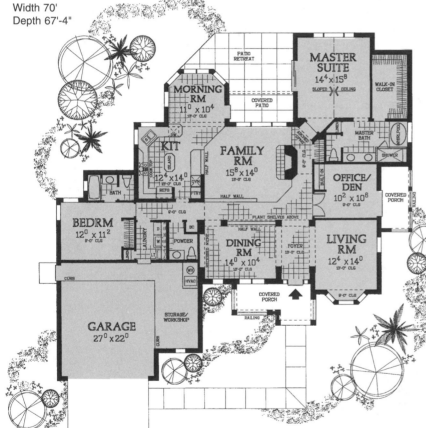

PATIO RETREAT

MORNING RM
11⁰ x 10⁴

COVERED PATIO

MASTER SUITE
14⁴ x 15⁸
SLOPED CEILING

WALK-IN CLOSET

KIT
12⁰ x 14⁰

FAMILY RM
15⁸ x 14⁰

MASTER BATH

SHOWER

BATH

HALF WALL

OFFICE/DEN
10² x 10⁶

COVERED PORCH

BEDRM
12⁰ x 11²

LAUNDRY

POWDER

PLANT SHELVES ABOVE

HALF WALL

DINING RM
14⁰ x 10⁴

FOYER

LIVING RM
12⁴ x 14⁰

GARAGE
27⁰ x 22⁰

STORAGE/WORKSHOP

HVAC

COVERED PORCH

RAILING

Design by
Home Planners

Design 3602

Square Footage: 2,312

L

● This lovely one-story home fits right into sunny regions—its stucco exterior with easily accessed outdoor living areas makes it an all-time favorite. Inside, the floor plan is especially good for newlyweds or empty-nesters. There is plenty of space for both formal and informal entertaining: living room, dining room, family room and morning room. An office/den has its own entrance and French doors that can be closed for privacy. Sleeping areas are split, with the master bedroom and bath on one side and a secondary bedroom and bath on the other. Additional special features include a warming hearth in the family room, a workshop/storage area in the garage and a covered rear patio.

QUOTE ONE®

Cost to build? See page 374 to order complete cost estimate to build this house in your area!

REAR ELEVATION

227

Design by
Home Planners

Design 3661/3665

Square Footage: 2,385/2,678

L

● A vaulted entry and tall windows complement a classic stucco exterior on this Floridian-style home. Inside, the great room offers a warming fireplace, an entertainment center and access to a patio retreat. The efficient island kitchen serves a sunny breakfast nook and a beautiful bayed formal dining room. A secluded master wing soothes the homeowner with a sumptuous bath and an inner retreat with access to a private patio/garden area. Both plans include two family bedrooms at the rear of the house and an office or guest room to the front. Design 3665 adds a fifth bedroom near the garage, while Design 3661 uses the space to make room for a third car.

Design 3661

Width 76'-6"
Depth 77'-4"

Design 3665

QUOTE ONE®

Cost to build? See page 374 to order complete cost estimate to build this house in your area!

Design 3633

Square Footage: 3,163

L

Design by
Home Planners

● A wraparound covered porch and an open courtyard plus a wonderful floor plan make a happy marriage of indoor-outdoor living. Art collectors will appreciate the entry gallery that showcases their favorite works. The formal dining room accommodates special occasions with style, while casual mealtimes are enjoyed at the country kitchen's snack bar or nearby breakfast room. The nucleus for formal and informal entertaining will be the great room with its raised-hearth fireplace flanked by built-in media centers. A guest suite and two family bedrooms are on one side of the plan, with the master suite providing a private retreat on the other. There you can relax in the sitting area, go outside to the covered arbor, or enjoy a pampering soak in the corner whirlpool.

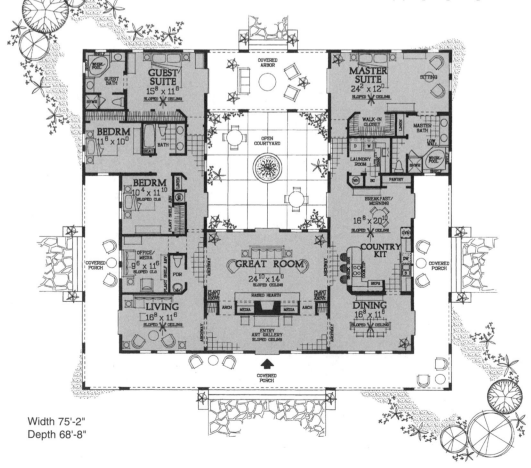

Width 75'-2"
Depth 68'-8"

Design 8682

Square Footage: 2,551
Bonus Room: 287 square feet

● Shutters and multi-pane windows dress up the exterior of this lovely stucco home. Formal and informal areas flow easily, beginning with the dining room sized to accommodate large parties and function with the adjacent living room. This area is joined to the family room by an archway, thus allowing easy circulation during large gatherings. A gourmet kitchen is complete with a walk-in pantry and is a step away from the breakfast nook. Double doors lead to the spacious master suite. The lavish master bath features His and Hers walk-in closets, a tub framed by a column archway and an oversized shower. Off the angular hallway are two bedrooms that share a pullman-style bath and a study desk. A bonus room over the garage provides additional space.

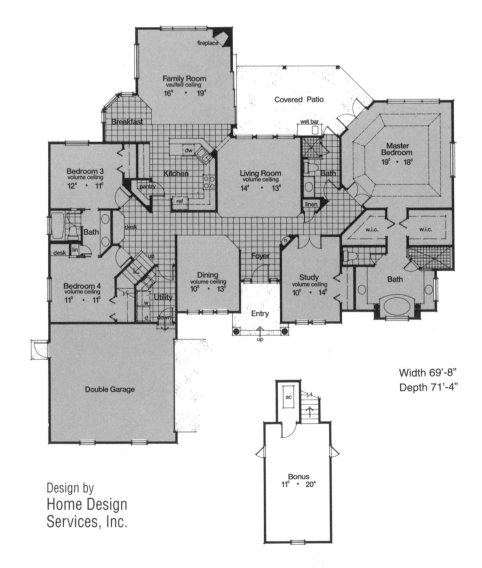

Width 69'-8"
Depth 71'-4"

Design by
Home Design
Services, Inc.

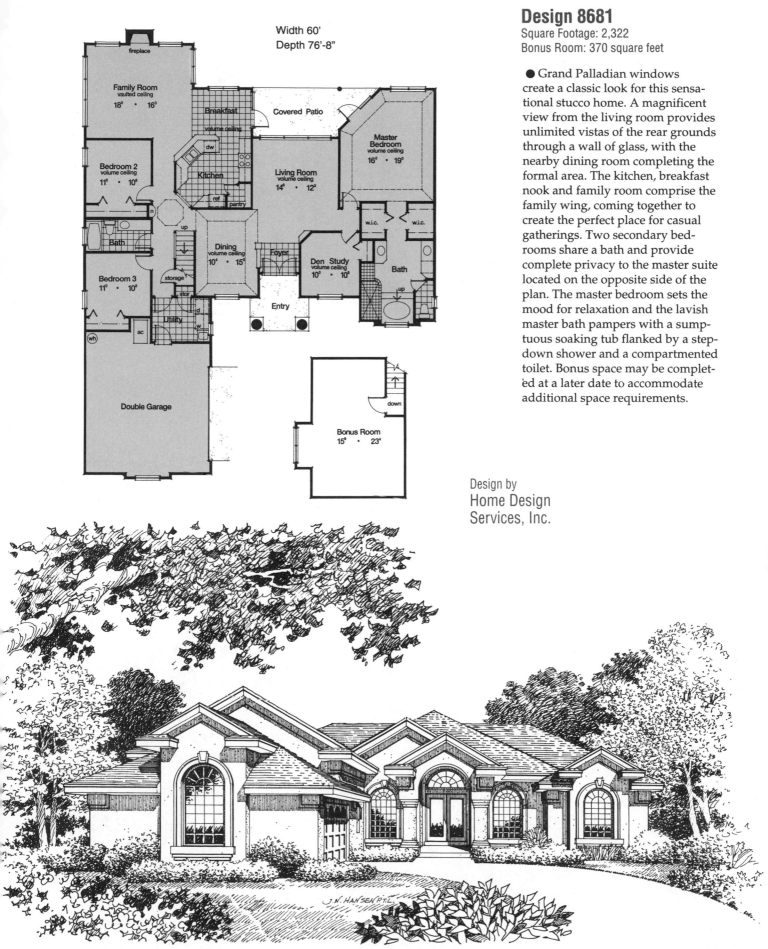

Width 60'
Depth 76'-8"

fireplace

Family Room
vaulted ceiling
18⁰ · 16⁰

Breakfast
volume ceiling

Covered Patio

Bedroom 2
volume ceiling
11⁰ · 10⁰

dw

Master
Bedroom
volume ceiling
16⁰ · 19⁰

Kitchen

Living Room
14⁴ · 12⁰

ref

pantry

Bath

up

w.i.c.

w.i.c.

Bedroom 3
11⁰ · 10⁰

Dining
volume ceiling
10⁴ · 15⁰

Foyer

Den Study
volume ceiling
10⁰ · 10⁰

Bath

storage

stor

up

Utility

Entry

ac

wh

Double Garage

Bonus Room
15⁰ · 23⁴

down

Design 8681

Square Footage: 2,322
Bonus Room: 370 square feet

● Grand Palladian windows create a classic look for this sensational stucco home. A magnificent view from the living room provides unlimited vistas of the rear grounds through a wall of glass, with the nearby dining room completing the formal area. The kitchen, breakfast nook and family room comprise the family wing, coming together to create the perfect place for casual gatherings. Two secondary bedrooms share a bath and provide complete privacy to the master suite located on the opposite side of the plan. The master bedroom sets the mood for relaxation and the lavish master bath pampers with a sumptuous soaking tub flanked by a step-down shower and a compartmented toilet. Bonus space may be completed at a later date to accommodate additional space requirements.

Design by
Home Design
Services, Inc.

J.N. HANSEN P.T.C.

Design 8600
Square Footage: 2,041

● The striking facade of this house is only the beginning to a very livable design. A dramatic foyer with columns branches off into the living room on one side, the dining room on the other. A spacious family room graces the center of the house—a true focal point. Beyond the kitchen and breakfast nook you'll find the master bedroom with private access to the covered patio. Three family bedrooms occupy the other side of the house.

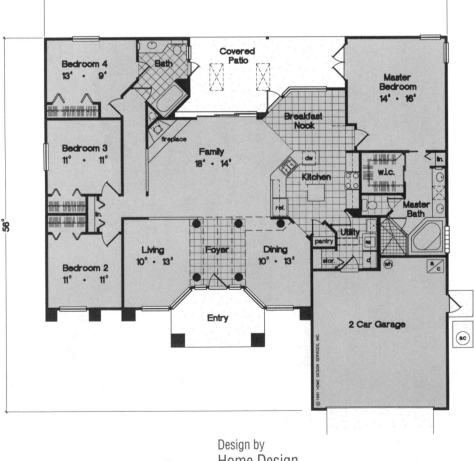

Design by
Home Design
Services, Inc.

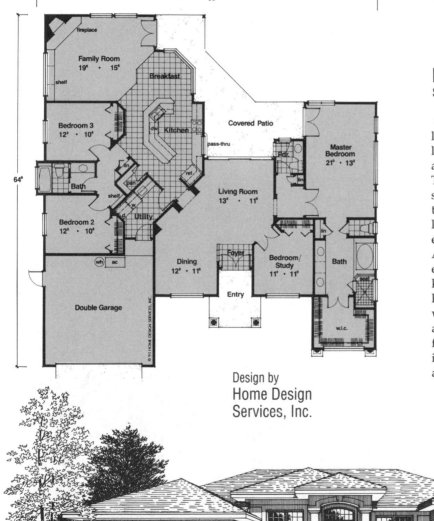

Design by
Home Design
Services, Inc.

Design 8647
Square Footage: 2,373

● This unique design takes the 90s lifestyle one step further. The formal living and dining space is in demand among families with young children. The "swing" room—bedroom/study—acts as the perfect guest room too. The master suite is replete with a luxurious bath, a huge closet, a shower built for two and vanity space. Angular design expertise creates an expansive feel in a very organized kitchen with access to the outdoor living area. The nook and family room with an angled media/fireplace creates excellent furniture arrangement for the active family. The huge walk-in pantry and generous laundry room are essential details in modern homes.

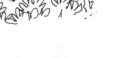

Design 9453
Square Footage: 3,524

● Just about any "extra"
you might ever conceive of
has been thoughtfully
incorporated into this striking one-story home. Tray
vaulted ceilings are found
in the breakfast nook, sitting room, master bed-
room, dining room and living room. The den and the
foyer are raised, also.
Notice the entertainment
center in the sunken family
room and the area set aside
for exercise with built-in
wet bar. The master suite
has an unbelievably large
walk-in closet and sky-
lights and spa in the bath.
The rear terrace could be a
fine precursor to a swim-
ming pool.

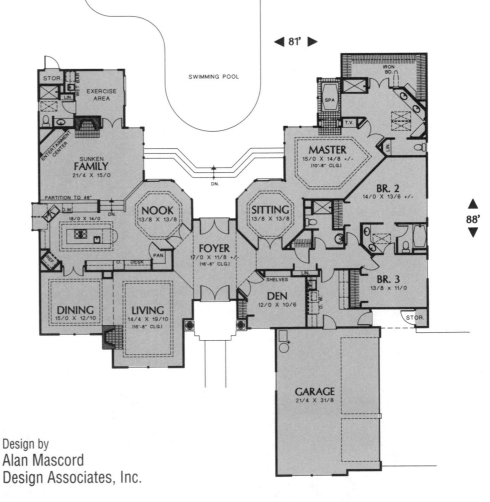

Design by
**Alan Mascord
Design Associates, Inc.**

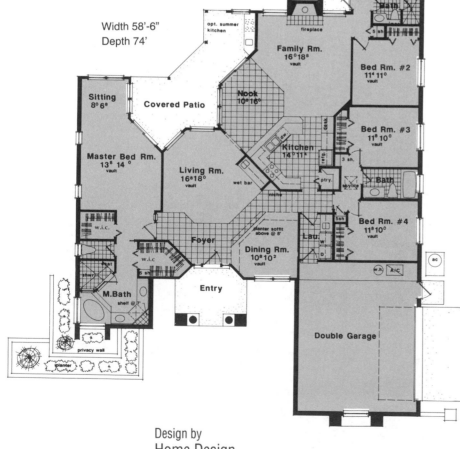

Width 58'-6"
Depth 74'

Sitting 8⁸ 6⁸

Covered Patio

Family Rm. 16⁰18⁸ vault

opt. summer kitchen

window above

fireplace

Bath 5 sh.

Bed Rm. #2 11⁴ 11⁰ vault

Nook 10⁰16⁰

Master Bed Rm. 13⁸ 14⁰ vault

Kitchen 14⁰11⁸

Living Rm. 16⁸18⁰ vault

wet bar

niche

ptry.

skylite

Bed Rm. #3 11⁸ 10⁰ vault

3 sh.

Bath

w.i.c.

Foyer

planter soffit above @ 8'

Dining Rm. 10⁸10² vault

Lau.

Bed Rm. #4 11⁸10⁰ vault

w.i.c

Entry

M.Bath shelf @'

w.h. A/C

ac

privacy wall

planter

Double Garage

Design by
**Home Design
Services, Inc.**

Design 8645
Square Footage: 2,224

● Arches crowned by gentle, hipped rooflines provide an Italianate charm in this bright, spacious, family-oriented plan. A covered entry leads to the foyer that presents the angular, vaulted living and dining rooms. A wet bar in the living room enhances livability. A kitchen with V-shape counter includes a walk-in pantry and looks out over the breakfast nook and family room with a fireplace. The master suite features a sitting area, two walk-in closets and a full bath with garden tub. Two additional bedrooms share a full bath located between them. A fourth bedroom, with its own bath, opens off the family room and works perfectly as a guest room.

Design by
**Home Design
Services, Inc.**

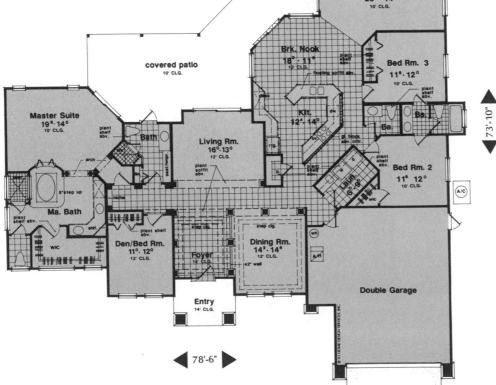

Design 8649
Square Footage: 2,691

● Italianate lines add finesse to the formal facade of this home. Strong symmetry, a soaring portico and gentle rooflines are the prized hallmarks of a relaxed, yet formal Italianate design. A stepped fourteen-foot ceiling highlights the entry foyer. To the right, columns and a stepped twelve-foot ceiling offset the dining room. A plant soffit heralds the living room which also has a twelve-foot ceiling. An angled cooktop counter adds flair to the kitchen, which also has a desk and walk-in pantry and serves the breakfast nook. A corner fireplace, a ten-foot ceiling and a patio enhance the family room. An arch opens the entry to the lavish master suite. Two additional bedrooms come with separate entries to a full bath.

Design 8669
Square Footage: 2,287

● This sunny home offers a wealth of livability in less than 2,300 square feet. The covered entry gives way to living and dining rooms. The kitchen is well equipped with a pantry and a breakfast room. The family room is a few steps away and delights with a fireplace. Two family bedrooms reside on this side of the plan. The master bedroom offers large proportions and an expansive bath with dual walk-in closets, a double-bowl lavatory, a whirlpool, a separate shower and a compartmented toilet. A den is located off the entry and can also serve as another bedroom.

Design by
Home Design
Services, Inc.

Width 63'-4"
Depth 62'-4"

Design 8621
Square Footage: 2,480

● This Florida contemporary
has been a best seller among
families who insist on formal
and casual living spaces. The
master's retreat, with a bay sitting area, is secluded away
from the family area for quiet
and solitude. The master bath
includes a sumptuous soaking
tub, shower for two, His and
Hers vanities and a huge walk-
in closet. The secondary bedrooms share a split bath,
designed for dual use as well as
privacy. The kitchen, nook and
family room all have magnificent views of the outdoor living
space. Note the media wall in
the family area—a must for
today's sophisticated buyers.

Design by
Home Design
Services, Inc.

Design by
Alan Mascord
Design Associates, Inc.

MASTER
12/8 X 15/6
(10'-4" CLG.)

BR 2
11/6 X 11/2
(9' CLG.)

FAMILY
15/0 X 18/0
(10'-4" CLG.)

NOOK
11/0 X 11/6

11/0 X 11/2

(14'-1" CLG.)

DINING
16/2 X 10/8
(10'-4" CLG.)

BR 3
10/4 X 12/0
(9' CLG.)

DEN
10/6 X 12/0
(10'-4" CLG.)

GARAGE
19/4 X 20/8

LIVING
13/0 X 14/6
(15'-4" CLG.)

Design 9578
Square Footage: 2,225

● This home exemplifies clever floor patterning. Casual living takes off in the kitchen, nook and family room. A fireplace here will warm gatherings. A dining room is nearby, as are a den and a living room. A see-through fireplace graces these areas. In the master bedroom suite, a garden tub and dual lavatories accommodate the owners. Two secondary bedrooms share a hall bath, also with dual lavatories. A laundry room connects the two-car garage.

QUOTE ONE®
Cost to build? See page 374
to order complete cost estimate
to build this house in your area!

Width 45'
Depth 73'

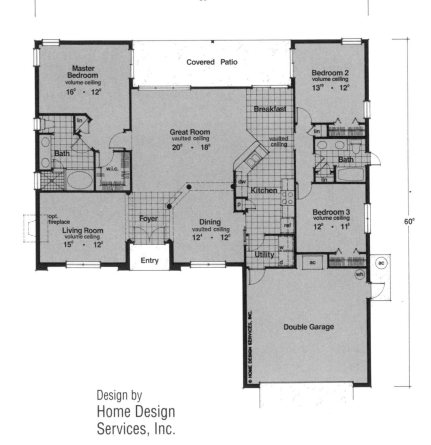

Design by
Home Design
Services, Inc.

Design 8662
Square Footage: 2,005

● A super floor plan makes this volume home that much more attractive. Inside you'll find a formal dining room—defined by columns—to the right and a living room—with an optional fireplace—to the left. Beyond this area is an expansive great room with a vaulted ceiling and openness to the kitchen and breakfast room. A covered patio in the back of the house enhances outdoor livability. Two secondary bedrooms complete the right side of the plan. Each features a volume ceiling, ample closet space and the use of a full hall bath with dual lavatories. The master bedroom enjoys its own bath with a whirlpool tub, separate shower, dual vanity and compartmented toilet.

Vaulted Family Room 17⁵ x 14⁰

Breakfast

TRAY CLG.

PANTRY

SERVING BAR

STEP DN

D.W.

Kitchen

ISLAND

SURFACE UNIT

DOUBLE OVEN

Sunken Living Room 14⁰ x 13⁴

11'-0" clg. height

TRAY CLG.

Master Suite 17⁰ x 13⁴

SHWR

LINEN

DRYING AREA

Vaulted M. Bath

VAULT

VAULT

TUB

K.S.

W.i.c.

OPT. CO.

Vaulted Bedroom 4/ Opt. Sitting Room 12⁵ x 11⁹

K.S.

Bath

LINEN

Laundry

D.   W.

Storage

DESK

REF.

STEP DN

Foyer 10'-4" clg. height

Dining Room 13⁵ x 11⁷

Bedroom 2 11⁰ x 12²

Bath

Bedroom 3 11⁰ x 12⁰

Garage 20⁵ x 20⁹

copyright © 1989 frank betz associates, inc.

Width 65'
Depth 68'-10"

Design by
Frank Betz
Associates, Inc.

Design P204

Square Footage: 2,302

● Attractive windows and gables welcome you to a well-designed interior. The formal dining room and sunken living room open from the foyer and separate the informal living areas from the sleeping zone. The vaulted family room offers plenty of space for relaxing in front of the fireplace as well as access to the rear property. The family cooks will enjoy the island kitchen with its peninsula serving bar, double ovens, built-in desk and walk-in pantry. Family and guests alike will tarry over coffee and conversation in the octagonal breakfast nook. The master suite boasts a tray ceiling, a door to the back yard and a deluxe private bath. Three family bedrooms—or make one into a sitting room—and two full baths complete the plan. Please specify basement, crawlspace or slab foundation when ordering.

Design by
Home Planners

Quote One®
Cost to build? See page 374
to order complete cost estimate
to build this house in your area!

Design 3603

Square Footage: 2,520

L

● This well-planned stucco home is
tailor-made for a small family or for
empty-nesters. Formal areas are situated
well for entertaining—living
room to the right and formal dining
room to the left of the foyer. A large
family room in the rear has access to a
covered patio and is warmed in the
cold months by a welcome hearth. The
efficient U-shaped kitchen features an
attached morning room for casual
meals and is near the laundry and a
powder room. The master suite provides
a private retreat and features a
fine bath and large walk-in closet. A
nearby office/den has a private porch.
Two secondary bedrooms are located
on the other side of the home and
share a full bath.

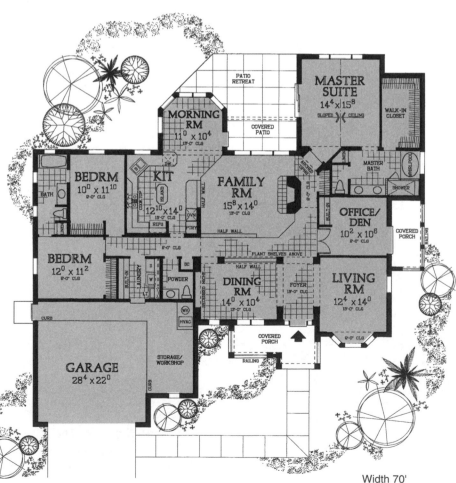

Width 70'
Depth 67'-4"

Design by
Home Design
Services, Inc.

Width 62'
Depth 83'-8"

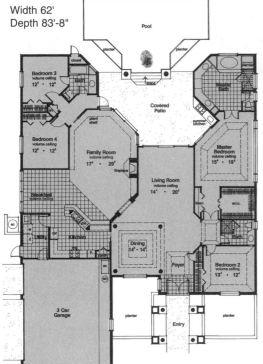

Design 8678

Square Footage: 3,091

● With elegant formal columns standing at attention around the entryway, this design starts off as impressive and only gets better. Inside, ceiling detail in the foyer and the formal dining room immediately reinforces the graceful qualities of this beautiful home. A large and airy living room awaits to accommodate any entertaining you might have in mind, while the spacious family room encourages more casual encounters with a warming fireplace and access to the covered patio. An angled kitchen is nearby and offers a sunny breakfast room for early risers. Three secondary bedrooms accommodate both family and friends, while a lavish master bedroom suite promises pampering for the fortunate homeowner.

Design by
Home Design
Services, Inc.

Design 8667

Square Footage: 2,258

● Columns add the finishing touch to a home with a choice of facades. The double-door entry opens to the foyer with a front-to-back view. The adjacent vaulted living room has sliding glass doors to the covered patio. The kitchen is open to both the living room and the bayed nook. A bow window and a fireplace define the rear of the family room. The tray-ceilinged master bedroom features covered patio access, dual walk-in closets and a spa tub. Two additional bedrooms share a full bath with a bay window. The plan includes both elevations.

ALTERNATE ELEVATION

Width 66'
Depth 73'-4"

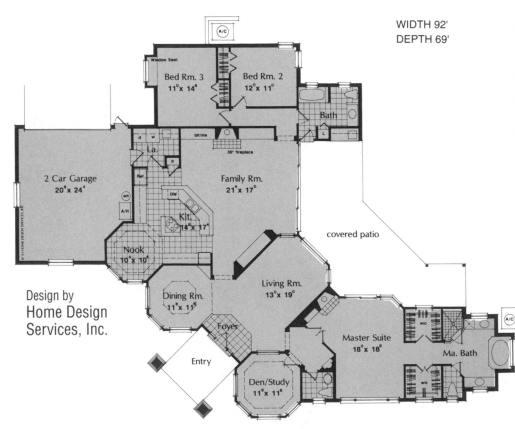

WIDTH 92'
DEPTH 69'

Design by
**Home Design
Services, Inc.**

Design 8603
Square Footage: 2,656

● A graceful design sets
this charming home apart
from the ordinary and tran-
scends the commonplace.
From the octagon foyer
paved in granite to the interesting breakfast nook, dining
room and den/study, this
well-executed plan incorporates rooms of varying
shapes but keeps its original
concept of spaciousness
intact. A large covered patio
adds to the living area.

Design 8653
Square Footage: 2,962

● Enter the formal foyer of this home and you are greeted with a traditional split living room/dining room layout. But the family room is where the real living takes place. It explodes onto the outdoor living space which features a summer kitchen. The ultimate master suite contains coffered ceilings, a "boomerang" vanity and angular mirrors that reflect the bayed soaking tub and shower. Efficient use of space creates a huge closet with little dead center space. The three-bedroom family wing contains one bedroom with a private bath for the ultimate privacy for guests. Two other bedrooms share a lavish bath that accesses the rear patio.

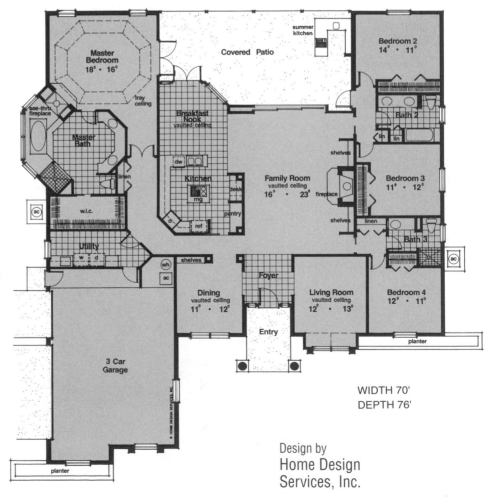

WIDTH 70'
DEPTH 76'

Design by
Home Design
Services, Inc.

245

Design 8601
Square Footage: 2,125

● A luxurious master suite is yours with this lovely plan—and it comes with two different options. Family bedrooms are on the opposite end of the home, separated from the master by the great room and kitchen/breakfast area. A formal dining room and den or study are to the front.

Design by
Home Design
Services, Inc.

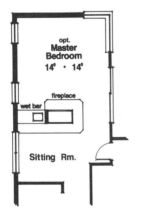

opt.
Master
Bedroom
14⁰ · 14⁰

wet bar   fireplace

Sitting Rm.

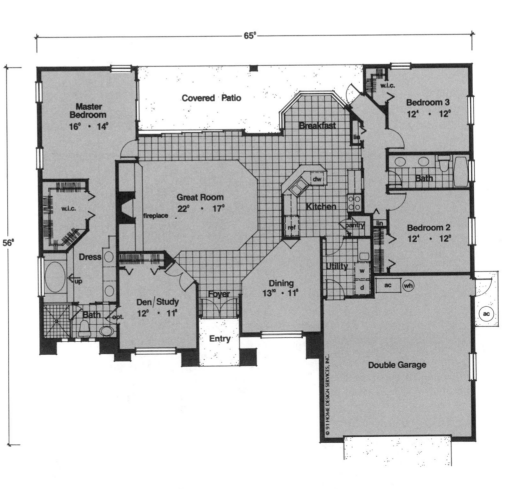

Design 8637
Square Footage: 2,089

● This four-bedroom, three-bath home offers the finest in modern amenities. The formal living spaces have a classic split design, perfect for quiet time and conversation. The unique design of the bedroom wing affords great flexibility for the family. Bedrooms 3 and 4 share their own bath while Bedroom 2 has a private bath with pool access, making it the perfect guest room. The huge family room, which opens up to the patio with twelve-foot, pocket sliding doors, has space for a fireplace and media equipment. The master suite, located just off the kitchen and nook, is private yet easily accessible. It has a double-door entry and a bed wall with glass above. The angled entry to the bath makes for a luxurious view of the corner tub. The step-down shower and private toilet room, walk-in linen closet, lavish vanity and closet make this a super bath!

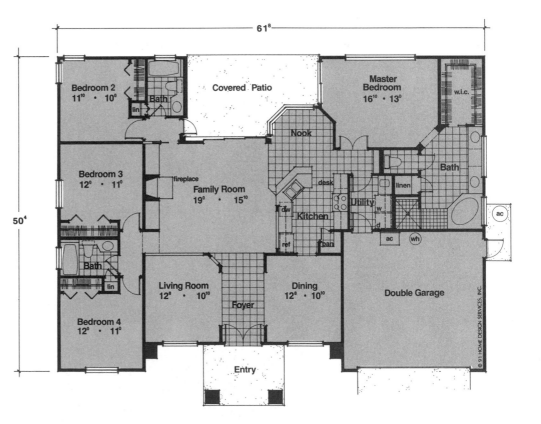

Design by
Home Design
Services, Inc.

Design by
Home Planners

QUOTE ONE®

Cost to build? See page 374
to order complete cost estimate
to build this house in your area!

Width 85'-9"
Depth 67'-10"

Design 3643

Square Footage: 2,092

L

● Stucco walls highlighted by simple window treatment and glass-block patterns introduce a fine, western-style home. High ceilings and open planning contribute to the spaciousness of the interior. To the left of the large foyer is the angular dining room with half-walls and tray ceiling. The formal living room has a high viga, or beamed, ceiling and a commanding corner fireplace with a raised hearth and banco, or bench. It also offers access to the covered rear patio. Past the built-in bookshelves of the family room is the hallway to the sleeping zone.

Design 3694

Square Footage: 2,226

L

● An impressive double-door entry to a walled courtyard sets the tone for this Santa Fe home. The expansive great room shows off its casual style with a centerpiece fireplace and windows overlooking the patio. The large gourmet kitchen has a pass-through to the dining room as well as an eating nook and snack bar for casual entertaining. Family room extras include a fireplace, entertainment built-ins and access to the front courtyard. Two family bedrooms are nearby, while the relaxing master suite is privately located off the back patio.

Width 103'-2"
Depth 78'

Design by
Home Planners

QUOTE ONE®

Cost to build? See page 374
to order complete cost estimate
to build this house in your area!

Design 3644

Square Footage: 2,015

● This Santa Fe-style home is as warm as a desert breeze and just as comfort-able. Outside details are reminiscent of old-style adobe homes, while the inte-rior caters to convenient living. The front covered porch leads to an open foyer. Columns define the formal dining room and the giant great room. The kitchen has an enormous pantry and a snack bar, and is connected to a break-fast nook with rear patio access. Two family bedrooms are found on the right side of the plan. They share a full bathroom with twin vanities. The master suite is on the left side of the plan and has a large walk-in closet and a bath with spa tub and separate shower. The home is completed with a three-car garage.

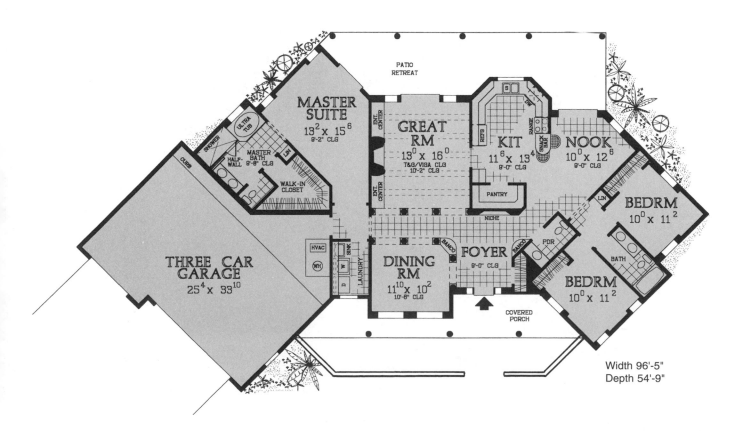

Design by
**Home Planners,
Inc.**

Design 3421
Square Footage: 2,145

L

● Split-bedroom planning makes the most of a one-story design. In this case the master suite is on the opposite side of the house from two family bedrooms. Gourmets can rejoice at the abundant work space in the U-shaped kitchen and will appreciate the natural light afforded by the large bay window in the breakfast room. A formal living room has a sunken conversation area with a cozy fireplace as its focus. The rear covered porch can be reached through sliding glass doors in the family room.

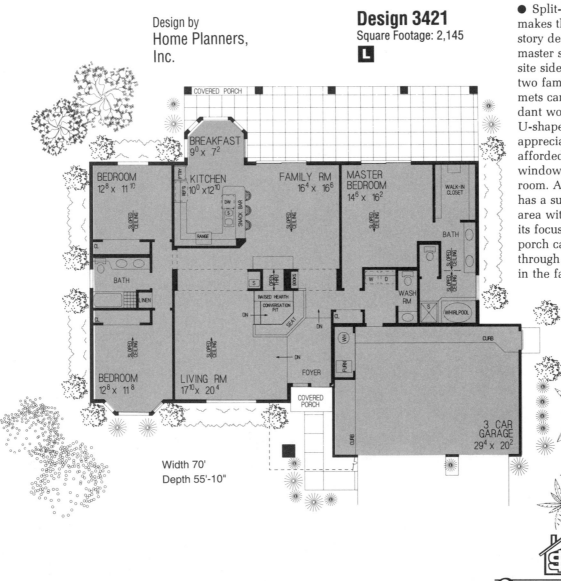

Width 70'
Depth 55'-10"

Design 3430

Square Footage: 2,394

L

● This dramatic design benefits from open planning. The centerpiece of the living area is a sunken conversation pit which shares a through-fireplace with the family room. The living room and dining room share space beneath a sloped ceiling. The open kitchen features a snack bar and breakfast room and conveniently serves all living areas. Split zoning in the sleeping area places the private master suite to the left of the plan and three more bedrooms, including one with a bay window, to the right.

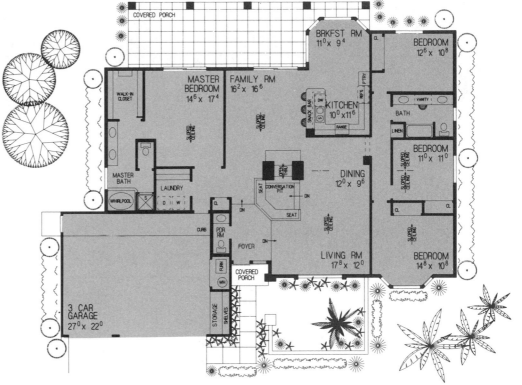

Width 72'
Depth 60'-6"

QUOTE ONE™

Cost to build? See page 374
to order complete cost estimate
to build this house in your area!

Design by
**Home Planners,
Inc.**

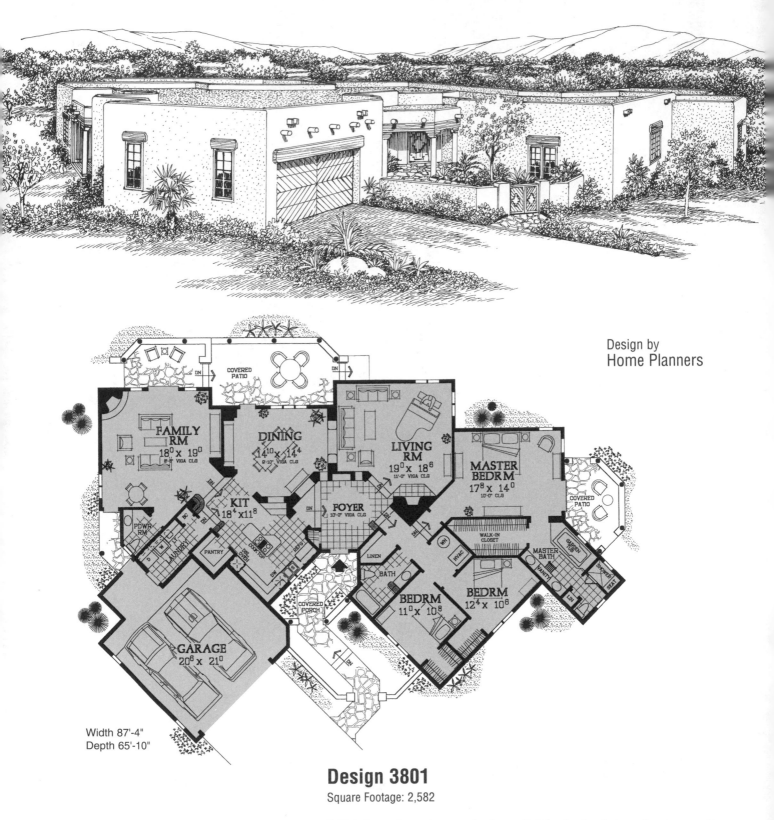

Design by
Home Planners

Width 87'-4"
Depth 65'-10"

Design 3801

Square Footage: 2,582

● This home is made to order for a slightly sloping lot—or have your site graded to fit its contours! The classic Pueblo styling includes projecting vigas, rounded corners and rough-sawn lintels. Enter by way of a walled courtyard that protects the entry. Down a step from the foyer, the living room features a massive corner fireplace and space for your grand piano. The formal dining room features a covered patio for *al fresco* meals and connects to the island kitchen for easy entertaining. For casual occasions, the family room serves up a corner fireplace and access to a second patio. The master suite has its own patio and a bath with a gigantic walk-in closet, garden tub and separate shower.

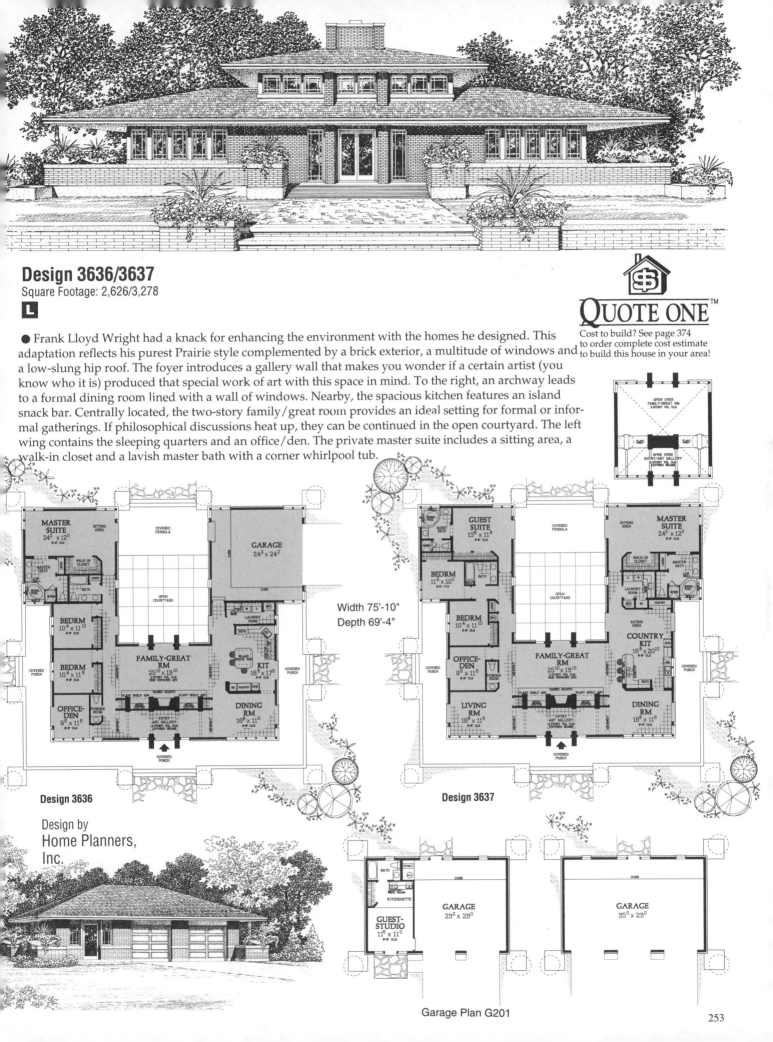

Design 3636/3637

Square Footage: 2,626/3,278

L

● Frank Lloyd Wright had a knack for enhancing the environment with the homes he designed. This adaptation reflects his purest Prairie style complemented by a brick exterior, a multitude of windows and a low-slung hip roof. The foyer introduces a gallery wall that makes you wonder if a certain artist (you know who it is) produced that special work of art with this space in mind. To the right, an archway leads to a formal dining room lined with a wall of windows. Nearby, the spacious kitchen features an island snack bar. Centrally located, the two-story family/great room provides an ideal setting for formal or informal gatherings. If philosophical discussions heat up, they can be continued in the open courtyard. The left wing contains the sleeping quarters and an office/den. The private master suite includes a sitting area, a walk-in closet and a lavish master bath with a corner whirlpool tub.

QUOTE ONE™

Cost to build? See page 374 to order complete cost estimate to build this house in your area!

Width 75'-10"
Depth 69'-4"

Design 3636

Design 3637

Design by
Home Planners, Inc.

Garage Plan G201

Design 3560

Square Footage: 2,189

L

● Simplicity is the key to the stylish good looks of this home's facade. A walled garden entry and large window areas appeal to outdoor enthusiasts. Inside, the kitchen forms the hub of the plan. It opens directly off the foyer and contains an island counter and a work counter with eating space on the living area side. A sloped ceiling, fireplace, and sliding glass doors to a rear terrace are highlights in the living area. The master bedroom also sports sliding glass doors to the terrace. Its dressing area is enhanced with double walk-in closets and lavatories. A whirlpool tub and seated shower are additional amenities. Two family bedrooms are found on the opposite side of the house. They share a full bath with twin lavatories.

California Engineered Plans and California Stock Plans are available for this home. Call 1-800-521-6797 for more information.

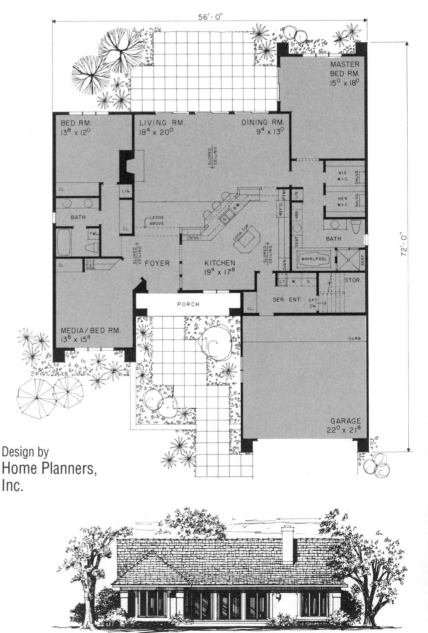

Design by
Home Planners,
Inc.

Quote One™

Cost to build? See page 374
to order complete cost estimate
to build this house in your area!

Design 3368
Square Footage: 2,720

L **D**

QUOTE ONE™

Cost to build? See page 374
to order complete cost estimate
to build this house in your area!

● Roof lines are the key to the interesting exterior of this design. Their configuration allow for sloped ceilings in the gathering room and large foyer. The master bedroom suite has a huge walk-in closet, garden whirlpool and separate shower. Two family bedrooms share a full bath. One of these bedrooms could be used as a media room with pass-through wet bar. Note the large kitchen with conversation bay and the wide terrace to the rear.

Design by
**Home Planners,
Inc.**

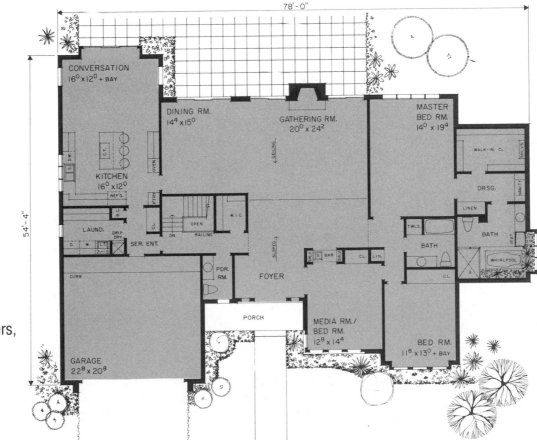

Design by
Home Planners,
Inc.

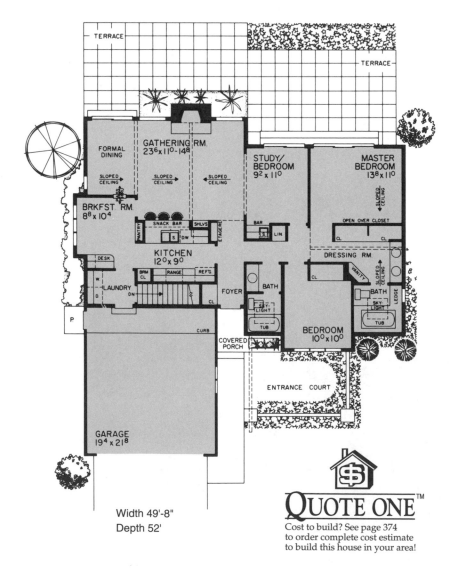

Design 2864

Square Footage: 1,387

L **D**

● Projecting the garage to the front of a house is very economical in two ways. One, it reduces the required lot size for building and, two, it protects the interior from street noise. Many other characteristics about this design deserve mention, too. Upon entering, the foyer will take you to the various areas. The interior kitchen has an adjacent breakfast room and a snack bar on the gathering room side. A study with a wet bar is adjacent. Sliding glass doors here and in the master bedroom open to the terrace.

California Engineered Plans and California Stock Plans are available for this home. Call 1-800-521-6797 for more information.

Width 49'-8"
Depth 52'

Design 3357
Square Footage: 2,913

L **D**

Design by
Home Planners,
Inc.

Width 82'-8"
Depth 74'

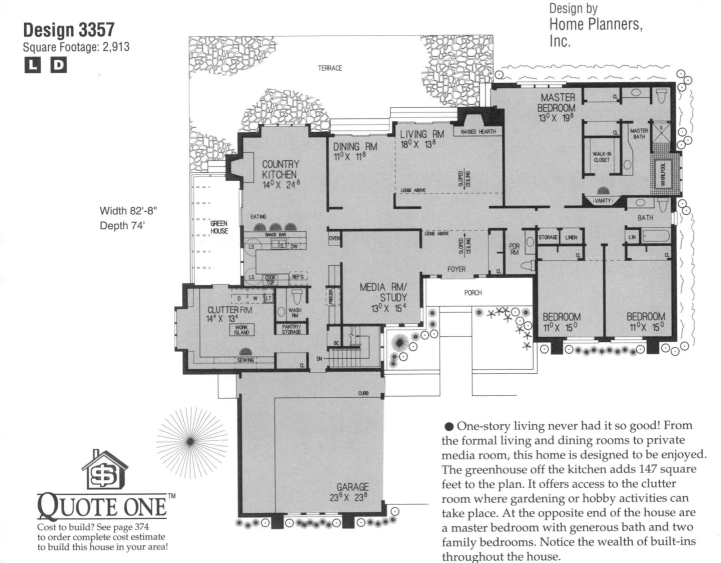

Quote One™
Cost to build? See page 374
to order complete cost estimate
to build this house in your area!

● One-story living never had it so good! From
the formal living and dining rooms to private
media room, this home is designed to be enjoyed.
The greenhouse off the kitchen adds 147 square
feet to the plan. It offers access to the clutter
room where gardening or hobby activities can
take place. At the opposite end of the house are
a master bedroom with generous bath and two
family bedrooms. Notice the wealth of built-ins
throughout the house.

257

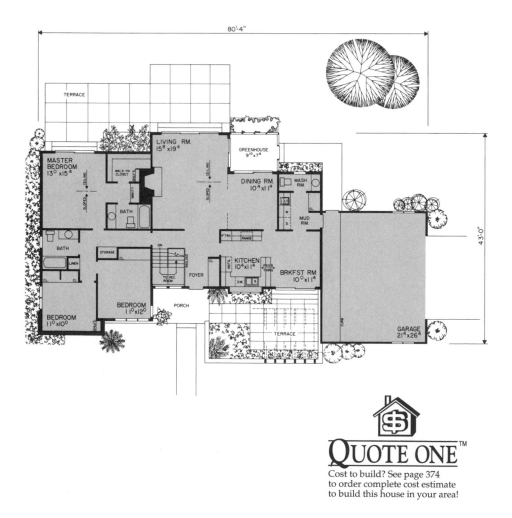

TERRACE

MASTER
BEDROOM
13⁰x15⁴

WALK-IN
CLOSET

LIVING RM.
15⁸x19⁴

GREENHOUSE
9¹⁰x7⁸

BATH

DINING RM.
10⁴x11⁴

WASH
RM.

W

MUD
RM.

BATH

STORAGE

LINEN

DN
TO REC.
ROOM

FOYER

KITCHEN
10⁴x11⁴

RANGE

REF'S.

BRKFST RM.
10⁰x11⁴

CURB

BEDROOM
11⁰x12⁰

PORCH

BEDROOM
11⁰x10⁰

TERRACE

GARAGE
21⁴x26⁴

80'-4"

43'-0"

Design by
Home Planners,
Inc.

Design 2871

Square Footage: 1,905

D

● A greenhouse area off the dining room and living room provides a cheerful focal point for this comfortable three-bedroom Trend home. The spacious living room features a cozy fireplace and sloped ceiling. In addition to the dining room, there's a less formal breakfast room just off the modern kitchen. Both kitchen and breakfast areas look out into a front terrace. Stairs just off the foyer lead down to a recreation room. Master bedroom suite opens to a terrace. A mud room and washroom off the garage allow rear entry to the house during inclement weather.

QUOTE ONE™
Cost to build? See page 374
to order complete cost estimate
to build this house in your area!

Design by
Home Planners,
Inc.

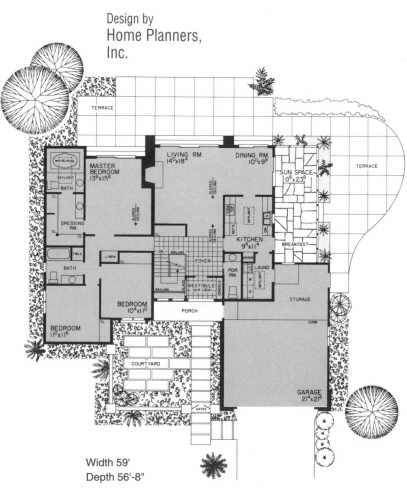

Width 59'
Depth 56'-8"

Design 2902

Square Footage: 1,632

L

● A sun space highlights this passive solar design. It has access from the kitchen, dining room and garage. It will be a great place to enjoy meals because of its location. Three skylights highlight the interior - one in the kitchen, laundrey and master bath. An air-locked vestibule helps this design's energy efficiency. Interior livability is excellent. The living/dining room has a sloping ceiling, fireplace and two sets of sliding glass doors to the terrace. This area will cater to numerous family activities. Additional activities can take place in the basement. Note its open staircase. Three bedrooms are in the sleeping wing. The square footage of the sun space is 216 and is not included in the above figure.

Cost to build? See page 374
to order complete cost estimate
to build this house in your area!

Quote One™

Cost to build? See page 374 to order complete cost estimate to build this house in your area!

● This is most certainly an outstanding contemporary design. Study the exterior carefully before your journey to inspect the floor plan. The vertical lines are carried from the siding to the paned windows to the garage door. The front entry is recessed so the overhanging roof creates a covered porch.

Note the planter court with privacy wall. The floor plan is just as outstanding. The rear gathering room has a sloped ceiling, raised hearth fireplace, sliding glass doors to the terrace and a snack bar with pass-thru to the kitchen. In addition to the gathering room, there is the living room/study. This

room could be utilized in a variety of ways depending on your family's choice. The formal dining room is convenient to the U-shaped kitchen. Three bedrooms and two closely located baths are in the sleeping wing. This plan includes details for the construction of an optional basement.

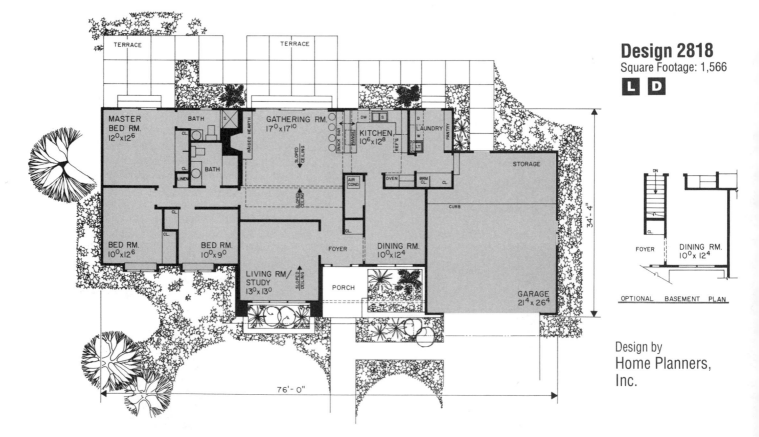

Design 2818
Square Footage: 1,566

L D

OPTIONAL BASEMENT PLAN

Design by
Home Planners,
Inc.

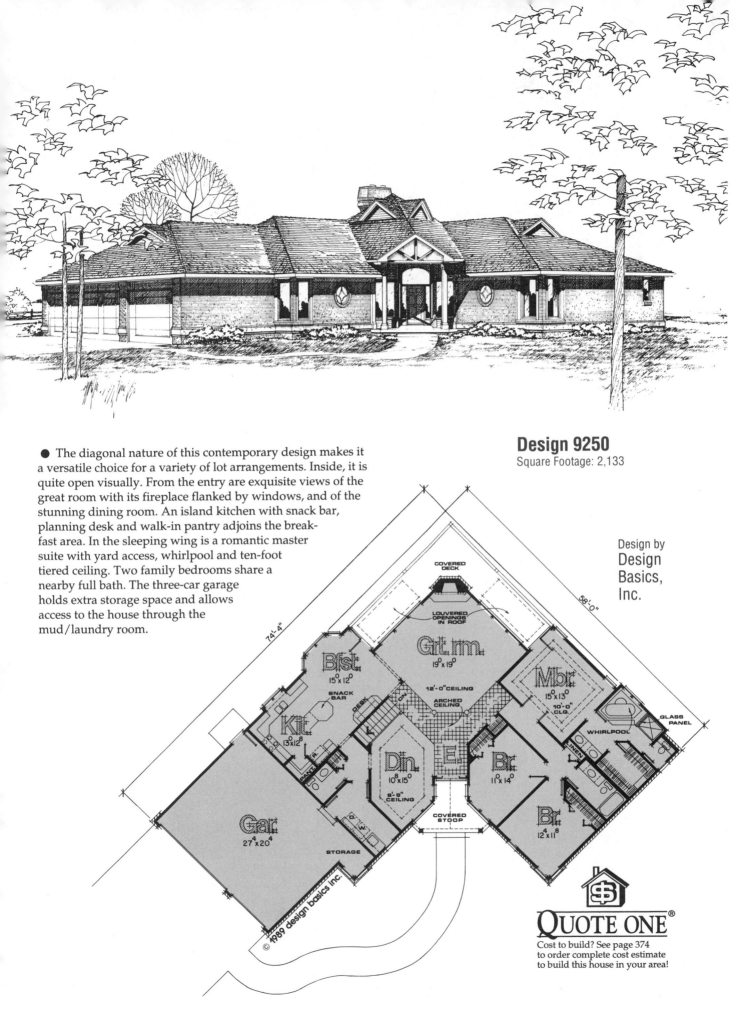

● The diagonal nature of this contemporary design makes it a versatile choice for a variety of lot arrangements. Inside, it is quite open visually. From the entry are exquisite views of the great room with its fireplace flanked by windows, and of the stunning dining room. An island kitchen with snack bar, planning desk and walk-in pantry adjoins the break-fast area. In the sleeping wing is a romantic master suite with yard access, whirlpool and ten-foot tiered ceiling. Two family bedrooms share a nearby full bath. The three-car garage holds extra storage space and allows access to the house through the mud/laundry room.

Design 9250
Square Footage: 2,133

Design by
Design
Basics,
Inc.

QUOTE ONE®
Cost to build? See page 374
to order complete cost estimate
to build this house in your area!

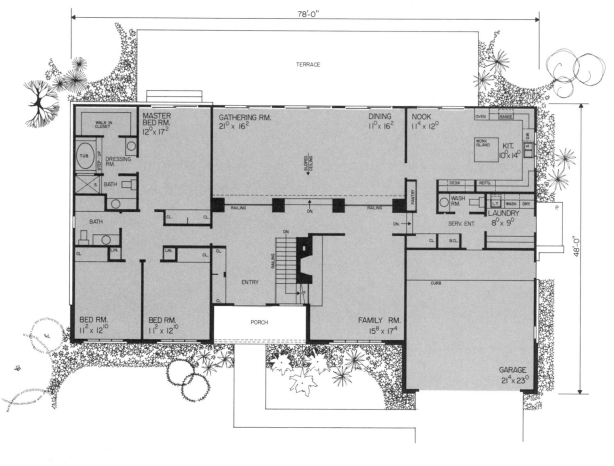

Design 2756

Square Footage: 2,652

L **D**

● This one-story, contemporary design is bound to serve your family well. It will assure the best in contemporary living with its many fine features. Notice the bath with tub and stall shower, dressing room and walk-in closet featured with the master bedroom. Two more family bedrooms are adjacent. The sunken gathering room/dining room is highlighted by the sloped ceiling and sliding glass doors to the large, rear terrace. This formal area is a full 32' x 16'. Imagine the great furniture placement that can be done in this area. In addition to the gathering room, there is an informal family room with a fireplace. You will enjoy the efficient kitchen and get much use out of the work island, pantry and built-in desk. Note the service entrance with washroom and laundry.

Design by
Home Planners,
Inc.

Design 2866
Square Footage: 2,371

● An extra living unit has been built into the design of this home. It would make an excellent "mother-in-law" suite. Should you choose not to develop this area as indicated, maybe you might use it as two more bedrooms, a guest suite or even as hobby and game rooms. Whatever its final use, it will complement the rest of this home. The main house also deserves mention. The focal point will be the large gathering room. Its features include a skylight, sloped ceiling, centered fireplace flanked on both sides by sliding glass doors and adjacent is a dining room on one side, study on the other. The work center is clustered together. Three bedrooms and two baths make up the private area. Note the outdoor areas: court with privacy wall, two covered porches and a large terrace.

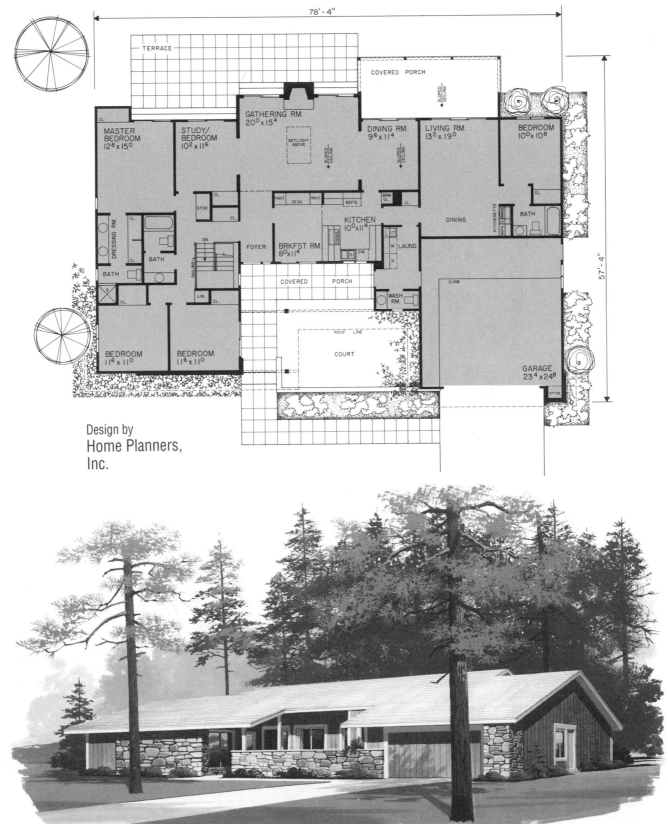

Design by
Home Planners,
Inc.

Design 2913

Square Footage: 1,835

D

● This smart design features multi-gabled ends, varied roof lines, and vertical windows. It also offers efficient zoning by room functions and plenty of modern comforts for Contemporary family lifestyle. A covered porch leads through a foyer to a large central gathering room with fireplace, sloped ceiling, and its own special view of a rear terrace. A modern kitchen with snack bar has a pass-thru to a breakfast room with view of the terrace. There's also an adjacent dining room. A media room isolated along with bedrooms from the rest of the house offers a quiet private area for listening to stereos or VCRs. A master bedroom suite includes its own whirlpool. A large garage includes extra storage.

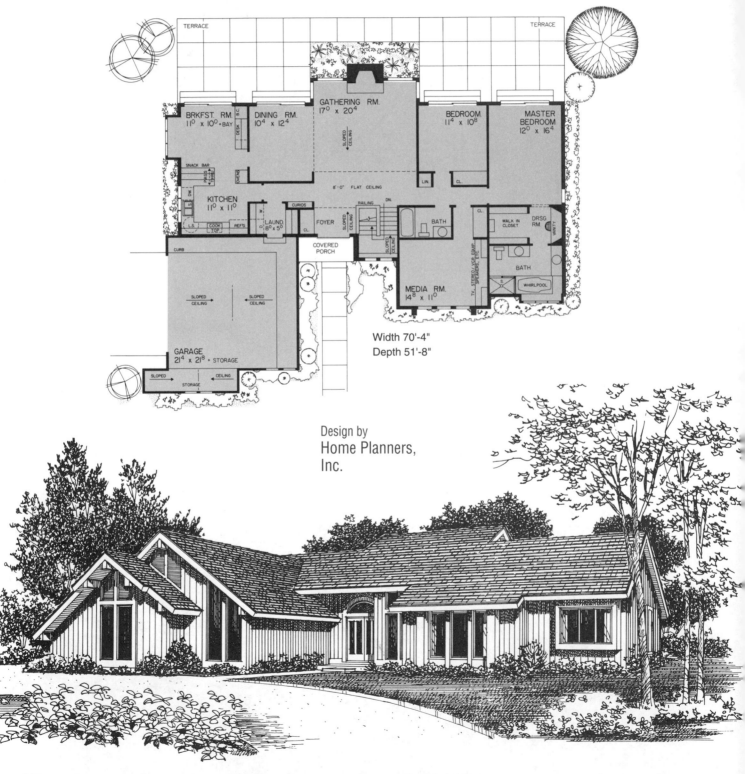

Width 70'-4"
Depth 51'-8"

Design by
Home Planners,
Inc.

Design 2915 Square Footage: 2,758

L **D**

● The features of this appealing contemporary design go far beyond the clutter and media rooms. The country kitchen is spacious and caters to the family's informal living and dining activities. While it overlooks the rear yard it is just a step from the delightful greenhouse. The size of the greenhouse is 8'x18' and contains 149 square feet not included in the square footage quoted above. The formal living and dining areas feature spacious open planning. The foyer is large and routes traffic to all areas. The sleeping zone is well-planned. Two children's bedrooms have good wardrobe facilities and a full bath. The master bedroom is exceptional and large enough to accommodate a sitting area. Two walk-in closets, a vanity area with a lavatory and a compartmented bath are noteworthy.

California Engineered Plans and California Stock Plans are available for this home. Call 1-800-521-6797 for more information.

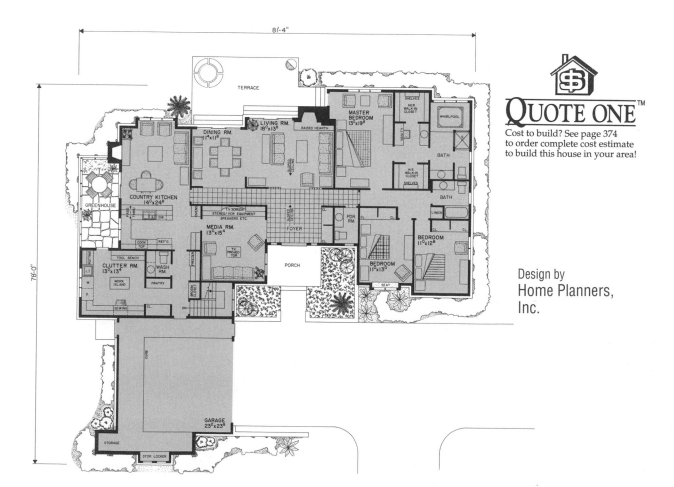

QUOTE ONE™

Cost to build? See page 374 to order complete cost estimate to build this house in your area!

Design by
Home Planners, Inc.

Design 1947

Square Footage: 1,764

● When it comes to housing your family, if you are among the contemporary-minded, you'll want to give this L-shaped design a second, even a third, or fourth, look. Inside, you will see a continuation of the contemporary theme with sloping ceilings, exposed beams and a practical 42-inch-high storage divider between the living and dining rooms. The family room warms with a fireplace. The U-shaped kitchen serves this area with a snack bar. Three bedrooms include a master bedroom with a private, compartmented bath.

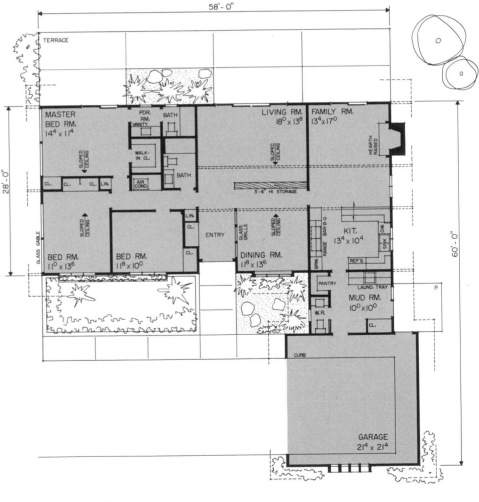

Design by
Home Planners,
Inc.

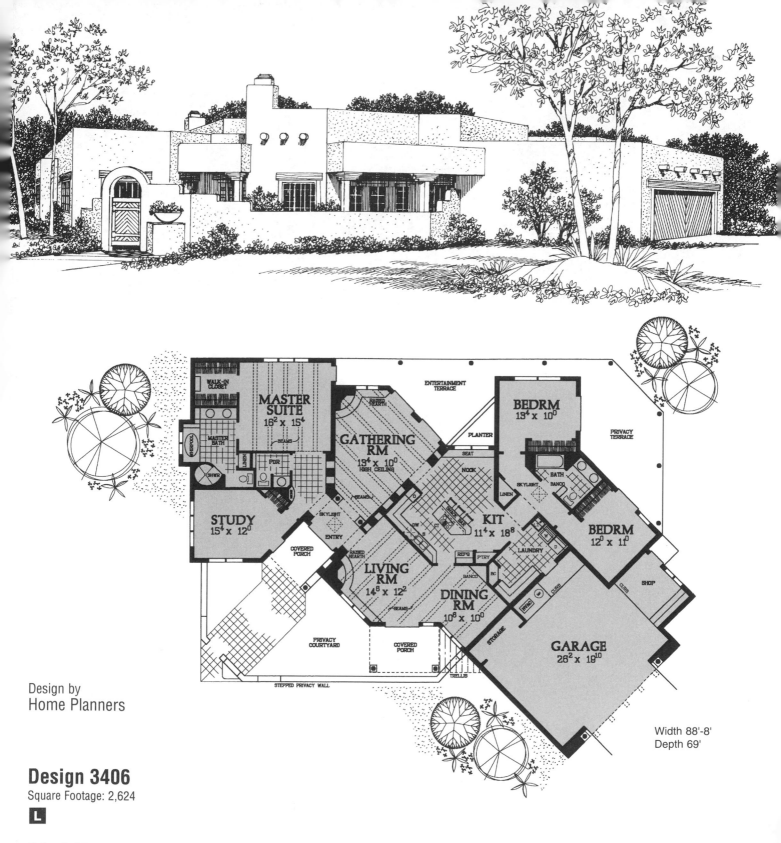

Design by
Home Planners

Design 3406
Square Footage: 2,624

L

● Angled living spaces add interest to this already magnificent Santa Fe home. From the offset entry you can travel straight back to the open gathering room—or turn to the right to enter the formal living and dining rooms. The huge kitchen is centralized and features an L-shaped work area with an island. Secondary bedrooms open to a side terrace and share a full bath. The master suite is complemented by a warm study and is separated from the secondary bedrooms for privacy.

Width 88'-8'
Depth 69'

Cost to build? See page 374
to order complete cost estimate
to build this house in your area!

Design 2793
Square Footage: 2,065

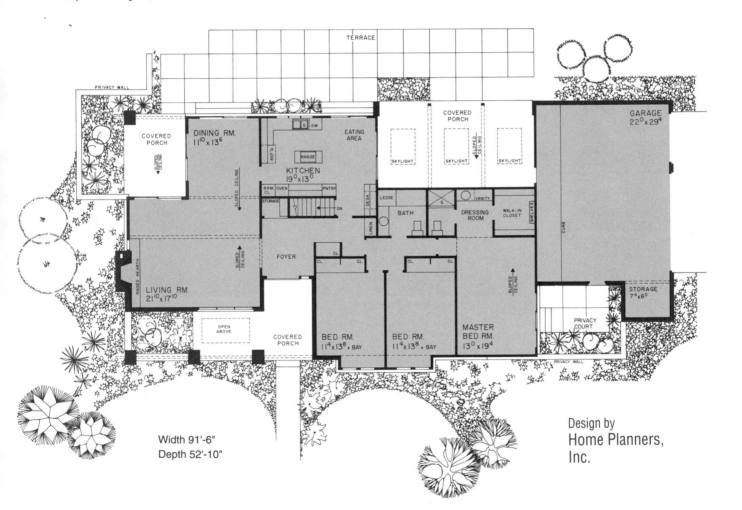

Width 91'-6"
Depth 52'-10"

Design by
Home Planners, Inc.

● Privacy will be enjoyed in this home both inside and out. The indoor-outdoor living relationships offered in this plan are outstanding. A covered porch at the entrance. A privacy court off the master bedroom divided from the front yard with a privacy wall. A covered porch serving both the living and dining rooms through sliding glass doors. Also utilizing a privacy wall. Another covered porch off the kitchen eating area. This one is the largest and has skylights above. Also a large rear terrace. The kitchen is efficient with eating space available, an island range and built-in desk. Storage space is abundant. Note storage area in the garage and its overall size. Three front bedrooms. Raised-hearth fireplace in the living room.

Design by
Home Planners,
Inc.

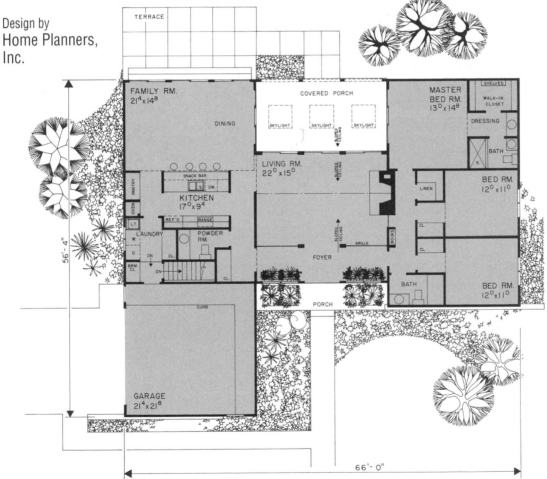

TERRACE

FAMILY RM.
21⁴x14⁸

DINING

COVERED PORCH

SKYLIGHT SKYLIGHT SKYLIGHT

SLOPED CEILING

MASTER
BED RM.
13⁰x14⁸

SHELVES

WALK-IN
CLOSET

DRESSING

BATH

PANTRY

SNACK BAR

S. DW.

KITCHEN
17⁰x9⁴

OVEN

REF'G RANGE

L.T.

LAUNDRY

W.

POWDER
RM.

D.

BRM
CL.

DN

DN

CL.

CL.

LIVING RM.
22⁰x15⁰

SLOPED CEILING

FOYER

LINEN

SLOPED CEILING

GRILLE

BOOKS

CL.

CL.

BED RM.
12⁰x11⁰

BATH

BED RM.
12⁰x11⁰

56'-4"

CURB

GARAGE
21⁴x21⁸

PORCH

66'-0"

Design 2790
Square Footage: 2,075

● Enter this comtemporary hip-roofed home through the double front doors and immediately view the sloped-ceilinged living room with fireplace. This room will be a sheer delight when it comes to formal entertaining. It has easy access to the kitchen and also a powder room nearby. The work area will be convenient. The kitchen has an island work center with snack bar. The laundry is adjacent to the service entrance and stairs leading to the basement. This area is planned to be a real "step saver". The sleeping wing consists of two family bedrooms, bath and master bedroom suite. Maybe the most attractive feature of this design is the rear covered porch with skylights above. It is accessible by way of sliding glass doors in the family/dining area, living room and master bedroom.

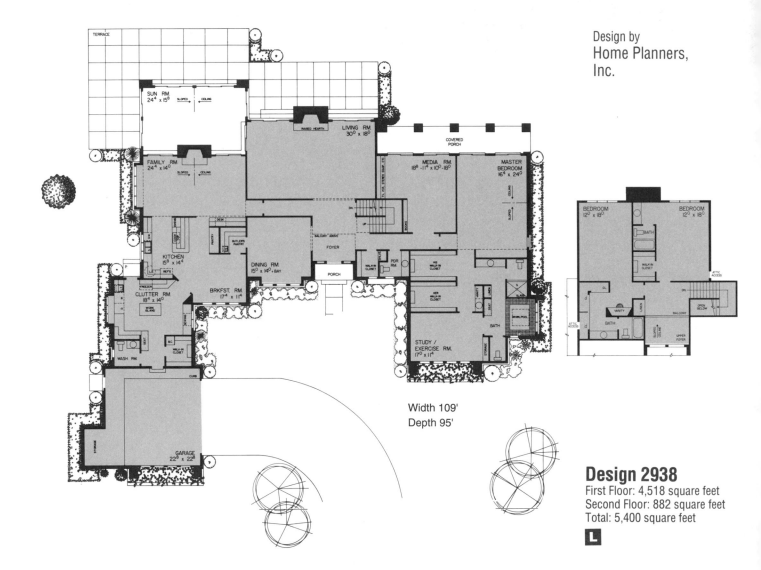

Design by
**Home Planners,
Inc.**

Width 109'
Depth 95'

Design 2938
First Floor: 4,518 square feet
Second Floor: 882 square feet
Total: 5,400 square feet

L

● A semi-circular fanlight and side-lights grace the entrance of this striking contemporary. The lofty foyer, with balcony above, leads to an elegant, two-story living room with fireplace. The family room, housing a second fireplace, leads to a glorious sunroom; both have dramatic sloped ceilings.

The kitchen and breakfast room are conveniently located for access to the informal family room or to the formal dining room via the butler's pantry. The large adjoining clutter room with work island offers limitless possibilities for the seamstress, hobbyist, or indoor gardener. An executive-sized, first-

floor master suite offers privacy and relaxation; the bath with whirlpool tub and dressing area with twin walk-in closets open to a study that could double as an exercise room. Two second-floor bedrooms with private baths and walk-in closets round out the livability in this gracious home.

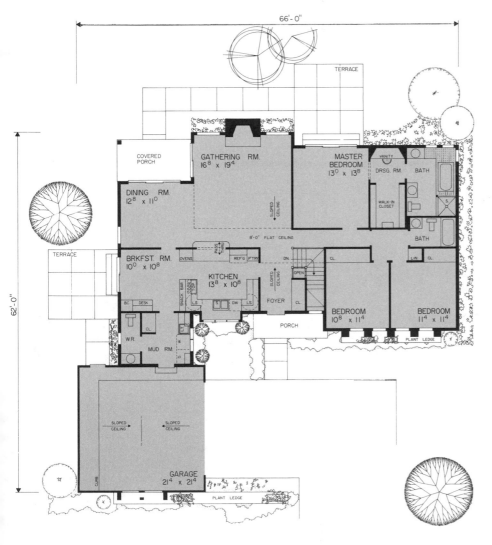

Design by
Home Planners,
Inc.

Quote One™

Cost to build? See page 374
to order complete cost estimate
to build this house in your area!

Design 2912

Square Footage: 1,864

● This modern design with smart Spanish styling incorporates careful zoning by room functions with lifestyle comfort. All three bedrooms, including a master bedroom suite, are isolated at one end of the one-story home for privacy and out of traffic patterns. Entry to a breakfast room and kitchen is possible through a mud room off the garage. That's good news for people carrying groceries from car to kitchen or people with muddy shoes during inclement weather. The modern kitchen includes a snack bar and cook top with multiple access to breakfast room, side foyer, and pass-thru to hallway. There's also a nearby formal dining room. A large rear gathering room features sloped ceiling and its own fireplace. Note the two-car garage and built-in plant ledge in front. Gabled end window treatment plus varied roof lines further enhance the striking appearance of this efficient design.

Design 3163
Square Footage: 1,552

OPTIONAL BASEMENT

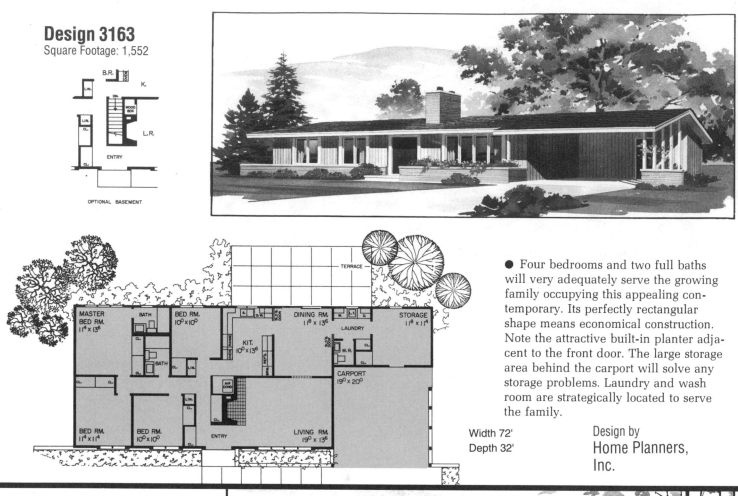

● Four bedrooms and two full baths will very adequately serve the growing family occupying this appealing contemporary. Its perfectly rectangular shape means economical construction. Note the attractive built-in planter adjacent to the front door. The large storage area behind the carport will solve any storage problems. Laundry and wash room are strategically located to serve the family.

Width 72'
Depth 32'

Design by
Home Planners, Inc.

Design 1021
Square Footage: 1,432

OPTIONAL BASEMENT PLAN

Design by
Home Planners, Inc.

Width 60'-8"
Depth 38'-5"

● Behind the double front doors of this straight-forward, contemporary design there is a heap of living to be enjoyed. The large living room with its dramatic glass wall and attractive fireplace will never fail to elicit comments of delight. The master bedroom has a whole wall of wardrobe closets and a private bath. Another two bedrooms and a bath easily serve the family.

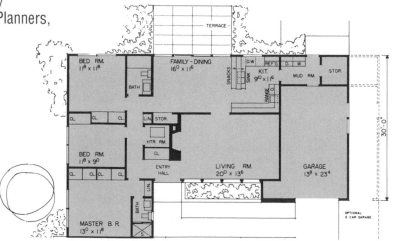

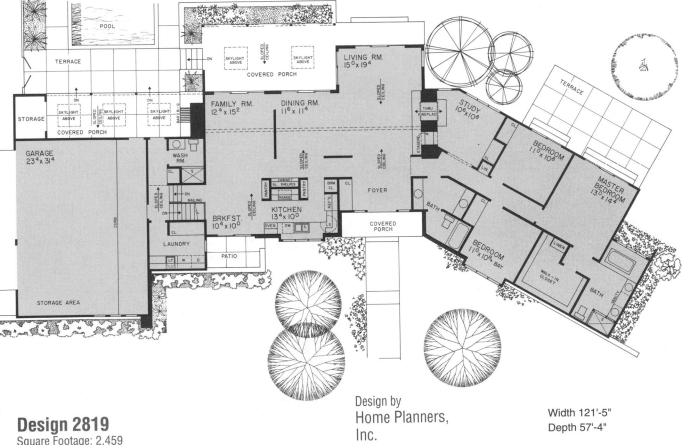

Design 2819
Square Footage: 2,459

D

● Indoor-outdoor living will be enjoyed to the fullest in this rambling one-story contemporary plan. Each of the rear rooms in this design, excluding the study, has access to a terrace or porch. Even the front breakfast room

Design by
Home Planners, Inc.

Width 121'-5"
Depth 57'-4"

has access to a private dining patio. The covered porch off the living areas, family, dining and living rooms, has a sloped ceiling and skylights. A built-in barbecue unit and a storage room will be found on the second covered porch.

Inside, the plan offers exceptional living patterns for various activities. Notice the thru-fireplace that the living room shares with the study. A built-in etagere is nearby. The three-car garage has an extra storage area.

Design 2796
Square Footage: 1,828

● This split-bedroom design has a great deal to offer. A front living room has a sloped ceiling and sliding glass doors, which lead to a front private court. The kitchen serves the family room with a snack bar. The dining room is conveniently located and has a built-in china cabinet. The master bedroom, the family room and one of the secondary bedrooms access a rear terrace. A full hall bath accommodates both secondary bedrooms while the master bedroom has its own bath with a dressing room.

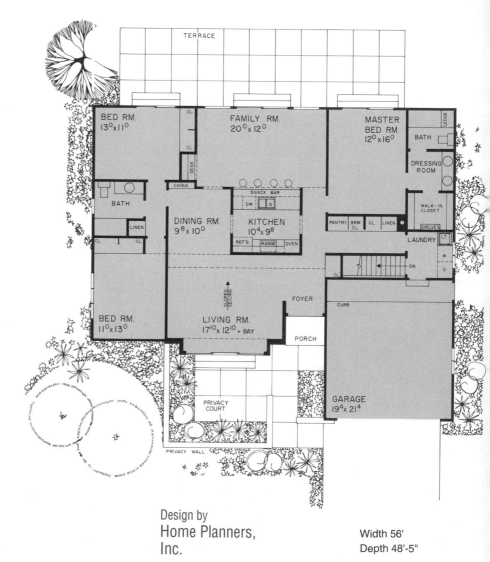

Design by
Home Planners, Inc.

Width 56'
Depth 48'-5"

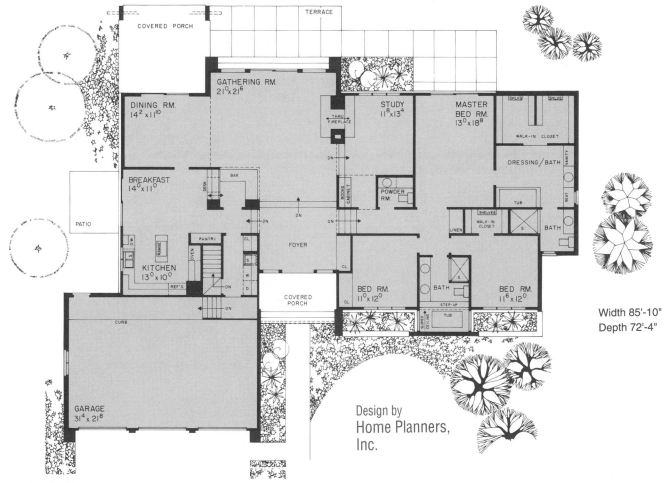

COVERED PORCH

TERRACE

GATHERING RM.
21⁰ x 21⁶

DINING RM.
14² x 11¹⁰

STUDY
11⁸ x 13⁴

MASTER
BED RM.
13⁰ x 18⁸

WALK-IN CLOSET

THRU
FIREPLACE

DRESSING / BATH

BREAKFAST
14⁰ x 11⁰

BAR

DESK

BOOKS
CABINET

POWDER
RM.

TUB

SEAT

VANITY

PATIO

PANTRY

SHELVES

WALK-IN
CLOSET

LINEN

BATH

RANGE

OVEN

DW

FOYER

KITCHEN
13⁰ x 10⁰

REF'G

W
D

BED RM.
11⁰ x 12⁰

BATH

BED RM.
11⁶ x 12⁰

STEP-UP

TUB

COVERED
PORCH

CURB

GARAGE
31⁴ x 21⁸

Width 85'-10"
Depth 72'-4"

Design by
Home Planners,
Inc.

Design 2789

Square Footage: 2,732

L **D**

● An attached three car garage! What a fantastic feature of this three bedroom contemporary design. And there's more. As one walks up the steps to the covered porch and through the double front doors the charm of this design will be overwhelming. Inside, a large foyer greets all visitors and leads them to each of the three areas, each down a few steps. The living area has a large gathering room with fireplace and a study adjacent on one side and the for-mal dining room on the other. The work center has an efficient kitchen with island range, breakfast room, laundry and built-in desk and bar. Then there is the sleeping area. Note the raised tub with sloped ceiling.

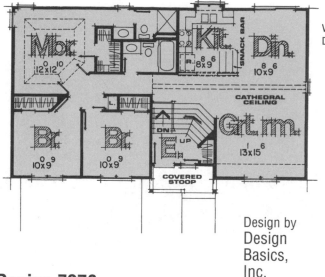

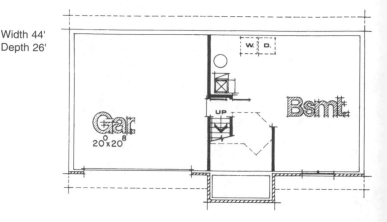

Width 44'
Depth 26'

Design by
**Design
Basics,
Inc.**

Design 7278

Square Footage: 1,125

● An angled staircase that leads to the great room adds a touch of drama to the large entry of this split-entry ranch home. A cathedral ceiling further expands the lofty feeling in the home. The efficient kitchen functions with a snack bar, a Lazy Susan and a window over the sink. A hallway leads to the bedrooms. Double doors open to a large master bedroom with a tray ceiling, a walk-in closet and a private bath. The secondary bedrooms share a convenient hall bath.

Design by
**Design
Basics,
Inc.**

Design 7279

Square Footage: 1,201

● Hilly sites are easily accommodated by this efficient home. The entry opens to a volume great room with a fireplace and a large boxed window. The conveniently located laundry room is only a half-flight down on the garage level. The well-planned kitchen features a wrapping counter, a corner sink with windows, a pantry, a Lazy Susan and a snack bar serving the sunny dining area. The master bedroom, with walk-in closet space and a compartmented toilet and shower, provides comfort and convenience. Two secondary bedrooms share a full hall bath and enjoy lots of privacy.

Width 44'
Depth 30'-8"

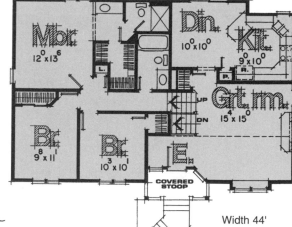

Design 2824
Square Footage: 1,550

● Low-maintenance and economy in building are the outstanding exterior features of this sharp one-story design. It is sheathed in long-lasting cedar siding and trimmed with stone for an eye-appealing facade. Entrance to this home takes you through a charming garden courtyard then a covered walk to the front porch. The garage extending from the front of the house serves two purposes; to reduce lot size and to buffer the interior of the house from street noise. Sliding glass doors are featured in each of the main rooms for easy access to the outdoors. A sun porch is tucked between the study and gathering rooms. Optional non-basement details are included with the purchase of this design.

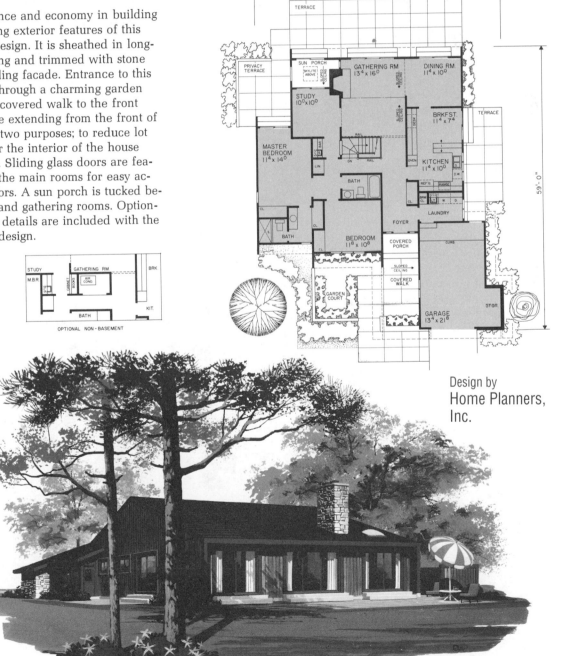

Design by
Home Planners, Inc.

Design by
**Home Design
Services, Inc.**

Design 8661

Square Footage: 1,817

● First impressions take off in this volume-look home. A traditional split entry finds the living room on the left and the dining room on the right. The latter shares a large, open space with the family room, made more impressive with its volume ceiling. The tiled kitchen and breakfast room manifest charm and efficiency. On one side of the plan, the master bedroom boasts a private sitting space and a lavish bath with shutter doors at the soaking tub and a room-sized walk-in closet. At the other side of the house, two family bedrooms each afford ample closet space and room to grow. A "kid's" door leads to the covered patio at the rear of the plan.

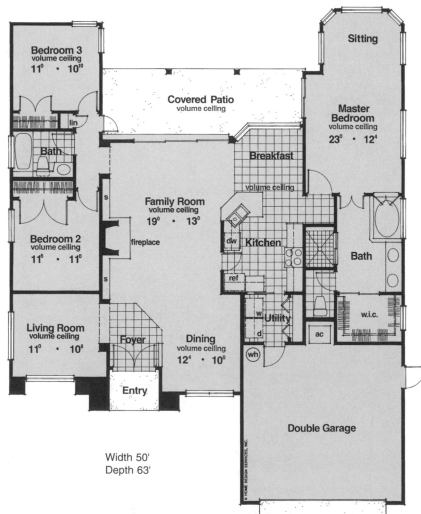

Width 50'
Depth 63'

Design by
**Home Design
Services, Inc.**

ALTERNATE ELEVATION

Width 42'-6"
Depth 55'-8"

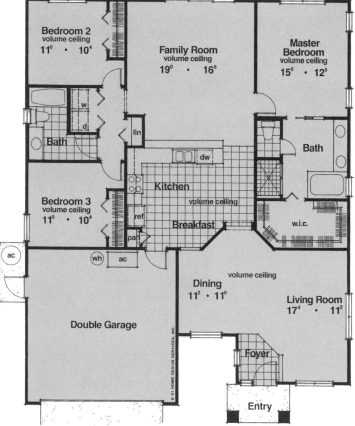

Bedroom 2
volume ceiling
11⁰ · 10⁴

Family Room
volume ceiling
19⁰ · 16⁶

Master
Bedroom
volume ceiling
15⁰ · 12⁰

w
d

Bath

lin

dw

Kitchen
volume ceiling

Bath

Bedroom 3
volume ceiling
11⁰ · 10⁴

ref

Breakfast

pan

w.i.c.

ac

wh   ac

volume ceiling

Dining
11² · 11⁰

Living Room
17⁴ · 11²

Double Garage

© '91 HOME DESIGN SERVICES, INC.

Foyer

Entry

Design 8632

Square Footage: 1,750

● This dapper design boasts two exterior elevation choices—both with true good looks. Inside,
a volume ceiling enlivens the combined living
and dining rooms. Interestingly, the kitchen acts
as the heart of the home, both in location and
style. A tiled floor and a volume ceiling set the
mood of the room while ample counter space
lends to its practicality. Casual living takes
precedence in the spacious family room. In the
master bedroom, you'll find a private bath that
includes dual lavatories, a private commode and
an expansive walk-in closet. The secondary bedrooms find privacy by design as well as convenience in the full bath that separates them. Note
the convenience of placing the washer and dryer
in a tidy alcove near these bedrooms.

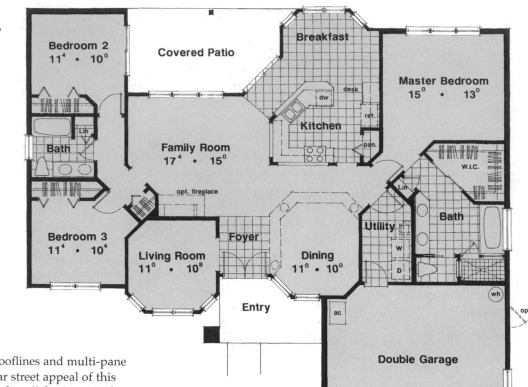

Width 59'
Depth 55'-4"

Bedroom 2
11⁴ • 10⁰

Covered Patio

Breakfast

Master Bedroom
15⁰ • 13⁰

Design by
Home Design
Services, Inc.

Bath

Family Room
17⁴ • 15⁰

Kitchen

desk
dw
ref.
pan.

W.I.C.

Bath

opt. fireplace

Utility

w
D

Design 8644

Square Footage: 1,831

Bedroom 3
11⁴ • 10⁴

Living Room
11⁰ • 10⁸

Foyer

Dining
11⁰ • 10⁰

Entry

ac

wh

opt.

Double Garage

● A two-story entry, varying rooflines and multi-pane windows add to the spectacular street appeal of this three-bedroom home. To the right, off the foyer, is the dining room surrounded by elegant columns. Adjacent is the angular kitchen, which opens to the bayed breakfast nook. The family room includes plans for an optional fireplace and accesses the covered porch. The master bedroom is tucked in the back of the home and features a walk-in closet and full bath with dual vanities, spa tub and oversized shower. Two additional bedrooms share a full bath.

Design 2795
Square Footage: 1,952

● This three-bedroom design leaves no room for improvement. Any size family will find it difficult to surpass the fine qualities that this home offers. Begin with the exterior. This fine contemporary design has open trellis work above the front, covered private court. This area is sheltered by a privacy wall extending from the projecting garage. Inside, the floor plan will be just as breathtaking. Begin at the foyer and choose a direction. To the left is the sleeping wing equipped with three bedrooms and two baths. Straight ahead from the foyer is the gathering room with through-fireplace to the dining room. To the right is the work center. This area includes a breakfast room, a U-shaped kitchen and laundry.

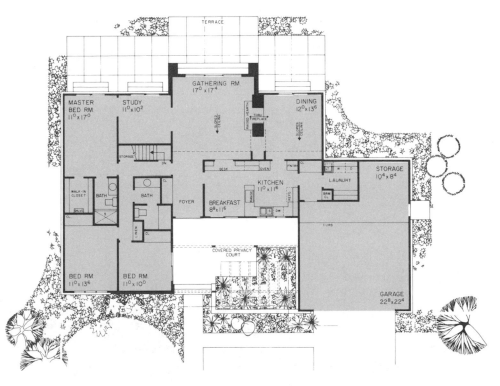

Width 73'-6"
Depth 52'-2"

Design by
Home Planners,
Inc.

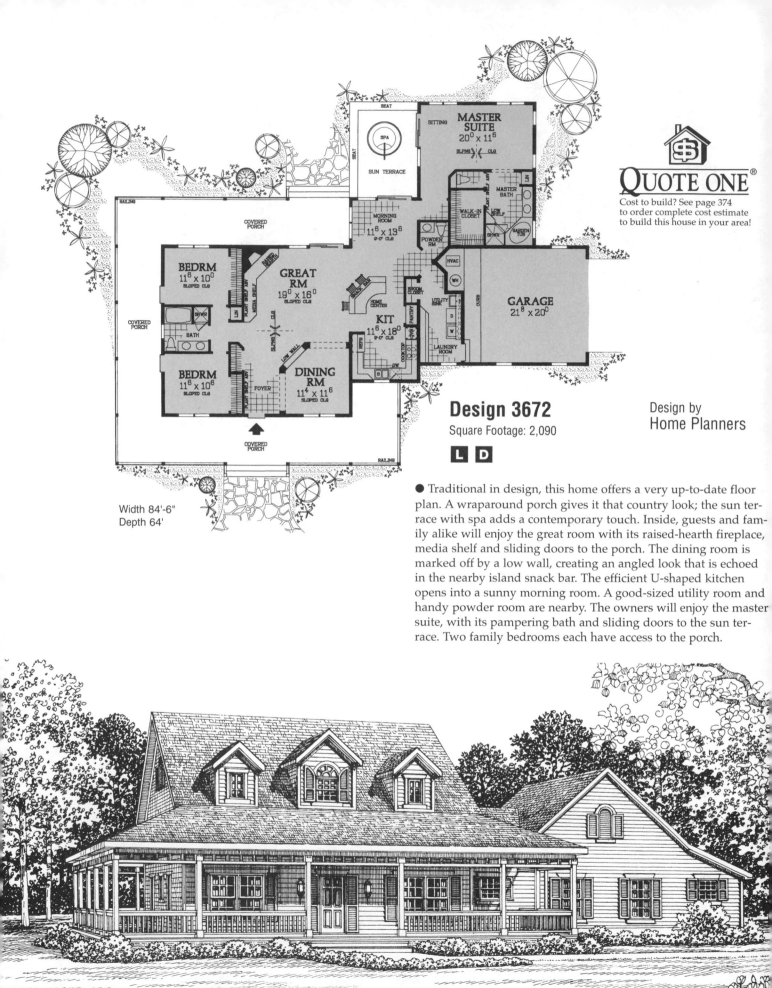

Design 3672

Square Footage: 2,090

L **D**

Width 84'-6"
Depth 64'

Quote One®

Cost to build? See page 374
to order complete cost estimate
to build this house in your area!

Design by
Home Planners

● Traditional in design, this home offers a very up-to-date floor plan. A wraparound porch gives it that country look; the sun terrace with spa adds a contemporary touch. Inside, guests and family alike will enjoy the great room with its raised-hearth fireplace, media shelf and sliding doors to the porch. The dining room is marked off by a low wall, creating an angled look that is echoed in the nearby island snack bar. The efficient U-shaped kitchen opens into a sunny morning room. A good-sized utility room and handy powder room are nearby. The owners will enjoy the master suite, with its pampering bath and sliding doors to the sun terrace. Two family bedrooms each have access to the porch.

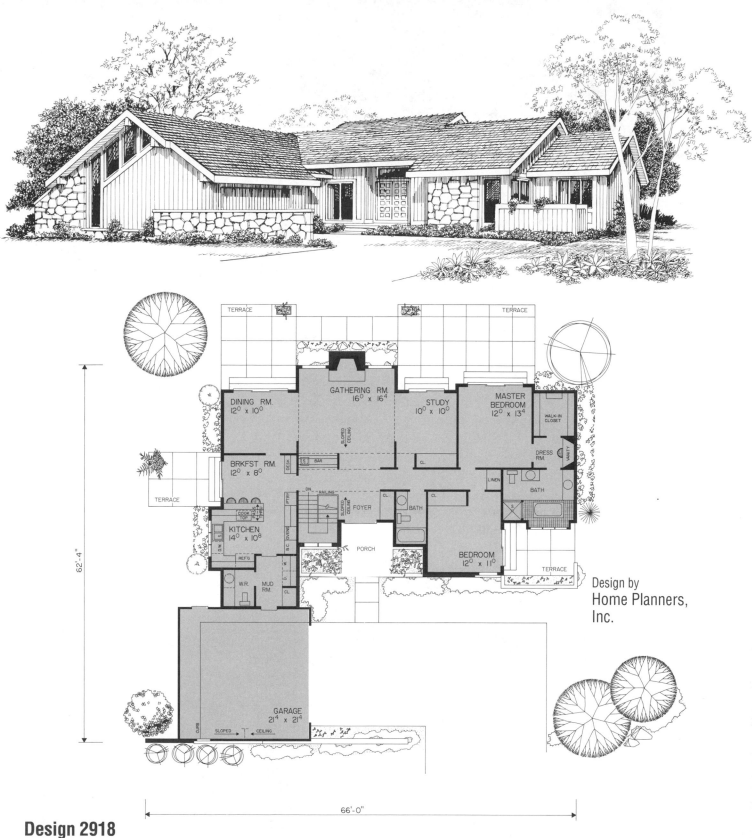

Design 2918

Square Footage: 1,693

D

● Alternating use of stone and wood gives a textured look to this striking contemporary home with wide, over-hanging roof lines and a built-in planter box. The design is just as exciting on the inside with two bedrooms, (or optional third bedroom), a rear gathering room with a fireplace and a sloped ceiling, a rear dining room and an efficient U-shaped kitchen with a pass-through to an adjoining breakfast room. A mud room and a wash room are located between the kitchen and the spacious, two-car garage.

California Engineered Plans and California Stock Plans are available for this home. Call 1-800-521-6797 for more information.

Design by
Home Planners,
Inc.

Design 2703

Square Footage: 1,445

D

● This modified, hip-roofed contemporary design will be the answer for those who want something both practical, yet different, inside and out. The covered front walk sets the stage for entering a modest-sized home with tremendous livability. The focal point will be the pleasant conversation lounge. It is sunken, partially open to the other living areas and shares the enjoyment of the through-fireplace with the living room. There are two bedrooms, two full baths and a study. The kitchen is outstanding.

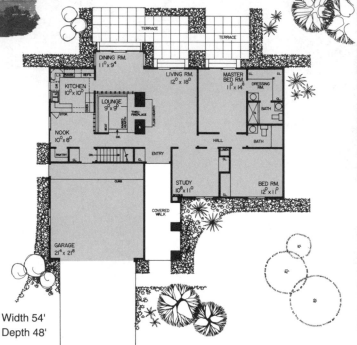

Width 54'
Depth 48'

Design 2351

Square Footage: 1,862

● A low-slung contemporary with affordable style, this plan has a number of key features, including a master suite separate from the other two bedrooms, a sunken living room, a large family room with a snack bar, an enormous utility room and loads of extra storage. Note, too, the covered entryway and rear terrace off the family room.

Design by
Home Planners,
Inc.

Width 56'-10"
Depth 48'-10"

Design by
**Donald A.
Gardner,
Architects, Inc.**

Design 7618

Square Footage: 1,972
Bonus Room: 398 square feet

● The arches of the covered porch make an attractive contrast to the pointed gables and dormers of this lovely home. Inside, spaciousness is the key word, as decorative pillars mark the boundaries of the foyer and formal dining room, and lead into the great room, with its cathedral ceiling and welcoming fireplace. In the kitchen, the cook will enjoy the glow from the fireplace as well as the large walk-in pantry and island work area. A cheerful breakfast nook offers lots of sunshine and access to the back porch. The master suite also has access to the porch and a sumptuous master bath. A full hall bath is shared by two bedrooms, one of which could serve as a study. Stairs off the kitchen lead to attic storage and a bonus room with a skylight.

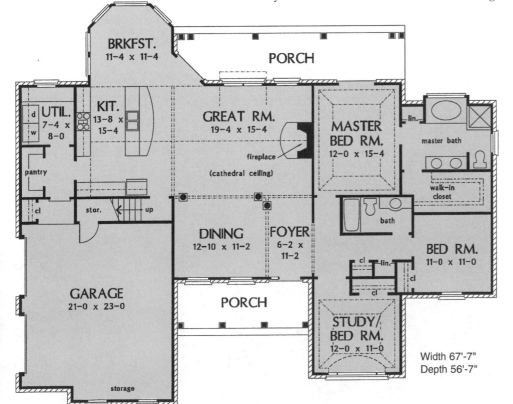

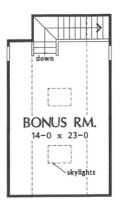

Width 67'-7"
Depth 56'-7"

Design 2343
Square Footage: 3,110

● If yours is a growing active family the chances are good that they will want their new home to relate to the outdoors. This distinctive design puts a premium on private outdoor living. And you don't have to install a swim- ming pool to get the most enjoyment from this home. Developing this area as a garden court will provide the in- door living areas with a breathtaking awareness of nature's beauty. Notice the fine zoning of the plan and how each area has its sliding glass doors to provide an unrestricted view. Three bedrooms plus study are serviced by three baths. The family and gathering rooms provide two great living areas. The kitchen is most efficient.

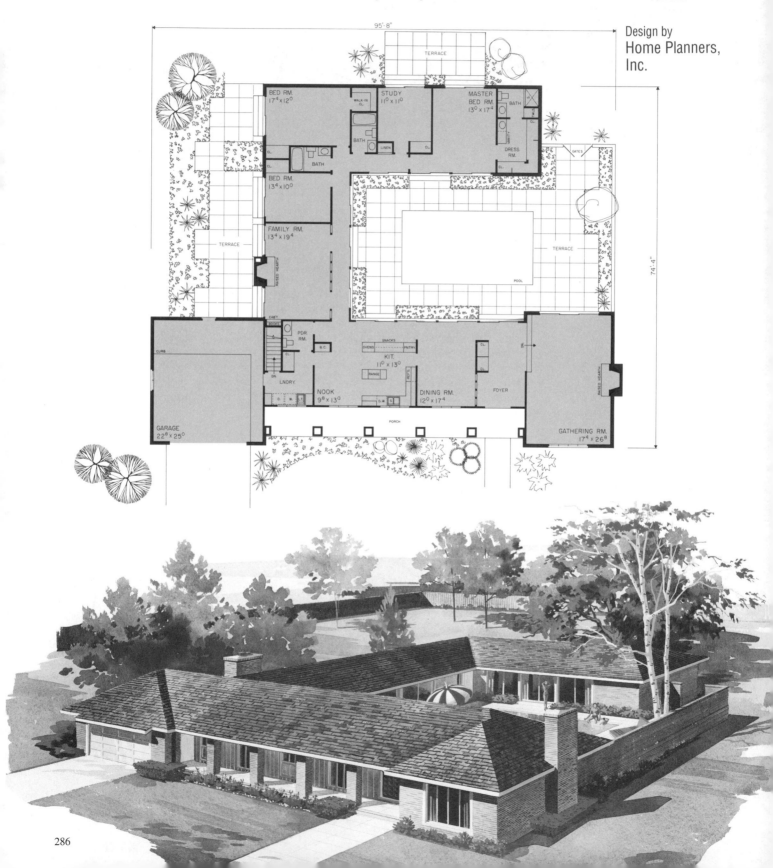

Design by
Home Planners, Inc.

Design 2744

Square Footage: 1,381

● Here is a practical and an attractive contemporary home for that narrow building site. It is designed for efficiency with the small family or retired couple in mind. Sloping ceilings foster an extra measure of spaciousness. In addition to the master bedroom, there is the study that can also serve as the second bedroom or as an occasional guest room. The single bath is compartmented and its dual access allows it to serve living and sleeping areas more than adequately. Note raised-hearth fireplace, snack bar, U-shaped kitchen, laundry, two terraces, etc.

Design by
**Home Planners,
Inc.**

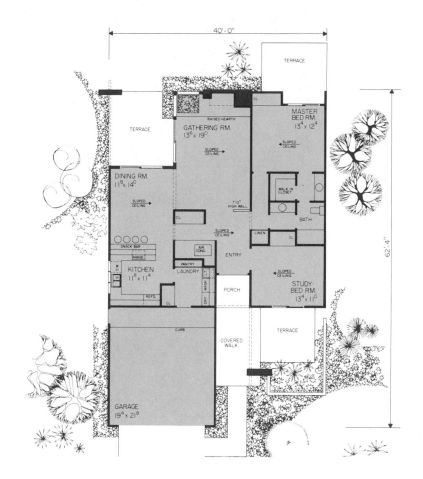

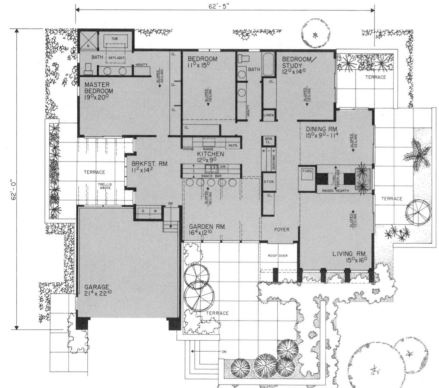

Design by
Home Planners,
Inc.

Design 2858

Square Footage: 2,231

● This sun oriented design was created to face the south. By doing so, it has minimal northern exposure. It has been designed primarily for the more temperate U.S. latitudes using 2 x 6 wall construction. The morning sun will brighten the living and dining rooms, along with the adjacent terrace. Sun enters the garden room by way of the glass roof and walls. In the winter, the solar heat gain from the garden room should provide relief from high energy bills. Solar shades allow you to adjust the amount of light that you want to enter in the warmer months. Interior planning deserves mention, too. The work center is efficient. The kitchen has a snack bar on the garden room side and a serving counter to the dining room. The breakfast room with laundry area is also convenient to the kitchen. Three bedrooms are on the northern wall. The master bedroom has a large tub and a separate shower with a four foot square skylight above. When this design is oriented toward the sun, it should prove to be energy efficient and a joy to live in.

● Earth shelters the interior of this house from both the cold of the winter and the heat of the summer. This three bedroom design has passive solar capabilities. The sun room, south facing for light, has a stone floor which will absorb heat. When needed, the heat will be circulated to the interior by opening the sliding glass doors or by mechanical means. Entrance to this home will be obtained through the vestibule or the garage. Both have a western exposure. A large, centrally located skylight creates an open feeling and lights up the interior of this plan where the formal and informal living areas are located. The sun room contains 425 sq. ft. not included in total to the right.

Design by
Home Planners, Inc.

Design 2862
Square Footage: 3,238

Design 8625

First Floor: 2,669 square feet
Second Floor: 621 square feet
Total: 3,290 square feet

● Rooflines, arches and corner quoins adorn the facade of this magnificent home. A porte cochere creates a stunning prelude to the double-door entry. A wet bar serves the sunken living room and overlooks the pool area. The dining room has a tray ceiling and is located near the gourmet kitchen with prep island and angled counter. A guest room opens off the tiled hall. The generous family room, warmed by a fireplace, opens to the screened patio. The master bedroom has a sitting room and a fireplace set into an angled wall. Its luxurious bath includes a step-up tub. Upstairs, two bedrooms share the oversized balcony and nearby observation room.

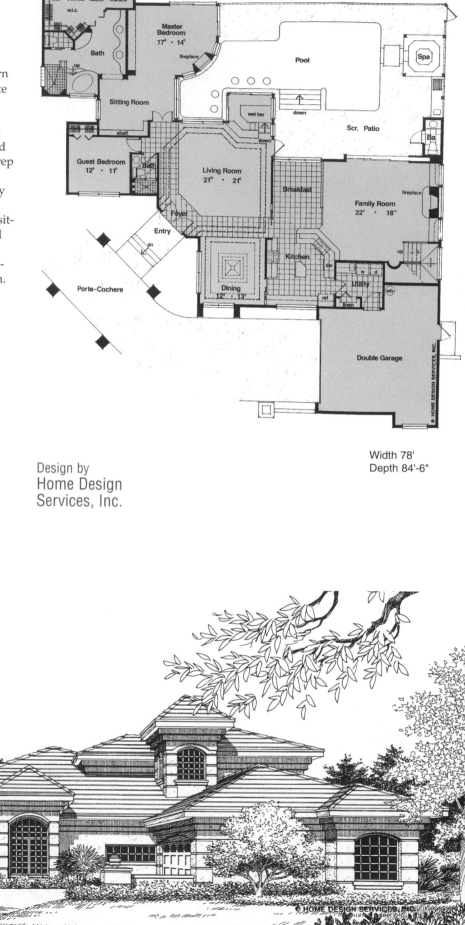

Width 78'
Depth 84'-6"

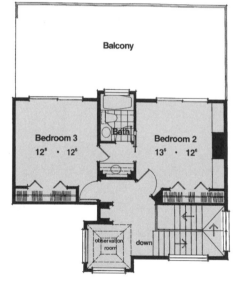

Design by
Home Design
Services, Inc.

Design 2832
Square Footage: 2,805 (Excluding Atrium)

D

● The advantage of passive solar heating is a significant highlight of this contemporary design. The huge skylight over the atrium provides shelter during inclement weather, while permitting the enjoyment of plenty of natural light to the atrium below and surrounding areas. Whether open to the sky, or sheltered by a glass or translucent covering, the atrium becomes a cheerful spot and provides an abundance of natural light to its adjacent rooms. The stone floor will absorb an abundance of heat from the sun during the day and permit circulation of warm air to other areas at night. During the summer, shades afford protection from the sun without sacrificing the abundance of natural light and the feeling of spaciousness. Sloping ceilings highlight each of the major rooms, three bedrooms, formal living and dining and study. The conversation area between the two formal areas will really be something to talk about. The broad expanses of roof can accommodate solar panels should an active system be desired to supplement the passive features of this design.

Design by
Home Planners,
Inc.

Width 69'-8"
Depth 70'-4"

Sunshine Design:

Homes from warmer climes

Design 3638

Square Footage: 2,861

L

● Double columns and an arched entry create a grand entrance to this elegant one-story home. Inside, arched colonnades add grace and definition to the formal living and dining rooms as well as the family room. The master suite occupies a separate wing, providing a private retreat. Treat yourself to luxury in the master bath which includes a bumped-out whirlpool tub, a separate shower and twin vanities. An office/den located nearby easily converts to a nursery. A snack bar provides space for meals on-the-go and separates the island kitchen from the bay-windowed morning room. Three additional bedrooms—one a guest room with an adjacent bath—share two baths.

Design by
Home Planners,
Inc.

Width 93'-4"
Depth 66'-6"

QUOTE ONE™

Cost to build? See page 374 to order complete cost estimate to build this house in your area!

94'-6"

79'-11"

COVERED PATIO

COVERED REAR PORCH

TRELLIS ABOVE

PRIVATE PATIO

FAMILY ENTERTAINMENT PATIO

TRELLIS ABOVE

KIT.
11⁰ x 10⁸
10'-0" CLG.

PANTRY

NOOK
8⁸ x 9²
10'-0" CLG.

LAUNDRY

LIVING RM
15⁰ x 15⁸
11'-6" CLG.

WET BAR

STUDY
11⁶ x 11⁰

MASTER BEDRM
16⁸ x 14²
10'-0" CLG.

MBA

LINEN

TUB

SEAT

SEAT

SHWR

WALK-IN CLOSET

FAMILY RM
12⁷ x 14⁰
10'-0" CLG.

DINING RM
15⁰ x 11⁰
11'-6" CLG.

SLOPED CEILING

FOYER

PDR

BEDRM
13² x 12⁶
10'-0" CLG.

BATH

LINEN

WALK-IN CLOSET

WALK-IN CLOSET

WORK SHOP

HVAC

STORAGE ROOM

COVERED PATIO

COVERED PORCH

PRIVACY WALL

BEDRM
15² x 10¹⁰
10'-0" CLG.

HVAC

PRIVATE PATIO

GARAGE
21⁸ x 29⁰

CURB

PRIVACY WALL

QUOTE ONE™
Cost to build? See page 374
to order complete cost estimate
to build this house in your area!

Design by
Home Planners, Inc.

Design 3436
Square Footage: 2,573

L

● This dashing Spanish home, with its captivating front court yard, presents a delightful introduction to the inside living spaces. These excel with a central living room/dining room combination. A wet bar here makes entertaining easy. In the kitchen, a huge pantry and interesting angles are sure to please the house gourmet. A breakfast nook with a corner fireplace further enhances this area. The master bedroom makes room for a private bath with a whirlpool tub and dual lavs. Each additional bedroom is highlighted by a spacious walk-in closet.

California Engineered Plans and California Stock Plans are available for this home. Call 1-800-521-6797 for more information.

Design 3641

Square Footage: 2,945

L

● A variety of hipped-roof planes with highly textured tiles cap this western hacienda. The stucco exterior wall surfaces are broken by effective window and door treatment. Fourteen-foot ceilings, columns, archways and a planter highlight a spacious and open-planned interior. Formal living and dining rooms flank the foyer. Straight ahead is the family's great room, which functions well with the outdoor entertainment lanai. This plan features children's sleeping facilities which are located at opposite ends of the plan from those of the parents. The master bedroom is large and has its own outdoor living area, complete with a fireplace and a spa.

Width 85'-10"
Depth 78'-5"

Cost to build? See page 374
to order complete cost estimate
to build this house in your area!

© 1992 The Sater Group, Inc.

Jenkins

Design 6640

Square Footage: 3,866

● This modern home adds a contemporary twist to the typical ranch-style plan. The turret study and bayed dining room add a sensuous look from the streetscape. The main living areas open up to the lanai and offer broad views to the rear through large expanses of glass and doors. The family kitchen, nook and leisure room focus on the lanai and the entertainment center and wet bar. The guest suites have separate baths and also access the lanai. The master bath features a curved glass shower, a whirlpool, and a private toilet and bidet room. Dual walk-in closets and an abundance of light further the appeal of this suite.

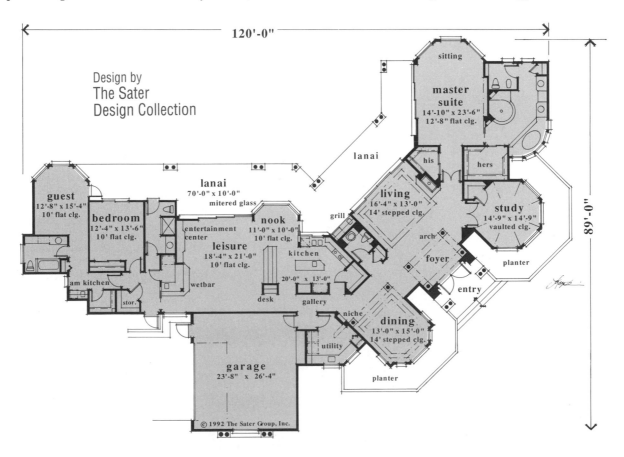

Design by
The Sater
Design Collection

Design by
Home Planners, Inc.

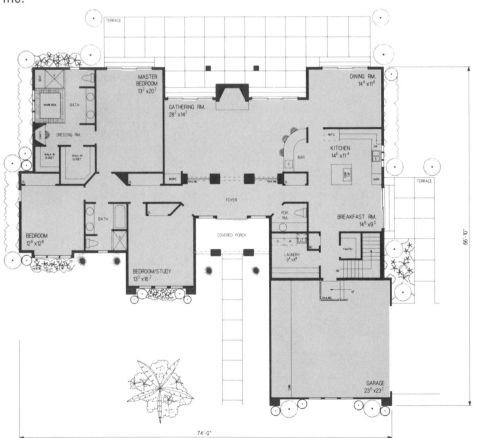

Design 2950
Square Footage: 2,559

● A natural desert dweller, this stucco, tile-roofed beauty is equally comfortable in any clime. Inside, there's a well-planned design. Common living areas—gathering room, formal dining room and breakfast room—are off-set by a quiet study that could be used as a bedroom or guest room. A master suite features two walk-in closets, a double vanity and a whirlpool spa. The two-car garage provides a service entrance; close by is an adequate laundry area and a pantry. A lovely hearth warms the gathering room and complements the snack-bar eating area.

California Engineered Plans and California Stock Plans are available for this home. Call 1-800-521-6797 for more information.

Cost to build? See page 374 to order complete cost estimate to build this house in your area!

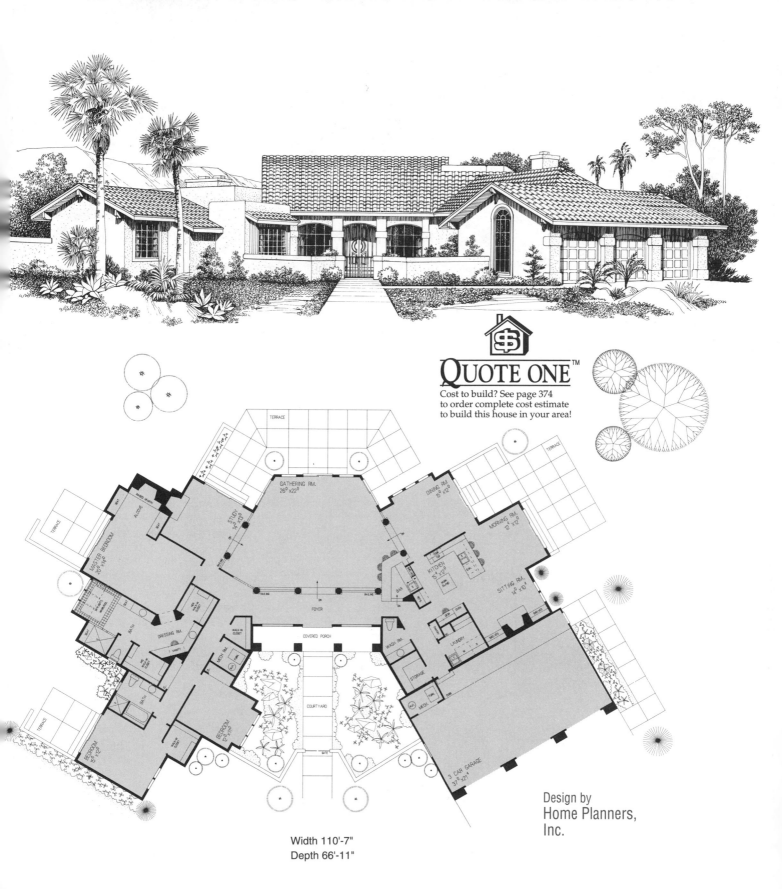

QUOTE ONE™

Cost to build? See page 374
to order complete cost estimate
to build this house in your area!

Design by
Home Planners,
Inc.

Width 110'-7"
Depth 66'-11"

Design 2922

Square Footage: 3,505

● Loaded with custom features, this plan seems to have everything imaginable. There's an enormous sunken gathering room and a cozy study. The country-style kitchen contains an efficient work area, as well as space for relaxing in the morning and sitting rooms. Two nice-sized bedrooms and a luxurious master suite round out the plan.

California Engineered Plans and California Stock Plans are available for this home. Call 1-800-521-6797 for more information.

Design 2948
Square Footage: 1,830

● Styled for Southwest living, this home is a good choice in many areas. Among its many highlights are a gathering room/dining room combination that includes a fireplace, a snack-bar pass-through and sliding glass doors to the rear terrace. The kitchen is uniquely shaped and sports a huge walk-in pantry plus a breakfast room with windows to the front covered porch. Bedrooms include a master suite with a sloped ceiling, access to the rear terrace, a whirlpool spa and a double vanity. Two additional bedrooms share a full bath. One of these bedrooms makes a fine study and features built-in shelves for books as well as a built-in cabinet.

California Engineered Plans and California Stock Plans are available for this home. Call 1-800-521-6797 for more information.

QUOTE ONE™

Cost to build? See page 374 to order complete cost estimate to build this house in your area!

Design by
Home Planners,
Inc.

Floor Plan Labels

TERRACE

WHIRLPOOL

MASTER BEDROOM 11¹⁰ x 17⁸

BATH — SEAT — SLOPED CEILING — SLOPED CEILING

VANITY

DRESS RM

GATHERING RM 15⁰ x 17⁸

SLOPED CEILING

DINING RM 12⁰ x 9⁸

SLOPED CEILING

LEDGE — LINEN — CL

BATH — BC — CL

SHELVES — SNACK BAR — DW — REF'S — PANTRY — OVEN

KIT. 14² x 12⁰

SHELVES — COOK TOP — DESK — DN

GARAGE 21⁴ x 22⁴ + STOR

CL — BOOKS CAB'T

FOYER — BRKFST RM 8⁸ x 10⁴ — LAUNDRY

BEDROOM 10⁶ x 11⁶

STUDY/ BEDROOM 11² x 11⁶

COVERED PORCH 'OPEN SKYLIGHTS'

STORAGE

CURB

43'-5"

75'-0"

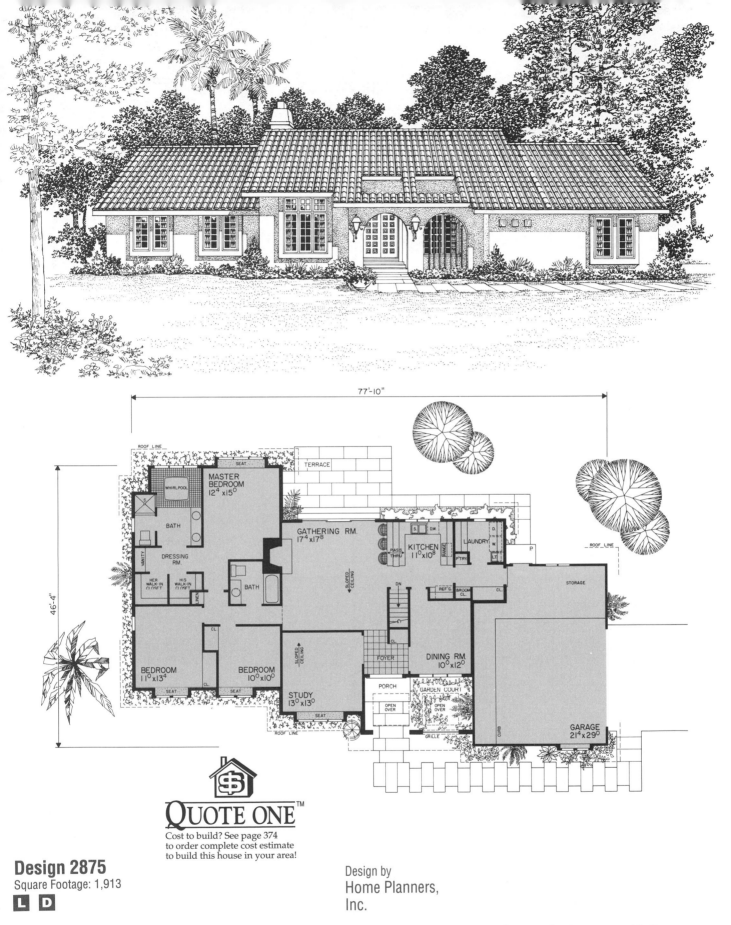

Quote One™

Cost to build? See page 374
to order complete cost estimate
to build this house in your area!

Design 2875
Square Footage: 1,913

L D

Design by
**Home Planners,
Inc.**

● This elegant Spanish design incorporates excellent indoor-outdoor living relationships for modern families who enjoy the sun and comforts of a well-planned new home. Note the overhead openings for rain and sun to fall upon a front garden, while a twin arched entry leads to the front porch and foyer. Inside the floor plan features a modern kitchen with pass-thru to a large gathering room with fireplace. Other features include a dining room, laundry room, a study off the foyer, plus three bedrooms including master bedroom with its own whirlpool.

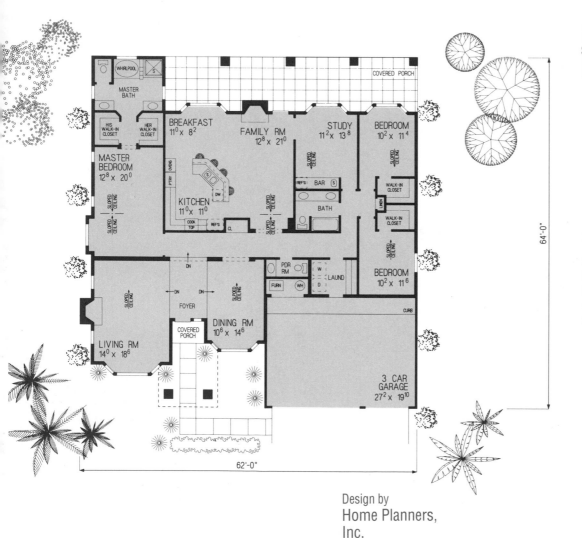

Design 3413
Square Footage: 2,517

L

● Though distinctly Southwest in design, this home has some features that are universally appealing. Note, for instance, the central gallery, perpendicular to the raised entry hall, and running almost the entire width of the house. An L-shaped, angled kitchen serves the breakfast room and family room in equal fashion. Sleeping areas are found in four bedrooms including an optional study and exquisite master suite.

QUOTE ONE™

Cost to build? See page 374 to order complete cost estimate to build this house in your area!

Design by
Home Planners, Inc.

Design 6661

Square Footage: 3,265

● A turret study and a raised entry with half-round columns add elegance to this marvelous stucco home. Inside, columns frame the living room, which features glass doors that open to the veranda and provide spectacular views of the rear grounds. A guest suite—adjacent to the leisure room—features a full bath, porch access and a private garden, making it perfect for use as an in-law suite. Secondary bedrooms share a full bath. The master suite accommodates a foyer with a window seat overlooking another private garden (with a fountain), bayed windows to the back yard and veranda access. The private bath has His and Hers closets, a garden tub and a walk-in shower with curved glass looking onto the garden.

Design by
**The Sater
Design Collection**

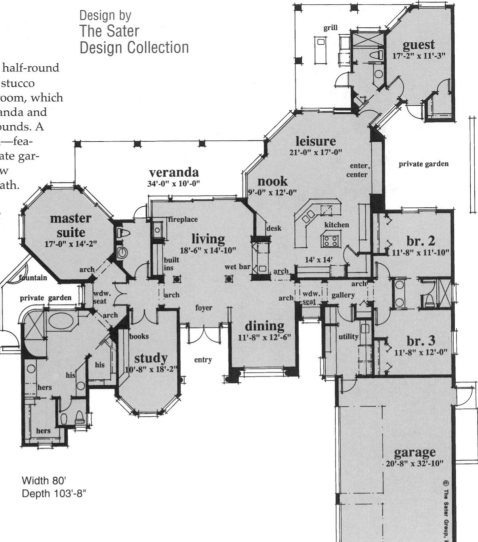

Width 80'
Depth 103'-8"

© The Sater Group, Inc.

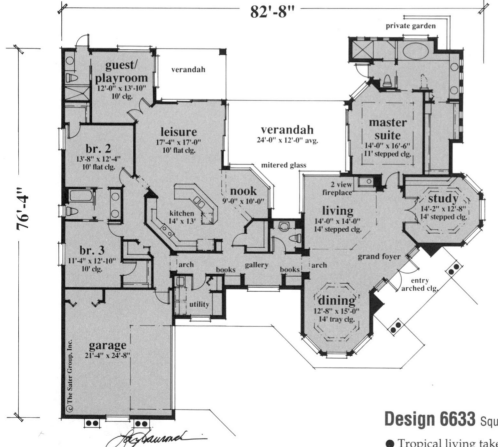

82'-8"

76'-4"

private garden

guest/playroom 12'-0" x 13'-10" 10' clg.

verandah

master suite 14'-0" x 16'-6" 11' stepped clg.

leisure 17'-4" x 17'-0" 10' flat clg.

verandah 24'-0" x 12'-0" avg.

br. 2 13'-8" x 12'-4" 10' flat clg.

mitered glass

2 view fireplace

study 14'-2" x 12'-8" 14' stepped clg.

nook 9'-0" x 10'-0"

kitchen 14' x 13'

living 14'-0" x 14'-0" 14' stepped clg.

br. 3 11'-4" x 12'-10" 10' clg.

grand foyer

arch books gallery books arch

entry arched clg.

utility

dining 12'-8" x 15'-0" 14' tray clg.

garage 21'-4" x 24'-8"

© The Sater Group, Inc.

Design by
The Sater
Design Collection

Design 6633 Square Footage: 2,986

● Tropical living takes off in this super one-story home. Double doors lead to a lovely formal living area consisting of a living room, dining room and study. Through an archway, a gallery adds an air of distinction. The kitchen is open to a sunny nook and a bright leisure area for delightful dining and relaxing. A play room opens off this area and is sure to please the kids of the house. A full bath here leads outside. Two bedrooms nearby each sport a walk-in closet and utilize a full bath in between. The master bedroom suite enjoys a private bath with a whirlpool tub, dual lavs, a large walk-in closet and a compartmented toilet and shower.

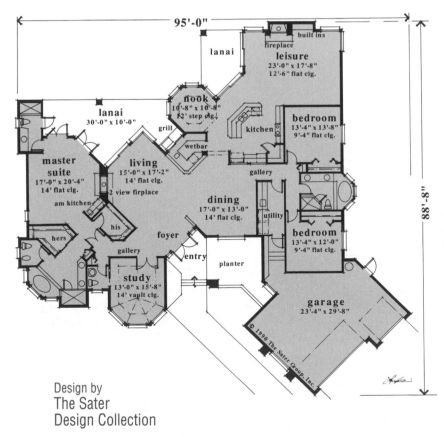

95'-0"

88'-8"

lanai

leisure
23'-0" x 17'-8"
12'-6" flat clg.

built ins
fireplace

nook
10'-8" x 10'-8"
12' step clg.

grill

lanai
30'-0" x 10'-0"

kitchen

bedroom
13'-4" x 13'-8"
9'-4" flat clg.

wetbar

master
suite
17'-0" x 20'-4"
14' flat clg.

living
15'-0" x 17'-2"
14' flat clg.

gallery

am kitchen

2 view firplace

his

dining
17'-0" x 13'-0"
14' flat clg.

hers

utility

bedroom
13'-4" x 12'-0"
9'-4" flat clg.

foyer

gallery

entry

planter

study
13'-0" x 15'-8"
14' vault clg.

garage
23'-4" x 29'-8"

© 1990 The Sater Group, Inc.

Design by
**The Sater
Design Collection**

Quote One®

Cost to build? See page 374
to order complete cost estimate
to build this house in your area!

Design 6634
Square Footage: 3,477

● Make dreams come true with this fine sunny
design. An octagonal study provides a nice focal
point both inside and outside. The living areas
remain open to each other and access outdoor
areas. A wet bar makes entertaining a breeze,
especially with a window pass-through to a grill
area on the lanai. The kitchen enjoys shared
space with a lovely breakfast nook and a bright
leisure room. Two bedrooms are located near
family living centers. They share a dapper hall
bath that includes a separate shower, a double-
bowl vanity and a bumped-out whirlpool tub. In
the master bedroom suite, luxury abounds with
a two-way fireplace, a morning kitchen, two
walk-in closets and a compartmented bath.
Another full bath accommodates a pool area.

Design 6645

Square Footage: 2,473

● Luxurious living begins as soon as
you step into the entryway of this
home. With columns and a barrel-
vaulted ceiling, it opens through double doors to the foyer and combined
living and dining rooms. The octagonal kitchen serves this area with a
pass-through counter. Two master
suites characterize this plan as the perfect vacation retreat. Two guest rooms
enjoy quiet locales and direct access to
the master baths. Outdoor living areas
include a master lanai and another
that stretches around the back of the
house. A pool bath is easily accessible
from the lanai. A two-car garage and a
utility room finish off the plan.

Design by
**The Sater
Design Collection**

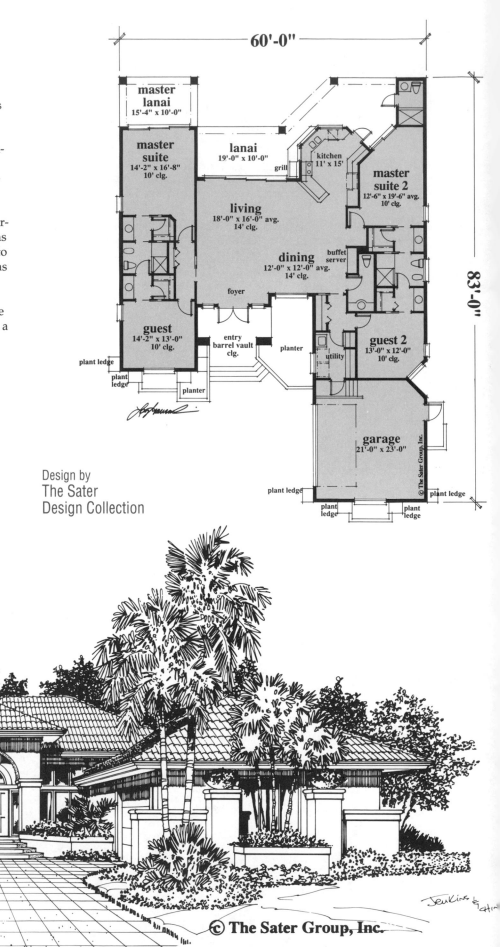

© The Sater Group, Inc.

© The Sater Group, Inc.

Design 6612

Square Footage: 1,487

● Here's an offer too good to pass up! Two elevations and a wealth of modern livability is presented in this compact one-story home. Inside, a great room with a vaulted ceiling opens to the lanai, offering wonderful options for either formal or informal entertaining. Step out onto the lanai and savor the outdoors from the delightful kitchen with its bay-windowed breakfast nook. Two secondary bedrooms (each with its own walk-in closet) share a full bath. Finally, enjoy the lanai from the calming master suite and pampering bath featuring a corner tub, a separate shower and a large walk-in closet.

58'-0"

58'-0"

lanai
48'-0" x 10'-0"

nook
9'-4" x 10'-0"
vaulted clg.

master suite
13'-0" x 15'-0"
8' clg.

great room
16'-0" x 14'-0"
vaulted clg.

br. 1
12'-0" x 10'-0"
8' clg.

br. 2
11'-8" x 12'-4"
8' clg.

foyer

dining
11'-6" x 10'-4"
vaulted clg.

util.

entry

garage
20'-0" x 21'-4"

© The Sater Group, Inc.

QUOTE ONE®

Cost to build? See page 374 to order complete cost estimate to build this house in your area!

© The Sater Group, Inc.

Design by
The Sater Design Collection

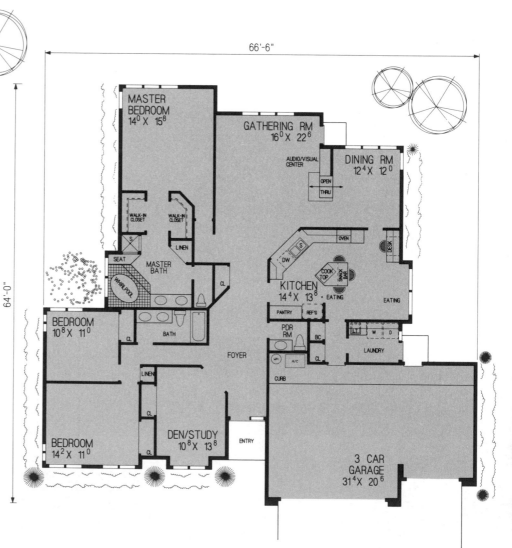

Design 3440
Square Footage: 2,290

L

● Pack 'em in! There's plenty of room for everyone in this three-, or optional four-bedroom home. The expansive gathering room welcomes family and guests with a through-fireplace to the dining room, an audio/visual center, and a door to the outside. The kitchen includes a wide pantry, a snack bar, and a separate eating area. Included in the master suite: two walk-in closets, shower, whirlpool tub and seat, dual vanities, and linen storage.

Design by
Home Planners,
Inc.

QUOTE ONE™
Cost to build? See page 374
to order complete cost estimate
to build this house in your area!

Floor plan labels:

- MASTER BEDROOM 14⁰ X 15⁸
- GATHERING RM 16⁰ X 22⁶
- DINING RM 12⁴ X 12⁰
- AUDIO/VISUAL CENTER
- OPEN THRU
- WALK-IN CLOSET
- WALK-IN CLOSET
- LINEN
- SEAT
- WHIRLPOOL
- MASTER BATH
- OVEN
- DESK
- COOK TOP
- SNACK BAR
- DW
- KITCHEN 14⁴ X 13⁸ • EATING
- EATING
- BEDROOM 10⁸ X 11⁰
- CL
- BATH
- PANTRY
- REF'S
- FOYER
- PDR RM
- BC
- W D
- LAUNDRY
- LINEN
- BEDROOM 14² X 11⁰
- DEN/STUDY 10⁸ X 13⁸
- ENTRY
- CURB
- 3 CAR GARAGE 31⁴ X 20⁶
- 66'-6"
- 64'-0"

Width 51'-6"
Depth 59'-6"

Quote One™

Cost to build? See page 374
to order complete cost estimate
to build this house in your area!

Design by
Home Planners, Inc.

Design 3478
Square Footage: 1,898

L

● Small but smart describes this one-story plan that provides a maximum of livability in a compact plan. The living and dining rooms project a sense of space with sloped ceilings, flat arches and plenty of space above for plants, decorative pots or family treasures. The kitchen shares space with the bayed breakfast nook, providing accessibility to the back yard through sliding glass doors. The adjacent family room enjoys a fireplace, creating a living area ideal for informal gatherings. Sleeping quarters consist of the master suite, a secondary bedroom and a study that may be used as a third bedroom if needed. The master bedroom boasts a whirlpool tub and a large walk-in closet.

Design 6663

Square Footage: 2,978

● The wonderfully balanced exterior of this Floridian design offers columns and circle-top windows at the covered entry. Inside, the formal living and dining rooms face the rear, with large glass doors providing excellent views to the veranda and beyond. The kitchen, nook and leisure room unite to provide a grand space for causal gatherings. The leisure room includes an optional wet bar. Bedrooms are planned for maximum privacy. The secondary bedrooms share a full bath; a separate lanai is available to Bedroom 2. The master wing includes a study that can serve as a reading room, a home office or a guest bedroom. It is conveniently located near the entry and has a powder room and coat closet. The master suite includes a bayed area and a master bath with a garden tub, a large shower and His and Hers walk-in closets.

Design by
**The Sater
Design Collection**

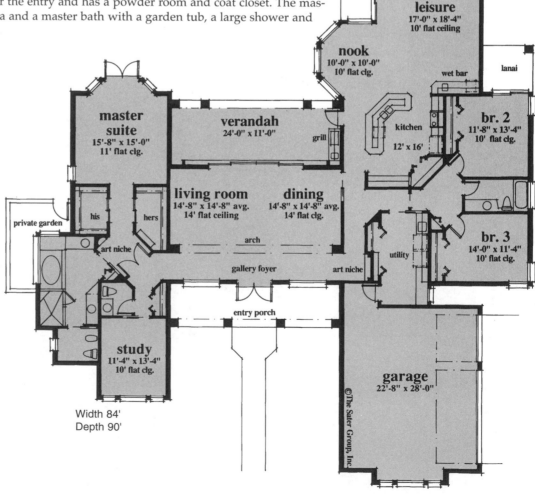

Width 84'
Depth 90'

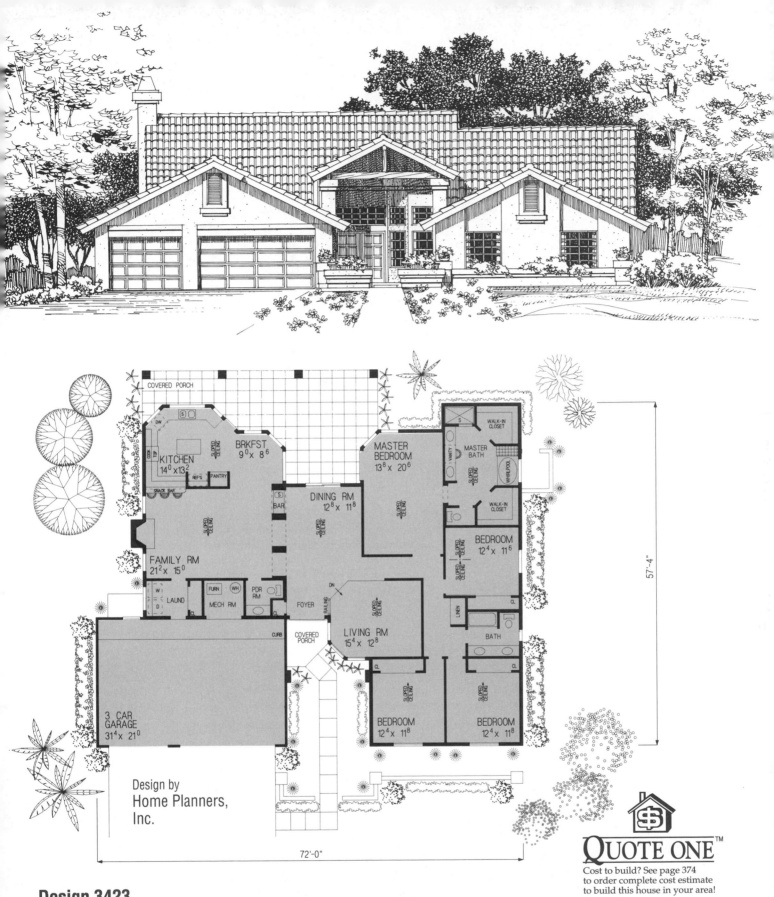

COVERED PORCH

KITCHEN
14⁰ x 13²

BRKFST
9⁰ x 8⁶

MASTER
BEDROOM
13⁸ x 20⁶

WALK-IN
CLOSET

MASTER
BATH

WHIRLPOOL

WALK-IN
CLOSET

DINING RM
12⁸ x 11⁸

BAR

PANTRY

REF'G

SNACK BAR

FAMILY RM
21² x 15⁰

BEDROOM
12⁴ x 11⁶

FURN

WH

PDR
RM

FOYER

RAILING

DN

LAUND

MECH RM

LINEN

BATH

CL

COVERED
PORCH

LIVING RM
15⁴ x 12⁸

CL

3 CAR
GARAGE
31⁴ x 21⁰

BEDROOM
12⁴ x 11⁸

BEDROOM
12⁴ x 11⁸

CURB

Design by
Home Planners,
Inc.

57'-4"

72'-0"

Design 3423
Square Footage: 2,577

● This spacious Southwestern home will be a pleasure to come home to. Immediately off the foyer are the dining room and step-down living room with bay window. The highlight of the four-bedroom sleeping area is the master suite with porch access and a whirlpool for soaking away the day's worries. The informal living area features an enormous family room with fireplace and bay-windowed kitchen and breakfast room. Notice the snack bar pass-through to the family room.

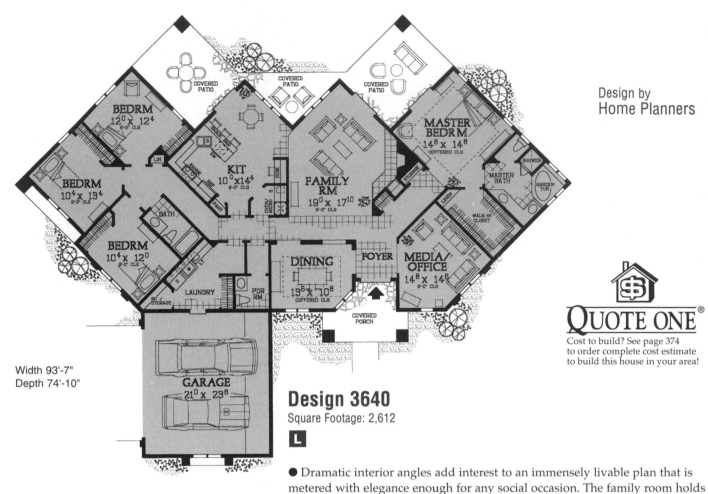

BEDRM
12⁰ x 12⁴
9'-0" CLG

BEDRM
10⁴ x 13⁴
9'-0" CLG

BEDRM
10⁴ x 12⁰
9'-0" CLG

KIT
10⁰ x 14⁴
9'-0" CLG

FAMILY
RM
19⁰ x 17¹⁰
9'-0" CLG

MASTER
BEDRM
14⁸ x 14⁸
COFFERED CLG

MASTER
BATH

SHOWER

GARDEN
TUB

WALK-IN
CLOSET

LINEN

MEDIA/
OFFICE
14⁸ x 14⁶
9'-0" CLG

FOYER

DINING
13⁶ x 10⁸
COFFERED CLG

COVERED
PORCH

LAUNDRY

PDR
RM

BATH

PANT

DESK

OVEN/
MICRO

STORAGE

LIN

SNACK
BAR

RANGE

BC
STORAGE

COVERED
PATIO

COVERED
PATIO

COVERED
PATIO

GARAGE
21⁰ x 23⁸

Width 93'-7"
Depth 74'-10"

Design by
Home Planners

Design 3640
Square Footage: 2,612

L

● Dramatic interior angles add interest to an immensely livable plan that is metered with elegance enough for any social occasion. The family room holds court at the hub of the plan and features a corner fireplace and covered patio access. A media room or home office offers a more secluded space just across the foyer from the formal dinning room. The spacious kitchen, with extra storage at every turn, has an eat-in nook and a door to the rear patio. Three family bedrooms share a hall bath to complete this wing. The master suite is split from the family area to ensure a private retreat. The large bedroom can easily accommodate a sitting area and has a luxurious bath, walk-in closet and sliding doors to a private patio.

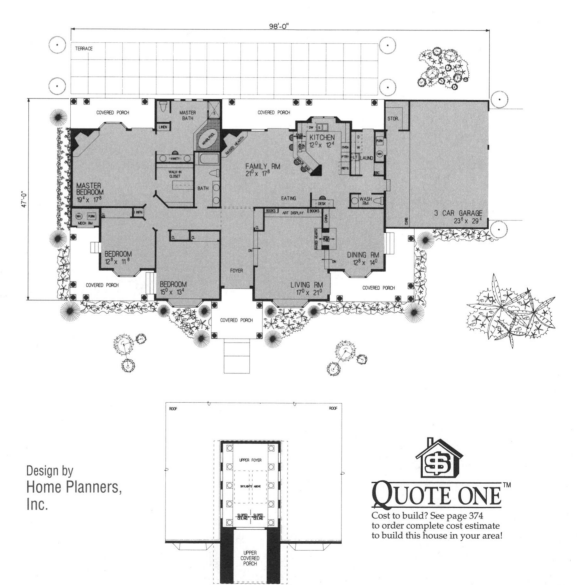

Design 3400
Square Footage: 2,784

L

● Abundant terrace space favors an outdoor lifestyle in this charming one-story. Each room has access to a porch or terrace; think of the added entertainment possibilities! Interior highlights include corner fireplaces in the master suite and family room, a dining room with bay window, and a regal master bath. Note the dramatic two-story foyer.

Design by
Home Planners, Inc.

QUOTE ONE™

Cost to build? See page 374 to order complete cost estimate to build this house in your area!

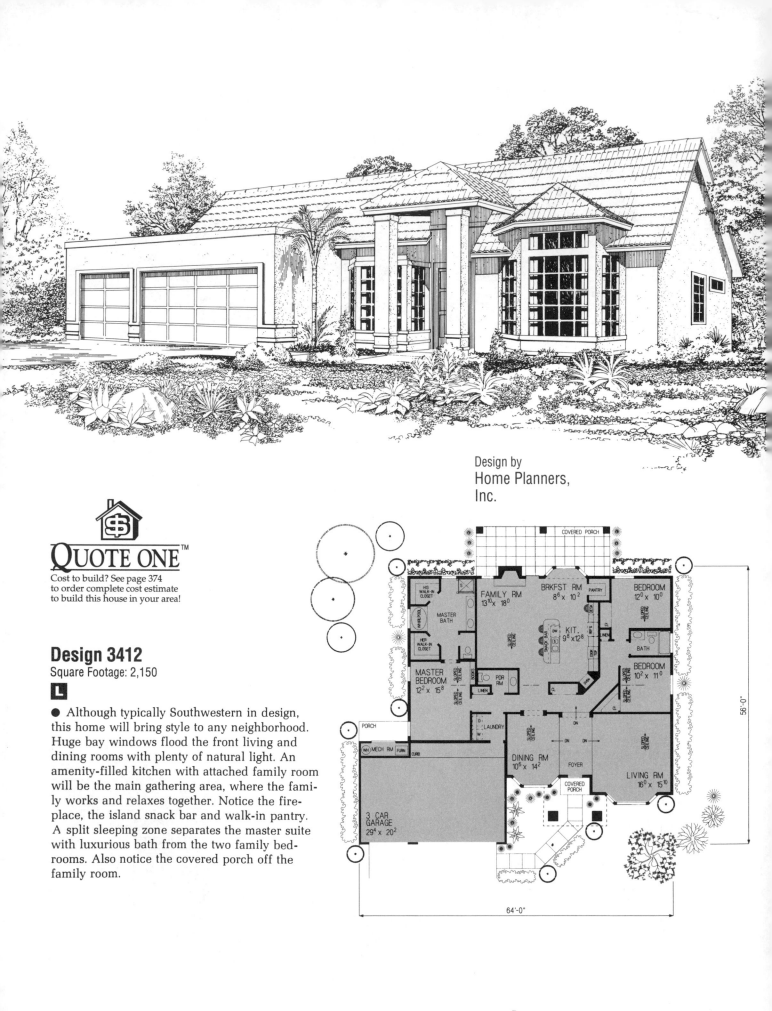

Design by
**Home Planners,
Inc.**

Quote One™

Cost to build? See page 374
to order complete cost estimate
to build this house in your area!

Design 3412

Square Footage: 2,150

L

● Although typically Southwestern in design,
this home will bring style to any neighborhood.
Huge bay windows flood the front living and
dining rooms with plenty of natural light. An
amenity-filled kitchen with attached family room
will be the main gathering area, where the family works and relaxes together. Notice the fireplace, the island snack bar and walk-in pantry.
A split sleeping zone separates the master suite
with luxurious bath from the two family bedrooms. Also notice the covered porch off the
family room.

Design by
Home Planners,
Inc.

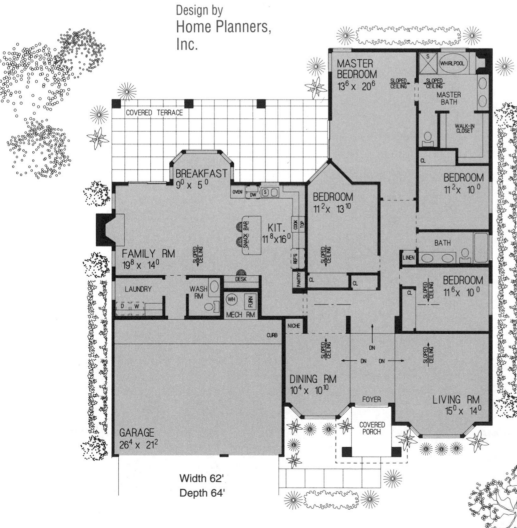

COVERED TERRACE

BREAKFAST
9⁰ x 5⁰

FAMILY RM
19⁸ x 14⁰

SLOPED CEILING

SNACK BAR

KIT.
11⁸ x 16⁰

OVEN DW S

COOK TOP

MASTER
BEDROOM
13⁶ x 20⁶

SLOPED CEILING

SLOPED CEILING

S WHIRLPOOL

MASTER
BATH

WALK-IN
CLOSET

CL

BEDROOM
11² x 13¹⁰

SLOPED CEILING

REF'S

PANTRY CL CL

BEDROOM
11² x 10⁰

BATH

LINEN

LAUNDRY

WASH RM

DESK

WH FURN

MECH RM

BEDROOM
11⁶ x 10⁰

CL

SLOPED CEILING

NICHE

CURB

SLOPED CEILING

DN DN

DN

GARAGE
26⁴ x 21²

DINING RM
10⁴ x 10¹⁰

FOYER

COVERED
PORCH

LIVING RM
15⁰ x 14⁰

SLOPED CEILING

Width 62'
Depth 64'

Design 3415

Square Footage: 2,406

L

● Relax and enjoy the open floor plan of this lovely one-story. Its family room with fireplace and space for eating are a suitable complement to the formal living and dining rooms to the front of the house. There are four bedrooms, or three if you choose to make one a den, and 2½ baths. Don't miss the large pantry and convenient laundry area.

QUOTE ONE™

Cost to build? See page 374 to order complete cost estimate to build this house in your area!

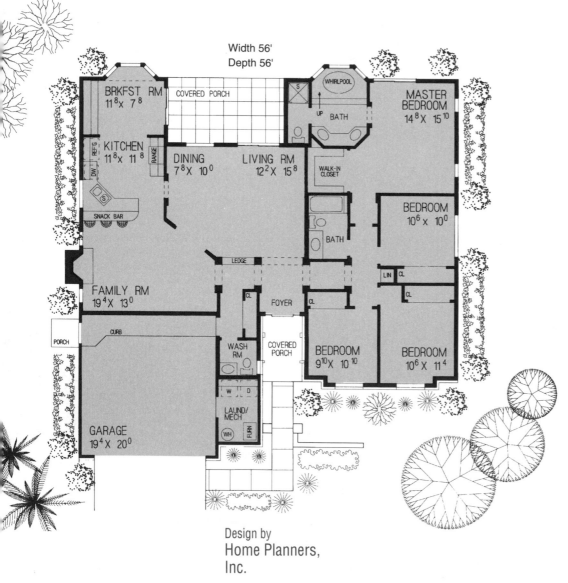

Width 56'
Depth 56'

BRKFST RM
11⁸ x 7⁸

COVERED PORCH

WHIRLPOOL

MASTER BEDROOM
14⁸ x 15¹⁰

KITCHEN
11⁸ x 11⁸

REF'G

DW

RANGE

DINING
7⁸ x 10⁰

LIVING RM
12² x 15⁸

BATH

UP

WALK-IN CLOSET

SNACK BAR

BEDROOM
10⁶ x 10⁰

BATH

FAMILY RM
19⁴ x 13⁰

LEDGE

LIN

CL

CL

CL

PORCH

CURB

FOYER

CL

WASH RM

COVERED PORCH

BEDROOM
9¹⁰ x 10¹⁰

BEDROOM
10⁶ x 11⁴

GARAGE
19⁴ x 20⁰

LAUND/ MECH

W   D

WH   FURN

Design by
Home Planners, Inc.

Design 3419

Square Footage: 1,965

L

● This attractive, multi-gabled exterior houses a compact, livable interior. The entry foyer effectively routes traffic to all areas: left to the family room and kitchen, straight back to the dining room and living room, and right to the four-bedroom sleeping area. The spacious family room provides an informal gathering space while the living and dining rooms are perfect for formal occasions. The highlight of the sleeping area is the master bedroom with its whirlpool, walk-in closet and view of the back yard.

QUOTE ONE™

Cost to build? See page 374 to order complete cost estimate to build this house in your area!

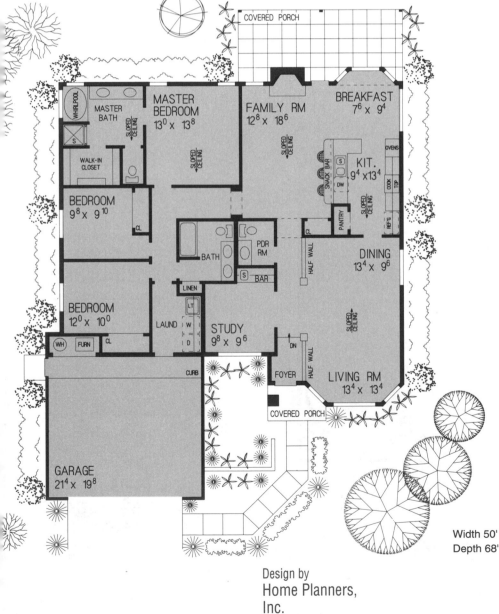

Design 3422

Square Footage: 1,932

L

● An enclosed entry garden greets visitors to this charming Southwestern home. Inside, the foyer is flanked by formal and informal living areas — a living room and dining room to the right and a cozy study to the left. To the rear, a large family room, breakfast room and open kitchen have access to a covered porch and overlook the back yard. Notice the fireplace and bay window. The three-bedroom sleeping area includes a master with a spacious bath with whirlpool.

QUOTE ONE™

Cost to build? See page 374 to order complete cost estimate to build this house in your area!

Width 50'
Depth 68'

Design by
Home Planners,
Inc.

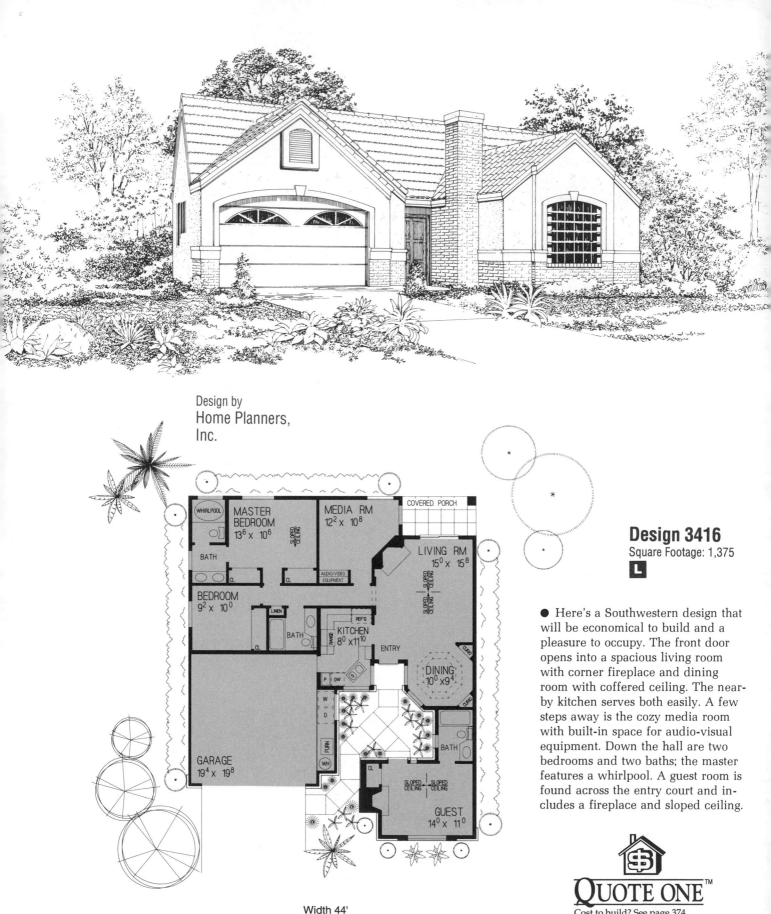

Design by
Home Planners,
Inc.

WHIRLPOOL

MASTER
BEDROOM
13⁶ x 10⁶
SLOPED CEILING

BATH

CL

BEDROOM
9² x 10⁰

CL

LINEN

BATH

MEDIA RM
12² x 10⁸

AUDIO/VIDEO
EQUIPMENT

CL

REF'S

RANGE

KITCHEN
8⁰ x 11¹⁰

P   DW

S

W
D

FURN

WH

GARAGE
19⁴ x 19⁸

COVERED PORCH

LIVING RM
15⁰ x 15⁸
SLOPED CEILING   SLOPED CEILING

ENTRY

DINING
10⁰ x 9⁴

CL/RD

CL/RD

BATH

CL

SLOPED
CEILING   SLOPED
CEILING

GUEST
14⁰ x 11⁰

Width 44'
Depth 52'-4"

Design 3416
Square Footage: 1,375

L

● Here's a Southwestern design that
will be economical to build and a
pleasure to occupy. The front door
opens into a spacious living room
with corner fireplace and dining
room with coffered ceiling. The nearby kitchen serves both easily. A few
steps away is the cozy media room
with built-in space for audio-visual
equipment. Down the hall are two
bedrooms and two baths; the master
features a whirlpool. A guest room is
found across the entry court and includes a fireplace and sloped ceiling.

QUOTE ONE™
Cost to build? See page 374
to order complete cost estimate
to build this house in your area!

Design 3411

Square Footage: 2,441

L

● You'll love the entry to this Southwestern home — it creates a dramatic first impression and leads beautifully to the formal living and dining rooms. Beyond, look for an open family room and dining area in the same proximity as the kitchen. Sliding glass doors here open to a backyard patio. Take your choice of four bedrooms or five, depending on how you wish to use the optional room. The huge master suite is not to be missed.

QUOTE ONE™

Cost to build? See page 374 to order complete cost estimate to build this house in your area!

Design by
Home Planners, Inc.

GUEST BEDROOM
11⁰ x 10⁶

COVERED PORCH

MASTER BEDROOM
13⁰ x 17⁶

MASTER BATH

WALK-IN CLOSET

WHIRLPOOL

BRKFST RM
9⁴ x 9⁰

BEDROOM
11⁴ x 9⁶

BATH

KITCHEN
12⁰ x 11⁸

BEDROOM
10⁸ x 10⁶

BATH

FAMILY RM
17⁶ x 14⁰

MECH RM

PANTRY

BEDROOM
11⁴ x 10⁴

LAUNDRY

3 CAR GARAGE
28² x 20⁸ + STORAGE

DINING RM
11⁶ x 12⁸

FOYER

LIVING RM
16⁰ x 13⁴

STORAGE

COVERED PORCH

63'-0"

70'-0"

Design 9744

Square Footage: 2,090

● This exciting Southwestern design
is enhanced by the use of arched windows and an inviting arched entrance.
The large foyer opens to a massive
great room with a fireplace and built-
in cabinets. The kitchen features an
island cooktop and a skylit breakfast
area. The master suite has an impressive cathedral ceiling and a walk-in
closet as well as a luxurious bath that
boasts separate vanities, a corner
whirlpool tub and a separate shower.
Two additional bedrooms are located
at the opposite end of the home for
privacy and share a full bath. This
plan is available with either a
crawlspace or slab foundation. Please
specify when ordering.

Design by
Donald A.
Gardner,
Architects, Inc.

Design 9755

Square Footage: 1,315

● Southwestern influences are evident in this design, from the tiled roof to the warm stucco exterior. A covered porch leads indoors where the great room gains attention. A cathedral ceiling, a fireplace and built-ins enhance this area. The dining room remains open to this room. In the kitchen, a pass-through cooktop counter allows the cook to converse with family and friends. Three bedrooms include two family bedrooms that share a hall bath and a master suite with skylights, a walk-in closet and a private bath. Please specify crawlspace or slab foundation when ordering.

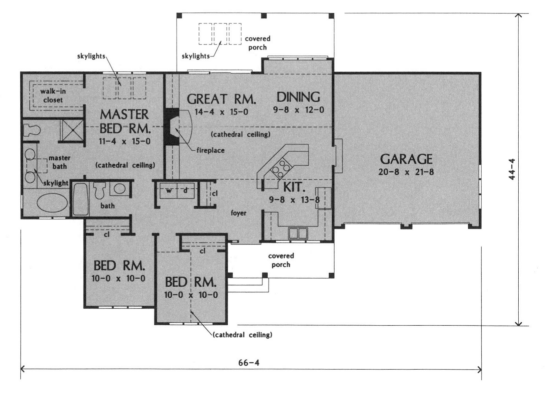

Design by
Donald A.
Gardner,
Architects, Inc.

Design 3344

Square Footage: 3,054

L

QUOTE ONE™

Cost to build? See page 374 to order complete cost estimate to build this house in your area!

QUIET TERRACE

PLAY TERRACE

WHIRLPOOL

MASTER BEDROOM
13⁰ x 17⁴

HER BATH

HIS BATH

DRESSING RM

VANITY

DINING RM
13⁰ x 11⁰

KITCHEN
10⁰ x 11⁴

BRKFST RM
8⁴ x 11⁴

DESK

LS

DW

REFG

COOK TOP

OVEN

S

FLOWER PORCH
13⁰ x 11⁸

SKYLIGHTS ABOVE

HER WALK-IN CLOSET

SHELVES

SHELVES

HIS WALK-IN CLOSET

ETAGERE

FAMILY RM
15⁴ x 19⁶

BEDROOM
10¹⁰ x 11⁰

LINEN

CL

BATH

SLOPED CEILING

SLOPED CEILING

SLOPED CEILING

SLOPED CEILING

PDR RM

BC

PANTRY

S

BAR

CL

RAISED HEARTH

SKYLIGHT

DN

SKYLIGHT

CL

BEDROOM
10¹⁰ x 14⁴

CL

LIVING RM
13⁰ x 19⁴

FOYER

STUDY
13⁰ x 11⁰

BAR

S

CL

LAUNDRY
7⁸ x 10⁰

LT

W

D

BEDROOM
11⁸ x 12⁰

TRELLIS ABOVE

COURTYARD

CL

70'-2"

Design by
Home Planners, Inc.

P

GARAGE
21⁴ x 21⁴

85'-8"

● This home features interior planning for today's active family. Living areas include a living room with fireplace, a cozy study and family room with wet bar. Convenient to the kitchen is the formal dining room with attractive bay window overlooking the back yard. The four-bedroom sleeping area contains a sumptuous master suite. Also notice the cheerful flower porch with access from the master suite, living room and dining room.

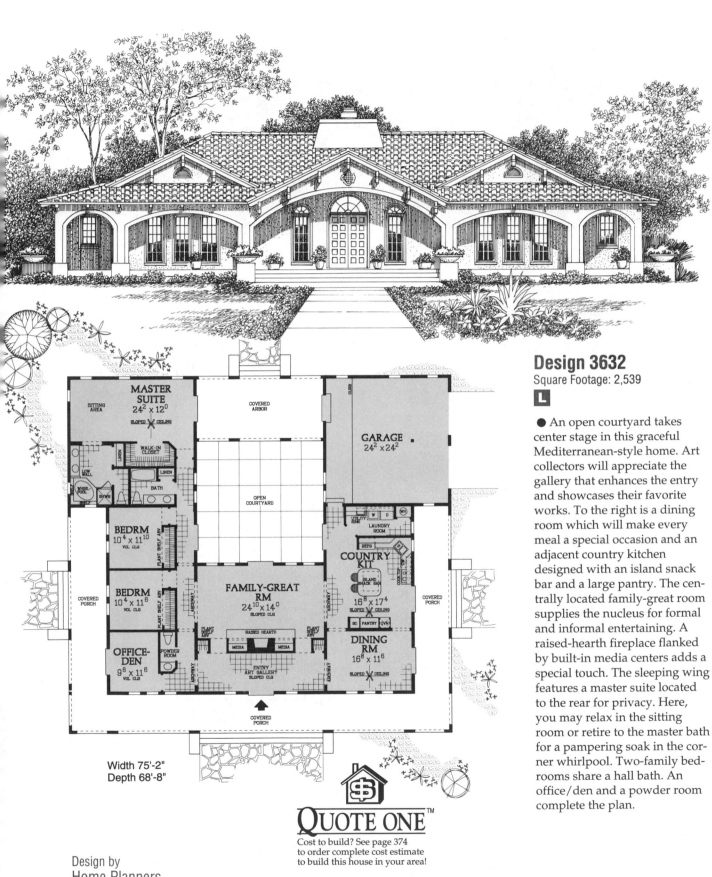

Design 3632
Square Footage: 2,539

L

● An open courtyard takes center stage in this graceful Mediterranean-style home. Art collectors will appreciate the gallery that enhances the entry and showcases their favorite works. To the right is a dining room which will make every meal a special occasion and an adjacent country kitchen designed with an island snack bar and a large pantry. The centrally located family-great room supplies the nucleus for formal and informal entertaining. A raised-hearth fireplace flanked by built-in media centers adds a special touch. The sleeping wing features a master suite located to the rear for privacy. Here, you may relax in the sitting room or retire to the master bath for a pampering soak in the corner whirlpool. Two-family bedrooms share a hall bath. An office/den and a powder room complete the plan.

Width 75'-2"
Depth 68'-8"

QUOTE ONE™
Cost to build? See page 374 to order complete cost estimate to build this house in your area!

Design by
Home Planners,
Inc.

Design by
Home Planners,
Inc.

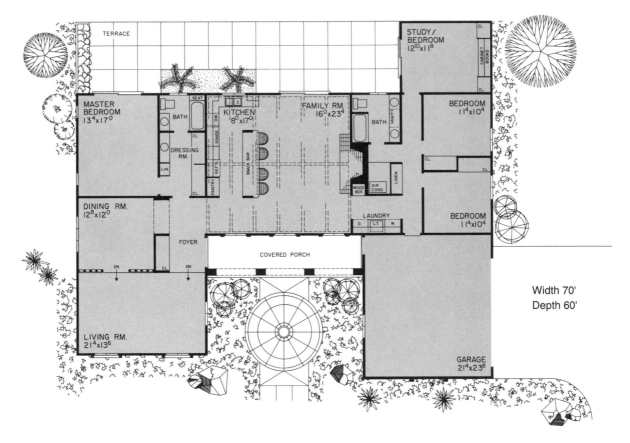

Width 70'
Depth 60'

Design 2236
Square Footage: 2,307

● Living in this Spanish adaptation will truly be fun for the whole family. It will matter very little whether the backdrop matches the mountains above, becomes the endless prairie, turns out to be the rolling farmland, or is the backdrop of a suburban area. A family's flair for distinction will be satisfied by this picturesque exterior, while its requirements for everyday living will be gloriously catered to. The hub of the plan will be the kitchen-family room area. The beamed ceiling and raised hearth fireplace will contribute to the cozy, informal atmosphere. The separate dining room and the sunken living room function together formally. The master bedroom will enjoy its privacy from the three children's rooms located at the opposite end of the plan.

Design 2820

Square Footage: 2,261

L D

● A courtyard with a pool and a trellised planter area makes coming home quite a pleasure. Inside, the front living room has sliding glass doors which open to the entrance court. The adjacent dining room features a bay window. The rear family room accommodates informal activities. A sloped, beamed ceiling, a raised-hearth fireplace, sliding glass doors to the terrace and a snack bar for quick meals characterize this area. The sleeping wing remains quiet, away from day-to-day living. A three-car garage is endowed with storage space.

California Engineered Plans and California Stock Plans are available for this home. Call 1-800-521-6797 for more information.

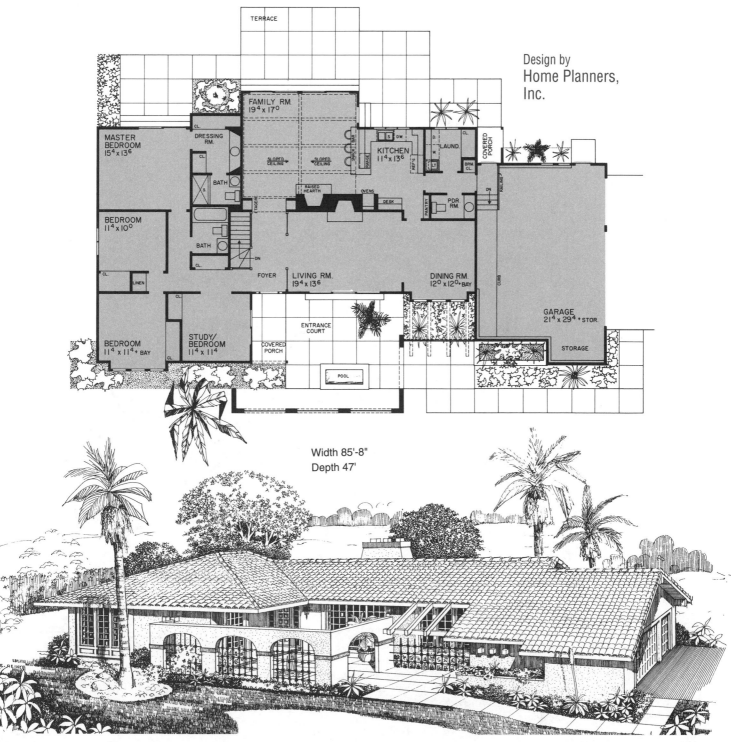

Design by
Home Planners, Inc.

Width 85'-8"
Depth 47'

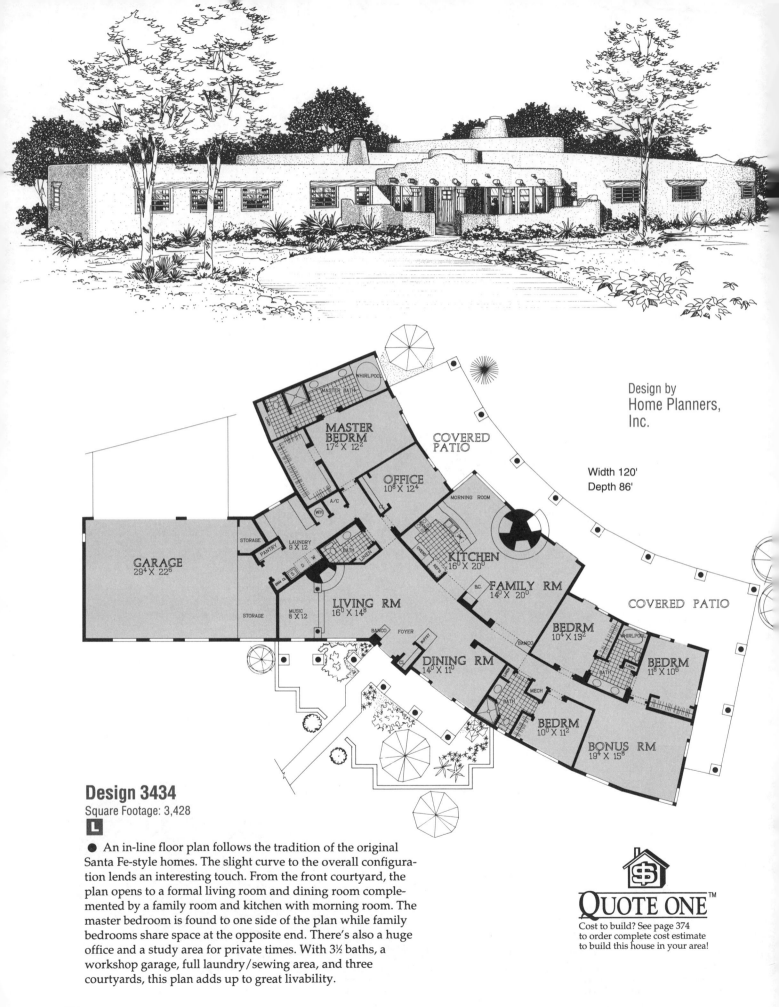

Design by
Home Planners,
Inc.

Width 120'
Depth 86'

MASTER BEDRM 17² X 12²

OFFICE 10⁸ X 12⁴

COVERED PATIO

MORNING ROOM

KITCHEN 16⁰ X 20⁰

FAMILY RM 14⁰ X 20⁰

COVERED PATIO

GARAGE 29⁴ X 22⁶

STORAGE

PANTRY

LAUNDRY 9 X 12

BATH

LINEN

STORAGE

MUSIC 8 X 12

LIVING RM 16⁰ X 14⁸

BEDRM 10⁴ X 13²

WHIRLPOOL

BEDRM 11⁸ X 10⁶

BANCO

FOYER

BUFFET

BANCO

BATH

DINING RM 14⁰ X 11⁰

BATH

MECH

BEDRM 10⁰ X 11²

BONUS RM 19⁴ X 15⁸

Design 3434

Square Footage: 3,428

L

● An in-line floor plan follows the tradition of the original Santa Fe-style homes. The slight curve to the overall configuration lends an interesting touch. From the front courtyard, the plan opens to a formal living room and dining room complemented by a family room and kitchen with morning room. The master bedroom is found to one side of the plan while family bedrooms share space at the opposite end. There's also a huge office and a study area for private times. With 3½ baths, a workshop garage, full laundry/sewing area, and three courtyards, this plan adds up to great livability.

QUOTE ONE™

Cost to build? See page 374
to order complete cost estimate
to build this house in your area!

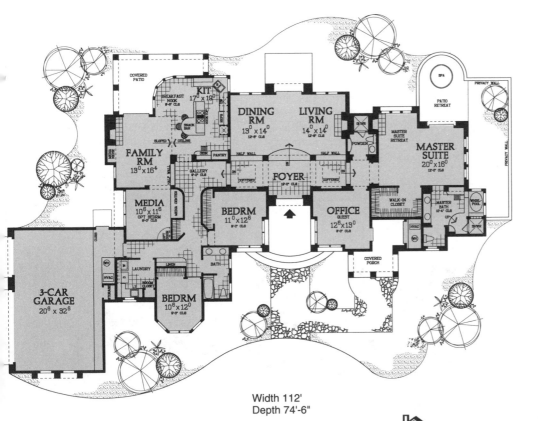

Width 112'
Depth 74'-6"

Design 3630

Square Footage: 3,034

L

● A grand entry enhances the exterior of this elegant stucco home. The office located at the front of the plan makes this design ideal for a home-based business. Formal areas combine to provide lots of space for entertaining. The kitchen, complete with a snack bar and a breakfast nook, opens to the family room which connects to the media room. The private master suite includes two retreats—one is a multi-windowed sitting area, the other contains a spa for outdoor enjoyment. Be sure to notice the walk-in closet and the luxurious bath. Two family bedrooms share a full bath.

QUOTE ONE™

Cost to build? See page 374
to order complete cost estimate
to build this house in your area!

Design by
Home Planners,
Inc.

Photo by Allen Maertz Photography

This home, as shown in the photograph, may differ from the actual blueprints. For more detailed information, please check the floor plans carefully.

Quote One™

Cost to build? See page 374 to order complete cost estimate to build this house in your area!

Design 3405

Square Footage: 3,144

L

● In classic Santa Fe style, this home strikes a beautiful combination of historic exterior detailing and open floor planning on the inside. A covered porch running the width of the facade leads to an entry foyer that connects to a huge gathering room with a fireplace and an adjacent formal dining room. The family kitchen allows special space for casual gatherings. The right wing of the home holds two family bedrooms and a full bath. The left wing is devoted to the master suite and a guest room or a study. Built-ins abound throughout the house.

California Engineered Plans and California Stock Plans are available for this home. Call 1-800-521-6797 for more information.

Design by
Home Planne
Inc.

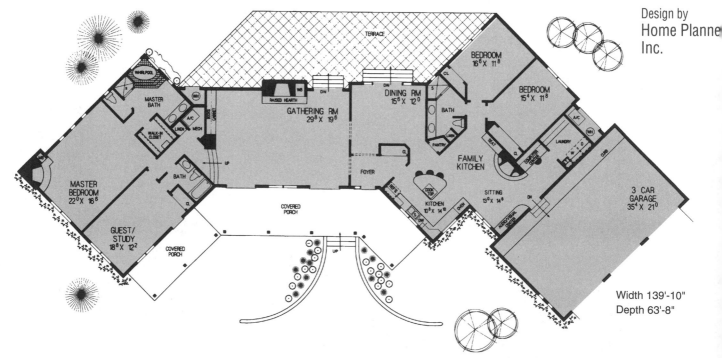

Width 139'-10"
Depth 63'-8"

Design by
Home Planners,
Inc.

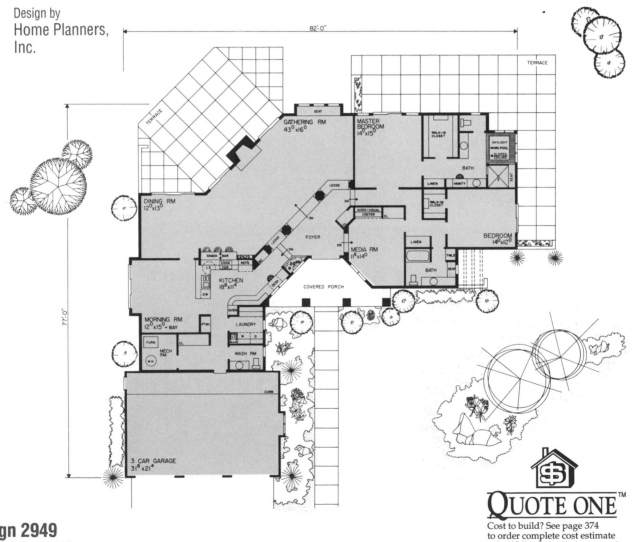

Design 2949
Square Footage: 2,922

● This one-story matches traditional Southwestern design elements such as stucco, tile, and exposed rafters (called vigas) with an up-to-date floor plan. The 43-foot gathering room provides a dramatic multi-purpose living area. Other unusual features include a morning room with a sunny bay and a media room which could serve as a third bedroom. The master bedroom contains a walk-in closet and an amenity-filled bath with a whirlpool tub. It shares a sunny terrace with a family bedroom that enjoys its own full bath.

California Engineered Plans and California Stock Plans are available for this home. Call 1-800-521-6797 for more information.

Design 3486

Square Footage: 2,000

● This classic stucco design provides a cool retreat in any climate. From the covered porch, enter the skylit foyer to find an arched ceiling leading to the central gathering room with its raised-hearth fireplace and terrace access. A connecting corner dining room is conveniently located near the amenity-filled kitchen that features an abundant pantry, a snack bar and a separate breakfast area. The large master bedroom includes terrace access and a master bath with a whirlpool tub, a separate shower and plenty of closet space. A second bedroom and a study that can be converted to a bedroom complete this wonderful plan.

Design by
Home Planners,
Inc.

QUOTE ONE™

Cost to build? See page 374
to order complete cost estimate
to build this house in your area!

Width 75'
Depth 55'

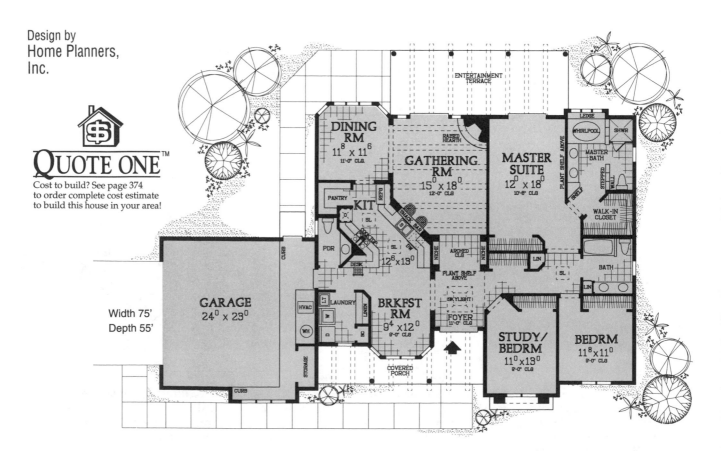

Design 3642

Square Footage: 2,945

● This Santa Fe delivers great livability. From three bedrooms for the family and a beautiful master suite for Mom and Dad to formal and informal living areas, the floor plan is designed for today's lifestyles. The living room opens directly from the foyer and is defined by a curve of glass overlooking the front entry. Across the hall and through double columns is the dining room which overlooks the rear patio. The family room is mega-sized and contains a wet bar, curved fireplace and other built-ins. It leads, through a utility area, to the three-car garage. The kitchen overlooks the rear patio and connects to a glass-walled breakfast nook. Don't miss the double walk-in closets in the master suite.

Design by
Home Planners, Inc.

Quote One™

Cost to build? See page 374 to order complete cost estimate to build this house in your area!

Width 73'
Depth 68'-10"

Outstanding Options:

One-story designs with an extra level

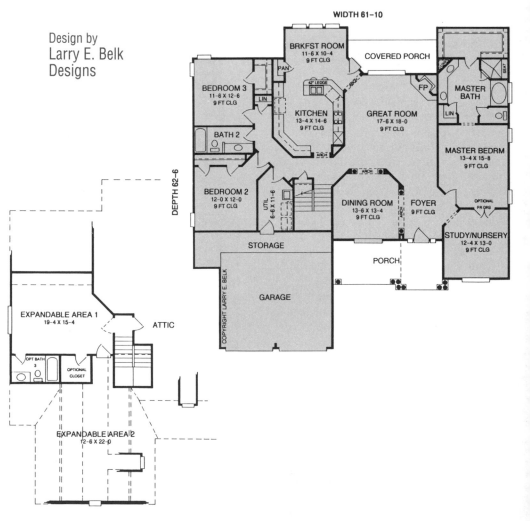

COPYRIGHT LARRY E. BELK

Design 8158

Square Footage: 2,366
Optional Second Floor: 622 square feet

● Cedar shingles and brick give this home the flavor of a country cottage. Inside, an up-to-date floor plan includes all of today's amenities. Nine-foot ceilings throughout give the plan a "big home" feel. The dining room is defined by elegant arched openings flanked by columns. A corner fireplace serves the great room. The kitchen features lots of counter and cabinet space along with a walk-in pantry and a 42" eating bar. The master suite includes optional access to a "flex" room that can be used as a study, a nursery or an in-home office. The optional second floor includes space for an additional bedroom, a bath and a large, expandable area over the garage. Please specify crawlspace or slab foundation when ordering.

Design by
Larry E. Belk
Designs

WIDTH 61-10

DEPTH 62-6

BRKFST ROOM
11-6 X 10-4
9 FT CLG

COVERED PORCH

BEDROOM 3
11-6 X 12-6
9 FT CLG

PAN

42" LEDGE

KITCHEN
13-4 X 14-6
9 FT CLG

GREAT ROOM
17-6 X 18-0
9 FT CLG

FP

MASTER
BATH

LIN

LIN

BATH 2

ARCH

BEDROOM 2
12-0 X 12-0
9 FT CLG

UTIL
6-6 X 11-6

DINING ROOM
13-6 X 13-4
9 FT CLG

ARCH

FOYER
9 FT CLG

MASTER BEDRM
13-4 X 15-8
9 FT CLG

OPTIONAL
FR DRS

STORAGE

PORCH

STUDY/NURSERY
12-4 X 13-0
9 FT CLG

GARAGE

COPYRIGHT LARRY E. BELK

EXPANDABLE AREA 1
19-4 X 15-4

ATTIC

OPT BATH
3

OPTIONAL
CLOSET

EXPANDABLE AREA 2
12-6 X 22-0

COPYRIGHT LARRY E. BELK

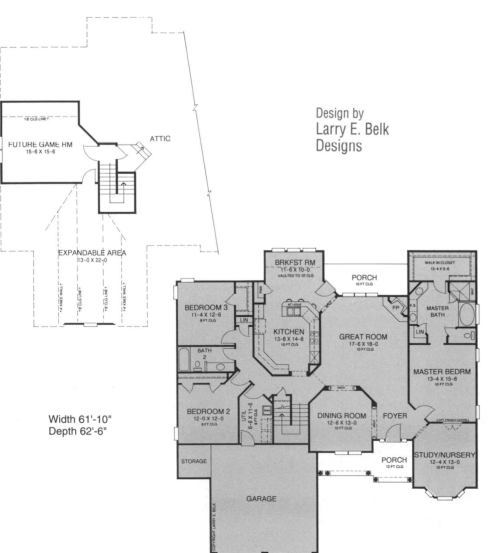

Width 61'-10"
Depth 62'-6"

Design by
Larry E. Belk
Designs

Design 8124

Square Footage: 2,350
Optional Second Floor: 286 square feet

● Traditional brick and an interesting accent of stucco give this home an elegant look. Designed with a split-bedroom layout, the plan provides an additional benefit with a study/nursery located adjacent to the master suite. The room can be used as a nursery when needed and converted to a study or home office later. The master suite has a fantastic, amenity-filled bath, which includes a huge walk-in closet. A sunny breakfast room is located at the rear of the home. The kitchen features a wealth of cabinets, counter space and an eating bar. A rear stair is provided for access to the second floor. Here, space is allocated for a future game room. Please specify crawlspace or slab foundation when ordering.

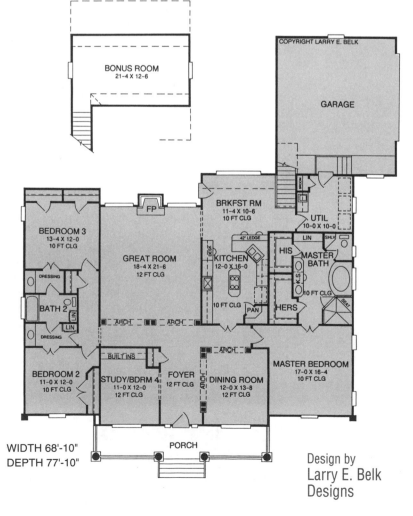

BONUS ROOM
21-4 X 12-6

GARAGE

BRKFST RM
11-4 X 10-6
10 FT CLG

UTIL
10-0 X 10-0

LIN   SHLV

FP

BEDROOM 3
13-4 X 12-0
10 FT CLG

GREAT ROOM
18-4 X 21-6
12 FT CLG

KITCHEN
12-0 X 16-0

DESK   42" LEDGE

HIS

MASTER
BATH

DRESSING

BATH 2

LIN

K.S.

10 FT CLG

SEAT

PAN   HERS

ARCH   ARCH

LIN

DRESSING

10 FT CLG

BUILT INS

ARCH

BEDROOM 2
11-0 X 12-0
10 FT CLG

STUDY/BDRM 4
11-0 X 12-0
12 FT CLG

FOYER
12 FT CLG

ARCH

DINING ROOM
12-0 X 13-8
12 FT CLG

MASTER BEDROOM
17-0 X 16-4
10 FT CLG

WIDTH 68'-10"
DEPTH 77'-10"

PORCH

Design by
Larry E. Belk
Designs

Design 8143

Square Footage: 2,648
Bonus Room: 266 square feet

● This vintage elevation has all the
extras desired by today's homeowners.
Inside, 12' ceilings give the study, the
dining room, and the great room a large,
spacious feeling. Graceful arches are
flanked by stately columns. The kitchen
features a cooktop work island, a pantry
and a 42" eating bar. An optional bonus
room over the garage is a great place for
a play room or an in-home office. The
master suite includes His and Hers closets and an amenity-filled master bath.
Bedrooms 2 and 3 feature roomy closets
and each has access to a private dressing
area off of Bath 2. Please specify
crawlspace or slab foundation when
ordering.

Design 8126

Square Footage: 2,127
Bonus Room: 338 square feet

● Three arched windows provide just the right touch of elegance and give this home a picturesque appeal. The large great room with a corner fireplace is located conveniently near the roomy breakfast area and kitchen. Ten-foot ceilings in all major living areas give the plan an open, spacious feel. The master suite includes a luxury bath with a coffered ceiling, large His and Hers closets, a whirlpool tub, a shower with a seat and His and Hers vanities with a seating area. This split-bedroom plan locates Bedrooms 2 and 3 on the opposite side of the home. A stair is provided leading to an expandable area on the second floor. Please specify crawlspace or slab foundation when ordering.

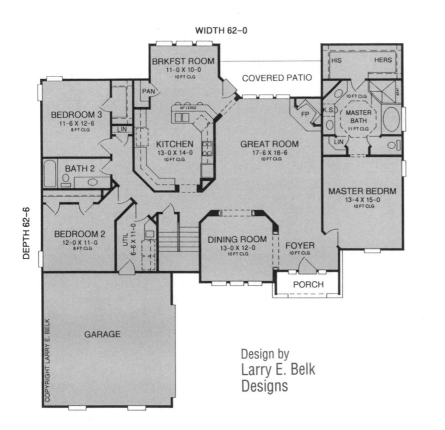

WIDTH 62-0

BRKFST ROOM
11-0 X 10-0
10 FT CLG

COVERED PATIO

PAN

HIS   HERS

42" LEDGE

10 FT CLG

BEDROOM 3
11-6 X 12-6
8 FT CLG

LIN

FP

K.S.

MASTER
BATH
11 FT CLG

KITCHEN
13-0 X 14-0
10 FT CLG

GREAT ROOM
17-6 X 18-6
10 FT CLG

LIN

BATH 2

DEPTH 62-6

MASTER BEDRM
13-4 X 15-0
10 FT CLG

BEDROOM 2
12-0 X 11-0
8 FT CLG

UTIL
6-6 X 11-0

DINING ROOM
13-0 X 12-0
10 FT CLG

FOYER
10 FT CLG

PORCH

GARAGE

Design by
Larry E. Belk
Designs

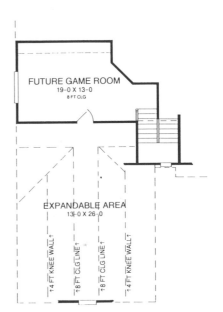

FUTURE GAME ROOM
19-0 X 13-0
8 FT CLG

EXPANDABLE AREA
13-0 X 26-0

4 FT KNEE WALL↑   8 FT CLG LINE↑   8 FT CLG LINE↑   4 FT KNEE WALL↑

Design by
**Frank Betz
Associates, Inc.**

Design P234

Square Footage: 2,622
Bonus Room: 478 square feet

● Multiple gables, corner quoins and a
variety of window treatments decorate
the facade of this stucco home. Inside,
high ceilings in the foyer, dining room
and living room add to the spaciousness
created by the open design. The vaulted
family room receives natural light from
a wall of windows that continues across
the back of the house. The L-shaped
kitchen includes an island work area
and serving bar, a large walk-in pantry,
a pass-through to the family room, and
the convenience of a sunny breakfast
bay with a built-in desk. The sleeping
zone is at the right of the plan, where
two front bedrooms share a full bath,
and an elegant master suite offers a
sunny sitting room and a luxurious
bath. Please specify basement or crawlspace foundation when ordering.

Width 69'
Depth 71'-4"

Design 9543

Main Level: 2,188 square feet
Lower Level: 1,049 square feet
Total: 3,237 square feet

● Carriage lamps and brick columns provide a dramatic element to the impressive entry to this one-story traditional. The well-designed floor plan flows nicely. The den is ideally located for use as an office if the need arises. To the left rests the formal living and dining area which provides nearby access to the step-saving kitchen. The family room is separated only by the breakfast nook, which provides access to the rear deck. The master suite, with its tray ceiling and luxurious bath, completes the first floor. The basement contains a recreation room, two secondary bedrooms (one with access to the rear grounds) and a full bath.

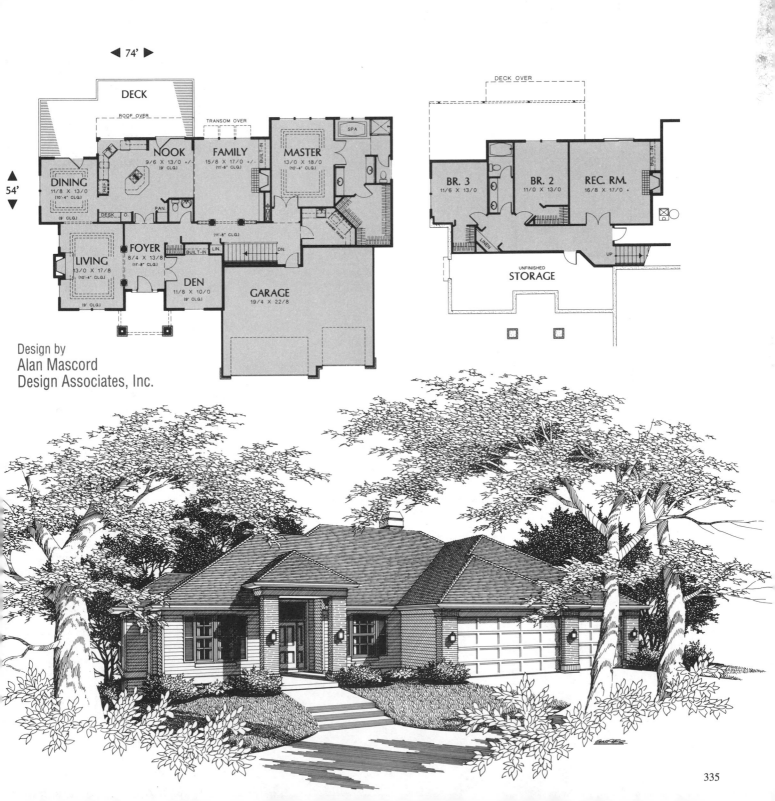

Design by
Alan Mascord
Design Associates, Inc.

335

Quote One®

Cost to build? See page 374
to order complete cost estimate
to build this house in your area!

Design 9831

Square Footage: 2,150
Expandable Lower Level: 2,150 square feet

● This home draws its inspiration
from both French and English country
homes. From the foyer and across the
spacious great room, French doors
give a generous view of the covered
rear porch. The adjoining dining room
is subtly defined by the use of
columns and a large triple window.
The kitchen, with its generous work-
island, adjoins the breakfast area and
keeping room with a fireplace, a
vaulted ceiling and an abundant use
of windows. A bedroom to the front of
the first floor may act as guest quarters. Another bedroom shares a bath
with this one. The home is completed
by a quiet master suite located at the
rear. It contains a bay window, a garden tub and His and Hers vanities.
Space on the lower level can be developed later.

WIDTH 64'
DEPTH 64'-4"

Design by
Design Traditions

Design by
**Frank Betz
Associates, Inc.**

Design P196

Square Footage: 2,193
Bonus Room: 400 square feet

● Arched windows, corner quoins and stonework accent the facade on this attractive stucco home. Inside, the family room stretches from the foyer to the back of the house, where a fireplace is flanked by windows. The spacious island kitchen is handy to the formal dining room, which is defined by columns and lighted by a massive multipane window. Other features of the kitchen include a pass-through to the family room, a good-sized pantry and a sunny breakfast area with a French door to the back yard. To the left of the foyer, the formal living room could be used as a family bedroom, joining two others on that side of the house. The luxurious master suite is on the right and includes a sitting room and a pampering bath. Please specify basement or crawlspace foundation when ordering.

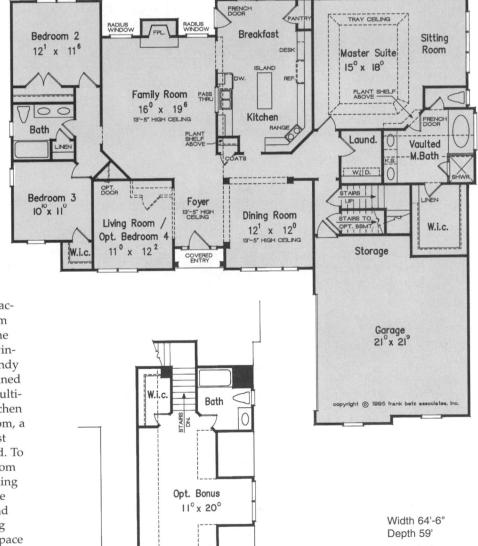

Width 64'-6"
Depth 59'

337

DECK

BREAKFAST
11'-4" X 8'-6"

BEDROOM NO. 3
11'-6" X 11'-0"

GREAT ROOM
14'-0" X 17'-6"

KITCHEN
11'-4" X 10'-0"

MASTER
BEDROOM
12'-4" X 15'-6"

BATH

DN

HIS

FOYER
6'-6" X 5'-0"

PWDR

MASTER
BATH

BEDROOM NO. 2
11'-0" X 12'-2"

DINING ROOM
11'-4" X 10'-6"

STOOP

LAUNDRY

HERS

TWO-CAR GARAGE
20'-4" X 19'-4"

Width 55'-6"
Depth 57'-6"

Design 9840

Square Footage: 1,684
Expandable Lower Level: 1,650 square feet

QUOTE ONE®

Cost to build? See page 374
to order complete cost estimate
to build this house in your area!

WORKSHOP/
STORAGE

FUTURE
FAMILY ROOM
14'-0" X 17'-6"

FUTURE
GAME ROOM
11'-4" X 18'-6"

FUTURE
GUEST BEDROOM
11'-10" X 14'-6"

MECHANICAL

STOOP
ABOVE

UP

FUTURE
BATH

STORAGE

SLAB ON GRADE

● Charmingly compact, this one-
story home is as beautiful as it is
practical. The impressive arch over
the double front door is repeated
with an arched window in the formal dining room. This room opens to
a spacious great room with fireplace
and is nearby the kitchen and bayed
breakfast area. Split sleeping
arrangements put the master suite
with His and Hers walk-in closets at
the right of the plan and two family
bedrooms at the left. Additional
space in the basement can later be
developed as the family grows.

Design by
Design Traditions

Design 9846
Expandable Lower Level: 2,295 square feet

● The abundance of details in this plan make it the finest in one-story living. The great room and formal dining room are loosely defined by a simple column at the entry foyer, allowing for an open, dramatic sense of space. The kitchen with prep island shares the right side of the plan with a bayed breakfast area and keeping room with fireplace. Sleeping accommodations to the left of the plan include a master suite with sitting area, double closet and separate tub and shower. Two family bedrooms share a full bath. Additional living and sleeping space can be developed in the unfinished basement.

Design by
Design Traditions

Width 69'
Depth 49'-6"

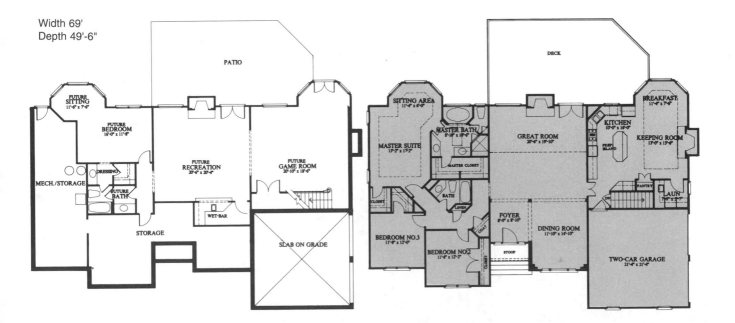

Width 64'
Depth 72'-4"

Covered Porch
Vaulted Family Room 15⁰ x 19⁴
Breakfast
Sitting Room 14⁵ x 10⁰
Living Room 14⁰ x 20⁸ 12'-5" HIGH CEILING
Master Suite 14⁰ x 16¹⁰
Vaulted M.Bath
Serving Bar
Pantry
Pwdr.
Kitchen
Laund.
Storage
Dining Room 13⁰ x 13⁰
Foyer 12'-5" CEILING
Bedroom 3 12⁰ x 10⁹ 12'-5" HIGH CEILING
Covered Porch
Bath
Vaulted Bedroom 2 11¹⁰ x 13⁰ 11'-6" HIGH CEILING
W.i.c.
Linen
Garage 20⁰ x 21⁹
copyright © 1995 frank betz associates, inc.

Opt. Bedroom 4 14⁰ x 12⁵
Opt. Bath
Stairs Dn.
Linen
Dining Room Below
Optional Bonus Room 10⁵ x 24¹

OPT. BASEMENT/ BONUS ROOM PLAN

Vaulted Family Room 15⁰ x 19⁴
Stairs Up
Built-ins
Pantry
Pwdr.
Living Room 14⁰ x 20⁸ 12'-5" CEILING
Oven
Coats
Kitchen
Stairs Dn.

OPT. BASEMENT/ BONUS STAIR LOCATION

Design P194

Square Footage: 2,491
Bonus Room: 588 square feet

Design by
Frank Betz Associates, Inc.

● Interesting rooflines, a stucco-and-stone facade and repeated arches at the entry give this home plenty of curb appeal. Inside, the formal dining and living rooms are separated by decorative columns. Large crowds can easily spill over into the vaulted family room, with its delightful fireplace, or to the back yard. A covered porch is reached from the breakfast nook that opens off the efficient kitchen. The sleeping zone includes a luxurious master suite and two family bedrooms. Please specify basement or crawlspace foundation when ordering.

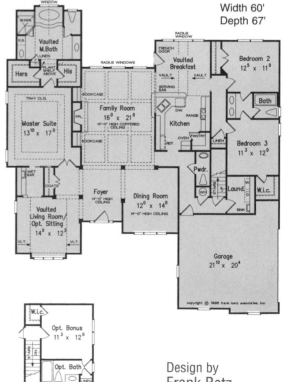

Design P176

Square Footage: 2,403
Bonus Room: 285 square feet

● The heart of this home will be the family room, with its attractive coffered ceiling, fireplace, built-in bookcases and views of the rear property. The spacious kitchen offers a right-angled serving bar to family room and sunny breakfast nook, and is not far from the formal dining room. Two family bedrooms are on the right, separated from the sumptuous master suite on the left. A vaulted living or sitting room and upstairs bonus space complete the plan. Please specify basement or crawlspace foundation when ordering.

Vaulted Breakfast
Linen
Bedroom 2 12⁵ x 11⁰
Kitchen
Bath
Bedroom 3 11³ x 12⁰
Pwdr.
Coats
Laund.

OPT. BASEMENT STAIRS LOCATION

Width 60'
Depth 67'

Radius Window
Shwr.
Vaulted M.Bath
K.S.
Hers
Plant Shelf Above
His
Radius Windows
French Door
Vaulted Breakfast
Bedroom 2 12⁵ x 11⁰
Tray Clg.
Bookcase
Master Suite 13¹⁰ x 17⁰
Family Room 16⁰ x 21⁰ 14'-0" HIGH COFFERED CEILING
Serving Bar
Dw.
Range
Kitchen
Oven
Pantry
Ref.
Bath
Bedroom 3 11³ x 12⁰
Bookcase
Fpl.
Wet Bar
Coats
Foyer 14'-0" CEILING
Dining Room 12⁰ x 14⁰ 14'-0" HIGH CEILING
Pwdr.
Laund.
W.i.c.
Vaulted Living Room/ Opt. Sitting 14⁰ x 12⁰
Garage 21¹⁰ x 20⁴
copyright © 1996 frank betz associates, inc.

W.i.c.
Opt. Bonus 11³ x 12⁰
Opt. Bath
Linen

OPT. BONUS ROOM

Design by
Frank Betz Associates, Inc.

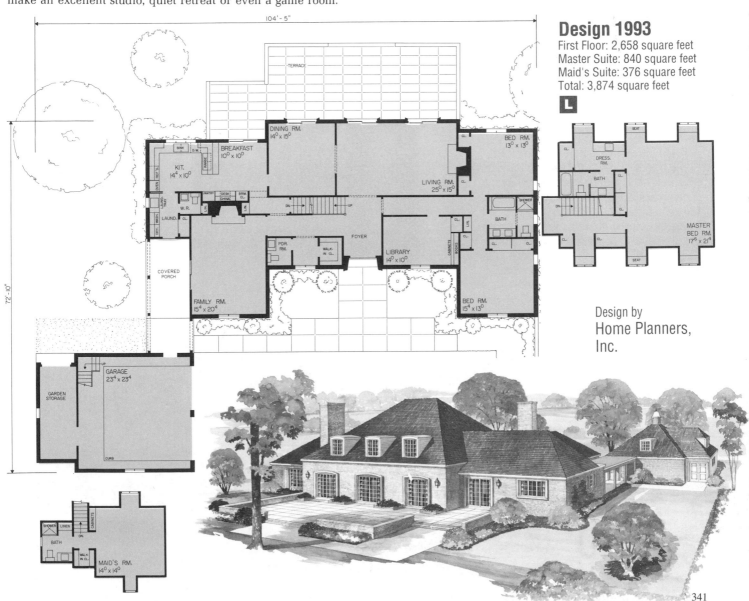

● The elegance of pleasing proportion and delightful detailing has seldom been better exemplified than by this classic French country manor adaptation. Approaching the house across the drive court, the majesty of this multi-roofed structure is breathtaking, indeed. An outstanding feature is the maid's suite. It is located above the garage and is easily reached by use of the covered porch connecting the laundry room's service entrance to the garage. If desired, it would make an excellent studio, quiet retreat or even a game room.

Design 1993

First Floor: 2,658 square feet
Master Suite: 840 square feet
Maid's Suite: 376 square feet
Total: 3,874 square feet

L

Design by
Home Planners, Inc.

Design 7229

Square Footage: 1,696

● This convenient split-entry ranch design features a great room with a volume ceiling, a fireplace flanked by bookcases and a floor-to-ceiling view of the back yard. The efficient double-L kitchen includes a sunny bay-windowed breakfast area. Box ceilings grace both the breakfast nook and the formal dining room. The laundry room is strategically located near the sleeping wing. Two secondary bedrooms offer abundant closet space and a shared full bath. The deluxe master bedroom includes a vaulted ceiling, a large walk-in closet and a bath with a whirlpool tub and a skylit dual vanity.

Width 54'
Depth 34'

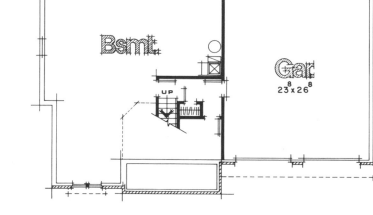

Design by
Design
Basics,
Inc.

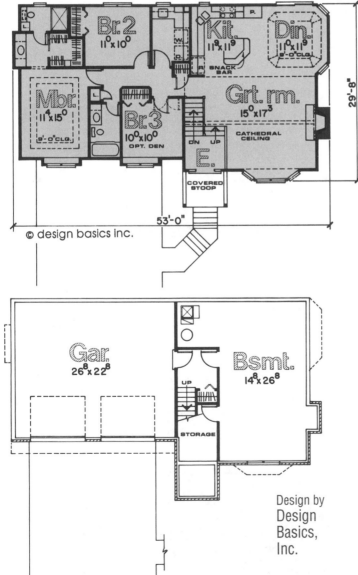

Design 7225

Square Footage: 1,385

● Three steps up from the entry, the great room contains a cathedral ceiling, a bayed window and a fireplace. A vaulted ceiling in the dining area furthers this feeling of loftiness. The kitchen offers a snack bar and a pantry. The nearby laundry room has a window and a soaking sink. Versatile Bedroom 3 can become a den by adding French doors. The private master bedroom features a boxed window and a tiered ceiling. The master bath includes a walk-in closet and a compartmented toilet and shower area.

Design by
Design
Basics,
Inc.

Design 3315

Square Footage: 3,248

L

● Besides the covered front veranda, look for another full-width veranda to the rear of this charming home. The master bedroom, breakfast room, and gathering room all have French doors to this outdoor space. A handy wet bar/tavern enhances entertainment options. The upper lounge could be a welcome haven.

Design by
Home Planners, Inc.

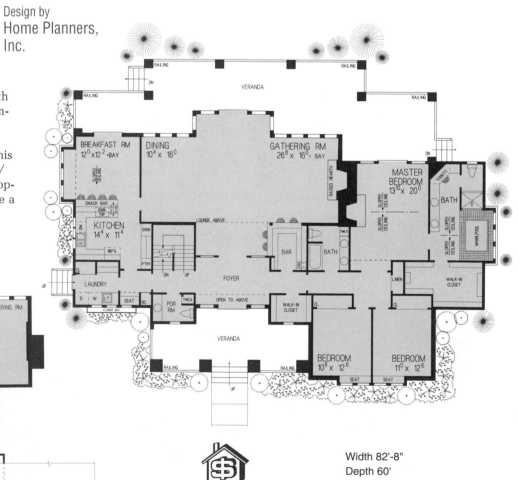

Width 82'-8"
Depth 60'

Quote One™
Cost to build? See page 374
to order complete cost estimate
to build this house in your area!

This home, as shown in the photographs, may differ from the actual blueprints. For more detailed information, please check the floor plans carefully.

Photos by Bob Greenspan

Width 97'
Depth 102'-8"

Design 2920

First Floor: 3,067 square feet
Second Floor: 648 square feet
Total: 3,715 square feet

L D

● This contemporary design has a great deal to offer. A fireplace opens up to both the living room and country kitchen. Privacy is the key word when describing the sleeping areas. The first floor master bedroom is away from the traffic of the house and features a dressing/exercise room, a whirlpool tub and shower and a spacious walk-in closet. Two more bedrooms and a full bath are on the second floor. The three-car garage is arranged so that the owners have use of a double garage with an attached single on reserve for guests. The cheerful sun room adds 296 square feet to the total.

California Engineered Plans and California Stock Plans are available for this home. Call 1-800-521-6797 for more information.

QUOTE ONE™

Cost to build? See page 374 to order complete cost estimate to build this house in your area!

Design by
Home Planners, Inc.

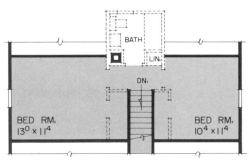

Design 1372

First Floor: 768 square feet
Second Floor: 432 square feet
Total: 1,200 square feet

● Low-cost livability could
hardly be better. Here is an
enchanting Colonial exterior
and a four-bedroom floor plan.
The family kitchen includes eating space and a door to the carport. The living room accommodates family activities. The first
floor offers two bedrooms and a
full bath. The second floor provides two additional bedrooms
and an optional bath. Note the
expansion space available in the
basement.

Design by
Home Planners,
Inc.

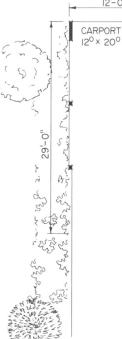

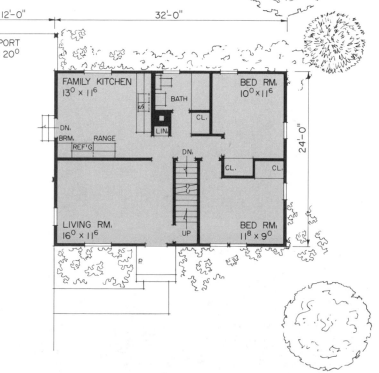

Design 1394

First Floor: 832 square feet
Second Floor: 512 square feet
Total: 1,344 square feet

L **D**

● This darling cottage home opens with a living room that shares views with the dining room. An efficient kitchen easily serves this area. A rear door leads to outdoor livability. Two bedrooms on the first floor utilize a bright hall bath. A nearby linen closet will be much appreciated. Upstairs, a large bedroom with a dressing room and another with a walk-in closet share a full bath.

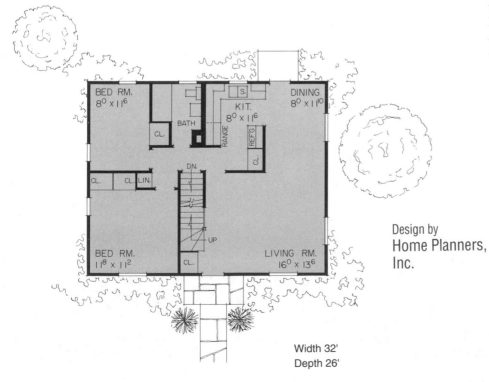

Design by
Home Planners, Inc.

Width 32'
Depth 26'

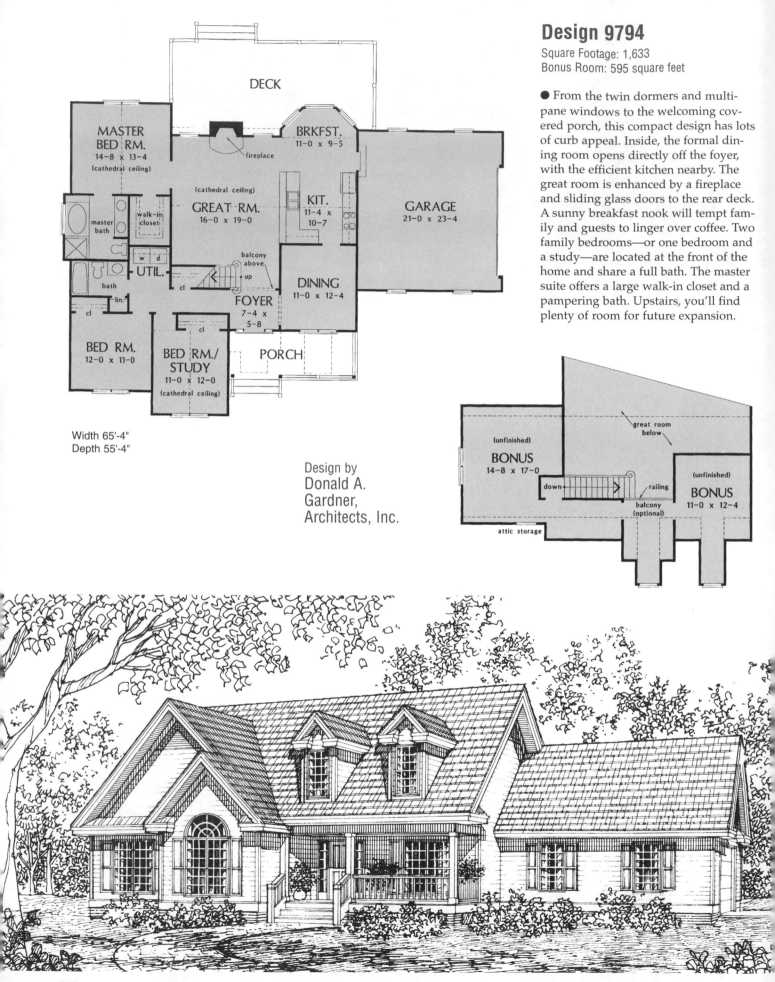

DECK

MASTER
BED RM.
14-8 x 13-4
(cathedral ceiling)

BRKFST.
11-0 x 9-5

fireplace

(cathedral ceiling)
GREAT RM.
16-0 x 19-0

KIT.
11-4 x
10-7

GARAGE
21-0 x 23-4

master
bath

walk-in
closet

balcony
above

up

UTIL.

w d

bath

cl

DINING
11-0 x 12-4

lin.

cl

FOYER
7-4 x
5-8

cl

BED RM.
12-0 x 11-0

BED RM./
STUDY
11-0 x 12-0
(cathedral ceiling)

cl

PORCH

Width 65'-4"
Depth 55'-4"

Design by
Donald A.
Gardner,
Architects, Inc.

Design 9794

Square Footage: 1,633
Bonus Room: 595 square feet

● From the twin dormers and multipane windows to the welcoming covered porch, this compact design has lots of curb appeal. Inside, the formal dining room opens directly off the foyer, with the efficient kitchen nearby. The great room is enhanced by a fireplace and sliding glass doors to the rear deck. A sunny breakfast nook will tempt family and guests to linger over coffee. Two family bedrooms—or one bedroom and a study—are located at the front of the home and share a full bath. The master suite offers a large walk-in closet and a pampering bath. Upstairs, you'll find plenty of room for future expansion.

great room
below

(unfinished)
BONUS
14-8 x 17-0

down

railing

(unfinished)
BONUS
11-0 x 12-4

balcony
(optional)

attic storage

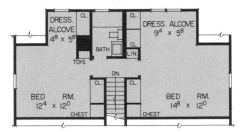

Design 3189 First Floor: 884 square feet
Second Floor: 598 square feet; Total: 1,482 square feet

D

● A large kitchen/dining area and living room are the living areas of this design. A rear terrace provides outdoor living space. Four bedrooms, two up and two down, compose the sleeping zone. Each floor also has a full bath. Note the dressing alcoves in upstairs bedrooms. A full basement and an attached garage will provide plenty of storage areas.

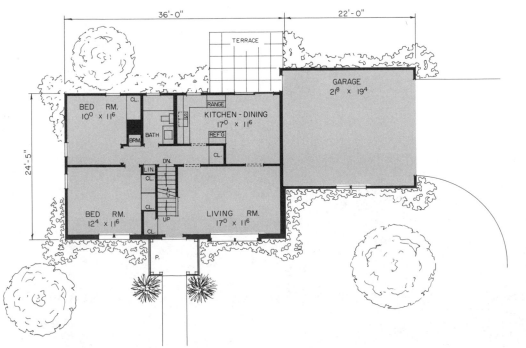

Design by
Home Planners,
Inc.

Photo by Andrew D. Lautman

This home, as shown in the photographs, may differ from the actual blueprints. For more detailed information, please check the floor plans carefully.

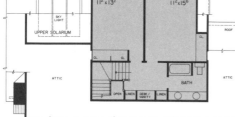

Design 2615

First Floor: 2,563 square feet
Second Floor: 552 square feet
Total: 3,115 square feet

L **D**

Design by
Home Planners,
Inc.

● The exterior detailing of this design recalls 18th-Century New England architecture. Enter by way of the centered front door and you are greeted into the foyer. Directly to the right is the study or optional bedroom or to the left is the living room. This large formal room features sliding glass doors to the sun-drenched solarium. The beauty of the solarium will be appreciated from the master bedroom and the dining room along with the living room.

QUOTE ONE™

Cost to build? See page 374
to order complete cost estimate
to build this house in your area!

This home, as shown in the photographs, may differ from the actual blueprints. For more detailed information, please check the floor plans carefully.

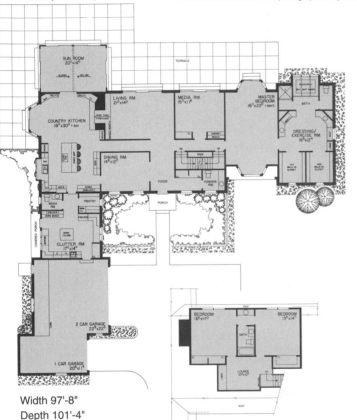

Width 97'-8"
Depth 101'-4"

Design by
Home Planners,
Inc.

QUOTE ONE™
Cost to build? See page 374
to order complete cost estimate
to build this house in your area!

Design 2921

First Floor: 3,215 square feet
Second Floor: 711 square feet
Total: 3,926 square feet
Sun Room: 296 square feet

L **D**

● Organized zoning by room functions makes this traditional design a comfortable home for living. Quiet areas of the house include a media room and luxurious master bedroom suite with a fitness area, a spacious closet and bath, as well as a lounge or writing area. Informal living areas of the house include a sun room, a large country kitchen and an efficient food preparation area with an island. Formal living areas include a living area and a formal dining room. The second floor holds two bedrooms and a lounge.

California Engineered Plans and California Stock Plans are available for this home. Call 1-800-521-6797 for more information.

Design 2699

First Floor: 2,188 square feet
Second Floor: 858 square feet
Total: 3,046 square feet

Design by
Home Planners,
Inc.

● Be the talk of the town in this spacious Cape Cod-style home. The foyer gives way to a living room endowed with a fireplace and two sets of sliding glass doors that offer passage to an expansive rear terrace. The dining room, as well as the country kitchen, access this area. The kitchen functions well with an island cooktop and lots of counter and cabinet space. A front media room accommodates TV time. The master bedroom suite has a lounge and a whirlpool bath. Upstairs, two secondary bedrooms flank a lounge that overlooks the living room.

Cost to build? See page 374
to order complete cost estimate
to build this house in your area!

Design 1967

First Floor: 1,804 square feet
Second Floor: 496 square feet
Total: 2,300 square feet

● This inviting home is sure to make a lasting impression with its horizontal siding, interesting roof lines and welcoming front porch. To the left of the entry is the winning combination of the breakfast room, kitchen and beamed-ceilinged family room warmed by a cheerful fireplace. For more formal occasions, the adjacent dining room leads to the living room, sharing views of the rear grounds. The master bedroom and two secondary bedrooms complete the first floor. Two bedrooms and a full bath are contained on the second floor for future use.

Design by
Home Planners,
Inc.

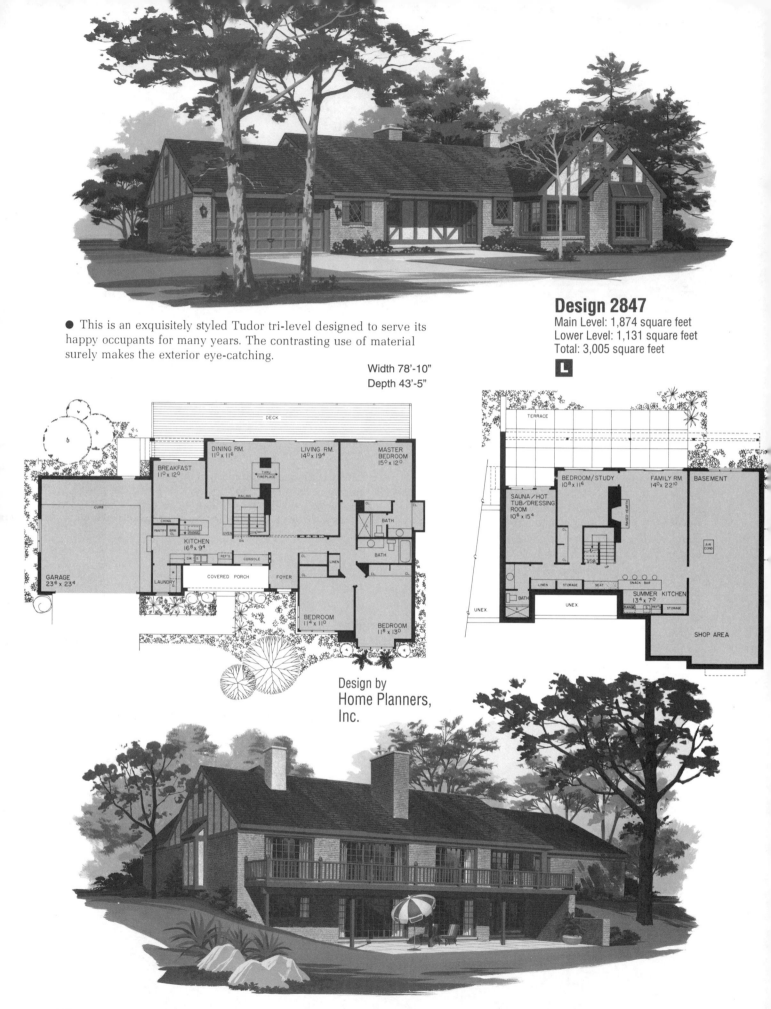

● This is an exquisitely styled Tudor tri-level designed to serve its happy occupants for many years. The contrasting use of material surely makes the exterior eye-catching.

Width 78'-10"
Depth 43'-5"

Design 2847
Main Level: 1,874 square feet
Lower Level: 1,131 square feet
Total: 3,005 square feet

L

Design by
Home Planners,
Inc.

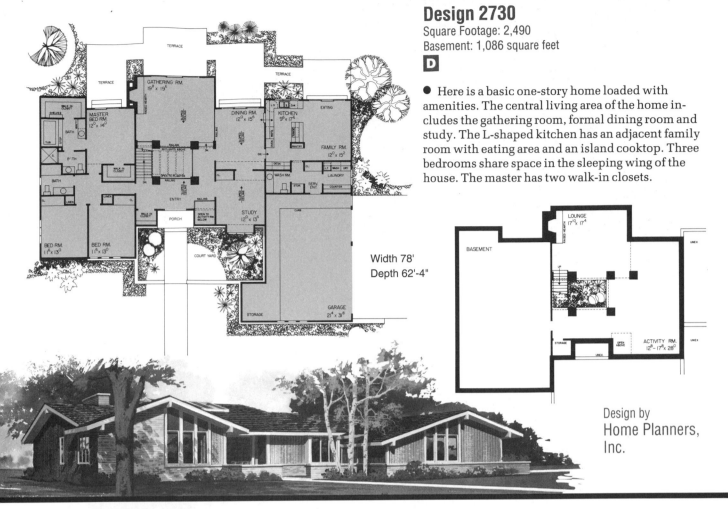

Design 2730

Square Footage: 2,490
Basement: 1,086 square feet

D

● Here is a basic one-story home loaded with amenities. The central living area of the home includes the gathering room, formal dining room and study. The L-shaped kitchen has an adjacent family room with eating area and an island cooktop. Three bedrooms share space in the sleeping wing of the house. The master has two walk-in closets.

Width 78'
Depth 62'-4"

Design by
Home Planners,
Inc.

Design by
Home Planners,
Inc.

Design 2549

Main Level: 2,260 square feet
Lower Level: 1,406 square feet
Total: 3,666 square feet

● This hillside home gives all the appearance of being a one-story ranch home; and what a delightful one at that! Should the contours of your property slope to the rear, this plan permits the exposing of the lower level. This results in the activities room and bedroom/study gaining direct access to outdoor living. The large and growing family will be admirably served with five bedrooms and three baths. An extra wash room and a separate laundry add to the convenient living pattern.

Width 86'
Depth 52'

Design 2879

Living Area Including Atrium: 3,173 square feet
Upper Lounge/Balcony: 267 square feet; **Total:** 3,440 square feet

● This plush modern design seems to have it all, including an upper lounge, upper family room, and upper foyer. There's also an atrium with skylight centrally located downstairs. A modern kitchen with snack bar service to a breakfast room also enjoys its own greenhouse window. A deluxe master bedroom includes its own whirlpool and bay window. Three other bedrooms also are isolated at one end of the house downstairs to allow privacy and quiet. A spacious family room in the rear enjoys its own raised-hearth fireplace and view of a rear covered terrace. A front living room with its own fireplace looks out upon a side garden court and the central atrium. There's also a formal dining room situated between the kitchen and living room, plus a three-car garage, covered porches, and sizable laundry with washroom just off the garage.

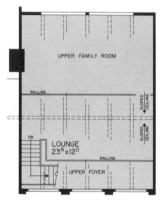

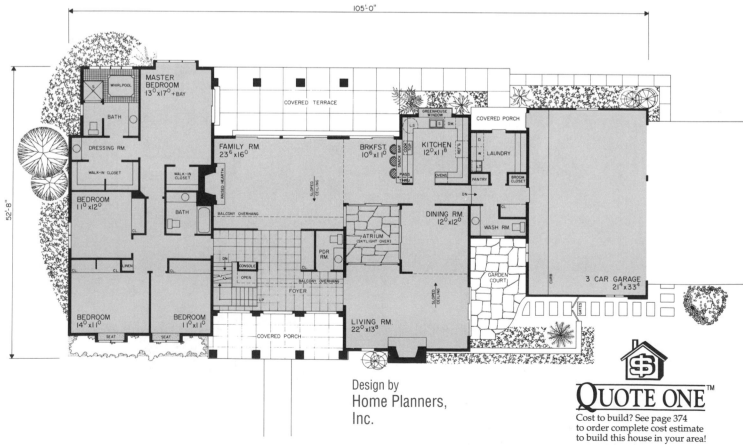

Design by
**Home Planners,
Inc.**

Cost to build? See page 374
to order complete cost estimate
to build this house in your area!

Design by
Home Planners,
Inc.

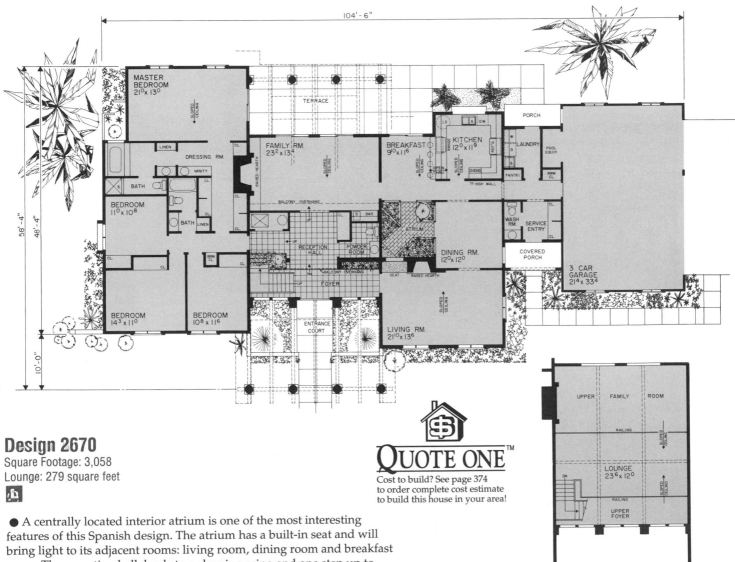

104'-6"

MASTER BEDROOM 21⁰ x 13⁰

TERRACE

PORCH

FAMILY RM. 23² x 13⁴

BREAKFAST 9¹⁰ x 11⁶

KITCHEN 12⁰ x 11⁹

LAUNDRY

POOL EQUIP.

LINEN

DRESSING RM.

VANITY

BATH

PANTRY

BRM CL.

BEDROOM 11⁰ x 10⁸

BATH LINEN

RECEPTION HALL

POWDER ROOM

ATRIUM

DINING RM. 12⁰ x 12⁰

WASH RM.

SERVICE ENTRY

COVERED PORCH

3 CAR GARAGE 21⁴ x 33⁴

BALCONY OVERHANG

FOYER

BRM CL.

BEDROOM 14³ x 11⁰

BEDROOM 10⁸ x 11⁶

ENTRANCE COURT

SEAT   RAISED HEARTH

LIVING RM. 21⁰ x 13⁶

58'-4"

48'-4"

10'-0"

Design 2670

Square Footage: 3,058
Lounge: 279 square feet

Quote One™

Cost to build? See page 374
to order complete cost estimate
to build this house in your area!

UPPER   FAMILY   ROOM

RAILING

LOUNGE 23⁶ x 12⁰

DN

RAILING

UPPER FOYER

● A centrally located interior atrium is one of the most interesting
features of this Spanish design. The atrium has a built-in seat and will
bring light to its adjacent rooms: living room, dining room and breakfast
room. The reception hall leads to a sleeping wing and one step up to
the family room. A railed lounge upstairs makes a fine study.

**California Engineered Plans and California Stock Plans are available
for this home. Call 1-800-521-6797 for more information.**

© The Sater Group, Inc.

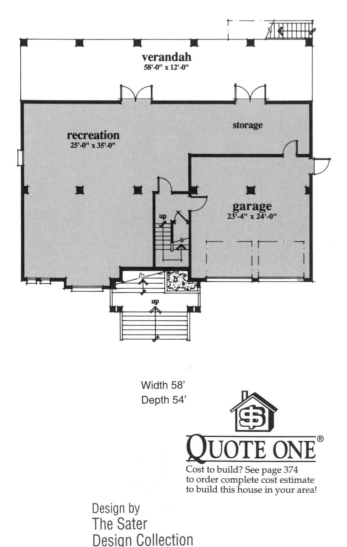

verandah
58'-0" x 12'-0"

recreation
25'-0" x 35'-0"

storage

garage
23'-4" x 24'-0"

up

up

Width 58'
Depth 54'

Design by
The Sater
Design Collection

Design 6622 Square Footage: 2,190

● A dramatic set of stairs leads to the entry of this home. The foyer leads to an expansive living room with a fireplace and built-in bookshelves. A lanai opens off this area and will assure outdoor enjoyments. For formal meals, a front-facing dining room offers a bumped-out bay. The kitchen serves this area easily as well as the breakfast room. A study and three bedrooms make up the rest of the floor plan. Two secondary bedrooms share a full hall bath. A utility area is also nearby. In the master suite, two walk-in closets and a full bath are appreciated features. In the bedroom, a set of French doors offers passage to the lanai.

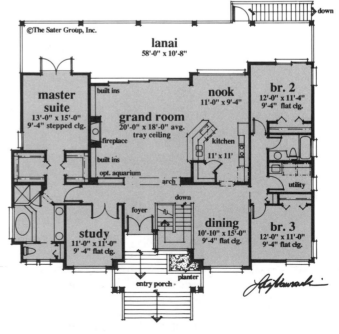

© The Sater Group, Inc.

lanai
58'-0" x 10'-8"

down

master suite
13'-0" x 15'-0"
9'-4" stepped clg.

built ins

nook
11'-0" x 9'-4"

br. 2
12'-0" x 11'-4"
9'-4" flat clg.

grand room
20'-0" x 18'-0" avg.
tray ceiling

kitchen
11' x 11'

fireplace

built ins

opt. aquarium

arch

utility

study
11'-0" x 11'-0"
9'-4" flat clg.

foyer

down

dining
10'-10" x 15'-0"
9'-4" flat clg.

br. 3
12'-0" x 11'-0"
9'-4" flat clg.

entry porch

planter

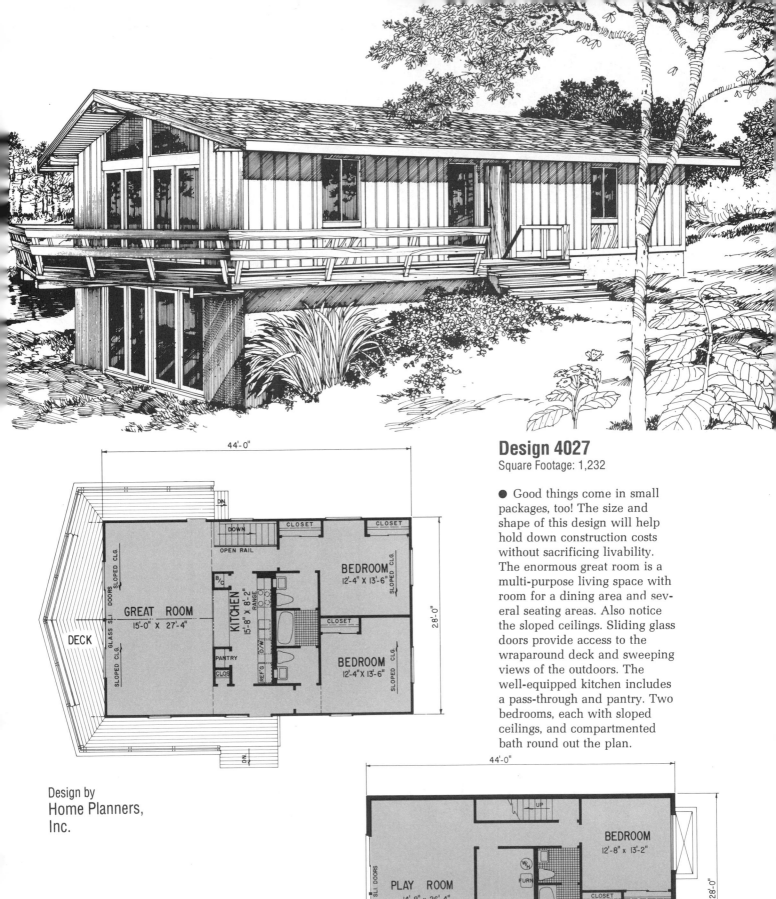

Design 4027
Square Footage: 1,232

● Good things come in small packages, too! The size and shape of this design will help hold down construction costs without sacrificing livability. The enormous great room is a multi-purpose living space with room for a dining area and several seating areas. Also notice the sloped ceilings. Sliding glass doors provide access to the wraparound deck and sweeping views of the outdoors. The well-equipped kitchen includes a pass-through and pantry. Two bedrooms, each with sloped ceilings, and compartmented bath round out the plan.

Design by
Home Planners,
Inc.

Optional Basement

Outdoor Trimmings:
A potpourri of yard & garden plans

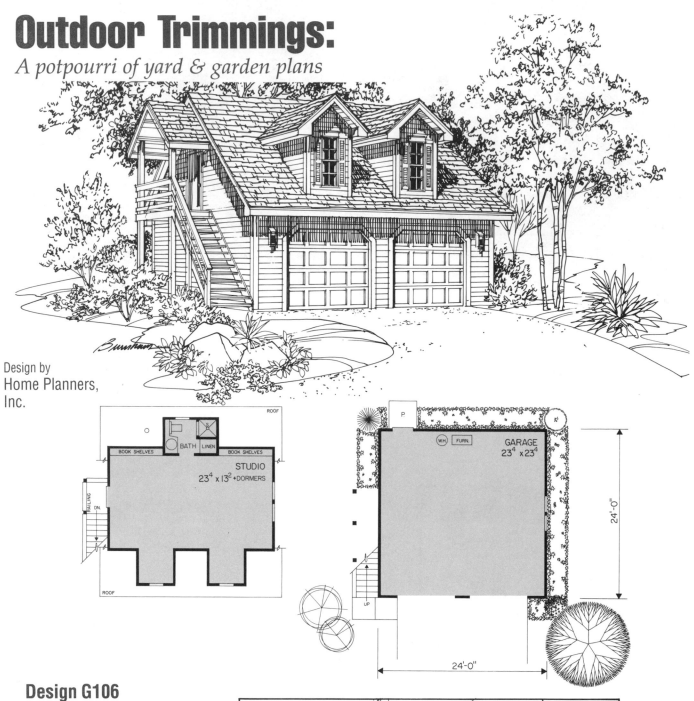

Design by
**Home Planners,
Inc.**

Design G106
Studio Garage

Can you top this? Our two-car garage has an artist's studio nestled snugly on the second floor. The Cape Cod-style design, with three dormers, large shutters, paneled doors, and characteristic proportions of roof to floor, makes a strong visual statement that would complement a large number of traditional housing styles. An exterior staircase, covered at the top, leads to 300 square feet of fully insulated studio space; adjacent is a full 4x7-foot bath with shower and linen storage.

Width 34'-4"
Depth 24'

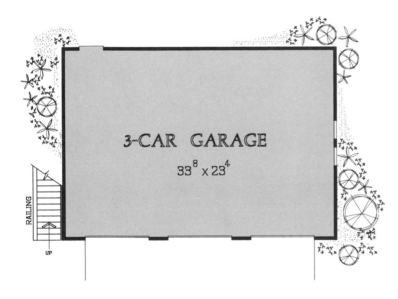

3-CAR GARAGE
33^8 x 23^4

RAILING

UP

BOOKSHELVES

REFG RANGE

KITCHEN

DW

SHWR

BATH

CLOSET

LIN

STUDIO/LOFT
33^8 x 14^2

CEILING CLIP

DN

RAILING

Design G206

Three-Car Garage

Full livability is available in the studio over this three-car garage. Should a child return to the nest or a renter come into the picture, this space perfectly accommodates the student. Three dormer windows brighten a roomy space that also includes a bath and an efficiency kitchen. With traditional style, this garage will complement a variety of housing styles.

Design by
**Home Planners,
Inc.**

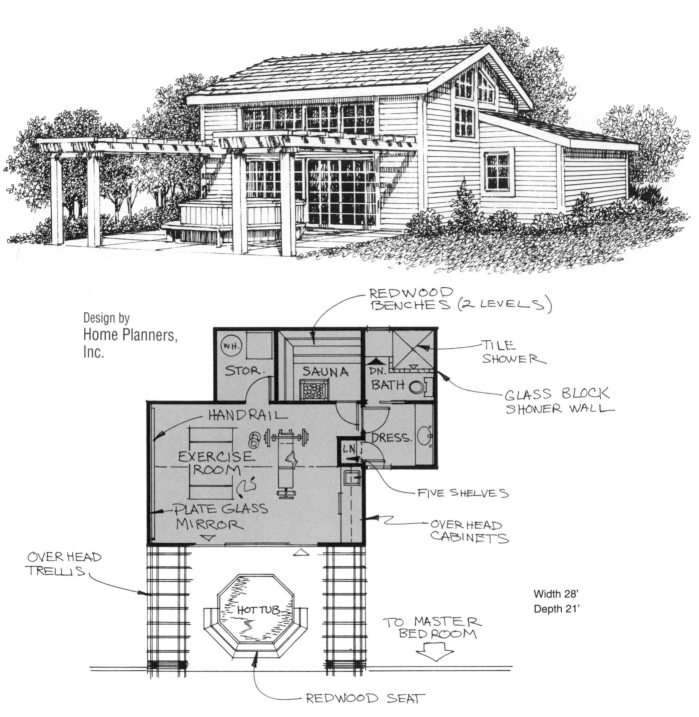

Design by
Home Planners, Inc.

REDWOOD BENCHES (2 LEVELS)

TILE SHOWER

GLASS BLOCK SHOWER WALL

W.H.

STOR.

SAUNA

DN.
BATH

HANDRAIL

EXERCISE ROOM

DRESS.

L.N.

FIVE SHELVES

PLATE GLASS MIRROR

OVER HEAD CABINETS

OVER HEAD TRELLIS

HOT TUB

Width 28'
Depth 21'

TO MASTER BEDROOM

REDWOOD SEAT

Design R129
Exercise Cottage

If you're looking for the ultimate in home exercise, this plan is sure to get you going on the right track. With over 250 square feet, the plan packs a powerful punch by providing a trellised hot-tub area, a sauna and a bath with a dressing room. Add over twelve feet of head room to arrive at plenty of space for large equipment. One wall supports mirrors and a ballet bar. For preparing sports drinks or juices, a wet bar with cabinets is tucked in a corner. Bright windows invite sunshine in.

Design by
**Home Planners,
Inc.**

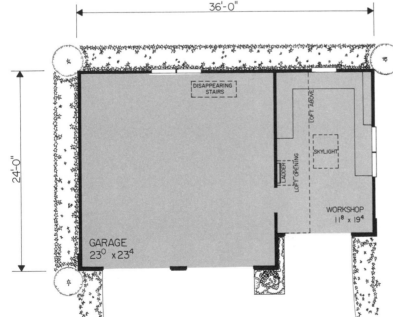

36'-0"

24'-0"

DISAPPEARING
STAIRS

LOFT ABOVE

SKYLIGHT

LADDER

LOFT OPENING

WORKSHOP
11⁸ x 19⁴

GARAGE
23⁰ x23⁴

Design G111
Workshop Garage

Here the appeal of Tudor
exterior styling is applied to
a free-standing workshop
garage. Distinctive roof lines,
simulated beamwork, stucco,
and stone set the character.
Three garage doors allow for
flexible access to the vehicular
and workshop areas. A
skylight provides an extra
measure of natural light for
shop projects. Fine wall space
provides plenty of area for
handy tool placement above
the U-shaped counter surfaces,
which have storage potential
below. For the storage of
project lumber, there is an
out-of-the-way loft. Around
the corner from the shop is the
folding stair unit in the garage.
This provides access to another
generous bulk storage area.
The home craftsman will love
this efficient above-ground
workshop, storage unit.

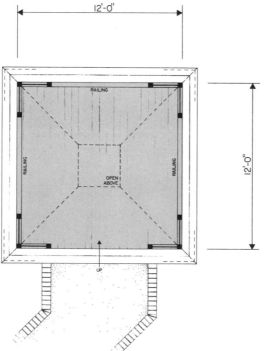

12'-0"

12'-0"

RAILING

RAILING   RAILING

OPEN
ABOVE

UP

Design G108
Neoclassic Gazebo

Our gazebo is a prime spot for
entertaining. At 200-plus square
feet, it has much surface space as
the average family room. Plus,
its just under 17½ feet tall, which
makes it the size of a typical one-
story house. As a result, it's best
suited for larger lots–at least a
half acre. Boasting a number of
neoclassic features–perfect proportions, columns, bases–it's also
a good match with solid, traditional housing styles. The cupola
is a homey touch that lets light in
to the decking below. Cedar or
redwood are the building materials of choice.

Design by
Home Planners,
Inc.

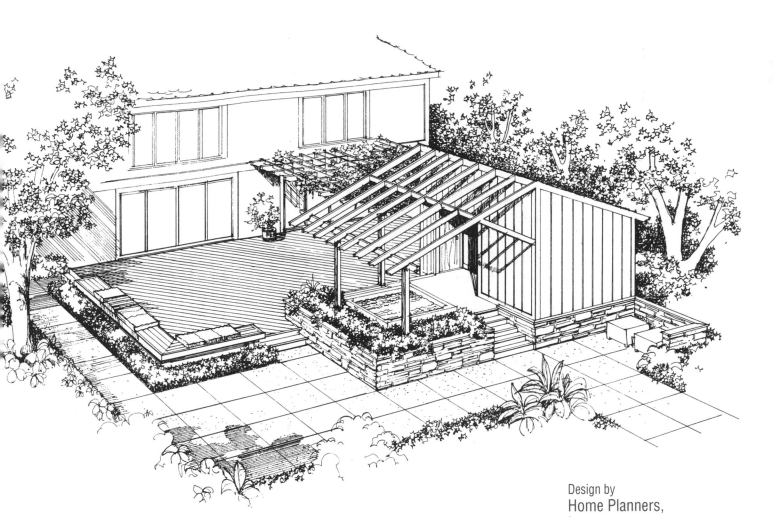

Design G112
Soothing Whirlpool/Sauna

Design by
Home Planners,
Inc.

A relaxing addition to back-yard space, this sauna and whirlpool spa combination promises respite from the hectic world. Joined to the house by wood decking and a sun-filtering trellis, the dry heat sauna has planked seating as well as a sink and shower and a bench seat in the dressing area. A small attached storage room neatly accommodates supplies and equipment. Just outside, raised planters flank the revitalizing whirlpool spa on two sides. The third side has a long bench seat. Additional bench seating borders the wood deck on two sides. Simple lines and open design allow this plan to blend perfectly with any style or type of house.

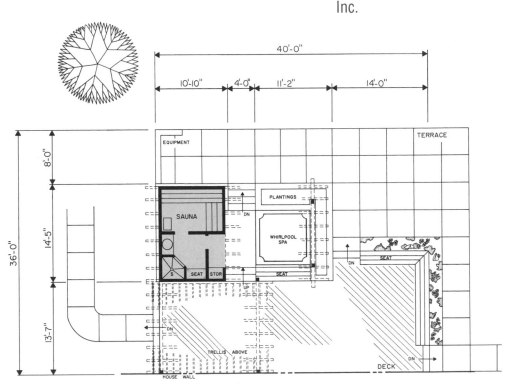

Design by
Home Planners,
Inc.

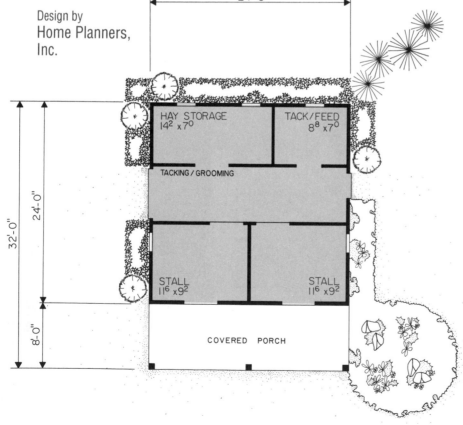

24'-0"

HAY STORAGE
14² x7⁰

TACK/FEED
8⁸ x7⁰

TACKING / GROOMING

STALL
11⁶ x9²

STALL
11⁶ x9²

COVERED   PORCH

32'-0"

24'-0"

8'-0"

Design G113
Country Stable

Charming, cross-hatched
Dutch doors and a steepled
roof are fitting country touches
for this free-standing stable.
Two horses and all their gear
share plenty of room in two
stalls, a tack and feed room,
and a hay storage area. A long
central corridor, with one wide
and one regular entrance, contributes space for grooming
your favorite mount or sad-
dling up for a morning ride.
The covered porch on the stall
side acts as a weather buffer,
keeping rain and hot sun away
from precious animals. Shuttered windows are accented
with window boxes. No
horses? With some simple
modifications, the stable becomes a writer's cottage or
gardening workshop.

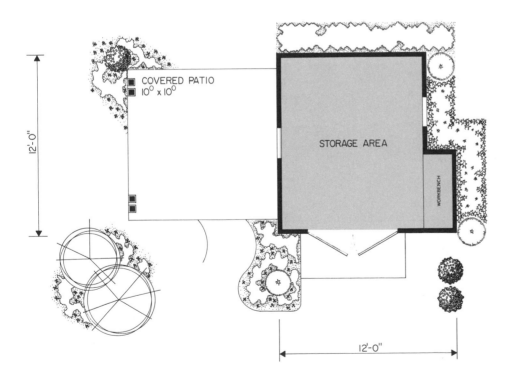

COVERED PATIO
10⁰ x 10⁰

STORAGE AREA

WORKBENCH

12'-0"

12'-0"

Design G107
Storage Shed With Patio

Here's a hard working storage shed with a number of bright touches. At 120 square feet, it's bigger than most. Cupola, bird-house, shutters and grooved ply-wood siding add up to a tradi-tional look that compliments many popular housing styles. It's a flexible design, too, and could also be a potting shed or a work-shop. The nicest feature may well be the covered patio. After you cut the grass, just stash the lawn mower, take a seat and sur-vey your handiwork.

Design by
Home Planners,
Inc.

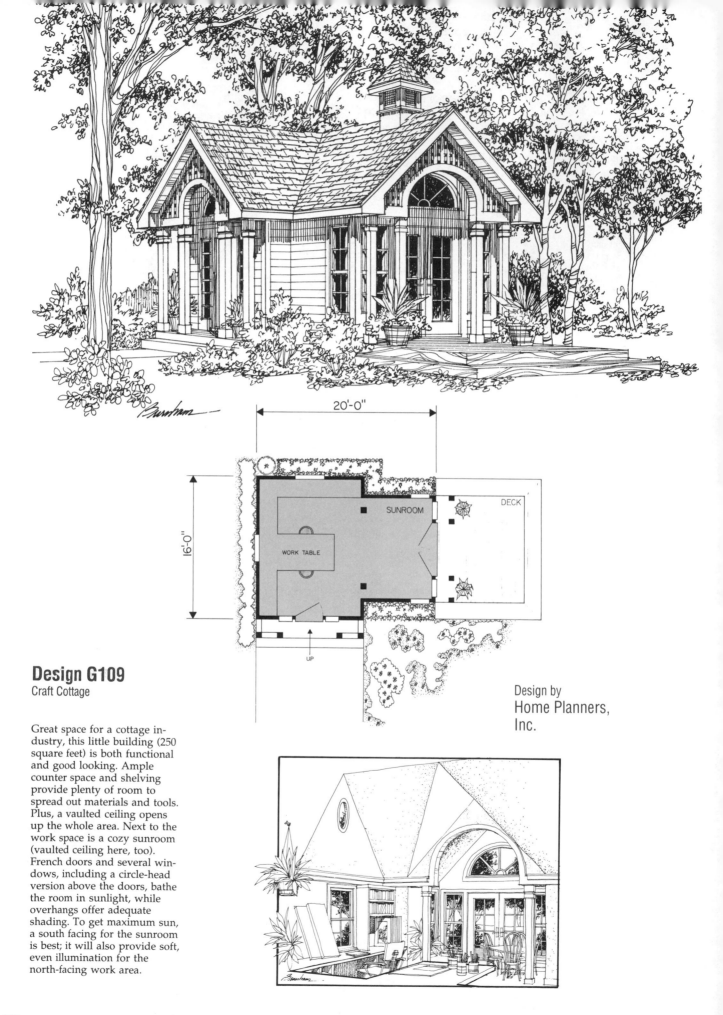

20'-0"

16'-0"

WORK TABLE

SUNROOM

DECK

UP

Design G109
Craft Cottage

Design by
Home Planners, Inc.

Great space for a cottage industry, this little building (250 square feet) is both functional and good looking. Ample counter space and shelving provide plenty of room to spread out materials and tools. Plus, a vaulted ceiling opens up the whole area. Next to the work space is a cozy sunroom (vaulted ceiling here, too). French doors and several windows, including a circle-head version above the doors, bathe the room in sunlight, while overhangs offer adequate shading. To get maximum sun, a south facing for the sunroom is best; it will also provide soft, even illumination for the north-facing work area.

Design by
**Home Planners,
Inc.**

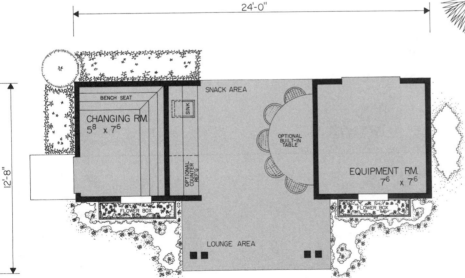

24'-0"

12'-8"

BENCH SEAT

CHANGING RM.
5⁸ x 7⁶

SINK

OPTIONAL COUNTER 'G

SNACK AREA

OPTIONAL
BUILT-IN
TABLE

EQUIPMENT RM.
7⁶ x 7⁶

FLOWER BOX

LOUNGE AREA

FLOWER BOX

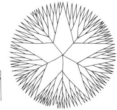

Design G110
Pool Cabana

Imagine this charming
structure perched adjacent to
your backyard swimming pool.
Its exterior highlights such
architectural features as hip
and gable roofs, a decorative
cupola, shuttered windows,
flower boxes, and horizontal
wood and shingle siding. Its
plan offers a spacious
sheltered party/lounge area
with counter, sink, and
refrigerator space. An optional
built-in table could assure no
rain-outs of those poolside
snacks. Flanking this practical
breezeway-type area are two
rooms equal in size and utility.
To the left is the changing
room with a convenient bench.
To the right is the equipment
room for the handy storage of
pool supplies and furniture.
Surely a fine addition to the
active family's backyard.

Design R126
Teen Retreat

Put a smile on your kids' faces with this neat plan. Designed to give kids plenty of room to "hang out", it features a French door that opens to a graffiti wall for unique decorating. Behind this wall is the perfect spot for a TV and video-game center. A raised, carpeted platform provides seating. A vaulted ceiling and interesting window placement contribute to the fun atmosphere. There's even a study center and a window seat for quieter pursuits. Able to blend with a variety of housing styles, this back-yard buildable is easily set apart by adding fanciful color.

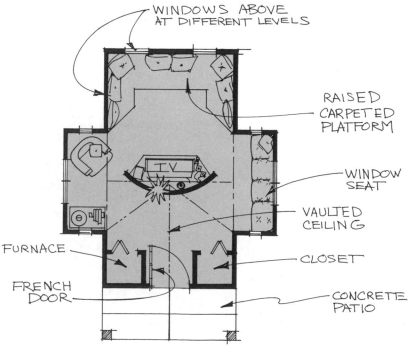

WINDOWS ABOVE AT DIFFERENT LEVELS

RAISED CARPETED PLATFORM

WINDOW SEAT

VAULTED CEILING

FURNACE

CLOSET

FRENCH DOOR

CONCRETE PATIO

Width 16'
Depth 22'

Design by
Home Planners,
Inc.

370

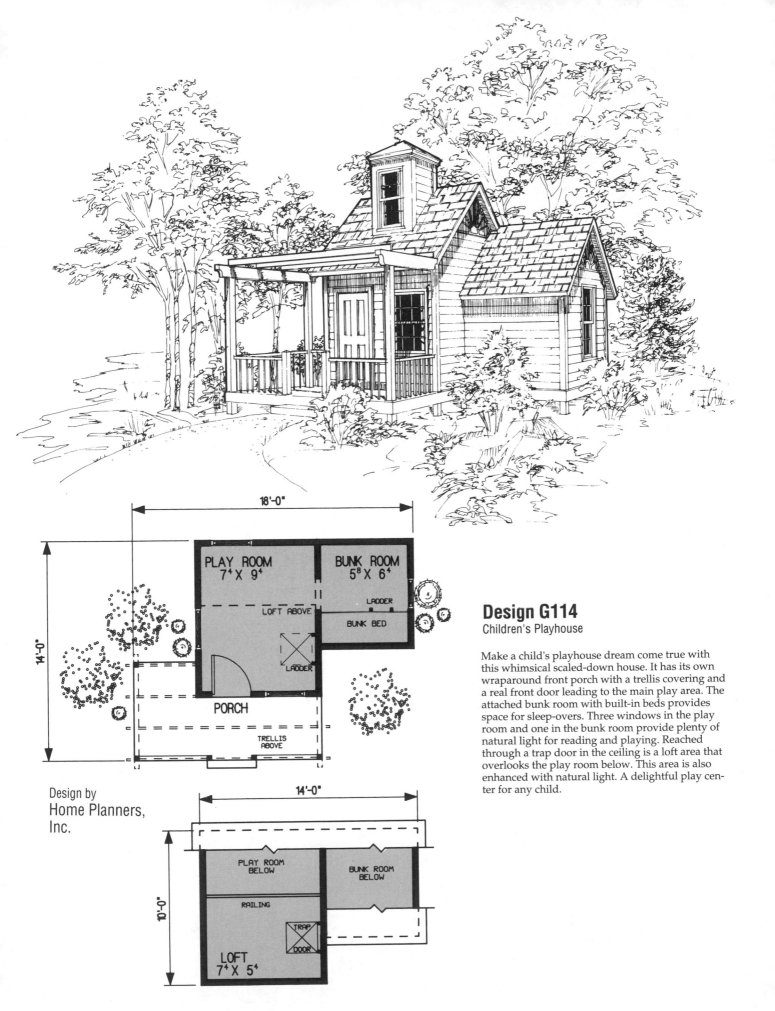

18'-0"

14'-0"

PLAY ROOM
7⁴ X 9⁴

BUNK ROOM
5⁸ X 6⁴

LOFT ABOVE

LADDER

BUNK BED

LADDER

PORCH

TRELLIS
ABOVE

Design by
Home Planners,
Inc.

14'-0"

10'-0"

PLAY ROOM
BELOW

BUNK ROOM
BELOW

RAILING

TRAP
DOOR

LOFT
7⁴ X 5⁴

Design G114

Children's Playhouse

Make a child's playhouse dream come true with this whimsical scaled-down house. It has its own wraparound front porch with a trellis covering and a real front door leading to the main play area. The attached bunk room with built-in beds provides space for sleep-overs. Three windows in the play room and one in the bunk room provide plenty of natural light for reading and playing. Reached through a trap door in the ceiling is a loft area that overlooks the play room below. This area is also enhanced with natural light. A delightful play center for any child.

When You're Ready To Order . . .

Let Us Show You Our Home Blueprint Package.

Building a home? Planning a home? Our Blueprint Package has nearly everything you need to get the job done right, whether you're working on your own or with help from an architect, designer, builder or subcontractors. Each Blueprint Package is the result of many hours of work by licensed architects or professional designers.

QUALITY

Hundreds of hours of painstaking effort have gone into the development of your blueprint set. Each home has been quality-checked by professionals to insure accuracy and buildability.

VALUE

Because we sell in volume, you can buy professional-quality blueprints at a fraction of their development cost. With our plans, your dream home design costs only a few hundred dollars, not the thousands of dollars that custom architects charge.

SERVICE

Once you've chosen your favorite home plan, you'll receive fast, efficient service whether you choose to mail or fax your order to us or call us toll free at 1-800-521-6797.

SATISFACTION

Over 50 years of service to satisfied home plan buyers provide us unparalleled experience and knowledge in producing quality blueprints. What this means to you is satisfaction with our product and performance.

ORDER TOLL FREE 1-800-521-6797

After you've looked over our Blueprint Package and Important Extras on the following pages, simply mail the order form on page 381 or call toll free on our Blueprint Hotline: 1-800-521-6797. We're ready and eager to serve you.

. . . .

Each set of blueprints is an interrelated collection of detail sheets which includes components such as floor plans, interior and exterior elevations, dimensions, cross-sections, diagrams and notations. These sheets show exactly how your house is to be built.

Among the sheets included may be:

Frontal Sheet
This artist's sketch of the exterior of the house gives you an idea of how the house will look when built and landscaped. Large ink-line floor plans show all levels of the house and provide an overview of your new home's livability, as well as a handy reference for deciding on furniture placement.

Foundation Plan
This sheet shows the foundation layout includ-

SAMPLE PACKAGE

ing support walls, excavated and unexcavated areas, if any, and foundation notes. If slab construction rather than basement, the plan shows footings and details for a monolithic slab. This page, or another in the set, may include a sample plot plan for locating your house on a building site.

Detailed Floor Plans

These plans show the layout of each floor of the house. Rooms and interior spaces are carefully dimensioned and keys are given for cross-section details provided later in the plans. The positions of electrical outlets and switches are shown.

House Cross-Sections

Large-scale views show sections or cut-aways of the foundation, interior walls, exterior walls, floors, stairways and roof details. Additional cross-sections may show important changes in

floor, ceiling or roof heights or the relationship of one level to another. Extremely valuable for construction, these sections show exactly how the various parts of the house fit together.

Interior Elevations

Many of our drawings show the design and placement of kitchen and bathroom cabinets, laundry areas, fireplaces, bookcases and other built-ins. Little "extras," such as mantelpiece and wainscoting drawings, plus moulding sections, provide details that give your home that custom touch.

Exterior Elevations

These drawings show the front, rear and sides of your house and give necessary notes on exterior materials and finishes. Particular attention is given to cornice detail, brick and stone accents or other finish items that make your home unique.

Frontal Sheet

Foundation Plans

Detailed Floor Plans

Exterior Elevations

Interior Elevations

House Cross-Sections

373

Important Extras To Do The Job Right!

Introducing eight important planning and construction aids developed by our professionals to help you succeed in your home-building project.

MATERIALS LIST & DETAILED COST ESTIMATE

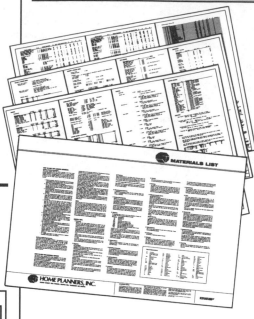

The **Materials List** outlines the quantity, type and size of materials needed to build your house. Included are framing lumber, windows and doors, kitchen and bath cabinetry, rough and finish hardware, and much more. This handy list helps you or your builder cost out materials and serves as a reference sheet when you're compiling bids.

The **Quote One® Detailed Cost Estimate** matches line for line over 1,000 items in the Materials List (which is included when you purchase this estimating tool). It allows you to determine building costs for your specific area and for your specific home design. Space is allowed for additional estimates from contractors and subcontractors. (See **Quote One®** below for further information.)

The Materials List/Detailed Cost Estimate package can be ordered up to 6 months after a blueprint order. Because of the diversity of local building codes, the Materials List does not include mechanical materials. Detailed Cost Estimates are available for select Home Planners plans only. Consult a customer service representative for currently available designs.

Make informed decisions about your home-building project with a customized materials take-off and a Quote One® Detailed Cost Estimate. These tools are invaluable in planning and estimating the cost of your new home.

SPECIFICATION OUTLINE

This valuable 16-page document is critical to building your house correctly. Designed to be filled in by you or your builder, this book lists 166 stages or items crucial to the building process. It provides a comprehensive review of the construction process and helps in making choices of materials. When combined with the blueprints, a signed contract, and a schedule, it becomes a legal document and record for the building of your home.

QUOTE ONE®

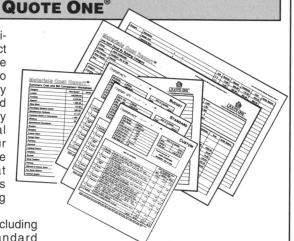

This new service helps you estimate the cost of building select Home Planners designs. Quote One® system is available in two separate stages: The Summary Cost Report and the Detailed Cost Estimate. The Summary Cost Report shows the total cost per square foot for your chosen home in your zip-code area and then breaks that cost down into ten categories showing the costs for building materials, labor and installation. The total cost for the report (including three grades: Budget, Standard and Custom) is just $19.95 for one home; and additionals are only $14.95. These reports allow you to evaluate your building budget and compare the costs of building a variety of homes in your area.

The Detailed Cost Estimate furnishes an even more detailed report. The material and installation (labor + equipment) cost is shown for each of over 1,000 line items provided in the Standard grade. Space is allowed for additional estimates from contractors and subcontractors. This invaluable tool is available for a price of $110 ($120 for a Schedule E plan) which includes the price of a materials list which must be purchased at the same time.

To order these invaluable reports, use the order form on page 381 or call **1-800-521-6797**.

CONSTRUCTION INFORMATION

If you want to know more about techniques—and deal more confidently with subcontractors we offer these useful sheets. Each set is an excellent tool that will add to your understanding of these technical subjects.

Plan-A-Home®

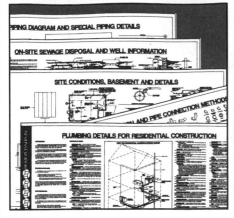

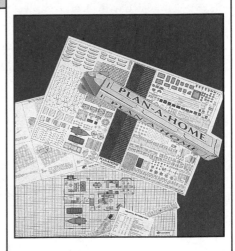

PLUMBING

The Blueprint Package includes locations for all the plumbing fixtures in your new house, including sinks, lavatories, tubs, showers, toilets, laundry trays and water heaters. However, if you want to know more about the complete plumbing system, these 24x36-inch detail sheets will prove very useful. Prepared to meet requirements of the National Plumbing Code, these six fact-filled sheets give general information on pipe schedules, fittings, sump-pump details, water-softener hookups, septic system details and much more. Color-coded sheets include a glossary of terms.

ELECTRICAL

The locations for every electrical switch, plug and outlet are shown in your Blueprint Package. However, these Electrical Details go further to take the mystery out of household electrical systems. Prepared to meet requirements of the National Electrical Code, these comprehensive 24x36-inch drawings come packed with helpful information, including wire sizing, switch-installation schematics, cable-routing details, appliance wattage, door-bell hookups, typical service panel circuitry and much more. Six sheets are bound together and color-coded for easy reference. A glossary of terms is also included.

Plan-A-Home® is an easy-to-use tool that helps you design a new home, arrange furniture in a new or existing home, or plan a remodel-ing project. Each package contains:

- **More than 700 reusable peel-off planning symbols** on a self-stick vinyl sheet, including walls, windows, doors, all types of furniture, kitchen components, bath fixtures and many more.

- **A reusable, transparent, 1/4-inch scale planning grid** that matches the scale of actual working drawings (1/4-inch equals 1 foot). This grid provides the basis for house layouts of up to 140x92 feet.

- **Tracing paper** and a protective sheet for copying or transferring your completed plan.

- **A felt-tip pen,** with water-soluble ink that wipes away quickly.

Plan-A-Home® lets you lay out areas as large as a 7,500 square foot, six-bedroom, seven-bath house.

CONSTRUCTION

The Blueprint Package contains everything an experienced builder needs to construct a particular house. However, it doesn't show all the ways that houses can be built, nor does it explain alternate construction methods. To help you understand how your house will be built—and offer additional techniques—this set of drawings depicts the materials and methods used to build foundations, fireplaces, walls, floors and roofs. Where appropriate, the drawings show acceptable alternatives. These six sheets will answer questions for the advanced do-it-your-selfer or home planner.

MECHANICAL

This package contains fundamental principles and useful data that will help you make informed decisions and communicate with subcontractors about heating and cooling systems. The 24x36-inch drawings contain instructions and samples that allow you to make simple load calculations and preliminary sizing and costing analysis. Covered are today's most commonly used systems from heat pumps to solar fuel systems. The package is packed full of illustrations and diagrams to help you visualize components and how they relate to one another.

To Order, Call Toll Free 1-800-521-6797

To add these important extras to your Blueprint Package, simply indicate your choices on the order form on page 381 or call us Toll Free 1-800-521-6797 and we'll tell you more about these exciting products.

L *The Landscape Blueprint Package*

For the homes marked with an **L** in this index, Home Planners has created a front-yard landscape plan that matches or is complementary in design to the house plan. These comprehensive blueprint packages include a Frontal Sheet, Plan View, Regionalized Plant & Materials List, a sheet on Planting and Maintaining Your Landscape, Zone Maps and Plant Size and Description Guide. These plans will help you achieve professional results, adding value and enjoyment to your property for years to come. Each set of blueprints is a full 18" x 24" in size with clear, complete instructions and easy-to-read type. To view the designs, call us to order your copy of *The Home Landscaper*, which shows all 40 front-yard designs in glorious full color.

Regional Order Map

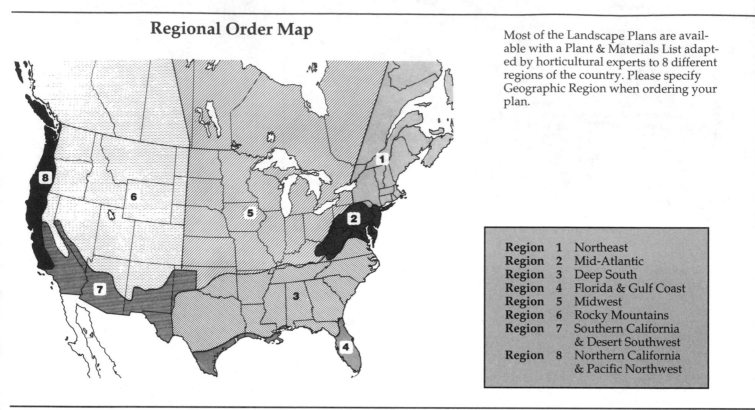

Most of the Landscape Plans are available with a Plant & Materials List adapted by horticultural experts to 8 different regions of the country. Please specify Geographic Region when ordering your plan.

Region	**1**	Northeast
Region	**2**	Mid-Atlantic
Region	**3**	Deep South
Region	**4**	Florida & Gulf Coast
Region	**5**	Midwest
Region	**6**	Rocky Mountains
Region	**7**	Southern California & Desert Southwest
Region	**8**	Northern California & Pacific Northwest

D *The Deck Blueprint Package*

Many of the homes in this index can be enhanced with a professionally designed Home Planners' Deck Plan. Those home plans highlighted with a **D** have a matching or corresponding deck plan available which includes a Deck Plan Frontal Sheet, Deck Framing and Floor Plans, Deck Elevations and a Deck Materials List. A Standard Deck Details Package, also available, provides all the how-to information necessary for building *any* deck. Our Complete Deck Building Package contains 1 set of Custom Deck Plans of your choice, plus 1 set of Standard Deck Building Details all for one low price. Our plans and details are carefully prepared in an easy-to-understand format that will guide you through every stage of your deck-building project. To view all 25 deck designs in our portfolio, call us to order your copy of our *Deck Planner* book.

See facing page for prices and ordering information.

 **Toll Free**
1-800-521-6797

Price Schedule & Plans Index

House Blueprint Price Schedule
(Prices guaranteed through December 31, 1998)

Tier	1-set Study Package	4-set Building Package	8-set Building Package	1-set Reproducible Sepias	Home Customizer® Package
A	$350	$395	$455	$555	$605
B	$390	$435	$495	$615	$665
C	$430	$475	$535	$675	$725
D	$470	$515	$575	$735	$785
E	$590	$635	$695	$795	$845

Prices for 4- or 8-set Building Packages honored only at time of original order.

Additional Identical Blueprints in same order ....$50 per set
Reverse Blueprints (mirror image) ....$50 per set
Specification Outlines...$10 each
Materials Lists (available only from those designers listed below):
▲ Home Planners Designs..$50
✳ Larry Garnett Designs..$50
≠ Larry Belk Designs...$50
† Design Basics Designs..$75
✴ Alan Mascord Designs..$50
◆ Donald Gardner Designs...$50
■ Design Traditions Designs...$50
● The Sater Design Collection...$50

Materials Lists for "E" price plans are an additional $10.

Deck Plans Price Schedule

CUSTOM DECK PLANS

Price Group	Q	R	S
1 Set Custom Plans	$25	$30	$35
Additional identical sets	$10 each		
Reverse sets (mirror image)	$10 each		

STANDARD DECK DETAILS
1 Set Generic Construction Details ....$14.95 each

COMPLETE DECK BUILDING PACKAGE

Price Group	Q	R	S
1 Set Custom Plans, plus 1 Set Standard Deck Details	$35	$40	$45

Landscape Plans Price Schedule

Price Group	X	Y	Z
1 set	$35	$45	$55
3 sets	$50	$60	$70
6 sets	$65	$75	$85

Additional Identical Sets....................................$10 each
Reverse Sets (mirror image)...............................$10 each

Index

To use the Index below, refer to the design number listed in numerical order (a helpful page reference is also given). Note the price index letter and refer to the House Blueprint Price Schedule above for the cost of one, four or eight sets of blueprints or the cost of a reproducible sepia. Additional prices are shown for identical and reverse blueprint sets, as well as a very useful Materials List for some of the plans. Also note in the Index below those plans that have matching or complementary Deck Plans or Landscape Plans. Refer to the schedules above for prices of these plans. All Home Planners' plans can be customized with Home Planners' Home Customizer® Package. These plans are indicated below with this symbol: ⌂. See page 381 for information. Some plans are also part of our Quote One® estimating service and are indicated by this symbol: ⌂ . See page 374 for more information.

To Order: Fill in and send the order form on page 381—or call toll free 1-800-521-6797 or 520-297-8200.

DESIGN	PRICE	PAGE	CUSTOMIZABLE	QUOTE ONE®	DECK	DECK PRICE	LANDSCAPE	LANDSCAPE PRICE	REGIONS
▲ 1021	A	272	⌂						
▲ 1025	A	87	⌂						
▲ 1075	A	87	⌂		D114	R	L225	X	1-3,5,6,8
▲ 1107	A	78	⌂		D112	R	L225	X	1-3,5,6,8
▲ 1113	A	79	⌂	⌂	D113	R	L202	X	1-3,5,6,8
▲ 1186	B	173	⌂						
▲ 1191	A	80	⌂		D114	R	L225	X	1-3,5,6,8
▲ 1228	D	200	⌂		D124	S	L217	Y	1-8
▲ 1305	A	170	⌂		D106	S			
▲ 1311	A	81	⌂				L225	X	1-3,5,6,8
▲ 1323	A	65	⌂	⌂	D117	S	L225	X	1-3,5,6,8
▲ 1325	B	91	⌂		D106	S	L225	X	1-3,5,6,8
▲ 1337	B	113	⌂						
▲ 1343	B	152	⌂				L226	X	1-8
▲ 1346	A	181	⌂						
▲ 1364	A	158	⌂		D117	S			
▲ 1367	A	113	⌂						
▲ 1372	A	346	⌂						
▲ 1373	A	81	⌂						
▲ 1382	A	170	⌂		D106	S			
▲ 1394	A	347	⌂		D105	R	L202	X	1-3,5,6,8
▲ 1761	C	94	⌂		D117	S	L217	Y	1-8
▲ 1786	C	155	⌂						
▲ 1788	C	177	⌂		D101	R	L206	Z	1-6,8
▲ 1829	B	153	⌂		D113	R	L226	X	1-8
▲ 1835	B	167	⌂		D100	Q	L225	X	1-3,5,6,8
▲ 1864	B	84	⌂		D103	R			
▲ 1890	B	110	⌂						
▲ 1892	B	198	⌂		D106	S	L225	X	1-3,5,6,8
▲ 1896	B	175	⌂						
▲ 1911	D	98	⌂						
▲ 1920	B	162	⌂	⌂			L225	X	1-3,5,6,8
▲ 1939	A	95	⌂		D117	S	L225	X	1-3,5,6,8
▲ 1947	B	266	⌂						
▲ 1950	B	182	⌂						
▲ 1952	C	174	⌂						
▲ 1967	B	353	⌂						
▲ 1980	B	152	⌂						
▲ 1989	C	225	⌂		D100	Q	L220	Y	1-3,5,6,8
▲ 1993	D	341	⌂				L213	Z	1-8
▲ 2153	A	114	⌂		D114	R			
▲ 2165	A	78	⌂						
▲ 2170	B	224	⌂				L221	X	1-3,5,6,8
▲ 2181	C	167	⌂		D100	Q	L226	X	1-8
▲ 2204	B	90	⌂						
▲ 2206	B	223	⌂	⌂			L220	Y	1-3,5,6,8
▲ 2220	C	202	⌂		D114	R	L217	Y	1-8
▲ 2236	C	322	⌂						
▲ 2261	B	108	⌂						
▲ 2316	B	101	⌂		D106	S	L225	X	1-3,5,6,8
▲ 2317	D	183	⌂						
▲ 2318	B	209	⌂				L220	Y	1-3,5,6,8
▲ 2343	D	286	⌂						
▲ 2351	B	284	⌂						
▲ 2505	A	85	⌂	⌂	D113	R	L226	X	1-8
▲ 2528	B	206	⌂		D100	Q			
▲ 2534	B	189	⌂	⌂			L227	Z	1-8
▲ 2544	C	180	⌂		D124	S			
▲ 2549	C	355	⌂						
▲ 2550	B	110	⌂		D112	R			
▲ 2565	B	115	⌂	⌂	D101	R	L225	X	1-3,5,6,8
▲ 2570	A	208	⌂		D113	R	L225	X	1-3,5,6,8
▲ 2573	A	210	⌂		D114	R	L220	Y	1-3,5,6,8
▲ 2597	B	163	⌂		D114	R	L226	X	1-8

Before You Order . . .

Before filling out the coupon at right or calling us on our Toll-Free Blueprint Hotline, you may want to learn more about our services and products. Here's some information you will find helpful.

Quick Turnaround
We process and ship every blueprint order from our office within 48 hours. Because of this quick turnaround, we won't send a formal notice acknowledging receipt of your order.

Our Exchange Policy
Since blueprints are printed in response to your order, we cannot honor requests for refunds. However, we will exchange your entire first order for an equal number of blueprints at a price of $50 for the first set and $10 for each additional set; $70 total exchange fee for 4 sets: $100 total exchange fee for 8 sets. . . *plus* the difference in cost if exchanging for a design in a higher price bracket or *less* the difference in cost if exchanging for a design in a lower price bracket. One exchange is allowed within a year of purchase date. **(Sepias are not exchangeable.** All sets from the first order must be returned before the exchange can take place. Please add $18 for postage and handling via ground service; $30 via 2nd Day Air; $40 via Next Day Air.

About Reverse Blueprints
If you want to build in reverse of the plan as shown, we will include an extra set of reverse blueprints (mirror image) for an additional fee of $50. Although lettering and dimensions will appear backward, reverses will be a useful aid if you decide to flop the plan.

Modifying or Customizing Our Plans
With such a great selection of homes, you are bound to find the one that suits you. However, if you need to make alterations to a design that is customizable, you need only order our Home Customizer® Package to get you started.

Architectural and Engineering Seals
Some cities and states are now requiring that a licensed architect or engineer review and "seal" your blueprints prior to building due to local or regional concerns over energy consumption, safety codes, seismic ratings or other factors. For this reason, it may be necessary to talk to a local professional to have your plans reviewed.

Compliance with Local Codes and Regulations
At the time of creation, our plans are drawn to specifications published by the Building Officials and Code Administrators (BOCA) International, Inc.; the Southern Building Code Congress (SBCCI) International, Inc.; the International Conference of Building Officials; or the Council of American Building Officials (CABO). Our plans are designed to meet or exceed national building standards. Some states, counties and municipalities have their own codes, zoning requirements and building regulations. Before building, contact your local building authorities to make sure you comply with local ordinances and codes, including obtaining any necessary permits or inspections as building progresses. In some cases, minor modifications to your plans by your builder, architect or designer may be required to meet local conditions and requirements.
Notice: Plans for homes to be built in Nevada must be re-drawn by a Nevada-registered professional. Consult your building official for more information on this subject.

Foundation and Exterior Wall Changes
Most of our plans are drawn with either a full or partial basement foundation. Depending on your specific climate or regional building practices, you may wish to change this basement to a slab or crawl-space. Most professional contractors and builders can easily adapt your plans to alternate foundation types. Likewise, most can easily change 2x4 wall construction to 2x6, or vice versa.

How Many Blueprints Do You Need?
A single set of blueprints is sufficient to study a home in greater detail. However, if you are planning to obtain cost estimates from a contractor or subcontractors—or if you are planning to build immediately—you will need more sets. Because additional sets are cheaper when ordered in quantity with the original order, make sure you order enough blueprints to satisfy all requirements. The following checklist will help you determine how many you need:

_____Owner

_____Builder (generally requires at least three sets; one as a legal document, one to use during inspections, and at least one to give to subcontractors)

_____Local Building Department (often requires two sets)

_____Mortgage Lender (usually one set for a conventional loan; three sets for FHA or VA loans)

_____TOTAL NUMBER OF SETS

Have You Seen Our Newest Designs?

Home Planners is one of the country's most active home design firms, creating nearly 100 new plans each year. At least 50 of our latest creations are featured in each edition of our New Design Portfolio. You may have received a copy with your latest purchase by mail. If not, or if you purchased this book from a local retailer, just return the coupon below for your FREE copy. Make sure you consider the very latest of what Home Planners has to offer.

Yes! Please send my FREE copy of your latest New Design Portfolio.

Offer good to U.S. shipping address only.

Name _____

Address _____

City_____State_____Zip _____

HOME PLANNERS, A Division of Hanley-Wood, Inc.
3275 WEST INA ROAD, SUITE 110
TUCSON, ARIZONA 85741

Order Form Key
| VO |

Toll Free 1-800-521-6797

Regular Office Hours:
8:00 a.m. to 8:00 p.m. Eastern Time, Monday through Friday
Our staff will gladly answer any questions during normal office hours. Our answering service can place orders after hours or on weekends.

If we receive your order by 4:00 p.m. Eastern Time, Monday through Friday, we'll process it and ship within 48 hours. When ordering by phone, please have your charge card ready. We'll also ask you for the Order Form Key Number at the bottom of the coupon.

By FAX: Copy the Order Form on the next page and send it on our FAX line: 1-800-224-6699 or 1-520-544-3086.

Canadian Customers
Order Toll-Free 1-800-561-4169

For faster service and plans that are modified for building in Canada, customers may now call in orders directly to our Canadian supplier of plans and charge the purchase to a charge card. Or, you may complete the order form at right, adding 40% to all prices and mail in Canadian funds to:

The Plan Centre 60 Baffin Place
Unit 5
Waterloo, Ontario N2V 1Z7

OR: Copy the Order Form and send it via our Canadian FAX line: 1-800-719-3291.

The Home Customizer®

"This house is perfect...if only the family room were two feet wider." Sound familiar? In response to the numerous requests for this type of modification, Home Planners has developed **The Home Customizer® Package**. This exclusive package offers our top-of-the-line materials to make it easy for anyone, anywhere to customize any Home Planners design to fit their needs. Check the index on page 377 for those plans which are customizable.

Some of the changes you can make to any of our plans include:

- exterior elevation changes
- kitchen and bath modifications
- roof, wall and foundation changes
- room additions and more!

The Home Customizer® Package includes everything you'll need to make the necessary changes to your favorite Home Planners design. The package includes:

- instruction book with examples
- architectural scale and clear work film
- erasable red marker and removable correction tape
- ¼"-scale furniture cutouts
- 1 set reproducible, erasable Sepias
- 1 set study blueprints for communicating changes to your design professional
- a copyright release letter so you can make copies as you need them
- referral letter with the name, address and telephone number of the professional in your region who is trained in modifying Home Planners designs efficiently and inexpensively.

The price of the **Home Customizer® Package** ranges from $605 to $845, depending on the price schedule of the design you have chosen. **The Home Customizer® Package** will not only save you 25% to 75% of the cost of drawing the plans from scratch with a custom architect or engineer, it will also give you the flexibility to have your changes and modifications made by our referral network or by the professional of your choice. Now it's even easier and more affordable to have the custom home you've always wanted.

For information about any of our services or to order call 1-800-521-6797.

BLUEPRINTS ARE NOT RETURNABLE

ORDER FORM

HOME PLANNERS, A Division of Hanley-Wood, Inc.
3275 WEST INA ROAD SUITE 110,
TUCSON, ARIZONA 85741

THE BASIC BLUEPRINT PACKAGE
Rush me the following (please refer to the Plans Index and Price Schedule in this section):

_____ Set(s) of blueprints for plan number(s) _____.	$_____
_____ Set(s) of sepias for plan number(s) _____.	$_____
_____ Home Customizer® Package for plan(s)_____.	$_____
_____ Additional identical blueprints in same order @ $50 per set.	$_____
_____ Reverse blueprints @ $50 per set.	$_____

IMPORTANT EXTRAS
Rush me the following:

_____ Materials List: $50
$75 Design Basics. Add $10 for a Schedule E plan Materials List. $_____
_____ **Quote One**® Summary Cost Report @ $19.95 for 1, $14.95 for
each additional, for plans _____ $_____
Building location: City _____ Zip Code _____
_____ **Quote One**® Detailed Cost Estimate @ $110 Schedule A-D; $120
Schedule E for plan_____ $_____
(Must be purchased with Blueprints set; Materials List included)
Building location: City _____ Zip Code _____
_____ Specification Outlines @ $10 each. $_____
_____ Detail Sets @ $14.95 each; any two for $22.95; any three
for $29.95; all four for $39.95 (save $19.85). $_____
❑ Plumbing ❑ Electrical ❑ Construction ❑ Mechanical
(These helpful details provide general construction
advice and are not specific to any single plan.)
_____ Plan-A-Home® @ $29.95 each. $_____
DECK BLUEPRINTS
_____ Set(s) of Deck Plan _____. $_____
_____ Additional identical blueprints in same order @ $10 per set. $_____
_____ Reverse blueprints @ $10 per set. $_____
_____ Set of Standard Deck Details @ $14.95 per set. $_____
_____ Set of Complete Building Package (Best Buy!)
Includes Custom Deck Plan _____.
(See Index and Price Schedule)
Plus Standard Deck Details $_____
LANDSCAPE BLUEPRINTS
_____ Set(s) of Landscape Plan _____. $_____
_____ Additional identical blueprints in same order @ $10 per set. $_____
_____ Reverse blueprints @ $10 per set. $_____
Please indicate the appropriate region of the country for
Plant & Material List. (See Map on page 376): Region _____

POSTAGE AND HANDLING	1-3 sets	4+ sets
DELIVERY (Requires street address - No P.O. Boxes)		
•Regular Service (Allow 4-6 days delivery)	❑ $15.00	❑ $18.00
•Priority (Allow 2-3 days delivery)	❑ $20.00	❑ $30.00
•Express (Allow 1 day delivery)	❑ $30.00	❑ $40.00
CERTIFIED MAIL (Requires signature)	❑ $20.00	❑ $30.00
If no street address available. (Allow 4-6 days delivery)		
OVERSEAS DELIVERY Note: All delivery times are from date Blueprint Package is shipped.	fax, phone or mail for quote	

POSTAGE (From box above) $_____
SUB-TOTAL $_____
SALES TAX (AZ. 5%, CA. & NY. 8.25%, DC. 5.75%,
IL. 6.25%, MI 6%, MN.6.5%) $_____
TOTAL (Sub-total and tax) $_____

YOUR ADDRESS (please print)
Name _____
Street _____
City _____ State _____ Zip _____
Daytime telephone number (_____) _____

FOR CREDIT CARD ORDERS ONLY
Please fill in the information below:
Credit card number _____
Exp. Date: Month/Year _____
Check one ❑ Visa ❑ MasterCard ❑ Discover Card

Signature _____
Please check appropriate box: ❑ Licensed Builder-Contractor
❑ Homeowner

Order Form Key
VO

ORDER TOLL FREE!
1-800-521-6797 or 520-297-8200

Helpful Books & Software

Home Planners wants your building experience to be as pleasant and trouble-free as possible. That's why we've expanded our library of Do-It-Yourself titles to help you along. In addition to our beautiful plans books, we've added books to guide you through specific projects as well as the construction process. In fact, these are titles that will be as useful after your dream home is built as they are right now.

ONE-STORY
1 448 designs for all lifestyles. 860 to 5,400 square feet. 384 pages $9.95

TWO-STORY
2 460 designs for one-and-a-half and two stories. 1,245 to 7,275 square feet. 384 pages $9.95

VACATION
3 345 designs for recreation, retirement and leisure. 312 pages $8.95

MULTI-LEVEL
4 312 designs for split-levels, bi-levels, multi-levels and walkouts. 224 pages $8.95

COUNTRY
5 200 country designs from classic to contemporary by 7 winning designers. 224 pages $8.95

MOVE-UP
6 200 stylish designs for today's growing families from 9 hot designers. 224 pages $8.95

NARROW-LOT
7 200 unique homes less than 60' wide from 7 designers. Up to 3,000 square feet. 224 pages $8.95

SMALL HOUSE
8 200 beautiful designs chosen for versatility and affordability. 224 pages $8.95

BUDGET-SMART
9 200 efficient plans from 7 top designers, that you can really afford to build! 224 pages $8.95

EXPANDABLES
10 200 flexible plans that expand with your needs from 7 top designers. 240 pages $8.95

ENCYCLOPEDIA
11 500 exceptional plans for all styles and budgets—the best book of its kind! 352 pages $9.95

AFFORDABLE
12 Completely revised and updated, featuring 300 designs for modest budgets. 256 pages $9.95

ENCYCLOPEDIA 2
13 500 Completely new plans. Spacious and stylish designs for every budget and taste. 352 pages $9.95

VICTORIAN
14 160 striking Victorian and Farmhouse designs from three leading designers. 192 pages $12.95

EASY-LIVING
15 216 Efficient and sophisticated plans that are small in size, but big on livability. 224 pages $8.95

LUXURY
16 154 fine luxury plans-loaded with luscious amenities! 192 pages $14.95

LIGHT-FILLED
17 223 great designs that make the most of natural sunlight. 240 pages $8.95

BEST SELLERS
18 Our 50th Anniversary book with 200 of our very best designs in full color! 224 pages $12.95

SPECIAL COLLECTION
19 70 Romantic house plans that capture the classic tradition of home design. 160 pages $17.95

COUNTRY HOUSES
20 208 Unique home plans that combine traditional style and modern livability. 224 pages $9.95

TRADITIONAL
21 403 designs of classic beauty and elegance. 304 pages $9.95

MODERN & CLASSIC
22 341 impressive homes featuring the latest in contemporary design. 304 pages $9.95

NEW ENGLAND
23 260 of the best in Colonial home design. Special interior design sections, too. 384 pages $14.95

SOUTHERN
24 207 homes rich in Southern styling and comfort. 240 pages $8.95

Landscape Designs

Outdoor Projects

SUNBELT
25 215 Designs that capture the spirit of the Southwest. 208 pages $10.95

WESTERN
26 215 designs that capture the spirit and diversity of the Western lifestyle. 208 pages $9.95

EASY CARE
27 41 special landscapes designed for beauty and low maintenance. 160 pages $14.95

FRONT & BACK
28 The first book of do-it-yourself landscapes. 40 front, 15 backyards. 208 pages $14.95

BACKYARDS
29 40 designs focused solely on creating your own specially themed backyard oasis. 160 pages $14.95

OUTDOOR
30 42 unique outdoor projects. Gazebos, strombellas, bridges, sheds, playsets and more! 96 pages $7.95

GARAGES & MORE
31 101 Multi-use garages and outdoor structures to enhance any home. 96 pages $7.95

DECKS
32 25 outstanding single-, double- and multi-level decks you can build. 112 pages $7.95

Design Software

BOOK & CD ROM	3D DESIGN SUITE	ENERGY GUIDE	BATHROOMS	KITCHENS	HOUSE CONTRACTING	WINDOWS & DOORS	CONTRACTING GUIDE

33 Both the Home Planners Gold book and matching Windows™ CD ROM with 3D floorplans. $24.95

34 Home design made easy! View designs in 3D, take a virtual reality tour, add decorating details and more. $59.95

35 The most comprehensive energy efficiency and conservation guide available. 280 pages $35.00

36 An innovative guide to organizing, remodeling and decorating your bathroom. 96 pages $8.95

37 An imaginative guide to designing the perfect kitchen. Chock full of bright ideas to make your job easier. 176 pages $14.95

38 Everything you need to know to act as your own general contractor...and save up to 25% off building costs. 134 pages $12.95

39 Installation techniques and tips that make your project easier and more professional looking. 80 pages $7.95

40 Loaded with information to make you more confident in dealing with contractors and subcontractors. 287 pages $18.95

ROOFING	FRAMING	VISUAL HANDBOOK	BASIC WIRING	PATIOS & WALKS	TILE	PLUMBING	TRIM & MOLDING

41 Information on the latest tools, materials and techniques for roof installation or repair. 80 pages $7.95

42 For those who want to take a more-hands on approach to their dream. 319 pages $19.95

43 A plain-talk guide to the construction process; financing to final walk-through, this book covers it all. 498 pages $19.95

44 A straight forward guide to one of the most misunderstood systems in the home. 160 pages $12.95

45 Clear step-by-step instructions take you from the basic design stages to the finished project. 80 pages $7.95

46 Every kind of tile for every kind of application. Includes tips on use installation and repair. 176 pages $12.95

47 Tackle any plumbing installation or repair as quickly and efficiently as a professional. 160 pages $12.95

48 Step-by-step instructions for installing baseboards, window and door casings and more. 80 pages $7.95

Additional Books Order Form

To order your books, just check the box of the book numbered below and complete the coupon. We will process your order and ship it from our office within 48 hours. Send coupon and check (in U.S. funds).

YES! Please send me the books I've indicated:

☐ 1:VO $9.95	☐ 25:SW $10.95	
☐ 2:VT $9.95	☐ 26:WH $9.95	
☐ 3:VH $8.95	☐ 27:ECL $14.95	
☐ 4:VS $8.95	☐ 28:HL $14.95	
☐ 5:FH $8.95	☐ 29:BYL $14.95	
☐ 6:MU $8.95	☐ 30:YG $7.95	
☐ 7:NL $8.95	☐ 31:GG $7.95	
☐ 8:SM $8.95	☐ 32:DP $7.95	
☐ 9:BS $8.95	☐ 33:HPGC $24.95	
☐ 10:EX $8.95	☐ 34:PLANSUITE . $59.95	
☐ 11:EN $9.95	☐ 35:RES $35.00	
☐ 12:AF $9.95	☐ 36:CDP $9.95	
☐ 13:E2 .... $9.95	☐ 37:CDB $8.95	
☐ 14:VDH $12.95	☐ 38:CKI $14.95	
☐ 15:EL $8.95	☐ 39:SBC $12.95	
☐ 16:LD2 .... $14.95	☐ 40:BCC $18.95	
☐ 17:NA $8.95	☐ 41:CGR $7.95	
☐ 18:HPG $12.95	☐ 42:SRF $19.95	
☐ 19:WEP $17.95	☐ 43:RVH $19.95	
☐ 20:CN $9.95	☐ 44:CBW $12.95	
☐ 21:ET $9.95	☐ 45:CGW $7.95	
☐ 22:EC $9.95	☐ 46:CWT $12.95	
☐ 23:NES $14.95	☐ 47:CMP $12.95	
☐ 24:SH $8.95	☐ 48:CGT $7.95	

Canadian Customers
Order Toll-Free 1-800-561-4169

Additional Books Sub-Total .... $ _____
ADD Postage and Handling .... $ 3.00
Sales Tax: (AZ 5%, CA & NY 8.25%, DC 5.75%,
IL 6.25%, MI 6%, MN 6.5%) .... $ _____
YOUR TOTAL (Sub-Total, Postage/Handling, Tax) $ _____

YOUR ADDRESS (Please print)

Name _____

Street _____

City _____ State _____ Zip _____

Phone (_____) _____ — _____

YOUR PAYMENT
Check one: ☐ Check ☐ Visa ☐ MasterCard ☐ Discover Card
Required credit card information:

Credit Card Number _____

Expiration Date (Month/Year) _____ / _____

Signature Required _____

Home Planners, A Division of Hanley-Wood, Inc.
3275 W Ina Road, Suite 110, Dept. BK, Tucson, AZ 85741

VO

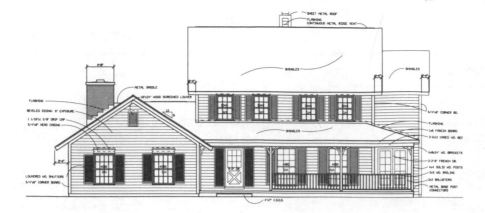

OVER 3 MILLION BLUEPRINTS SOLD

"We instructed our builder to follow the plans including all of the many details which make this house so elegant... Our home is a fine example of the results one can achieve by purchasing and following the plans which you offer... Everyone who has seen it has assured us that it belongs in 'a picture book.' I truly mean it when I say that my home 'is a DREAM HOUSE.'"

S.P.
Anderson, SC

"We have had a steady stream of visitors, many of whom tell us this is the most beautiful home they've seen. Everyone is amazed at the layout and remark on how unique it is. Our real estate attorney, who is a Chicago dweller and who deals with highly valued properties, told me this is the only suburban home he has seen that he would want to live in."

W. & P.S.
Flossmoor, IL

"Home Planners' blueprints saved us a great deal of money. I acted as the general contractor and we did a lot of the work ourselves. We probably built it for half the cost! We are thinking about more plans for another home. I purchased a competitor's book but my husband only wants your plans!"

K.M.
Grovetown, GA

"We are very happy with the product of our efforts. The neighbors and passersby appreciate what we have created. We have had many people stop by to discuss our house and kindly praise it as being the nicest house in our area of new construction. We have even had one person stop and make us an unsolicited offer to buy the house for much more than we have invested in it."

K. & L.S.
Bolingbrook, IL

"The traffic going past our house is unbelievable. On several occasions, we have heard that it is the 'prettiest house in Batavia.' Also, when meeting someone new and mentioning what street we live on, quite often we're told, 'Oh, you're the one in the yellow house with the wrap-around porch! I love it!'"

A.W.
Batavia, NY

"I have been involved in the building trades my entire life... Since building our home we have built two other homes for other families. Their plans from local professional architects were not nearly as good as yours. For that reason we are ordering additional plan books from you."

T.F.
Kingston, WA

"The blueprints we received from Home Planners were of excellent quality and provided us with exactly what we needed to get our successful home-building project underway. We appreciate Home Planners invaluable role in our home-building effort."

T.A.
Concord, TN